SOME FAMILY

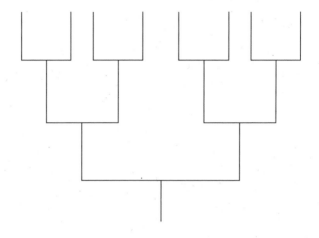

Some Family

THE MORMONS AND HOW HUMANITY
KEEPS TRACK OF ITSELF

DONALD HARMAN AKENSON

McGILL-QUEEN'S UNIVERSITY PRESS | Montreal & Kingston | London | Ithaca

ISBN 978-0-7735-3295-3

Legal deposit third quarter 2007
Bibliothèque nationale du Québec

Printed in Canada on acid-free paper that is 100% ancient forest free
(100% post-consumer recycled), processed chlorine free.

McGill-Queen's University Press acknowledges the support of the
Canada Council for the Arts for our publishing program. We also
acknowledge the financial support of the Government of Canada
through the Book Publishing Industry Development Program (BPIDP)
for our publishing activities.

Library and Archives Canada Cataloguing in Publication

Akenson, Donald Harman, 1941–
    Some family: the Mormons and how humanity keeps track
of itself / Donald Harman Akenson.

Includes bibliographical references and index.
    ISBN 978-0-7735-3295-3

    1. Genealogy. 2. Church of Jesus Christ of Latter-Day Saints.
Family History Library – History. I. Title.

CS14.A38 2007   929'.1   C2007-903804-2

This book was typeset by Interscript in 10.5/13 Baskerville.

For Citizen Harcourt

Contents

Figures and Tables

SOME FAMILY

Prologue
(a time-gambler's tip sheet)

1 Perhaps – flip a coin, this is a 50/50 proposition – by 2050 *most* people on this planet will learn of their familial history and how it fits into the pattern of world history from information provided by the Church of Jesus Christ of Latter-day Saints (the Mormons).

2 Very probably – you can bet your farm on this – by 2025 *more* human beings will learn their family histories and how world history has evolved through the Mormons' data and theologic-history than from any other source. Try to find a compulsive gambler with deep pockets.

3 And absolutely certainly – at the present time the largest pool of information on specific, identifiable individuals who have comprised the human race has been assembled by the Latter-day Saints. Bigger than any governmental data pool ever will be. The standard release form that the LDS asks owners of family histories and other data bases to sign explains that, this is "so the data from your materials can be used to create a common pedigree of mankind." Immodest, hubristic, monumental, heroic, and in many ways engagingly humble, for it is all in the service of recreating the divine chain of being, from God to humanity.

Before you place your bets, how, why and how well this project is proceeding might be worth considering.

PART ONE

Getting in Touch

1 *Yesterday's News*

"Genealogical workers of the world, unite!" Karl Marx might have urged, had he lived a century later than he did. And he would have heard the reply, "why bother? The Mormons are busy doing everything already."

That situation takes some explaining and, more importantly, evaluating. Whether one thinks of the members of the Church of Jesus Christ of Latter-day Saints as the advancing proletariat of the ultimate theological revolution or as affrighted creatures, clinging like limpets on a battered seashore, they are a massive, if usually underestimated, cultural force. Their present goal (among other faith-driven objectives) is to create an accurate and comprehensive genealogical tree of the entire human race: or, to put it another way, to establish, piece by piece, soul by soul, the narrative of humankind since the beginning of civilization. They intend to create the master narrative into which each one of us fits.

That these outwardly modest people are silently driven by a hubris that is well beyond that of the most megalomaniacal of world imperializers (even Alexander of Macedon set out to conquer only the peoples of the world he lived in, not the entire past of humanity), and that they are so irritatingly nice and vexingly and smilingly optimistic in their work, makes them, at minimum, something special.

The Church of Jesus Christ of Latter-day Saints (usually called "the Mormons" by outsiders in reference to one of the church's holy books: a reference LDS members accept as a convenient shorthand and often use themselves) claims to have roughly 12–14 million adherents. Somewhat fewer than half of these are found in North America.

The dimensions of the collective project they are working on are so big that it is hard to comprehend, much less grapple with. You can acquire a sense of its potential size by sitting down with a calculator and doing the simple math: start with yourself as the (imaginary) only soul on the planet and assume that a human generation over time has averaged twenty-five years and that, for the sake of simplicity, there has been no inbreeding and that there has been only one child per family in each generation (and, of course, two parents in each preceding generation). Even by these severely limiting assumptions, by the time Christopher Columbus blundered into the New World, you are the product of 1,048,576 ancestors. So, if you are interested in your own lineage, there is a bit of genealogical digging for you to do. And, if you were to be ambitious and take things back to the time of Jesus of Nazareth, the number of people you were seeking as ancestors would, in conventional numerical notation, stretch all the way across the page. (Think of the number "6" with twenty-three zeros after it and you will be close enough.)

Of course matters are a bit more complicated than that. You are not the only person on earth and, obviously, our assumption of one child per family per generation is a simplification that is way out of touch with reality. (The world records for fecundity are the more than 1,400 progeny sired by Moulay Ismail, an eighteenth-century emperor of Morocco, and on the female side, the 69 children of Fedora Vassilyev, an eighteenth-century Russian woman.)[1] Thus, if the Mormons are going to make a world pedigree, it would seem they have their work cut out for them.

What saves their task from being completely inconceivable is the simple fact that human beings interbreed quite promiscuously. Not just third cousins, or second, but first cousins, uncles and nieces, brothers and sisters, fathers and daughters, nephews and aunts, wives and brothers-in-law, and on and on. Most of the closest inbreedings are covered up by social convention and by skilled lying. Unless your parents come from totally separate populations (say, from Africa and from China), you would not have to go back many generations to find some of your mother's people procreating with your father's – would not, that is, if the records were complete and accurate, which they are not. And, in any case, your mother's people were procreating with each other, as were your father's: the only question is how genetically close the inbreeders were.

The simplest way to indicate the degree of human inbreeding is to compare the number of people who were required to explain your own existence in, for example, the era of Jesus of Nazareth – 6×10^{23} – with the actual number of people who were probably alive at that time. Admittedly, this is a speculative form of demographic work, but the two best estimates – those of Carl Haub and of Glen Paige – agree that a reasonable "guestimate" for the world's population at the beginning of the Common Era (the year 1 "AD") is 300 million persons.[2]

Whether or not one likes this basic fact of frequent human inbreeding, it provides a valuable set of advantages for genealogists and geneticists. It means, first, that any individual will have a lot fewer distinct genealogical lines to trace than if there had been no inbreeding. This is because an individual's several genealogical lines intersect with each other multiple times in any long genealogical chain. And, secondly, for genealogists (like the Mormons) who are devoted to tracing large groups of people, it means that individual persons in one genealogical line will also be more frequently found in the genealogical lines of other persons than if there had been no in-breeding. The limited original population from which we all stem means that we are all interrelated; and, if there were a full genealogy of every human being, we would discover that not only are we all related, but that our ancestors intersected each other several times in a great genetic tangle. This may be messy, but it permits the multiple usage of a single cell of data: information on your twenty-third grandfather will probably fit into the family tree of several score of people, though none of you will be known to each other.

So, the Mormons' project is not so totally chimerical as it first appears to be. They are a practical people and they have already collected as raw data at least 2 billion names: records of real people who left at least a minimal footprint on the historical record of humanity – that is, their names and some information concerning their dates and place of existence.[3] That is a huge data base. Of these 2 billion names, approximately 1 billion have been vetted (for duplication and for internal self-consistency) and are available as units that can be fitted into the swirling helix that is humanity's genealogical and genetic story.[4]

What is the proper frame for adjudging the Latter-day Saints' data base? Clearly, it is the one directly defined by their own intent – namely, the total number of people who have ever lived. Currently, demographers accept an estimate of approximately 6 billion people as being alive on earth at the present time and 96–100 billion as having lived sometime previously – for a total of 102–106 billion persons.[5] This is the number against which to judge the Mormons' work.

If one assumes that electronic technology will speed the Mormons' acquisition of further large patches of written data, that they will considerably improve their collection and transcription of oral sources, and that they will discover methods of efficiently mining the massive genealogical reservoirs of China and Japan, then I think it is realistic to suggest that they will collect as many as 5 billion names of real people before they hit the wall of forgetfulness. This wall is formed by cultures and by social castes in which names were not written down and, therefore, almost all individual members of those groups are forever beyond the memory line of even the most skilled of oral remembrancers.

Still, if they have the potential of recovering evidence for the existence of even 4 or 5 percent of the individuals who ever lived on earth – evidence for their existence as *individuals*, not as indistinguishable members of some social aggregate – the Mormons will have captured and made widely available more demotic history than is approachable through any other single source. Granted, their material is not, nor will it ever be, statistically representative of the entire human race: record-keeping and genealogy-memorizing groups will be privileged. Nevertheless, to be able to observe the genealogical plaiting of even one-twentieth (heavens, of even one-fiftieth) of all the humans who have ever lived, that indeed would be a wondrous vision.

————

This way of viewing the Mormons' activities makes it seem as if the Latter-day Saints are in alliance with a group that, in fact, comprises their natural enemies: historical geneticists. In a sense, the two groups are in the same business and use similar modes of thought, albeit much different forms of evidence.

In principle, these two modes of thought, genealogical and genetical, are simple enough, although they are extremely complicated in their details. Both large-scale genealogical projects and historical genetical projects have a similar goal: to show the scheme of development from the First Parents of humanity to the present world population.[6] (See Figure 1.1).

Figure 1.1
The genetic pyramid

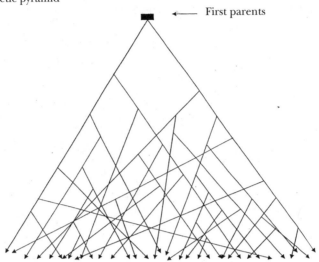

← First parents

PRESENT POPULATION OF THE WORLD —
AROUND 6 BILLION

The two groups of scholars, however, employ very different forms of evidence. In the usual case, historical geneticists collect genetic material from present-day populations and from the occasional well-preserved early human specimen, and then are able to fill in the specimen's genetic tree by mathematical techniques that make it possible to skip over distinct individuals and, indeed, over entire generations. The collective genetic coding is enough. In contrast, within a genealogical system of evidence collection each individual counts, and there is no skipping over anyone: for to lose an individual often means that knowledge of a line-of-descent is lost. This becomes very confusing for the individual genealogist, for although the investigator knows that the overall project is intended to produce a genetic tree of humanity that is shaped like a pyramid, the research on any given line usually expands outward. It resembles the frame of an ill-used and broken umbrella, turned inside-out by a strong wind (see Figure 1.2).[7]

This is confusing in its ever-distracting complexity. The most common response I have encountered recently among Mormon genealogists is that the computer will sort it all out. This is said with a sigh.

Figure 1.2
The genetic umbrella

HORIZON LINE — A SEEMINGLY INFINITE NUMBER OF LINEAGES

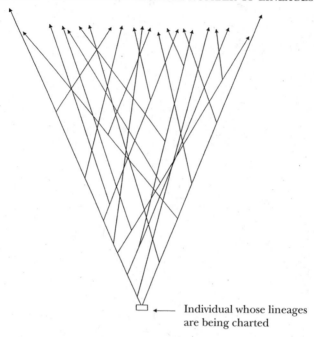

Individual whose lineages
are being charted

Now, in the unusual (but by no means rare) case of lines-of-descent that are well-recorded, the researcher hits a point where "genetic collapse" or "lineage collapse" or "pedigree collapse" occurs. (The terms are equivalent.) This is the point where the limits of the genetic material open to any human breeding population become obvious. A set of genetic lines that began with one individual in the present day expands backward in time and then begins to diminish, thus forming a diamond pattern in which the final, top portions are implied rather than precisely defined, as shown in Figure 1.3.[8]

That looks very nice schematically, but in practice the individual diamond pattern is hard to discern. That is because this is a *collective* enterprise and therefore we encounter two causes of immense, befuddling messiness. The first is that the entire business is trapped in the clash-of-the-duelling-umbrellas. By this I mean that the immense number of genealogical lines that spike downwards from the Ur-parents (as in Figure 1.1) cross-thatch with the lineages that reach upward from any specific individual (as in Figure 1.2). Secondly, rich as the confusion may be for any given individual tracing

Figure 1.3
The diamond of perspective

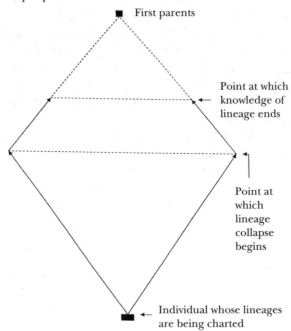

his or her own roots, the collective picture is insanely complex, for (at the limit of possibility) we are talking about 6 billion individual lineages that begin in the world's population today and which criss-cross each other and, finally, end up with Father Adam.

Maybe the Mormons are crazy. Maybe they should pay attention to the words ascribed to St. Paul: "Neither give heed to fables and endless genealogies" (Timothy 1:4). Yet they have faith, and faith, the scriptures say, can move mountains (Matthew 17:20).

Where historical geneticists and Mormon genealogists completely lose touch with each other is in their notion of who our First Parents were and how we find them. In this regard, historical geneticists are humble, in the sense that they are aware that they are making a set of approximations and that they will never have a final answer. Each iteration of their efforts, however, should be a little closer to the never-quite-recoverable final reality. In contrast, the Mormons are confident to the point of arrogance (quiet arrogance, but nevertheless cocksure). They know that humanity came into existence as described in the Book of Genesis in the Hebrew scriptures. This was in the year 4004 BCE, or thereabouts, according to the now-classical chronology of Archbishop James Ussher, the seventeenth-century Church of Ireland archbishop of Armagh. Unlike the geneticists, the Mormons have the advantage of knowing in advance the point where all their processing of information on human lineages will arrive. In their confident and patriarchal way, they trace all humanity not merely to the First Parents, but to Father Adam. Mother Eve plays second violin in this orchestra, but she is definitely there.

In defence of the Mormons' ideologically determined position, one can put forward two pragmatic suggestions. The first of these is that, from one statistical perspective, in their cutting from their massive genealogical project all people who lived before approximately 4000 BCE, they are not doing much harm. If one takes the best guesstimates by historical demographers of early populations, one can infer a human population of between 12 and 30 million at the date when the Garden of Eden myth is set.[9] These figures, and the total number of people who have ever lived up to that point depend upon how long one believes the human species has been on earth (50,000 and 1,000,000 years are the figures used in the above guesstimates) and what one thinks birth and death rates were over any period of time. The point is that the Mormons' cutoff date loses for them only a few score million persons, and this, out of the 102–106 billion individuals who have ever lived on earth is so small as to be insignificant, or so one could argue.

That, of course, is special pleading, for the earliest ancestors of humanity have a determinative importance out of all proportion to their mere numbers, a point the Latter-day Saints recognize in their own ideology: for them, Father Adam is a big deal indeed.

Equally pragmatic, but more compelling, is the argument from human psychology – namely, that it is hard to identify emotionally with an abstract entity. There is no continuously inhabited city on earth that is more than 6,000 years old; nor any monument before that date with which any present culture has had unbroken continuity. There are some weird and mysterious constructions that are older (who in the world built New Grange or Dun Aengus?, for example), but none with which we can feel the emotional tug, the assertion that, yes, they were made by our people. The Mormons, by limiting their search for human continuity to the eras in which "our" civilizations existed, are letting their followers stay within the zone of history where it is possible to identify comfortably emotionally. The long grey ages of human time before their date for Father Adam are like the astronomers' calculations for distances to far galaxies: intellectually impressive, aesthetically elegant but, for most observers, emotionally unsatisfying.

———

I think that most readers will recognize that this is a book about people I like: not just the industrious Mormons, but old-fashioned anthropologists, ardent amateur genealogists, optimistic geneticists, rabbinic Sages of Blessed Memory, Russian Formalists, New Historicists, and (may heaven forgive me), the most architectonically rigorous of French structuralists. What they all have in common is that they are not ironic or self-protecting in their own quests and they, like the Latter-day Saints, are willing to exhibit that quality which is much too rare in present-day scholarly work: sheer, unembarrassed enthusiasm.

Further, I hope it is clear that I do not share the disdain that most professional historians have for genealogists, amateur or professional. Professional historians, like all skilled tradespeople, have their own status rules. One of the most basic of these – so basic that our postgraduate students do not even need to be told, so clearly do we silently communicate our snobbery – is this: do not ever become involved with the practice of genealogy: it is a necropolis of the mind and anyone who enters there can only return as a zombie. This is absolute rubbish and fortunately a few very skilled historians in the academy go against the grain. Still, if one looks at the postgraduate curriculum of the top twenty rated history programs in North America, not a single one requires students to have or to acquire even the most elementary skills in genealogical research. More fools, us.

This book is really about how humanity keeps track of itself. That is an extremely immodest topic and it can never be successfully mastered, but the climb is the point, not the inevitable failure to reach the summit. I would not even take a step on the journey were it not for the contagious enthusiasm of genealogists for their own work, and especially the Mormon savants of lineage. Their optimism, bordering on orthonoia, is wonderful and it buoys one. Moreover, by using the Mormons and their own faith in genealogy as an entry point, one can ease into an examination of how our species tries to keep from being overcome by swirl and flux.

In the discussion that follows, the main assertion is simple. Genealogy – which is the most fundamental form of humanity's collective history – is best understood as narrative. And there is only one
basic narrative that lies behind all literature, history, plant-, animal-
and human-biology. Yes, there are lovely twists and turns, chro-
matic, mimetic, ironic arabesques, but nevertheless there is only
one story that counts: someone, some living thing, is born, survives
for a time, begets – maybe – and dies, certainly. We all need the
sense of being part of a succession for our own lives to be licit. That
succession can be scientific, genealogical, mythological, empirical,
ideological, and religious all at once. In each case, the human
mind understands what humanity is by walking through the door
that opens to succession-thinking. Ultimately, that leads to a consideration of the fundamental mystery: origins, especially our own.
Gibbon and Homer, Marx and Maimonides, Genesis and Darwin –
they are all writing the same narrative and, if we join them, at least
we are in good company.

2   What Do the Mormons Think ... ?

What do the Mormons think they are doing anyway, in attempting to capture individual by individual, the history of the whole human race? Like everyone else, *what* they think is determined largely by *how* they think. Above all, the Mormons are a scriptural people – a people of the books. Their scriptures are the cultural matrix of their tribe (in the biblical sense of the term). And their mission, to retro-save the world, is embedded in their scriptures with the same imperative force that the mission of "redeeming" the land of Canaan was the ground-base of the Hebrew scriptures. Nothing about the Mormons makes sense unless one accepts that the context of their present-day actions depends upon four volumes of scripture, three of which were written almost in their entirety in the first half of the nineteenth century. Once one discovers through these works how the Mormons think, their specific doctrines become understandable. These doctrinal points probably are not convincing to outsiders, but they are comprehensible; and the behaviours of present-day Mormons as a group become predictable and, indeed, somewhat comforting.

———

Because they define themselves as special (and what religious group does not?), we have to introduce a few definitions to clarify our discussion. The Mormons have their own special vocabulary that must be made to mesh with our own secular words. About the name of the group: when first formed in April 1830, they called themselves the "Church of Christ." In May 1834, they adopted the title, "The Church of Latter-day Saints" and in April 1838, this was expanded to the present form, "The Church of Jesus Christ of Latter-day Saints."[1] There are several splinter groups with names that have changed over time, but our focus here is on the main line of the church. Today, most outsiders refer to members of the church as "Mormons," a usage that began in the 1830s (the form then was "Mormonite") and most members use the term "Mormon" themselves, and they do not take offence when outsiders employ it. The situation is similar to the development of the term "Tory" in eighteenth- and nineteenth-century English politics. It began as a term of political abuse – meaning a highwayman or an Irish outlaw – and was applied to conservative politicians so frequently that they adopted the name and thus turned a term of opprobrium into one of pride. So, frequently we will use "Mormon" and "LDS" as convenient abbreviations for the full official title of the church and of its members.[2]

In theological language, however, church members have a special set of names for themselves and for non-members, and these we cannot employ unreservedly because they splash messily into secular terms that already have meaning and which draw different distinctions than do the LDS's terms. Thus, the church refers to its members as "Saints," (always capitalized) and this is a bit demeaning to the millions of other Christians who have some affinity for the term. More confusing is the use of "Gentile" (rarely capitalized) to mean non-Mormons. Such usage is boggling because, as employed in LDS literature, it usually means all non-Mormons, including Jews: confusing, and not something that most Jews find acceptable. And, when using "Jews," as distinct from other non-Mormons, the LDS historical and theological material has evinced a frequent oscillation in its nearly two centuries of development. Sometimes "Jew" is employed in its most specific sense, to refer to the descendants of the ancient tribe of Judah. At other times, it means everyone who most non-Mormons would call Jewish, namely, everyone allegiant religiously or ethnically to the ancient house of Israel – the Chosen People of the Hebrew scriptures.

One final term that we cannot adopt except in specific ritual descriptions: "priest." The Church of Jesus Christ of Latter-day Saints has no professional clergy. The church for the last century has been run by successful businessmen and a "priest" usually means an adult male member in good standing. (There are levels of priesthood and it is technically possible, though unusual, to be an adult male member and not a priest, but that is a side issue.) Normally, a young man takes the first step to priesthood and becomes a "deacon" at age twelve to fourteen: consider this first step as the equivalent of a bar-mitzvah. Ordinarily, he progresses from being a "deacon" to being a "teacher," and then, at age eighteen or so, a bearer of the "Aaronite priesthood." (No points for intuiting that the claim to being priest-of-Aaron results in some sharp differences with Jewish persons, not least the Cohens, who claim direct genetic descent from Moses' brother, Aaron. This, even though the LDS church recognizes as liturgically valid the priestly orders of anyone who can claim direct biological descent from Aaron, which would include most Cohens.)

Mormonism to an outsider seems fairly weird on the surface and even stranger the more one learns about the church's beliefs. In fact, Mormonism is no more banjaxed mentally than are any of the major western religions with which it competes: it's just that we are apt to be more familiar with these others, so they do not seem bizarre. If one could encounter with an innocent eye all the variants of the religions that sprang from the ancient Yahweh-faith – dozens of brands of Judaism, scores of Islamic sects, hundreds of Christian denominations – and engage a conspectus of their belief-systems and observe the pageants of their myriad rituals, one would think one were encountering a merry-go-round of psycho-hallucinating nutters. Yet, most of us are familiar with at least some of these systems and we know that they work as ways of giving meaning to individual life and cohesion to social groups. Thus, we tolerate them and try to understand them, even if we do not find all, or perhaps any, of them especially attractive for our own lives. So, give the Mormons the same break one gives, say, to the Haredi sects or the Coptic church. One does not have to embrace them, but try, try to understand.

This is crucial in our present task – dealing with the Latter-day Saints' genealogical fixation – because the way the Mormons approach genealogy is a function of the church's broader view of world history. The first step in construing the emerging LDS genealogical *imperium* is to examine the way their basic scriptures were delivered to the faithful. From this one can infer some basic beliefs, not only about what their "salvation history" is, but how history works and how history's workers (the "Saints") will operate in the everyday world, including in their genealogical work. In examining these matters, I am acting as a secular historian. I have no interest in proving or disproving Mormon beliefs, something that, in any case, I think is beyond the scope of a mere academic historian. My goal is simply to outline a series of events that happened in the secular world. For Mormons, these are sacred events but, as a professional historian, I am just reading the newspaper, not a holy parchment; these events affected thousands and eventually millions of minds, and are thus important historically, whether the authorized LDS version is accurate or not. Beliefs matter.

Above all else, the Mormons are a scriptural people. Their scriptures, however, are not the same as those of any other faith. They are four-plus in number.

The first two are the ones that those nice LDS missionaries who knock on your front door (however do these young men – and, increasingly, young women – get that just-scrubbed look, and does the church have a warehouse full of crisp white shirts?) always talk about. (1) the Christian Bible and (2) the "Book of Mormon." What they rarely talk about are two volumes that are more revealing of the way the church thinks and works historically: (3) The "Pearl of Great Price" and (4) the most important and also most historically revealing document in the Mormon canon, usually called "The Doctrine and Covenants." These are the "Standard Works of the Church."[3] In other words, the Mormon scriptures.

To them must be added an item that is similar in position to the books of the scriptures that the Protestants call the Apocrypha and Catholics term the Deutero-Canon. It is an item that is not as authoritative as the four Standard Works but it is used to supplement them (it includes a good deal of original material) and to provide faith-dating for some of the material in the Standard Works. This is the "History of the Church of Jesus Christ of Latter-day Saints," dictated mostly by Joseph Smith, the Prophet. He began the manuscript in 1838[4] and had written enough by the time of his martyrdom in 1844 to fill six heavy volumes (material for a seventh volume was added later by church leaders). The printed version, edited and annotated by church authorities, was first published in 1909–12.[5] The fact that the original manuscript still exists and that church-prepared printed versions also exist potentially provides a rare opportunity to assay the manner in which LDS authorities have treated historical material that bears upon their system of beliefs. Unhappily, the highest church authorities have not permitted public access, nor even what would be more anodyne from their point of view, "the production of a modern scholarly edition."[6] Because the Prophet's historical writing is so problematic (and not recognized as a fully canonical book by the church), we will limit our discussion to the four Standard Works.

The Bible is the plinth on which the whole enterprise is based. Yet, it is the least revealing document of the four Standard Works as far as the development of the unique faith of the Church of Jesus Christ of Latter-day Saints is concerned. That should not be surprising, really: the foundation course of a cathedral is a lot less interesting and much less revealing of the beliefs of the builders than are vaulted arches, painted ceilings and statues of saints.

But which Bible? From its earliest days, the LDS adopted the Tanakh (that is, the Hebrew scriptures) as the first half of its Bible. (That to adherents of the Jewish faith this is the entire Bible is a fact worth remembering.) They assimilated this, the "Old Testament" (offensive phrase, that, but unavoidable in the present context) in the unfortunate form that fourth-century Christianity adopted. That is, instead of preserving intact the books that are the Primary Unity of the Hebrew scriptures (Genesis, Exodus, Leviticus, Numbers, Deuteronomy, Joshua, Judges, Samuel and Kings), the Christians interrupted the narrative by inserting the adventitious Book of Ruth between Judges and Samuel. Worse, the Church Fathers moved the books of Ezra, Nehemiah and Chronicles from the back of the scriptures, where they provide a rhetorical balance to the Primary Unity, to the middle of the text. This major artistic error would not be relevant here except that these early canonical decisions left the screeching fulminations of the prophet Malachi as the final tones that reverberate from the Christian version of the Hebrew scriptures. And, as we will see later, Joseph Smith, the Prophet, grabs on to Malachi's words and uses them as a trot-line to tether to the ancient Hebrew texts some of his most unusual and innovative doctrines.

The other half of the Mormon's Bible is the standard Christian "New Testament."

Key to the LDS church's usage of the Bible is the version they chose. They embraced the incandescent translations done by William Tyndale in the first half of the sixteenth century and subsequently assimilated into the Authorized Version of the English Bible. This edition, produced by a committee of fifty scholars between 1604 and 1611, was referred to in American usage as the "King James Bible," (hereafter KJB). In the church's early days, none of the leaders of the Latter-day Saints knew Latin, Greek, and Hebrew (though some, including Smith himself, later studied Hebrew), so when they quoted the Word of God, they used the words of the KJB as if they were those of the original texts. From their enthusiasm for the KJB, one gains the impression that the early "Saints" felt that the Almighty had done his best work in English, and perhaps he had.

Here let me repeat the question: "Which Bible?," for things were not quite as they seem on the surface. In the Articles of Faith of the Church of Jesus Christ of Latter-day Saints, written by the Prophet, there is a revealing back-handed swipe at the King James Bible. "We believe the Bible to be the word of God *as far as it is translated correctly*; we also believe the book of Mormon to be the word of God."[7] Note the phrase "as far as it is translated correctly." Obviously, writing in 1842, Smith is comparing the Bible, which can have translation errors, even in the supernal King James version, and the Book of Mormon, which raises no such worries, since it was given directly to the Prophet Smith himself and, therefore, can have no translation errors. The invidiousness of the comparison leaves the Book of Mormon superordinate to the Bible.

And yet that is only a tithe of the meaning here conveyed to the "Saints," for "translation" was a code word, part of the secret vocabulary of the faith. Yes, "translation" could be construed to purvey meaning from one language to another, and in that narrow sense one could argue for the superiority of the Book of Mormon (which started out in English) to the Christian scriptures. That is fussing around the edges. As we will see a bit later, Joseph Smith and his followers used "translation" in a sense entirely their own. Smith employed it to mean his taking a direct revelation from the Almighty and putting it on paper. His divine revelations sometimes took the form of additions of entire books of scripture to the existing Bible; at other times, Smith introduced major appendices to existing passages of the Jewish and Christian scriptures; and at still other moments he used the direct revelation of the "Almighty" to himself to show where the Bible was wrong. So mention of "translation" in the eighth Article of Faith really meant (1) the Book of Mormon was superior to the Bible for philological reasons, but (2) much more importantly, the Bible was the word of God *only* if it was corrected, amended, and amplified by the divinely revealed material passed into print by the Prophet Joseph Smith. Myriad examples will be cited later. For the moment the point is the one any secular historian would immediately note: it is interesting when one encounters an individual who has acquired the right to rewrite some of the most pivotal documents in human history. Of course, the Prophet declared that he was merely the instrument for the restoration to pristine purity of God's Word.[8]

———

With the Prophet's epic false modesty in mind, it comes as a surprise to encounter Joseph Smith's first written revelation, the Book of Mormon, for it is relatively circumspect in the claims it makes for itself and very respectful towards the Bible in terms of its mode of presentation. Still, the publication of the Book of Mormon in Palmyra, New York, in late March 1830, revealed the optimism that has been such a noteworthy and perduring characteristic of the faith: 5,000 copies of the book of roughly 275,000 words were printed (so many copies that one of Joseph Smith's most faithful followers had to mortgage his farm to pay the printer's bill). With his basic scriptures to hand (the Bible and the Book of Mormon), the Prophet now was able to organize his own church. On 6 April 1830 in Fayette, New York, six of his closest followers and another two dozen disciples formally founded their new faith.[9]

The Book of Mormon is massively complex in its details, but is easily summarized. It is the story of the fates of three separate peoples. One of these, the Jaredites, who survived the Tower of Babel (set at 2247 BCE in Archbishop Ussher's chronology of biblical history, which the Mormons frequently employ) and eventually escaped to central America in eight sea-going barges. There they took to fighting among themselves and in approximately 600 BCE they wiped themselves out. They were a side-light to the other two groups, the sons of a previously unknown Israelite patriarch called "Lehi" (the word is a biblical place in the Palestinian lowlands). He has two sons, "Nephi" (a shortening of the name of the pre-flood giants mentioned in the Bible in Genesis, chapter six), and "Laman" (probably an adaptation of the name of the brother of the giant Goliath). The family of Lehi listens to the Almighty and flees from the Land of Israel in roughly 600 BCE, which means they escape the Babylonian Exile of 587/586 BCE. They traverse long stretches of desert and then build ships and sail to North America. There the two branches, the Nephites and the Lamanites, engage in a series of fratricidal wars, reconciliations, apostasies and repentances. The interesting point is that they have a pre-knowledge of Jesus Christ long before his birth. Moreover, in 34 CE, soon after his crucifixion and resurrection, Jesus appears in America and does some excellent preaching. But the wars between the two endogamous (and increasingly differentially pigmented) frateries continue, and eventually the Nephites, the white-skinned good guys, are wiped out in 421 CE: not, however, before their history is written on sacred metallic plates. (This was a practice the Jaredites had also engaged in, and eventually Joseph Smith claimed to possess four sets of metallic plates he translated into the Book of Mormon.) The bad guys, the dark-skinned Lamanites, survived intact and became the ancestors of the Amerindians who, by the time European explorers encounter them, have forgotten that they were ultimately part of the tribe of Joseph and therefore among the Chosen People.

Now, one of the silliest criticisms made of the Book of Mormon is that it is an heretical and plagiaristic rehash of the Hebrew and Christian scriptures. The Mormon defence against this has been twofold: No, it is not a plagiary because the material in it is new – or: No, it is not heretical because everything in it agrees with the Bible. Forget this. Of course the Book of Mormon is a rewriting of the Bible, but except at rare points it is compatible with the scriptures. It fills in parts that conceivably could have been in the Hebrew and Christian scriptures and does so with the same vocabulary, the same set of dramatic conflicts that make the Bible – especially the Tanakh – so strong. Harold Bloom, a masterful exegete of religio-cultural phenomena (and a very sympathetic observer of early Mormonism) has noted that "Mormonism is a wonderfully strong misprision, or creative misreading of the early history of the Jews."[10]

Notice: Joseph Smith had a pattern, an example to follow, namely, the way the "New Testament" was created. To anyone deeply familiar with the Tanakh, the "New Testament" is nothing more than a creative misreading and the Book of Mormon is no more a plagiary than are the Christian scriptures. Indeed, every single verse of the Christian scriptures has a source, if only a phrase or tone, in the Hebrew original. The early Christian authors did not really steal from the Tanakh; rather they were so saturated in the vocabulary, imagery, and dialectics of the Hebrew original that they could not think of religious truth except with the conceptual tools that the ancient scriptures gave them. Of course the inventors of the Christian scriptures creatively misread and imaginatively rearranged hundreds and thousands of the little tiles they appropriated from the Tanakh, and thus they made their own massive mosaic. Since they had a different base-story than that of ancient Israel to tell (Yeshua of Nazareth's story was rather different from that of Adam and the patriarchs), the resultant new artifact was beautiful, in parts sublimely frightening, in places hideously so, and at once both highly original and almost entirely within the ideational vocabulary of the ancient Jewish texts.[11]

The same pattern – though not the same level of artistic achievement – holds for the Book of Mormon. What terms other than biblical imagery, vocabulary, and dramatic structure does one expect Joseph Smith to think in? He was a young, semi-literate, largely unemployable farm labourer from the back-of-beyond and you expect him to have the intellectual tool kit of a Thomas Jefferson? Catch yourself on: the Book of Mormon is a strong misreading of the Bible (mostly of the "Old Testament") and a heroic one at that.

There are only two fundamental problems with it. The first is one of structure. The Book of Mormon can best be seen in literary terms as an example of the nineteenth-century three-volume novel and it is a clunker. The three sections do not balance. The third section (the "Book of Ether"), dealing with the Jaredites, takes up less than one-twentieth of the text and even then it is cut off by a codicil (the "Book of Moroni"). This still-born third "volume" of material on the Jaredites (who, recall, preceded the Nephites and Lamanites into America by about a millennium-and-a-half) reads like a failed attempt to begin a long biblical narrative, one that the author abandoned but kept in his stockpile as potentially useful in future. The middle "volume" of this three-volume novel runs from the confusingly named "The Words of Mormon" through the equally confusing "Book of Mormon" (neither of which should be confused with the overall term, the Book of Mormon). It takes up roughly two-thirds of the entire volume and is coherently presented and has a ring of confidence. The first "volume" of the novel, less than one-third of the whole, has a laboured, distracted quality that contrasts sharply with the confident tone of the second "volume." Some of its shorter segments (the "Book of Enos," the "Book of Jarom," and the "Book of Omni") seem to exist chiefly to cover big lengths of time quickly and thus to affect a cincture with the "Words of Mormon" that begins the compelling middle sector of the Prophet's creation. The reasons for this odd and off-putting imbalance in structure will become clear in

a moment when we look at the provenance of the entire Book of
Mormon. (That LDS apologists see the compositional weakness of
the Book of Mormon as a warrant of the volume's historicity is an argument that is here irrelevant.)

Briefly, though, some of the other literary qualities of the Book
of Mormon bear notice. Its early enemies said that it had a hugger-
mugger quality to it, but that is unfair. Nineteenth-century readers
were not as accustomed to the use of flashbacks-within-flashbacks
and to characters running from one tale to another as were later
readers. Once the reader becomes comfortable with these devices,
the real problem is just the opposite of hugger-mugger: instead of
being frantic and disordered, each individual tale is rigidly ordered.
This book is not the dance of dervishes but the step-step-step of
heavy boots, up one corridor, down another, back and forth, tramp-
ing through the days and nights and sounding with each passing tale
more and more like a hypnotic and soporific metronome. The
Prophet could write in only one register. And one can become vexed
with the author for his laziness: when he encounters writer's block,
his favourite way out is to insert a large chunk of the King James Bible into one of his tales.[12] But mostly one just chaffs under the
writer's remorseless humourlessness (a big contrast to the Hebrew
scriptures which are full of witty puns and some scabrous linguistic
jokes). If the Almighty in the Book of Mormon is given even a single
chance to show that he understands that his creation and his creatures have some amusing foibles, I have missed finding it.

And so did contemporaries. Instead, nineteenth-century reviewers
of the Book of Mormon often laughed at the literary solipsisms the
Prophet let slip in. The most famous of these is Smith's decision to
have a "Book of Ether." Now, even in rural areas in the late 1820s,
someone who could read a newspaper (and Joseph Smith was func-
tionally literate to that degree) would have known that whiffing ni-
trous oxide ("ether") was an evening's hilarious diversion for
adventurous young people in both city and countryside. And the
medical uses of "laughing gas" were beginning to be appreciated.[13]
Naming a book "Ether," even if that had ancient theological over-
tones, invited ridicule,[14] as did many other names created by the
Prophet. Dozens of false-Semitic names invite derisive English-
language puns, so one is actually relieved when the Prophet makes a
linguistic miscue and names the "exceedingly curious" Nephite who
builds ships for exploration of the "west sea," the Indo-European

"Hagoth." (Book of Alma 63:5). A bit of stereotyping, perhaps, when just Goth, Hun, or Burgundian would have done.

Actually, the unconscious self-parody in the Book of Mormon was caught only by outsiders, not by Smith's disciples. But one item drew the "Saints'" attention and caused long-term soul-searching. This was the Amerindian issue, and a real issue it was. Most white Americans of Joseph Smith's time were both fascinated by the Native Americans and deeply hostile to them. The Book of Mormon straddled that same line, but in a more conciliatory fashion than was usual. The First Nations of North America were presented in the Book of Mormon as being ancient brothers of the "Saints" because the Indians hailed from the biblical tribe of Joseph, via Manasseh. In the Hebrew Bible, Manasseh was the brother of Ephraim, the Israelite tribe from whom Mormons claim descent. So the Book of Mormon presented the "Saints" with the problem of dealing with their distant kin. These kin, mind you, were darkly coloured because unrighteousness besmirched human pigment and the darker a person was, the farther that person was from righteousness. As early as October 1830, the Mormons appointed four elders to visit Amerindian tribes in the west to spread the Prophet's revelations.[15] When some of the dark-skinned Indians converted and were baptized, Mormons were disappointed that they did not emerge from the waters as "white and delightsome people."[16] (Whether or not the new converts were also disheartened is not recorded.) Eventually, as the Church of Jesus Christ of Latter-day Saints moved westward, it havered: Indian lands were taken, but, whenever possible, compensation was paid; Indians were denominated in the Mormon scriptures as morally inferior, yet the same scriptures implied that they could be raised to the level of white Mormon civilization. Thus, condescension and compassion warred within the hearts of the faithful and on this issue it still does. In the twentieth century, several thousand Native Americans became Mormons and in 1975 George Patrick Lee, a full-blooded Navaho (and thus a full-blooded Lamanite) became the first Amerindian to be named to the First Quorum of Seventy, one of the church's upper echelons.[17] Issue partially resolved, apparently, although George Lee later became disaffected and was excommunicated.

————

A moment ago I mentioned that two fundamental problems bedevil Joseph Smith's work and they are serious enough to threaten to tip over the megalith that is the Book of Mormon. One of these, as already discussed, is the book's overall structure. It has no natural balance point, for its three sections are out of proportion to each other and to the total creation. The second basic problem is the book's provenance, and I think it is demonstrable that the difficulties with the book's provenance are directly responsible for the unbalanced form that the Book of Mormon finally assumes. Let us begin at the beginning. Joseph Smith was born 23 December 1805, the third son of a Vermont family that was barely successful in clawing a living out of the thin soil that covered its rocky farm. After several moves, the family (now with eight children and a ninth in train) fetched up in Palmyra, New York, in 1816. This was a reasonably prosperous town, close enough to the Erie Canal to be a potential commercial centre. The family struggled along and was not greatly helped by young Joseph's aversion to education (he did not take seriously to learning until his mid-twenties) and his even more distinct aversion to hard labour. By the time he was twenty years old, he was operating on the moral border between being a superstitious savant and a confidence-man.

His chosen idiom had various names: crystal-gazing, money-digging, peep-stoning. Think of it as an equivalent of dowsing for water but using a stone that had semi-supernatural qualities that allowed an adept to see through the earth and to discern valuable objects. This kind of thing was widespread in early America, but was especially popular in places such as the districts in north-central New York where there were large Indian burial grounds that often did include artefacts of some value, including brass utensils. Smith was credited with being able to see as far as twenty-four feet through the earth's crust with his special seers-stone – one that his wife later described as not quite dark in colour and that fits with the description of the seers-stone he later used when translating parts of the Book of Mormon.[18] In his early money-dowsing, Smith's usual mode of application was to place his seers-stone in his upturned hat and to bury his face in the hat and seek through the seers-stone the treasure that might be buried beneath his feet. Smith later (in the 1830s) admitted that he had been a money digger, but denied he had gone through any hocus-pocus or, indeed, had made much money.[19] However credulous these activities make young Smith's neighbours appear, they were within the rules. He was operating inside the boundaries of folk-belief and he was not fleecing anybody.

In 1826, however, he went over the line and became a confidence-man, as defined by his own society. He got greedy and took a well-off local farmer for a complainable sum of money: much of it went to men Smith had digging various holes for the treasure he had spotted, but the project also kept Smith in spending money and room and board for five months. No treasure was found and in March 1826 the aggrieved mark had Smith charged with using his seers-stone to fraudulently spy out potential gold mines and chests of money on the victim's property. The trial took place in Bainbridge, New York, where Smith had recently been attending, at age twenty, the local elementary school. Smith seems to have had both a pre-trial hearing and an actual trial, where he was found guilty and was given the choice of jail or of leaving town for a while. He left.[20]

This business upset later Mormon historical apologists a great deal, but one wonders why. So, Joseph Smith was a confidence-man. Acording to the Bible, the Almighty works his will with all sorts. A good con-man is fully capable of conning himself, and what starts out as a trick becomes a self-conversion. The final results of a good confidence game can be nothing less than sublime and the very act of producing a sublime trick can lead to a sublimated life for the trickster. Give young Joseph and the Almighty a chance to work things out.

Joseph Smith eloped with a young woman, Emma Hale, originally from Harmony, Pennsylvania, and was married 18 January 1827. They returned to his family's residence in Palmyra and the local authorities let him settle there in peace. But now he had responsibilities and needed money in hand. Thus was born his Big Con, the one that rambled out of control and eventually turned him from a small-time confidence trickster into the one authentic religious prophet to rise from the soil of rural America. The original trick was pretty basic. In the summer of 1827, Smith let it be known to his own family that he had found some golden plates, with writings on them, and that when the supernatural guardians of these items permitted him, he would present them, or at least what they said, to the public.

No one knows what he had in mind: at minimum an epic novel that would make his fortune, the more so because of the spectacular way the saga was announced, bordering on the supernatural. Joseph, although still not able to write an acceptable cursive hand, had both the ability to read quite well and an extraordinary facility with story-telling. So, before we view his whisking the cloth away from the golden plates, we can know with considerable certainty what the major components of his epic novel would be. These would be, first, the Bible. Second, America. That is, a biblical-style saga could be made to occur in the western hemisphere and mostly in what is now the United States of America. Third, he would deal with the native inhabitants. A salient feature of the land around Palmyra were numerous "Indian mounds" (mostly burial sites) and Smith and other treasure-diggers had often burrowed into them in search of booty. Fourth, Smith was willing to lift basic ideas from other people's work. It long has been suggested that he stole part of his early writing from unpublished writings of the Rev. Solomon Spaulding, who allegedly wrote two different versions of the story of the Israelites in America. In my judgment, the case here is just barely plausible, but highly improbable.[21] However, it is highly probable that Smith was acquainted with at least the outlines of the work of the Rev. Ethan Smith's (no relative of Joseph) *View of the Hebrews; or, Tribes of Israel in America* (Poultney, VT: Smith and Shute, orig. ed. 1823; sec. ed. 1825). By fortuitous coincidence, Poultney, Vermont, was the home in the mid-1820s of Oliver Cowdrey, who became one of Joseph Smith's chief secretaries in writing out the Book of Mormon. Comparative studies of *View of the Hebrews* and of the Book of Mormon show major structural similarities.[22] However, what I see does not involve direct plagiarism so much as Joseph Smith using an idea that Ethan Smith had come up with first. Perhaps the Prophet got his inspiration independently. It matters not for, as movie agents are forever saying, "You can't copyright an idea." The Prophet's book resembles the Rev. Mr. Smith's volume because they are both pieces of fictional logic that are based on the same ideational premise. Think: ancient Israel lived in America.

On 22 September 1827, Smith told his family that a special angel had given him permission to unearth some mysterious and sacred golden plates from the outskirts of Manchester, New York. The angel also had provided him with what, without impiety, we may describe as magical translating glasses. These were called the "Urim and Thummim" and, since they have forever disappeared (as have all the plates from which the Prophet eventually "translated"), they are difficult to describe. Their origin, however, is clear, for they are a direct lift from Exodus 28:30 where Aaron is told to put inside his priest's "breastplate of judgement, the Urim and the Thummim" (KJB).

These were taken in Joseph Smith's time to mean stones in some way attached to the high priest's regalia. These holy stones, or crystals, which go back to Aaron, are used by Joseph Smith to "translate" from a language he does not know into biblicalesque English. Mind you, he is careful not to show either of these devices or the golden plates to his family, for to behold their glory would be instant death. He does, however, allow his intimates to feel the plates when they are in a heavy piece of sacking; but see them, no.

For a time Joseph Smith tried to translate the golden plates at home in his family's residence, dictating to his wife, Emma, but there were too many distractions for him to get any work done: neighbours heard about the find and kept dropping in and asking to see the golden plates. (Smith, of course, refused, but let them feel some metallic objects that were wrapped in a linen table cloth.) So, Joseph and Emma moved to her family's home near Harmony, Pennsylvania. This move was financed by Martin Harris, Smith's first real mark and one of the most perduring. (It is he who eventually mortgages his farm to pay for the Book of Mormon to be published.) There, in his father-in-law's home, with Emma and, increasingly, Martin Harris as a scribe, the Prophet begins to translate. He has a curtain set up to separate him from the sight-lines of Emma, Harris, and anyone else in the house and then, using the Urim and Thummim as his spiritual eyes, he dictates from the golden plates.

The project moved haltingly, but Smith said that the plates were in "reformed Egyptian," so it was a hard job even with supernatural eyewear. To keep skeptics at bay, Smith copied off onto a piece of parchment samples of the "Caractors" he was encountering.[23] Some of these inscriptions were used on early posters advertising the Book of Mormon but, more importantly, a seven-line sample was preserved by the "Reorganized Church," now called the "Community of Christ" (a post-1844 splinter who prided themselves on keeping the pure Mormon record), and it is widely available.[24] The sample shows unambiguously that at this point Joseph Smith was still engaged in a complete scam (not a holy sham): the material is risible, being a jumble of mock-Hebrew, Ogam, pictographs, misformed Greek letters, and glyphs made to look vaguely Egyptian. It is the sort of thing a smart twelve-year-old would do.

If the actual "translation" went slowly, by mid-June 1828, Smith had dictated 116 pages of hand-scribed material from behind his curtain.[25] He was roughly one-sixth of the way through his three-volume novel and pre-publication interest was high.

Then disaster struck. The con-man was conned. The wife of Martin Harris, who was sick of his spending all his time and most of the family's spare cash on Joseph Smith's project, convinced Harris to bring the 116 completed pages home for her to see. She pushed hard and Smith had to give in against his better judgment. Mrs. Harris stole and eventually destroyed the original manuscript and told Martin Harris: "If this be a divine communication, the same being who revealed it to you [Joseph Smith] can easily replace it."[26]

Of course he could not.

This was one of the primary turning-points on the corkscrew road that is Mormon history. Most con-men, thus exposed, would have quietly slipped away. In July 1829 Joseph Smith had a major nervous breakdown and then, amazingly, effected a comeback. So resilient was the Prophet that he was dictating again by late autumn and the winter of 1828–29 was a feverish period of "translation" with new amanuenses (including Oliver Cowdrey – schoolmaster of the town where Ethan Smith had written and published his book on *Tribes of Israel in America* – who was drafted in to keep up with the now-epic flow). Mind you, Smith changed his mode of operation. The Almighty told him not to retranslate the original golden plates, but instead to use an abridged set, the "plates of Mormom," which fortuitously contained the core of his original material (the "plates of Nephi"). And the Urim and Thummim were taken from Smith, as punishment for his carelessness with the previous material. Now the Prophet had to return to the method he had used in his old money-digging days. He placed a seers-stone in the bottom of his hat, shoved his face into it, and came out with phrases for his secretaries to copy down. And didn't the man dictate!: by July 1829 the work was done[27] and there remained only the tiresome process of dealing with the printer.

Earlier, I mentioned that the three compositional sections of the Book of Mormon were out of balance and that this was a function of the provenance of the book. Here is how I would speculate on the relationship (I am confident of the first and second points, and slightly hesitant about the third: (1) The first section of the epic as we have it, with its awkward compression and skip–fast abridgements, was composed after the con-man trap was sprung by Mrs. Harris. The material is a replacement for the original 116 pages that Smith could not duplicate, retentive as his own memory was, and wisely he did not try. (2) The second section, the middle two-thirds of the Book of Mormon, is strong and coherent within the boundaries of its rhetorical assumptions and was written after Joseph Smith had recovered from his breakdown and was fully back in charge of his mind and imagination. (3) The third section, which should have been one-third of a successful three-volume novel, is the shrivelled "Book of Ether." It begins its narrative in approximately 2250 BCE and dies abruptly with the extinction of the Jaredites. It is totally out of phase with the main narrative of the Book of Mormon, which begins in approximately 600 BCE. I suspect that this is the vestige of an initial effort Joseph Smith made to recover his work after he had been unmasked as a confidence-man by Mrs. Harris. It is a bash at doing biblical history from the time of the patriarchs and I think Smith was wise to give it up: the thumping animation that characterizes his story-telling in full spate just is not there. The words, the register, the timbre, are those of a broken man, one who is trying to recover his spirit. This was material that the Prophet did not wish to throw away (what author likes to waste his own words?), but he probably should have.

Paradoxically, when Mrs. Harris purloined the first pages of Joseph Smith's magic-spectacles-derived dictation, she made the Mormon faith possible. That, though, was in the long run. The short-run question is: what does one make of the transformation of Joseph Smith after his debacle? Obviously, he showed himself a man of great character and of considerable shrewdness. But what did he become after being shown up as a con-artist? It seems to me that he took the first step towards becoming a towering figure. This occurred in stages. Here, in completing the Book of Mormon under a Chinese puzzle of circumstances, he turned himself into a voluble story-teller. That is a much under-rated skill and if his narratives are not polished, they were what his audience of rural proles wanted. Note, however, he did not set down any of the words himself. He was not yet sufficiently confident of his own written literacy, although he was studying assiduously. This first stage, as master oral story-teller was soon replaced (as we shall see in a moment) by very bold ventures into full written authorship – and he later developed a bravura voice, not just in the pulpit, but with his pen.

Somewhere along the line, Joseph Smith became a full-fledged prophet in the biblical sense of the term. Yet, crucially, one should not assume that his prophetic incandescence stopped his usage of many of the methods of the confidence trickster. As we shall see, at least through the year 1842 he was engaged in forgeries that were so easily detectable as to be embarrassing. Stating that, however, is merely secular history; if one is a "Saint," these actions should perhaps be thought of as God's enjoying a bit of sleight-of-hand.

As for the Book of Mormon, one must understand that the rough manuscript the Prophet dictated was very far from the polished item we read today. The printer received not a set of copperplate-on-foolscap, like, say, a lawyer's brief, but batches of two dozen pages each day, and these had no capitalization, few indications of the end of sentences, and virtually no punctuation. The typesetter, John Gilbert, did what he could to make the work look like a coherent and normal book.[28] Later, Joseph Smith was to work over some of the details and several of his followers ironed out infelicities and grammatical errors. An important turning-point was the polishing of the Book of Mormon by Smith's followers in England, who went over the volume for publication in London in 1841 and to which Brigham Young and Willard Richards added an index.[29] In the course of the various editings of the Book of Mormon, more than 4,000 changes were made between the 1830 edition and the one we know now.[30] These were matters of literary felicity, not substantive content. However, the most effective change was visual. After Smith's death, some of the more scholarly of the "Saints" arranged the Book of Mormon into chapters and verses and printed the book in double columns: in other words, they made it look like the King James Bible in format. All those were future changes, however. The first readers of the Book of Mormon encountered a long story that was not very easy to read and, because it had no internal reference system (as had the existing scriptures), it was hard to refer to precisely in discussion: a tough chaw.

The 1830 version, however, contained two informative items that were scissored out of later editions. Each was a terrible error of judgment on Smith's part. Firstly, the title page of the original edition declared that this literary property was "by Joseph Smith, Jun., author and proprietor," and he signed the preface as "The Author."[31] This assertion of authorship is revealing. It indicates that in the last days of preparing the Book of Mormon, Joseph Smith was still unsure as to how he planned to profit by his production: sell it as a Bible novel or use it to start a sect. In the latter case, he was breaking one of the most fundamental rules of the "grammar of biblical invention," as established in the Hebrew scrip-

tures.[32] He was asserting his own authorial power and creativity, something that ancient biblical writers were never allowed to do: even when
using their own names (as did some of the prophets), they made it
clear that they were not the author of anything, but merely a conduit
for the words of Yahweh. A frightful mistake on Smith's part, and
equally bad was his second miscue: he included in the preface that he
signed as "The Author" an explanation of why he had not re-trans-
lated the 116 pages that had been stolen from him by the cunning
Mrs. Harris. It was all a satanic trap, he said, for if he had "translated"
the original material again, then his satanic foes would have altered
his previous translation and then claimed that he was a fake because
the two versions were not the same![33] Obviously, it was well-known
among his acquaintances and followers that he had been caught in
Mrs. Harris's con-trap and he felt he had to justify himself. (Clearly,
Smith did not know if Mrs. Harris had destroyed the original manuscript or not.) This preface was immensely counter-productive – indeed, deeply stupid – for it broadcast widely (5,000 printed copies) a
scandal that previously had been merely local and it did so in the relatively permanent form of print.

These two mistakes were corrected in the next edition of the
Book of Mormon, which deleted the preface and had the title page
changed to declare that the book was (in the Mormon sense of the
term) "translated by Joseph Smith, Jun."

As eventually cleaned up and burnished, the Book of Mormon
was a splendid success: a Bible not just for the USA, but *of* it. Being
modest in its narrative – in the sense of mostly keeping within biblical tramlines, the Prophet was shrewd. That he made the occasional tactical error is inevitable and that he almost inadvertently
altered some fundamental Christian doctrines was a peripheral occurrence that we can mention later. The clear point is that Joseph
Smith had invented a great religious text (not a good novel, a great
religious text), and he knew it. In 1841, he reflected that his creation was "the most correct of any book on earth."[34] This was something he had foreseen distantly, like the viridescent glow of foxfire
in a northern swamp: for in the mouth of Joseph in Egypt, he had
placed the prophecy that a seer would some day come to take his
place as patriarch, "and his name shall be called after me; and it
shall be after the name of his father." This man would, by the power
of the Lord "bring my people unto salvation."[35]

Joseph Smith, Junior, son of Joseph Smith, Senior.

———

Because our long-range concern is to understand why and how present-day members of the Church of Jesus Christ of Latter-day Saints are engaged in writing the historical narrative of the whole human race, person by person, we must look more at their scriptures, especially those that are more robust, more singularly Mormon than is the Prophet's first book. The reasoning here is simple: the way that the Prophet established historical truth in some ways influenced his followers, and the way his followers assimilate both his doctrines (as found in his historical texts) and his methods is still salient today. These are the things that determine why and how the "Saints" do genealogy and aim to form the deep-story of every person who has ever lived.

Almost immediately after the Book of Mormon appeared, Joseph Smith took up a new style and method of scripture writing. The resultant pieces are found in The Pearl of Great Price. The items by Joseph Smith were written between 1830 and 1842 and published in Liverpool, England, by F.D. Richards in 1851. (Two additional pieces, one by Smith, which is available elsewhere, and one revelation by the then-president of the church, uttered in 1918, were added in 1976 but are not here relevant.) The Prophet's items in The Pearl of Great Price that are most revealing are materials that he claimed had been excluded from the true Bible because of the wickedness of the Hebrews and had only now been revealed to him: a Book of Moses, a Book of Enoch (which failed and was scrunched by later editors into the Book of Moses), a Book of Abraham "translated" from papyri that came into Smith's hands; and an extension of the twenty-fourth chapter of the Gospel of Matthew.[36]

Sound tiresome? Anything but, actually, for Joseph Smith, in June 1830, having just issued a new version of the Christian Bible and having founded a new church (*the* church, he declared), somehow discovered the fire, imagination, and unbridled hubris to begin lighting the sky with pyrotechnic new revelations. These had none of the modesty of the Book of Mormon for, from this point onward, the Prophet unashamedly corrected the Hebrew and Christian scriptures when producing his new documents. And he had a new method. No more using secretaries: he now could write a cursive hand well enough for compositional purposes. No more dealing with the awkwardness of golden plates or of peering into a seers-stone in his hat: the revelations came to him directly from God and that was that. He never again fell into the tactical error of describing himself as an "author," although he still made the mistake in two cases of letting a text come into existence that could potentially be checked against an external original. Still, from now on, Joseph Smith – the Prophet – was God's voice on earth.

In the Book of Mormon (1 Nephi 5:11 and 19:23) there is mention that the golden plates of Nephi include the canonical Books of Moses. Now Joseph Smith makes a titanic jump and writes as a separate entity his own Book of Moses. How fearless an effort this was cannot be underestimated. In traditional Jewish and Christian thought, Moses is the author of the first five books of the Hebrew scriptures and, moreover, it is his unique theophany on Mount Sinai that is the occasion of Yahweh giving the basal Commandments to his Chosen People. Moses is the one figure in the "Old Testament" that one does not mess with, just as Jesus is the one untouchable figure in the "New." Amazingly, Joseph Smith both upstages Moses and simultaneously redefines Jesus and does so without apology, for he is only straightening out the historical record. "And now of this thing Moses bore record; but because of wickedness it is not had among the children of men" (Pearl: Book of Moses 1:23). So, through direct revelation the Prophet provides a rewrite of Genesis, chapters 1–5. He corrects a number of matters that the Hebrew scriptures had wrong. The most important are that all the ancient Hebrew writers and most of the Christian Church Fathers had misapprehended the basic mechanics of world-creation. It was not done by the Almighty alone. Rather, Jesus, the only-begotten son of Yahweh, was present at the Creation and he and his father worked together to put the earth and its inhabitants into existence (Pearl: Book of Moses 2:26; this is a notion that a handful of the early Church Fathers endorsed, based on their reading of 1 Cor.8:6 and John 1:3). Further, Smith introduces a distinctly non-Judaeo-Christian notion, one that he will develop intricately later, namely, the pre-Creation and, obviously, pre-natal, existence of the human soul. (Pearl: Book of Moses 3:7). The LDS term for this is "pre-existence."

One could spend months parsing the fascinating way that Joseph Smith redesigned the Creation story. What counts most, however, is his simple hubristic declaration – that the Bible began incompletely, and therefore wrongly, and that by direct revelation from the Almighty, he had set it right: it's here on this paper that I have written, he said, and his people believed.

Exactly where the Prophet originally intended to end his "translation" of the Book of Moses is unclear, since the church authorities edited The Pearl of Great Price after his death. I think it ended at 6:11, with "And Jared taught Enoch in all the ways of God." This suggestion stems from the fact that it is documented that, at this same volcanic period of creativity, Joseph Smith was also writing a Book of Enoch[37] and this (now vanished) item actually starts here (at verse 6:12 of the Book of Moses) and provides a mighty prophecy by Enoch.

But why Enoch?, especially given that it was easier to sell an edition or a revision of a book of the Bible that actually existed or which the Bible listed as being lost. For example, the "Book of the Chronicles of the Kings of Israel" (2 Kings 1:18; 15:26; 15:31; 15:36), the "Book of the Chronicles of the Kings of Judah" (2 Kings 15:36; 16:19; 20:20; 21:17; 21:25), the "Book of the Acts of Solomon" (1 Kings 11:41) the "Book of the Wars of Yahweh" (Numbers 21:14), the "Book of Jashar" (Joshua 10:13), the "Book of Samuel the Seer," the "Book of Nathan the Prophet," and the "Book of Gad the Seer" (1 Chronicles 29:29), in addition to various lost letters of St Paul which are referred to elliptically in the surviving epistles. These were easy targets, pre-sold. Yet there is no clear biblical reference to a Book of Enoch,[38] so it was a harder task and, unlike the rewriting of Genesis 1–5 in his Book of Moses, Smith had no model to work with.

Yet Enoch was a temptation Joseph Smith could not resist, for the biblical figure of Enoch was a precursor of the modern prophet, Smith himself. In the Hebrew scriptures, Enoch is the seventh male in direct line from Adam and he is the son of Jared (whom Smith had tried somewhat unsuccessfully to make a major character-line in the Book of Mormon) and the father of Methuselah, who had lived longer than anyone else recorded in the Hebrew scriptures – 969 years (Genesis 5:27). Enoch, though, beat Methuselah's record, albeit in a singular way. He was such a holy man that he was said to have walked with the Almighty and therefore, after 365 years on earth, was taken away by God without having to undergo death. (See Genesis 5:22–24.) A man of nearly unparalleled piety, an intimate of the Almighty, and an immortal was Enoch: how could Joseph Smith resist "translating" a Book of Enoch, of a man who was so ... so ...

just like me, the Prophet. Amid the jeremiads, prophecies, and visions of Enoch, as presented by Smith,[39] one goes from the pre-Creation Son of God to the Garden of Eden, through numerous battles, into the city of Zion (built by Enoch) and one sees the cosmic engagement with Satan and partakes of a vision of the Son of Man coming to earth at the start of the millennium.

This is Joseph Smith at his best.

Yet, when The Pearl of Great Price was published in 1851, there was no Book of Enoch, as such. It was intercalated into the Book of Moses and its title was erased. No Book of Enoch had been written by the Prophet: that, clearly, was the message. Why?

The answer is absurdly simple. Once again, as in the disagreeable matter of his "translation" of the golden plates (where indeed had they gone?) and of the first 116 pages of his original manuscript, the Prophet had placed himself in a position to be shown up as a less-than-perfect prophet, although one of sublime talents in many regards. You see, although there is no biblical reference to a scriptural Book of Enoch (Smith had misread Jude 1:14), there was a real *Book of Enoch* and it was just being appreciated in the late 1830s and 1840s. This volume (sometimes referred to as *1Enoch*) had been very well known in the religious community of Palestine just before and just after the beginning of the Common Era, and had greatly influenced both Jewish and early Christian thought. This *Book of Enoch* was accepted by the Church Fathers until well into the fourth century, but thereafter it fell into disfavour and was preserved only by the Ethiopic Church. As far as the young Mormon church was concerned, this book had two toxic characteristics. Firstly, it was rediscovered in the western world at an inopportune moment. The work was brought back from Africa by a Scottish traveller and in 1821 an obscure English edition appeared. The Prophet apparently did not get wind of this original and therefore he proceeded as if he had a free field to work in. By the 1840s, however, senior Mormon authorities were well-enough informed of the *Book of Enoch* to be frightened not only of its existence but of the second property of this volume: in its 108 chapters, it is among the most intoxicating, visionary, hallucinatory, apocalyptic, and prophetic of any one of the scriptures or para-scriptures. (Today it is usually grouped with the Pseudepigrapha.) It includes many of the topical references Joseph Smith employed – Methuselah, the Son of Man, and several apocalypses – and it does so in such a mixture of literary greatness and god-drunken religious swirl that, were Joseph Smith's work to be placed alongside it, the Prophet's Book of Enoch would have been swept away like a dry seed in a whirlwind.[40] So, prudentially, the Prophet's Book of Enoch was interred, using the Book of Moses as its shroud. Of course, to do this was to destroy the integrity of a revelation that Joseph Smith had recorded. History, though, sometimes needs to be restrained in order to protect religious truth and, therefore, documents perforce must be modified.

In his rich god-speaking years after 1830, when revelations by way of "translations" proceeded from his pen as if there were an angel sharpening his quill, Joseph Smith wrote an entirely new twenty-fourth chapter of the Gospel of Matthew, "Commencing with the last verse of the twenty-third chapter, King James' version." Given that this displaced one of the Christian scriptures' most-treasured sermons, Jesus' Olivet Discourse, the Prophet's telling the reader what Jesus actually had said on the Mount of Olives indicates a fair degree of historical self-confidence. It was taken into The Pearl of Great Price as being authoritative LDS scripture.

Yet, within The Pearl of Great Price was one more Mormon scripture that equalled this in its brass-necked courage: the Book of Abraham. In 1835 Smith, whose Book of Mormon, it will be recalled, was from "Reformed Egyptian," was called upon by Michael Chandler, an impresario-cum-antiquarian who was travelling the country with an exhibit of Egyptian curios. Chandler asked for Smith's help in deciphering the meaning of some of the papyri. The Prophet could offer little immediate help, but bought several of the papyri for the sum of $2,400.[41] Smith set to cracking the glyphs, but it was hard work: by early 1838 he had only broken enough of the code to fill a chapter and a half. That Smith sorted out any of the Egyptian text would have been remarkable, since only in 1799 had a stone slab which gave Greek and Egyptian scripts in a parallel form been found near Rosetta at the mouth of the Nile. This discovery made possible the decoding of ancient Egyptian hieroglyphics by French scholars. Their results were published in English only in 1837. Baulked by the difficulty of traditional modes of decipherment, Smith in 1838 took to his more rapid mode of "translation," in that he let the Almighty declare the meaning of the rest of the papyri to him.[42] The results, both the "translation" and the engraved versions of the original Egyptian text, were printed in a Mormon periodical in 1842 and then in 1851 in the canonical book of LDS scripture, The Pearl of Great Price.

Now, since his last spate of "translations" in 1830–33, Smith had studied a lot and he was a man with a very sharp upward learning curve. From a Rabbi, Joshua Seixas, he had learned some Hebrew and discovered that there are several different gods mentioned in the Tanakh and also that one of the god-names used is a plural (Elohim). Dangerous knowledge. Equally stimulating to Smith's all-too-easily stimulated imagination was his digesting a volume entitled *Philosophy of a Future State* (Brookfield, Mass, 1830), which argued that God did not create the universe from pure emptiness but from material that he already had in existence.[43] (This is not such a brilliant idea, but never mind; Smith liked it.) The Prophet put together his new ideas and some of his old enthusiasms and announced that he had discovered and "translated" the Book of Abraham, written by the ancient Patriarch in his own hand.

This was an amazing call, for Abraham trumps even Moses in Hebrew patrimony. He is regarded as nothing less than the father of the Chosen People. Moreover, in printed form, first in a periodical in 1842 and then in The Pearl of Great Price in 1851, the Prophet's "translation" was literally sensational. He included not only his own five-chapter Book of Abraham but also engraved reproductions of some of the Egyptian papyri from which he had worked. And he showed how many of the individual glyphs were to be interpreted.

Within his "translated" text was a direct dialogue between Abraham and "Jehova" (meaning Yahweh) and also an assertion by Abraham that he possessed the Urim and Thummim which had been given directly to him by the Lord. Theologically the most interesting points were, first, that Jehova was a physical being. Abraham walked and talked with him and they clasped hands together (Book of Abraham 3:11–12.). Second, the idea of the pre-natal existence of human souls, which Smith had mentioned in his Book of Moses, was confirmed. "Now the Lord had shown unto me, Abraham, the intelligences that were organized before the world was, and among these were many of the noble and great ones" (Book of Abraham 3:22). These were souls, many of which later were to be born on earth. Third, the Prophet reconfigures the Creation story. Instead of being created by the Father and the Son (as he had previously stated in the Book of Moses), Smith now reveals that the heavens and the earth were created by several gods who were doing the bidding of the Lord and of the Son of Man and they worked with pre-existing physical material (Book of Abraham, chapters 4 and 5). Notice the word "gods." Joseph Smith had become convinced that there was a whole orchestra of gods playing a celestial symphony. Some were more important than others, granted, but the Prophet believed that he had rediscovered the true nature of the ancient Hebrew faith: polytheism.

These would be fairly big lumps of suet for most Christians to swallow, but the "Saints" did so with little difficulty. Even though Egyptology developed quickly during the nineteenth century and doubts were expressed about the Prophet's "translation," the revelation seemed safe: this because when Smith was martyred in 1844, the papyri were passed to his brother William and then (so it was believed) incinerated in the Great Chicago Fire. In fact, eleven of the fragments the Prophet had employed survived, and in the 1960s they resurfaced in the collection of New York City's Metropolitan Museum. Scholars, now being able to read such material, were fascinated to find that they bore no relation whatsoever to the Prophet's "translation." The papyri that Smith had used were from the first century of the Common Era (quite a distance from Abraham's traditional date of c.1800 BCE) and they were part of the Book of Breathings, a common Egyptian funeral manual.[44] "Significantly, this translation has caused nary a ripple among the faithful," a leading historian of Mormonism has noted. This, because they "are secure in the knowledge that scholarly apologists are at work reconciling the seeming discrepancy."[45]

Strangely, one aspect of the "translation" of the Book of Abraham that has given the Latter-day Saints disquiet centres on the figure of the Pharaoh who dealt with Abraham. Strangely? Actually, no, because this is the heart of the Big Black Problem that so long bedevilled the "Saints." It had begun in almost syllogistic form in the Book of Mormon where the good tribe was white and the bad one was not. At that point, however, the issue was whites vs. Amerindians, with the deeper problem – what do we do with *really* black people? – left unstated. Then, in the Book of Enoch (as found in the Book of Moses, 7:22) it was said that all the seed of Adam were of one sort, save "for the seed of Cain were black, and had not place among them." Obviously, Joseph Smith was working out his own doctrine of the racial inferiority of blacks. This was only fully articulated in the Book of Abraham (1:21–22) where the Egyptian king "was a descendant from the loins of Ham and was a partaker of the blood of the Canaanites by birth. From this descent sprang all the Egyptians ..." Now, in classical Christian racism (the sort used to justify slavery in the American South and later to justify apartheid in South Africa)[46] the erroneously named "curse of Ham" was the primary operative biblical text. Ham was the second son of the three sons of Noah and he was cursed, it is said, for having seen his father naked, so that "a servant of servants shall he be unto his brethren" (Genesis 9:25). With considerable alacrity, whites had taken this to mean that the blacks should be the servants of whites and forever inferior, but the textual proof was a bit ambiguous, since the curse was upon Canaan, the son, not on Ham, the father. Joseph Smith, though, removed all ambiguity in his Book of Abraham. Not only were Ham and Canaan equated but he situated the Curse of Ham in a cosmic battle between some of the good gods (he now was a polytheist, remember) and the evil gods. His key new invention is that, in this story, "the land of Egypt being first discovered by a woman, who was the daughter of Ham ... and thus from Ham sprang the race which preserved the curse in the land" (Book of Abraham 1:23–24). These black people and their descendants were forever denied the "right of Priesthood" (Book of Abraham 1:31). So, by 1842, the historical documents "translated" by Joseph Smith had developed a strange and ugly palpus, an organ that allowed Mormons to sniff out people with black ancestry and to deny them full membership in the Church of Latter-day Saints. (Granted, one could be a black male member of the church, although not eligible for priesthood – like the case of children and women – because of one's biological characteristics. Few black men took advantage of this Jim Crow privilege.)

The development of such a morally vulnerable appendage was perhaps not wise, considering the slave question in the United States in the 1840s; its preservation was even less wise 120 years later with the rise of the American civil rights movement. Should we reject this doctrine of perpetual racial inferiority and, if so, why and how?, the Saints asked. Their method of amputating the anti-black palpus reveals a great deal about the Mormon mode of making and breaking history. No, in the 1960s they were not going to give up a fundamental church doctrine just because a lot of outsiders considered it to be in error: the Mormons were a separate and holy people and the disapproval of outsiders merely confirmed their own righteousness and the rightness of the doctrine the outsiders opposed. Effectively, Martin Luther King never existed; nor the secular scholars who showed that the Book of Abraham, as "translated" by Joseph Smith, was a fictional entity and, therefore, it could be argued, not a binding moral revelation as concerning black inferiority. None of that mattered. What finally forced the church to deal with its Big Black Problem was the embarrassing matter of Second and Third World countries where converts were adhering to Mormonism in growing numbers. What was to be done in, say, Brazil, where some members of a family were fairly white and others quite black? And, really difficult, what about the extraordinary case of thousands of Ibo tribespeople in Nigeria who had converted themselves to Mormonism – this, without the benefit of missionaries, but simply by reading the Mormon scriptures and proselytizing literature? They were deeply sincere and deeply black.[47]

The way out was for the First Presidency of the church to have its own revelation. This, in early June 1978: suddenly, any male, without regard to race or colour, was eligible for the priesthood – meaning eligible to become a full "Saint." It was a wonderfully brilliant finesse: in one swoop, the church had repudiated its Curse of Ham doctrine and had totally redefined its criteria for membership, and yet had done so without in any way admitting that there were problems either with the theology of the Book of Abraham or with that volume's origins.

It remained untouched, a valid historical document.

————

According to the modern historians of the Latter-day Saints, Joseph Smith had between 120 and 140 direct revelations from the Almighty, not including his "translation" of the Book of Mormon: a goodly number, in any case. The most revealing of these, from the viewpoint of our trying to understand how the Mormon sense of history emerged, are found in the fourth of the Standard Works of scripture of the Church of Jesus Christ of Latter-day Saints. This set of scriptures is an extraordinary document, for it looks and reads like a memorandum ledger to Smith from God and from the Almighty's prophet to the Almighty's people. It was first published in 1833 under the title *Book of Commandments* (Independence, Missouri: W.W. Phelps and Co.) and then, rearranged and augmented, appeared in 1835 as *Doctrine and Covenants of the Church of the Latter*

Day Saints (Kirtland, Ohio).[48] Usually referred to as The Doctrine and Covenants, the volume has grown to 138 specific revelations in its present form, most of which had been communicated by the Prophet himself. That The Doctrine and Covenants grew not only in Smith's lifetime but thereafter provided no difficulty for the church because Article Nine of the church's statement of faith affirmed that "We believe all that God has revealed, all that He does now reveal, *and we believe that He will yet reveal many great and important things pertaining to the Kingdom of God.* (Italics mine.)[49] That is, the "Saints" believed in the doctrine of continuing and progressive revelation, so they had no trouble with a body of scripture that just kept growing and growing.

Such a broad sprawl is The Doctrine and Covenants that summarizing it is impossible. Instead, let us simply categorize the types of revelation – four, I think – that the Prophet communicated to his people. Each of these involves a different sort of historical thinking from the others and is revealing in its own way about the LDS mindset.

First, there is material that can be described as "necessary backfill" for the period between Joseph Smith's announced apprehension of the golden plates in mid-1827 and the publication of the Book of Mormon in the spring of 1830. These were historical events, but they needed tying together and tidying up because between Smith's announcing that he had the golden plates and his book's appearing he had been unmasked as a scam artist, had suffered a nervous breakdown, and had recovered and functioned at a high level of volubility. So, in the original (1833) version of what became The Doctrine and Covenants there were fifteen revelations, arranged chronologically, that covered the problem of the missing 116 pages that Mrs. Harris had snatched, the loss of the Urim and Thummim and the golden plates, and sundry exhortations to Smith's helpers in the publication of the Book of Mormon. In florid biblicalesque language, occasionally broken by lapses into awkward demotic, these sections show a man pulling himself together after a major setback and then directing a tiny guerilla band of warriors in his initial spiritual campaign.[50] If hard to accept literally, the material probably indexes accurately the historical course of Joseph Smith's self-repair after the Mrs. Harris disaster. And they really were necessary stories, for they answered questions about matters that his early followers keenly wanted to know.

Much less necessary and less indicative of any verifiable historical reality were later sections found in The Doctrine and Covenants and in The Pearl of Great Price (and in Smith's autobiographical History of the Church, which he began in 1838). This second set of revelations retro-filled the historical period before 1827. There really was no need for Smith to talk about his own life before the guardian angel let him take the plates for "translation," and the quieter he kept about his early life, when he was a small-time con-artist, the better. The Bible and Jewish and Christian histories are full of people who were sinners and then God took their hands and they were given a free slate so they could start over righteously. All Smith had to do was invoke this Repentance Clause. Instead, he retrofitted his own holiness and did so in a terribly counter-productive manner. In the mid-1830s Smith told some of his intimates that, when only fourteen years of age, in 1820, he had a massive vision. He wrote this in 1832.[51] This is first mentioned in print in a Mormon periodical in 1840[52] and in a brilliant passage of the "Wentworth letter" of 1842, from whence it becomes a real historical document, if not necessarily a document about real history.[53] At age fourteen (according to the middle-aged Joseph Smith), he had called upon the Lord to help him escape from the maddening overlay of conflicting religious opinions, each Christian denomination shouting over the top of the other. He retired to a secret grove and there was met by "two glorious personages, who exactly resembled each other in features and likeness, surrounded with a brilliant light which eclipsed the sun at noon day. They told me that all religious denominations were believing in incorrect doctrines ..." This vision was followed three years later, he said, in September 1823 by the appearance of the angel Moroni who revealed to him that on the side of a hill near Manchester, New York, was a stone box and golden plates and the Urim and Thummim. However, a divine messenger also told Smith that he should not remove any of the treasures until four years' time had passed.[54]

Well, it all fitted in a chrome-plated sort of way. That is, this material on the 1820 and 1823 visions fit with the shininess of the golden plates in 1827 and the publication of the Book of Mormon in 1830, but it fit too well to be convincing. (Notice the too-neat way the period 1820–30 is divided.) Chiefly, however, the retrofit of Mormon history failed because it left out the real-life Joseph Smith of the mid-1820s: peep-stone seer, Indian-mound digger, and court-convicted confidence-man.

Yet, this biographical material is actually not central to The Doctrine and Covenants, nor is the third sort of material in the document – items that resemble nothing so much as a bundle of divine inter-office memos – really of much consequence to the way "Saints" believe and act in our own time. There are some diverting moments, but it is hard to keep reminding oneself that these are actually scripture, part of the Standard Works: Emma, the Prophet's wife, is given an entire revelation all to herself, "the voice of the Lord your God" tells her to stop her backchat and to be more of "a comfort unto my servant, Joseph Smith, Jun., thy husband, in his afflictions, with consoling words, in the spirit of meekness" (Doctrine and Covenants, section 25). Martin Harris has the voice of Christ (via Joseph Smith) tell him to keep all the commandments and, by the way, the Book of Mormon has yet to be paid for. "Pay the debt thou hast contracted with the printer. Release thyself from bondage" (Doctrine and Covenants, section 19:35). The Prophet, using his own voice, augmented by divine authority, gives the dimensions and location of the house to be built for himself in Kirtland, Ohio (Doctrine and Covenants, section 94).

What counts most in The Doctrine and Covenants, however, is the fourth sort of material which consists of frequent and hugely audacious rewrites of parts of the Bible. These surpass anything in the Book of Mormon and equal the most ambitious parts of The Pearl of Great Price. Several involve using the voices of major figures, including Jesus-the-Christ, to amend and to contradict (ah, "translate" correctly) what had been said in the canonical Christian and Hebrew scriptures. A simple example is that in April 1829, while the Book of Mormon still was in progress, the Prophet dictated to one of his secretaries a "translation" of a piece of parchment he had somehow acquired (and, not surprisingly, which was later lost before anyone else could see it). This parchment, relatively small, was said to contain a segment of scripture written by the author of the Gospel of John. On it, Jesus queried the apostle, "John, my beloved, what desirest thou?" John replied, "Lord, give unto me power over death that I may live and bring souls unto thee." And Jesus agreed that John could stay on earth and prophesy until the Second Coming (Doctrine and Covenants, section 7).

Nothing unambitious there. Nor in the Prophet's taking over the voice of St. Paul and rewriting part of 1 Corinthians, chapter seven.

This is a very difficult passage in Christian theology, for it deals in verses 10 through 17 with a matter on which Paul disagreed with his master, Jesus of Nazareth: Paul accepted that in some circumstances divorce between a man and a woman was necessary. Jesus did not. (Compare the words of Paul with Jesus' words in Matthew 5:31–32, doubled in Matthew 19:9.) Joseph Smith, who had a strong predisposition against divorce, especially if it involved freedom for a woman to remarry, simply rewrote the Bible to make it agree with his own view. He excised verses 15–17 and then continued on in a pseudo-Pauline voice (it is a hard voice to imitate) about circumcision (Doctrine and Covenants, section 74). Thus was one of the "New Testament's" thorniest issues solved: the difficult text was erased.

Mostly, these "translations" are fairly sure-handed in their details, if unsure in timbre and register. The biggest gaffe occurs in a "translation" given to the Prophet in April 1836. There, in ringing tones, he has two primary biblical prophets appear to him sequentially. First, "Elias appeared, and committed the dispensation of the gospel of Abraham ... After this vision had closed, another great and glorious vision burst upon us, for Elijah the prophet, who was taken to heaven without tasting death, stood before us ..." (Doctrine and Covenants, section 111:12–13). Joseph Smith, who was progressing quickly with his studies of biblical languages, had not yet acquired much, if any, Greek, and did not realize that "Elias" was simply the Greek name for "Elijah." In his searching out useful figures in the Bible for his "translations," he had created two characters out of one.

In the "translations" that appear in The Doctrine and Covenants, all sorts of biblical characters pop up; they are easy enough to digest rhetorically. What still must be a difficult bolus for any biblical scholar to swallow (whether or not that person is a believer or a secular scholar) is the dozens of times that the Prophet speaks in the voice of Jesus-the-Christ. There is no profit in my here parsing case after case – you have to read this material for yourself. Whether or not Jesus of Nazareth ever actually uttered a single word that is ascribed to him in the "New Testament" is here irrelevant. What is relevant is that the canonical Christian scriptures had, by mid-fourth century of the Common Era, become a set of historical documents that had an integrity of their own as documents – whatever one thinks of their contents. In The Doctrine and Covenants is evinced most clearly and more ambitiously the exercise of an entitlement that is unique: the right to alter these documents, by excision, amendment, and *pure laine* creation.

———

In the emergence of the unique scriptures of the Church of Jesus Christ of Latter-day Saints, we have been observing a set of attitudes towards history that eventually will enwrap millions of "Saints." Of course, in focusing upon the several scriptures, upon their mode of production, and upon the way they were interwoven with the Jewish and Christian scriptures (and, ultimately, took precedence over them, like an upas-tree upon its host), we have been looking at only half the story. The consumers of these scriptures are always there. That someone was willing to buy the product is just as important as there having been someone available to produce it.

So, taken together, we have an uneasy pair of paradoxes. The "Saints" accepted the right of the Prophet and his successors to revise existing sacred documents and to create new ones virtually at will. Ancient Jewish and Christian historical documents were treated as being made of soft plastic, useful for remoulding to the Mormon purpose. Yet, once the revelations of Joseph Smith and of his successors were canonized, they were to be taken literally and not to be questioned by the faithful. That is the first paradox: the "Saints" as consumers of historical knowledge were willing to be extremely generous in accepting new revelations, and then became extremely costive in protecting those revelations from any critical historical investigation.

And yet a second paradox lies behind the first. This is that if the church authorities declared a new revelation that contradicted an earlier one (as in the case of the church's Big Black Problem), the "Saints" could accept both the new historical document (all revelations become historical documents the moment they are recorded), and still not conclude that the previous, now-corrected document had contained an error. That takes a power of mind, an ability to enforce mind-over-reality, that is truly humbling.

This, though, has nothing to do with the massive Mormon genealogical project, right?

3   The Indomitable
Overcoming the Inevitable

Of course it does – the great Mormon genealogical project is the conjoint result of the way the several Mormon scriptures were produced and the paradoxical way in which the "Saints" came to approach history.

The beginning of the massive Mountain of Names that the LDS preserves in Utah is found in scriptures that Joseph Smith articulated in the last four years of his life. Much of the monumental genealogical project has to do with baptism. This is ritual cleansing, a practice that almost all of the religions that are descendants of the ancient Yahweh-faith engage in. The most common rituals involving complete immersion (and sometimes a thorough washing of the body); other methods involve the sprinkling of water on the head and sometimes upon the heart, or the cleansing of certain parts of the body as a metonym for cleansing the entire body. The age of the person baptized varies greatly.

Among the "Saints" there was no ambiguity about which form to follow. In the Book of Mormon, the Lord God commanded "all men that they must repent and be baptized in his name, having perfect faith in the Holy One of Israel, or they cannot be saved in the kingdom of God." (2 Nephi 9:23). The baptism of little children was unnecessary (Book of Moroni 8:10–15), for it was only an adult who could be aware of his sins and repent. And, the model for baptism was that conducted by John-the-Baptizer with Jesus of Nazareth (2 Nephi 31:5), and that had involved full immersion in the Jordan River.

In 1836 Joseph Smith began to break the baptism of the "Saints" out of the rubrics of all the other faiths by initiating a mediation that resulted in the Mormon practice of baptizing dead people: by proxy. In the Christian misarrangement of the Hebrew scriptures, the last words of the text are those of the prophet Malachi, speaking for the Lord. "Behold I will send you Elijah the prophet before the coming of the great and dreadful day of the Lord." And here is what counted greatly to Smith: "*And he shall turn the heart of the fathers to the children, and the heart of the children to their fathers, lest I come and smite the earth with a curse*" (Malachi 4:5–6). The italics are mine, but Smith would have seconded them, for he brooded upon them: how could the hearts of fathers and the hearts of their children be joined? Fortunately, the ancient Hebrew prophet Elijah appeared to Smith and to Oliver Cowdrey, one of Smith's outriders, on 3 April 1836. Elijah's words were again ambiguous, but they concluded this way: "To turn the hearts of the fathers to the children, and the children to the fathers, lest the whole earth be smitten with a curse." Yes, yes, we have heard that before in the book of Malachi. What came next? "Therefore the keys of this dispensation are committed into your hands; and by this ye may know that the great and dreadful day of the Lord is near, even at the doors" (Doctrine and Covenants, sect. 111:15–16). But the keys of exactly what dispensation? (The previous words in the revelation about keys and dispensations had been pretty muddy.) Well, LDS scholars take this to mean (and I think correctly) that Joseph Smith was beginning to invent the baptism of the dead.

There are portions of the "New Testament" that can be taken as endorsing, or at least bearing witness to this practice. In 1 Peter 3:18–19, Jesus is presented as preaching to the dead after his own demise. And St. Paul appears to argue for the effectiveness of someone's being baptized for a dead person (1 Corinthians 15:29). So, Joseph Smith seems to have been working his way towards the revival of a custom that the Christian church had given up by the fourth century, a way to regenerate souls after their earthly demise.

Unusually for the Prophet, he developed his doctrine slowly, rather than by sudden revelation. He talked among his intimates about the doctrine of baptism of the dead and by August 1840 he was writing to his travelling representatives in England that he had recently mentioned the matter in a funeral sermon. "The Saints have the privilege of being baptized for those of their relatives who are dead, whom they believe would have embraced the Gospel, if they had been privileged with hearing it ..."[1] The doctrine clearly had an appeal to the "Saints," for they conducted the first proxy baptism for dead persons in the Missouri River near Nauvoo, Illinois, in the autumn of 1840.[2]

Then, suddenly, in January 1841, the Prophet told them to cease.[3] This was not because Joseph Smith failed to understand the attraction to the "Saints" of the baptism of the dead, but rather because he intuitively realized that he was on to something so central to the human condition of America in his own time that he had to proceed not with mere caution but with perfection. As Klaus Hansen has presciently noted, ante-bellum America had a high child-mortality rate and that resulted in a forever-fear: the fear of losing a child whom one loved and, more heart-wrenchingly, the fear of loving any of one's children too much, for to do so was to invite heartbreak as the tides of child mortality swept down upon them.[4] You see, the baptism of the dead was not just about one's forebears: in Joseph Smith's time it was as much about one's children, especially those who died in childhood. Being able to be sure that their souls were saved was a healing balm to any parent. And – critical to the development of what later observers see, accurately, as the close Mormon family structure – it gave parents licence to love their children. The natural impulse in a society where childhood deaths were common was for adults to freeze out their vulnerable children emotionally. Smith's revelation overcame that for the family would meet again as baptized "Saints" in the celestial world. At such moments of apperception, Joseph Smith was a prophet indeed.

A full revelation eventually was involved, for on 19 January 1841, the Prophet was informed by the Almighty that there was no baptismal font on the entire earth that was worthy for the celestial baptisms and that "baptisms for your dead shall not be acceptable unto me" unless the "Saints" "build a house to me wherein the ordinance for the dead belongeth" (Doctrine and Covenants 124:32–33). Joseph Smith was on to something big for, despite his decree of January 1841, "Saints" kept baptizing their dead in the river and in October he had to repeat his prohibition and make it clear that no more baptisms for the dead could be conducted until they could be done properly in the ill-fated Nauvoo temple, whose construction was moving ahead quickly.[5] On the 21st of November 1841, with the walls of the Nauvoo temple still rising around it, a baptismal font was dedicated. This was the mother of all Mormon fonts, literally, for all subsequent temple fonts follow this model.

And a fearsome model it is. The classic Mormon font consists of a baptistry that rests on the back of twelve oxen, representing the twelve tribes of Israel. These were to be high-finish five-year-olds. (Cattle fattened much more slowly in the nineteenth century, so think of, say, a dozen grain-fattened two-year-old Charlois steers.) And on their twelve backs was a tongue-and-grove timber pool; 16 x 12 feet, large and deep enough so that in most present-day municipalities such an entity has to have safety fencing: quite enough to drown in.[6] The demand for proxy baptism, for dead parents, for dead children, for dead spouses, was immense, and the LDS ritual as yet not fully set. Men were baptized for women, women for men: innocent "irregularities," as they later were denominated.[7] The thirst certainly was there. Thus in an epistle of 6 September 1842, Joseph Smith, speaking in the voices of the Archangel Michael and of Sts. Peter, James, and John, instructed his people further about baptism for the dead. Crucially, good records were to be kept of the dead people baptized. Witnesses were required in each case, for the names of these people were being recorded in heaven as well as on earth. Smith even used one of his recently learned Latin tags, *summum bonum* and, incongruous as that is linguistically, it fits perfectly with the spirit of what he is telling his people. It is wonderful news, for now there is hope for an eternally welded link between human generations. Therein lies much (not all; there is more), but much of the preternatural optimism that makes Mormonism so difficult for outsiders to understand. The "Saints" can overcome not only their own death, but that of their children, and of their ancestors. Of course that leads to overflowing happiness: "Let the mountains shout for joy, and all ye valleys cry aloud ... And ye rivers and brooks, and rills, flow down with gladness ... And again I say, how glorious is the voice we hear from heaven, proclaiming in our ears, glory, and salvation, and honor, and immortality, and eternal life ..."(Doctrine and Covenants, section 128, esp v. 23).

———

Brilliant, resonant with the present-day LDS obsession with genealogy, but not as straight-ahead as it first appears. That is something one has to keep re-learning: that the Mormon theology and the theologically derived behaviour of the "Saints" are never as simple as they appear on the surface. To the world, the Mormons have always wished to appear more like a tea-party held by the Anglican

Church Women than as a meeting of the bishops of Byzantium, which they often closely resemble. These are complicated people and their doctrines are sinuous: not dishonest, just complex in some places and almost everywhere intertwining with each other, so that one faith-statement cannot be interpreted without reference to another one and no single faith-act is a simple faith-act.

All the time Joseph Smith was working out the basic concept of proxy-baptism-for-the-dead, he was engaged in planning a much more complex cosmic drama. This involved his seemingly weird romance – I am sorry, there is no other word than weird – with Freemasonry. Although in his earliest writings the Prophet had shown an antipathy to the Freemasons, they were fated eventually to bond, for the Masons traced many of their beliefs and rituals to the First Temple (that of King Solomon), and Smith claimed Semitic antiquity for the origin of many of his own doctrines. So Masonic ritual had the potential of being a smooth meld with Mormon theology. And that is what occurred.[8]

In December 1841 a lodge of Freemasons was founded in Nauvoo and immediately Mormon men swarmed to it, including Joseph Smith and his leading acolytes. Soon, a Masonic temple was started (completed in 1844), and at the lodge's formal opening on 15 March 1842, Joseph Smith set a *Guinness Book of Records* standard for ascent of the Masonic ladder: he went from being a neophyte to being a 33rd degree Mason within a single twenty-four hour period.[9] Most of the adult Mormon males of Nauvoo joined the lodge, and this put the fear of, well, the Lord, into the Freemasons of Illinois in general: the total non-Mormon membership of Masonic lodges in Illinois was 227; and the number of Mormon members or candidates-for-membership was 286.[10] So they had the Nauvoo lodge suspended from late in 1842 until October 1844, when rapidly increasing general persecution of the Mormons made Freemasonry an irrelevant side issue to everyone involved. For the moment, though, in 1842 and 1843 the "Saints" kept up their Freemasonry and absorbed Masonic rituals like parched wanderers in a desert. This Masonic base is still clearly recognizable at the heart of present-day Mormon temple ceremonies. At the time, the Masonic initiation and progression up the ladder of secret knowledge involved a ritual washing of the body of the candidate by a senior Mason, the donning of a special undergarment (essentially a decorated and ritually slashed union suit), and then, while wearing white robes over this sacred underwear, the candidate was initiated into some of the secrets of Freemasonry through allegorical drama. As the individuals gained more esoteric knowledge (usually this took years of study), there were more dramas and more and more oaths and secret signs and passwords.[11]

Remember that the Prophet had become a Freemason on 15 March 1842. In May 1842, he brought together in the upper room of a store in Nauvoo several selected "Saints" and introduced to them the concept of the *endowment ceremony*. "Endowment" became the LDS shorthand for the fuller term "Endowment of Power." This was to be a series of progressive rituals that would be engaged when the Nauvoo temple was completed. Like the Masonic sequence of dramas that increasingly inducted the Mason into new levels of ancient esoteric knowledge, the Mormon endowment ceremony would be a series of cleansings, anointings and of allegorical dramas that brought the "Saint" ever-closer to the godhead. This sequential "endowment" was to be available both to men and women, and Smith's first wife, Emma, was the first to receive the blessing.[12] Thus by mid-1843, Smith had his "Saints" in a fever: they were working heroically at building a massive temple; even as the walls of the temple rose around them, they were engaging in proxy baptisms for the dead and, by word of mouth, the "Saints" were learning that the Prophet has some unimaginable spiritual gifts to reveal to them and that these gifts – called "endowment of power" – would be given to them in a series of sacred ceremonies in the new temple. Rise quickly!

The fever became a paroxysm when, on 12 July 1843, the Prophet uttered his most famous, and certainly his most cosmically ambitious revelation. This revelation, given entirely in the voice of the Almighty, is frequently misconstrued, for it contains the divine command for polygamy (or, "plural marriage" as the "Saints" have preferred to call it, inaccurately, as it really is only male plural marriage). Believe it or not, that was only a minor part of this incredible vision. "For behold," says God, "I reveal unto you a new and an everlasting covenant; and if ye abide not by that covenant, then are ye damned" (Doctrine and Covenants 132: 4). The Almighty continues, through his Prophet, "my servant Joseph," to explain that "all covenants, contracts, bonds, obligations, oaths, vows, performances, connections, associations, or expectations, that are not made and entered into and *sealed by the Holy Spirit* ... have an end when men are dead" (132:7, italics mine). Note that word, "sealed," for it is the prepotent action-word in all Mormon theology. Everything is temporary and merely mortal until it is "sealed by the Holy Spirit," and the representative of the Holy Spirit on earth is Joseph Smith or his spiritual heir. What needs to be sealed? Marriage for one thing. "If a man marry him a wife in the world, and he marry her not by me nor by my word ... they are not bound by any law when they are out of the world" (132:15). Granted, according to Mormon theology, in heaven they become angels, doing odd jobs for the Almighty and his servants, but they are separate and single and not particularly blessed. But, if a couple undergoes "the new and everlasting covenant, and it is sealed unto them by the Holy Spirit of promise, by him whom I have appointed ...," they are sealed together forever (132:19).

This is *celestial marriage*. So, if married in the new temple, a couple will be sealed for all eternity, and if they are already married, Smith had made it clear to his intimates that there could be retro-sealings, so that a man and wife could spend eternity in celestial bliss. And he had explained that the children of a marriage performed by the LDS priesthood, under the Prophet's authority, would be part of an eternal family also. And there were sealing ceremonies planned for living children (of unsealed marriages) and for dead children.[13] Families were forever. And, since the "Saints" already were knowledgeable about baptizing the dead, families could be retro-baptized and retro-sealed backwards in time.

Yet there was more, much more. Celestial marriage was one step towards the ultimate form of polytheism (a doctrine which, earlier, we saw the Prophet embrace, as a result of his studying ancient Hebrew). "Then shall they be gods" [the sealed man and wife] ... "Then shall they be gods, because they have all power, and the angels are subject unto them" (Doctrine and Covenants 132: 20). That is some big promise: follow the instructions of the Almighty, the biggest of the many gods in the celestial world, and you can become a god yourself.

Where, though, does polygamy enter the picture? It enters through the trap door of logic. God reminds his listeners that some of the most important of his servants – Abraham and King David, for example – had many wives and/or concubines. Now, the logic here is simple: if one can become a god through one marriage, then how much better to engage in two, or twenty, or whatever number of marriages? And these male plural marriages, though made on earth, are, when sealed by the church, celestial marriages. Although the Prophet was not so crude in this revelation as to have the Lord spell out the final conclusion of the theological syllogism, it went like this: if a single temple-sealed celestial marriage made a man (and his wife, but that was always a sidebar for the Prophet), into a god, then how much bigger and better a god would that man be in the celestial world of eternity if he had several celestial marriages?

Quite a bit bigger and better, if Joseph Smith's own actions are any indication. A recent work of Mormon apologetics suggests that Smith probably had received his revelation about polygamy in 1831 and that certainly by 1835 he had engaged in one such marriage, to a nineteen-year-old (or younger) serving girl in his house.[14] Other informed LDS sources suggest that he had begun his own practice of polygamy in 1833[15] although, in any case, he did not reveal the doctrine to his followers until several years later. A minimalist count is that eventually the Prophet had thirty-two plural wives, ten of whom were also married to other men. A rather generous assessment of his motives is that "Like Abraham of old, Joseph yearned for familial plenitude. He did not lust for women so much as he lusted for kin."[16] Apparently the Prophet's first wife, Emma, was not pleased with all this marital clutter, for the Almighty (still using Smith's voice), had to admonish her at some length and tell her to "receive all those that have been given unto my servant Joseph ..." (Doctrine and Covenants 132:52). One hesitates to criticize the Almighty, but it seems somewhat mean-spirited for him to have added, "And I command mine handmaid, Emma Smith, to abide and cleave unto my servant Joseph, and to none else" (132:54).

How all this would have played out – the baptism of the dead, the Jacob's Ladder of "endowment" and the associated Masonic-derived rituals, the theology of celestial marriage and practice of earthly polygamy, and the belief that the "Saints," if they acted according to directions, could literally become gods – if Joseph Smith had not been martyred on 27 June 1844 is unknowable. It is clear that the "Saints" were deliriously keen on the promised system. The virtual completion of the Nauvoo temple in December 1845 sent them into a collective paroxysm. The demand for sealing and endowment was so great that for a while the temple had to run twenty-four hours a day.[17]

Perhaps the Prophet, like his predecessor Enoch, had left this earth for the celestial realm at just the right moment.

––––

The rest of Mormon history in the nineteenth century is well-known, or so it seems: the election of Brigham Young as the new leader in August 1844, the evacuation of Nauvoo in 1846, and the re-enactment of the biblical Exodus from persecution, involving wars, incredible physical hardship, and the founding of a holy city of refuge in the Great Salt Lake Valley (which was in Mexican territory when the Exodus began, but was ceded to the USA in 1848). Oh, they took some time to sort out the polygamy issue but, that done, the "Saints" became the most hard-working and patriotic of Americans.

If it were that simple, the reason the Mormons are so keen today on genealogy would simply be that their theological doctrines make it a very rewarding practice. Sealing dead souls, especially one's own ancestors, for all eternity is a good way to spend earthly time. Actually, during the second half of the nineteenth century, the "Saints" as a collective entity were being wound tighter and tighter, like a piece of spring-steel, and it was only when that tension was released that they turned forcefully to genealogical work.

The brute fact is that during the second half of the nineteenth century the Mormons were at war with the world. As I mentioned earlier, there always has been a Byzantine aspect to the "Saints," and much of it stretches back to the mental habits of the Prophet himself. Only since the pioneering work of Klaus Hansen in the 1960s has it been documented that Joseph Smith planned a Kingdom of God in the literal sense, and this was quite different from the spiritual entity that was his church. One of the secret acts of his foreshortened life was to create a "Council of Fifty" in Nauvoo. This group was to be part of the Prophet's millennial strategy. They were to be "princes" and the Prophet to be the "king" and they were to set up a dominion on this earth that would be the first step to ushering in the reign of God. This would be an imperium that would spread over the entire earth. Now, it is just barely possible to read this as mere metaphor on the Prophet's part, but that is special pleading, for the Council of Fifty planned in detail for the economic, practical, and moral discipline of their satrapy, and it was this-world planning, practical and literal. Moreover, the Council of Fifty continued after the Prophet's martyrdom and in Utah they did in fact try to promote the creation of a little country run by their God-derived rules.[18]

That the idea of a Kingdom of God on earth as a reachable goal was eventually abandoned does not mean it was not attempted. In practice, the Mormon utopia in Utah (Utah became a geographically defined territory in 1850) had three characteristics. First, and most importantly, it was a theocracy. Brigham Young, though careful always to make clear that he was not claiming the full spiritual abilities of the Prophet, let no one doubt that he wore his mantle. He issued bales of directives (his collected discourses reached twenty-six volumes) and seems to have created a remarkably able centralized bureaucracy. Secondly, the Mormon kingdom was communistic – not in the sense of then-emerging European revolutionary communism but in the sense of communitarianism and self-imposed economic isolation. The Utah "Saints" tried to isolate themselves from the capitalist economy of the USA (they even issued their own money). As outside merchants moved close – aided by the completion of the transcontinental railroad in 1867 – the LDS leaders managed a boycott of non-Mormon businesses which lasted from 1868 until 1882.[19] Even after the boycott was dropped, cooperative Mormon farms and businesses kept the "Gentiles" at bay.

Almost inevitably, the USA and its capitalist economy and individualistic society would have worn down God's desert kingdom, but the entire process was speeded up by the American public's dislike of the Mormons' "peculiar practice" – a term used first for the South's slave-holding and later applied to the "Saints'" polygamous marriage pattern. If there is one thing most adult Americans knew about the Mormons it was that the men practised plural marriage. And if there was one thing that Brigham Young was keen to preserve it was polygamy. One finds him in August 1873 delivering an astonishing but extraordinarily effective sermon on the topic at Paris, Idaho, where there was a colony of "Saints." Young had none of the biblicalism of the Prophet, but he had the tone of an old uncle who could badger his nephews and nieces with effect. In this sermon he mostly dealt with the nephews and their laziness, as close a thing as there is to a mortal sin in the Mormon vocabulary. He reminded his listeners of the July 1843 revelation of the Prophet concerning celestial marriage and male plural marriage. "If we could make every man upon the earth get him a wife, live righteously and serve God, we would not be under the necessity, perhaps, [Why the "perhaps"?, a few of his unmarried auditors might have wondered] of taking more than one wife. But they will not do this; the people of God, therefore, have been commanded to take more wives. The women are entitled to salvation [Ah, it's for the benefit of the women; but of course] if they live according to the word that is given to them; and if their husbands are good men, and they are obedient to them, they are entitled to certain blessings and they will have the privilege of receiving certain blessings that they cannot receive unless they are sealed to men who will be exalted. [That is, the men will become gods in the next life; quite right, too.] Now, where a man in the Church says, 'I don't want but one wife, I will live my religion with one,' he will perhaps [Why the "perhaps" again?, some may have wondered] be saved in the celestial kingdom; but when he gets there he will not find himself in possession of any wife at all. *He has had a talent that he has hid up.*" One can hear Young thump the pulpit and feel the collective intake of breath. He has hit the perfect note: a reference to Jesus' Parable of the Talents in which the man who did not increase his single talent was called wicked and slothful and thrown into outer darkness (Matthew 25:14–30). Brigham Young has actually improved upon the Prophet's doctrine of celestial marriage: he has announced that if you are too lazy to have at least two wives, then in the celestial world you will not have any wife at all.[20] Brigham Young preached well and practised better. He was married twenty-seven times and at his final reviewal in 1877, seventeen wives were present on the widows' bench.

Having fought a war against secession and slavery, the federal government of the United States was not inclined to allow a potentially independent, non-capitalist, and polygamous kingdom to develop within the borders of the constantly expanding American empire. No single legislative or administrative act of the federal government was enough to break the Mormons, but the USA kept moving forward, constricting the LDS, pushing the "Saints" ever-more onto the defensive. An anti-bigamy act of 1862 (the Morrill Act) was unenforceable as local courts refused to convict their co-religionists. However, the 1874 Poland Act established that federal law and federal administration controlled the legal system. Thereafter the United States district courts possessed the sole power to prosecute on bigamy and related criminal matters. Then in 1882, the Edmunds Act, applying only to Utah, provided for the US president to appoint both the governor and a five-man administrative commission to run most things in the territory, including elections, and a "test" was required if one was to vote, namely that the citizens (only males could vote) had to swear that they were not bigamists. None of these attempts was completely effective, but the garrote around the Mormons' neck became tighter and tighter. In 1887 the Edmunds-Tucker Act legally dissolved the church and began confiscating all of its property above the total value of $50,000. All these attacks were made through legal mechanisms and, in fact, the US Supreme Court upheld the Edmunds-Tucker Act by adjudging that the Latter-day Saints "church was an organized rebellion against the government, distinguished by the practices of polygamy and ecclesiastical control of its members."[21] At the same time the Mormons were being beaten by this stick they were being tempted by the carrot of statehood for Utah, if only they would behave outwardly like most other Americans. And tempting it was, for if Utah became a state, Mormon voters would control its government and, although it would mean the surrender of the Prophet's Kingdom of God, it would indeed be a Pretty Good Place.

Thus, in a series of compromises between 1890 and 1908, the "Saints" decided to join America. The signal event was the manifesto of Wilford Woodruff (who had become President of the church in 1884 and thereby was the lineal spiritual descendant of the Prophet) issued on 25 September 1890. The document declared that the church no longer taught plural marriage or permitted anyone to enter into a plural marriage. Apparent surrender, but palatable: recall that Joseph Smith had articulated as a basic item of faith the doctrine of progressive revelation. Woodruff, as the heir to Smith, declared that his decision was the result of a direct divine revelation. On that basis it was accepted reluctantly, but obediently, by most "Saints." Some indication of the unpopularity of the Woodruff decision was that despite its being a direct revelation from the Almighty, it was not included in The Doctrine and Covenants of the church until 1908, and then as an unnumbered item at the back.[22] The church kept its word and stopped permitting polygamous unions, although rebel fundamentalists were let slide by until the 1907 federal inquiry into the eligibility of the apostle Reed Smoot to sit in the senate.[23]

Simultaneously, though with no great manifesto, the Church of Jesus-Christ of Latter-day Saints gave up Joseph Smith's idea of a

Kingdom of God on earth: not forever, but for the foreseeable future. The Council of Fifty was ineffective by the early 1890s. The
Mormon's separate political party was disbanded in 1891, and
thereafter the "Saints" distributed their votes among the secular
parties. The Kingdom of God having been temporarily cancelled,
Utah was granted statehood in 1896.

At the same time, the communitarian economic structures of the
church were infiltrated and then etiolated by the capitalist economy of the wider society.

The cumulative result of all these changes was amazing. Between
1890 and, roughly, 1918, the Church of Jesus Christ of Latter-day
Saints had gone from being a real-world Kingdom of God on earth,
one that was communistic and polygamous, to being solely a kingdom of the spirit (at least until the present), one that forbade anything but monogamy and which, with a rapidity that was almost
obscene, became one of the most capitalistic, success-striving societies in the world.

That is revolution.

Yet, the true wonder is that the church did not break. It was
strong like a willow, not like an oak; and just as a willow usually
makes it through a roaring gale with less damage than does an adamantine oak, so the LDS church, compromising with the prevailing
and overwhelming forces of the US federal state, kept its identity
and self-respect intact.

Of course, the Prophet's doctrine of continuous and progressive revelation was crucial; but there was more than that. As we
will see in several instances relating to the genealogical work of
the church, there has also been a remarkable constant social characteristic at play. This is an ability to quietly, almost silently,
change beliefs and practices while at the same time refusing to
choke upon the undeniable fact that these things are being altered. Granted, between 1890 and the end of World War I, the
"Saints" repudiated many of their core beliefs and practices, but
they did not change their ideology – in the sense that they still
were the Latter-day Saints, no matter what. Any organization that
could survive what the church went through in the late nineteenth and early twentieth centuries could be expected to prosper
in the succeeding decades, for the institution was flexible enough
to adapt to a world where nothing stayed the same one year after
another – and at the same time the LDS church was sufficiently

sure of itself not to let the world's ebbing-and-flowing tides wash away its cohesion. Amazing indeed.

———

Revolutions almost always release or redirect immense amounts of energy. So, in a sense, the historian now engages a question of physics: what happened to all the energy that previously had been directed towards maintaining the Kingdom of God on this earth and to promoting a unique family structure that has promised to bring the "Saints" to the status of gods in the celestial realm? Some of it dissipated, unchannelled; much of it went into the search for success in business. (If ever there were a people who illustrated the possibilities of Max Weber's thesis, it is the Mormons.) And, a surprising and continually increasing amount of energy went into genealogical work, which was now redefined and given greater and greater emphasis.

In his revelation of 1890, Wilford Woodruff, president of the church, had served as the pivot for an ideological revolution among the "Saints" and in another revelation of 1894 he turned his attention to problems with various liturgical services conducted on behalf of the dead. This was a good time to straighten out such matters, for the temple in Salt Lake City was completed in 1893 and immediately upon completion it became a centre for services for the living and the dead. But, in reflecting upon this beehive of activity, President Woodruff concluded that things were being conducted in a haphazard fashion. For one thing, genealogy was being done in an innocently sloppy way. While most Mormons had their deceased parents proxy-baptized, it was common practice for everyday members to declare themselves "adopted" by some LDS personage of high rank then, sealed liturgically to that person, thereby followed his line back into antiquity and forward into eternity. By 1893, just before Woodruff's revelation intervened, roughly 13,000 such adoption-sealings had been completed.[24] To an outside observer this is merely bad genealogy, but to President Woodruff it was much worse: bad doctrine, for these adoptions meant that the line of genealogy the ancient prophet Malachi and the Prophet Joseph Smith had desired – the joining of father and son – was being aborted. Woodruff's divine revelation was that "Saints" should work only on their own family lines and that they should not merely baptize their ancestors but effect the liturgical endowment and sealing

for each generation. "We want the Latter-day Saints from this time
to trace their genealogies as far as they can, and to be sealed to
their fathers and mothers. Have children sealed to their parents
and run this chain through as far as you can get it ...This is the will
of the Lord to his people ..."[25]

This revelation in April 1894: it is not accidental that in November 1894 the Genealogical Society of Utah was incorporated. There
had to be a library, a standard set of recording procedures and, ultimately, a bureaucracy, if genealogy was to be done properly. *This is
the will of the Lord*, President Woodruff had declared and from that
revelation came, eventually, one of the world's best reference libraries and humanity's most ambitious attempt to narrate its collective story.

One should not overstate the initial pace of this eventual achievement. Most ordinary Mormons were too busy to spend time in serious genealogical research. However, in this early era, genealogical
work attracted two very forceful figures, both of them with the best
of LDS bloodlines. One of these was Susa Young Gates. She was one
of the daughters of Brigham Young, a mother of thirteen, a suf-
frage crusader, and a person of fearsome will power. (Some contemporaries called her the thirteenth apostle.) She supported
historical lineage work on a variety of fronts, developed the first set
of classes in genealogical methods, tyrannized the church leader-
ship when it under-funded the library and, incidentally, in 1908 set
a precedent for which non-Mormons should be deeply grateful: she
forced the library to rescind its rule limiting use of the library's material to members of the Church of Jesus Christ of Latter-day
Saints.[26] Her own volume of 1918, cryptically titled *Surname Book
and Racial History*, was a template for what all Mormon genealogy
would reveal. That is, unlike secular students of history, Susa knew
where human genealogical research would wend its way: back to
Father Adam and his wife. (Mrs. Gates was very strong on propriety;
those two were married.) She therefore began a manual on tracing
one's ancestors – and a very thick manual it was: 576 pages – not
with how to go backwards but with a story that went forward. From
Adam, down through the Hebrew scripture's founders of the three
major races – Ham, Shem, and Japheth – through Jacob and his
son Joseph (and his second son Ephraim, from whom almost all
Mormons of Gates's era were thought to descend), into the New
World via Joseph's first son, Manasseh, and thence to the peoples

THE INDOMITABLE OVERCOMING THE INEVITABLE 65

described in the Book of Mormon, and finally to the big empty spots where genealogies were weak: from about 1800 back to the ancient Chosen People on both sides of the Atlantic Ocean. If one can get over this initial melange, Gates's book contains a good many sensible suggestions on how or where Mormons should look for their own personal genealogical background: in the British Isles, mostly, and in Western Europe.[27] Three thousand copies of the book were printed and it was force-fed to virtually every historical and genealogical society and library in North America and in Europe.[28] The details and method of LDS genealogical work have become infinitely more sophisticated since Gates's time, but her paradigm has remained.

The second energizing figure in the genealogical sector in the era of the Mormon cultural revolution, 1890–1918, was Joseph Fielding Smith, whose father in October 1901 had become the sixth person to be president of the Church. (Both of these men had the same name – Joseph Fielding Smith, the father, was always referred to as "Joseph F. Smith" and the son by the full three-part name) He was a grand-nephew of the Prophet and a grandson of the martyred brother Hyrum. From his return from missionary service in 1901 onwards, Smith minor was the spine of the church's historical and genealogical work, much as Mrs. Gates was the mouthpiece. Indeed, he worked for it tirelessly until January 1970 when he became the ninth successor to the Prophet.[29] Given that Joseph Fielding Smith was the oldest person ever to become president of the Church of Jesus Christ of Latter-day Saints – he was ninety-three years, six months of age when anointed – it is not surprising that he served less than two-and-a-half years before "passing through the veil," in Mormon terminology.

What he did for the Genealogical Society and for family research in local wards has been well memorialized by LDS historians. What is not recorded is the high probability that it was his influence that led his own father (spiritual heir to the Prophet) to have a major revelation in 1918 that expanded the doctrine of the redemption of the dead. In his vision, President Joseph F. Smith's vision actually saw Jesus Christ visit the spirit world and work there to evangelize the dead who had not yet been saved. This was a ratification and expansion of the view that Joseph Smith, the Prophet, had put forward. Now, in President Smith's vision, departed "Saints" were to preach to those "Gentiles" who had not accepted the gospel while alive. The Lord himself organized these missionaries, revealed President Joseph F. Smith: "From among the righteous, he appointed messengers ... even to all the spirits of men; and thus was the gospel preached to the dead."[30] Hence, in concert with the millions of "Saints" who were expected to be missionaries on earth, there was a comparable number who preached to the billions of the dead who were in "spirit prison."

This revelation helped to spur genealogical work. Obviously, in a general way, the vision emphasized that the cause of the dead was an important duty. More directly, however, was a shrewd doctrinal proviso: that although the great missionary work in the spirit world certainly would produce an army of posthumous believers, they could not become true "Saints," and thus enjoy the full joy of living among their fellow gods, unless church ordinances – baptism, endowment, sealing – were performed for them by persons on this present earth. And how can one perform ordinances unless we know the names of these people? The only way we can do so is through genealogical research. Now, although only a small percentage of the Latter-day Saints actually were engaged in serious genealogical work in the middle years of the twentieth century,[31] the genealogical system was a litmus item that indexed the new contours that the church was assuming and, especially, the new confidence and post-Victorian "niceness" it embraced.

The period 1918–76 was a distinct era in church history. The former date is President Joseph F. Smith's vision of the mission-to-the-dead and the latter date is its adoption as holy scripture by the church. Think for a moment about the concept of performing holy liturgies for the dead and about the belief that dead "Saints" could go on mission to the billions who had departed this life without having heard the gospel. Whatever else this was, the continual emphasis upon this post-1918 doctrine was nothing if not both immensely self-confident and extremely generous (the more so considering the kicking the Mormons had taken at the behest of US society in general). None of this save-ourselves-and-everyone-else-is-damned for the "Saints." The church, following the 1918 revelation of Joseph F. Smith, was the most inclusive organization in this world and the next. And generous: it was willing to preach to anyone who ever was.

Interestingly, in this era, 1918–76, the church's view of the afterlife softens. It had never been very harsh, but the Prophet had cast some very Hebraic curses at his enemies. These fade away, mostly. The Mormon's three-tiered heaven – it is a theological construct that I have never seen explained in words that I can understand; my fault, doubtlessly – has this characteristic: even the bottom level is not bad. It is close to the Catholic idea of purgatory, but not one in which sinners are tortured in the classic Augustinian manner, for even there the glory of the Almighty makes post-death existence fine beyond mere understanding.[32] And almost nobody goes to the Mormon equivalent of Hell. Originally, the Prophet had decreed that eternal damnation would be visited upon those who had received the Holy Spirit and then denied it. Also, those who had shed innocent blood were banned from the Lamb's Book of Life and had no chance of celestial glory, but were to burn in the eternal lake of fire (Doctrine and Covenants 76:35–36 and 132:19). However, these provisions seemed excessively harsh to "Saints" in their era of growing confidence and inclusiveness so, after World War I (when Mormons fought on both sides, for there had long been LDS missions to European countries), they quietly dropped the issue of the taking of human life and let the Almighty sort that out. As for sins-against-the-Holy-Spirit, although the foundation texts remained the same, the meaning was transformed. Originally, it had been a curse against apostate Mormons. By the mid-twentieth century, it was limited to those few mega-sinners who had defected from the Holy Ghost, and the only one anyone could name with certainty of universal acceptance among the "Saints" was Judas Iscariot."[33] Ineluctably, the Church of Jesus Christ of Latter-day Saints was becoming so generous, so optimistic, so non-threatening, that it could with full confidence preach that virtually every human being had a decent future in the next world and, with proper spiritual tutelage from "Saints," dead or alive, depending on the circumstances, everyone could expect to move ever-upwards on the celestial ladder: providing they heeded the call.

This expansiveness, optimism, and self-confidence can be seen by any outside observer in two mundane (meaning this-world) developments among the Mormons. One of these was the creation of a Mormon form of ecclesiastical architecture. As dozens of temples rose around the North American continent (and, increasingly, elsewhere), their Sacred Basilisk school of architecture became as unmistakable as Stonehenge and just about as easy on the eyes. It ruled until, roughly, 1980, proclaiming the presence of the Prophet's true faith, and cried out Bauhaus-we-ain't. Simultaneously, a Mormon school of decorative art emerged, representational and unselfconscious. The school was needed, first, to provide gripping illustrations of scenes from the Book of Mormon for proselytizing purposes and, second, to decorate temple interiors with vast murals. This latter practice had begun in 1884, with the Logan temple wherein separate rooms were set aside for each of the sacred temple ceremonies and the walls were covered with huge symbolic paintings – symbolic, but employing representational figures. This decorative period dominated until the mid-1950s.[34] It is still popular today in booklets and framed prints. Visually and iconically it is easily recognizable: just think of Maxfield Parrish as a "Saint" on steroids and you're there.

Although heavy-duty genealogical work was actually performed by only a minority of Mormons – Monday night was genealogy night in the tightly-packed LDS weekly calendar – it became an increasingly common semi-avocational activity in the 1930s. In part, this was because adults without jobs had more time for eternal pursuits. However, more directly influential in the long-run was the decision in October 1930 to include a requirement in the training of the "Aaronic priesthood" – roughly, boys aged twelve to seventeen or eighteen, preparing for the higher "Melchizedek priesthood" – of one lesson a month in genealogy.[35] Here a batch of sequential activities is set the teens (for each of them they received a paste-on symbol from which they could build up their own personal coat-of-arms):

– write the story of your life;
– make a record of your own family;
– fill out completely your own pedigree chart;
– write brief stories of the lives of any five of your direct ancestors;
– make out correctly one or more baptism sheets from the family record of your parents. Send these sheets to be approved at the Index Bureau in readiness for baptism;
– be baptized for 100 of your kindred dead;
– find by your own efforts one new progenitor not known to your family before;
– teach another to compile a pedigree chart and family group record.[36]

The direct effect of such lessons for the young probably was minimal – church authorities kept complaining that many "Saints" routinely went to temple and, while neglecting their own ancestral kindred, were satisfied to take part in proxy ceremonies with any name they were given – but in the long run the effect was considerable, for now a generation of young Mormon males was being brought up, each of whom had done at least some genealogical work, and some of whom became quite keen on it. This trend was confirmed a generation later, in 1961, when the performance of genealogical work was designated by the First Presidency as one of the four functions of the LDS priesthood, these now being missionary activity, welfare provision, home teaching, and genealogy.[37]

The most obvious physical manifestation of the exponential increase in commitment by the church to genealogical work in the 1918–76 era was an immense construction project that was took place in Utah. In mid-1960, an extraordinary underground storage site for the millions of family records the LDS had collected was begun. In what approached fulfillment-of-prophecy, the site was Little Cottonwood Canyon where the stone for the supernal Salt Lake temple had been hewn, three quarters of a century earlier. This subterranean site – it reminds one of the heroic underground labours of the Cappadocian Christians in the years of Roman persecution – was to house the data for the salvation of billions of souls and, ultimately, it was hoped, the material for the narrative of the entire human race. It opened in 1963 and it is the world's largest storage facility for temperature-sensitive historical data, such as microfilm and, increasingly, for electronic data forms that are surprisingly unstable under even moderate ambient stress.[38] What a palace to the eternal: no wonder that when Alex Shoumatoff published his 1985 book, subtitled *A History of the Human Family*, he chose as his main title, *The Mountain of Names*, a direct homage to this Mormon votive site of which any pharaoh would have been proud.

Coincident with this achievement was another step in LDS outreach. Beginning in 1961, with the establishment of the Logan, Utah, branch library, a system was set in place to provide widespread access to material that previously had been searchable only in Salt Lake City. This became a formal branch library program in 1964[39] and by the end of the twentieth century most Mormon wards of any size had "family history libraries." This is a benison not solely to Mormon genealogists but to anyone doing family studies, for they are open to "Gentiles," and, in my own experience, in a most pleasant fashion. One of their admirable characteristics is

that, besides being very good on the records of their specific local-
ity, these family history libraries give efficient inter-library loan access to microfilms of fugitive printed and manuscript materials that
often are not in the Library of Congress, the National Library of
Canada, or in the British Library.

Generous, amazing, hubristic, perhaps: the "Saints" were on the
edge of their Big Push for the salvation of the entire family-of-man.
This was made clear in 1969 when the church began the auto-
mated processing of its genealogical files of those for whom temple
ordinances had been performed.[40] In Silicon Valley, Mormons
were among those in the forefront of several research programs
and much of this expertise came back to Salt Lake City: the LDS
church would be on the leading edge of the computer acquisition
and manipulation of genealogical data.

This march to the front of one form of computer data-management
was coterminous with an ideological affirmation. Recall that in 1918,
Joseph F. Smith had experienced a mighty vision concerning Jesus'
ministering to the dead and of "Saints" who had passed through the
veil of death becoming missionaries to the deceased. In 1976, this vision, and one of the Prophet's of January 1836, were declared by the
general conference of the church to be scriptures. They were added
to The Pearl of Great Price and to The Doctrine and Covenants, as
sections 137 and 138.[41] The affirmation of President Smith's 1918 vision as a genuine revelation, on a par with any in the Bible or in any
other Mormon scripture, was no idle gesture. It said that the Church
of Jesus Christ of Latter-day Saints, which was engaged in a worldwide
expansion involving millions of new members each decade, was going
to pin much of its resources on church activities (especially temple
ceremonies) that depended upon massive amounts of genealogical
data to keep the faithful liturgically busy. The growth of the Mormon
family on earth, therefore, depended upon the growth of the Mormon family in heaven.

PART TWO

The Course of Adam

4   *What's the Plot?*

In the autumn of 2004 a thick, celebrity-endorsed book entitled *The Seven Basic Plots: Why We Tell Stories* appeared. Its author, Christopher John Penrice Booker, sometime editor of *Private Eye*, solid BBC scriptwriter, and longtime Sunday *Telegraph* and *Daily Telegraph* columnist, had begun to write this book in 1969 and it took him nearly three-and-half decades to finish drafting it. So perhaps one should not begrudge him even a single one of his 700-plus pages and, anyway, big topics frequently require big books. "To spend half a lifetime writing a single book is obviously ridiculous," Booker confessed in an "author's personal note" near the end of the volume. He employed that self-deprecating modesty the English use when they mean just the opposite.[1] Actually, Booker's assertion at the start of his study, that he stands in an authentic critical tradition, was somewhat more accurate. Dr. Samuel Johnson had told his running-dog James Boswell that the same images had served the authors of fiction over and over with little variation. And, indeed, Johann Wolfgang von Goethe had been fascinated by the assertion of his friend Carlo Gozzi, the defender of the traditional Italian *commedia dell'arte*, that there were only thirty-six dramatic situations.[2] Intrigued by this speculation, Georges Polti, a serious scholar, managed to come up with thirty-six plots which, when taken together, made up the paintbox of all literature – and of all narrative, storytelling, gossip, and dreams, for that matter. They included things such as Pursuit, Madness, Remorse, and Recovery of a Lost One. Furrow-browed though Polti's work may have been, it had no logic as an analytic typology and, in any case, the result was a set of unresolved situations, not of plots.[3]

Plots require resolution (otherwise they are just situations), so one admires the straight-ahead courage of William Foster-Harris who in 1959 presented *The Basic Patterns of Plot*. These boiled down to three fundamental plots in all literature: "Type A," wherein the I-character makes an apparently illogical sacrifice for someone else and a happy ending results; "Type B," in which the I-character does what appears to be logically right, but somehow fails to make the necessary sacrifice and an unhappy ending ensues; and "Type C," the so-called 'literary plot," in which the tale proceeds backwards, running from an ending (either happy or unhappy) to the place where fate (or whatever one calls it) had determined events. "Type C" is the plot of Greek tragedies, Foster-Harris suggests. None of these are objectionable as plot-types, but how can they be seen as all-encompassing? To take the lowest level objection to Type A: what about the situation in which the I-character makes a logical self-sacrifice (why does it have to be *ill*-logical? one wonders) and everything works out. And so on.[4]

As for Christopher Booker's *The Seven Basic Plots*, he is convinced that he has found a set of furrows deep in the human psyche and that "the general approach to stories set out in this book will come to be widely accepted, simply because it opens up our understanding of why we tell stories in a way which makes it scientifically comprehensible."[5] Admirable ambition. However, if plot analysis is to become a scientific activity, the categories of plot must be rigorously defined indeed. Booker's seven plots, then, bear attention, not least because he is claiming to chart the grooves by which human beings narrate their own existence. They are: (1) Overcoming the Monster, which covers everything from the triumph of James Bond to, one infers, the resurrection of Jesus Christ. (2) Rags to Riches, putting David Copperfield and Cinderella under the same blanket. (3) The Quest. (4) Voyage and Return, which is hard to distinguish from The Quest. (5) Comedy. (6) Tragedy and (7) Rebirth. Actually, how anyone can see either comedy or tragedy as a single plot beggars the imagination: a single ending in the respective cases (happy, or unhappy), but single plots? From such sloppiness can arise no rigour. But one remains curious how Booker could ever raise the suggestion of this sort of thing being "scientific" thought? Then one realizes: he has suffused his whole massive book with a thick gravy that gives off the irridentist sheen produced by the admixture of Jungian archetypes and feel-good spiritualism.

In creating the universe and forming story-telling humanity, Booker tells us, "the cosmic mind which had originally set all this in motion had at last created an organism which could, however dimly, share a tiny bit of its own consciousness; which could become aware of its own transcendent existence; which could sense that behind all creation and all the universe was one unifying power which bound it all together, as one substance, one structure, one all-connecting impulse and one spirit which ..." Oh dear, he just goes on and on.[6]

Now, why are you being subjected to this? Observing how these plot analyzers operate (and I have saved you from some beauties)[7] is like watching a series of crashes on a toy railway system: kind of fun at first, but not instructive on any real-world scale. Why watch? First, one looks at such mini-minds because it makes one appreciate the true first-rate talents in the field. These are people who became known as "narratologists," even though some of them were uncomfortable with that label. Second, because I think that genealogy is actually an extended form of narrative and therefore has a plot-structure. And, third, because it is profitable to look for a grammar of genealogy in the same way that narratologists look for a grammar of stories of all sorts. If I cannot put forward a single grammar of genealogy, I can at least suggest the limited number of forms that the sequential narrative of human existence has taken.

———

The start of a sensible way of looking at narrative that has an applicability to matters of genealogy grew out of the Russian Formalists of the first half of the twentieth century. They attempted to put literature on a "scientific" footing in the sense that poetry (their chief interest) and narrative have ways of working that operate irrespective of specific content. In other words, literature is not current events, but system. At the edge of this group was Vladimir Propp, who was less wedded to high culture than the other Formalists, and much more willing to use material that was empirical and verifiable in constructing his system. (Here I should recognize that the words "empirical" and "verifiable" are anathema to most postmodern literary critics, save the New Historicists but, ultimately, we are not playing in their world, but one in which such things as life and death actually take place.) Propp amassed a large data base of Russian folk tales (alternately called "magic tales," or "fairy tales") and, as he did so, he realized that they were remarkably similar in basic ways. In 1928 he published in Russian a book that filtered its way into French literary scholarship and in 1958 was rendered into English in an obscure research monograph[8] and then in 1968 into a well-distributed university press volume as *Morphology of the Folktale*.[9] His theory of the Russian folk tale was based on two formulations. First, the concept of *functions*. By this he meant the act of a character in a story as defined by the significance of the act for the overall course of action. There are, Propp said, four clear rules of functions in Russian tales: (1) The functions of characters serve as constant elements in a story, no matter who fulfills them. They are therefore the fundamental components of a tale. (2) The number of functions in the entire range of Russian fairy tales is limited. (3) The sequence of functions is always identical. And (4) all the fairy tales from which he worked had only one basic structure, by which he meant a linear mode.

Notice that in point "3" he employs his second pivotal concept, *sequence*. According to Propp, there were thirty-one possible plot elements – and no more – in Russian folk tales. The full list of generic elements would be a distraction at this point. The key point in viewing his entire sequential list[10] is to understand that the full line of each of these elements is not found in any single tale, but that no tale can be constructed without employing some of the components of his list, and that there are in Russian folk tales no compositional elements additional to his list. In recent years, a useful convention among critics has fined down Propp's initial thirty-one elements into five "moves" that each traditional story possesses: (1) protagonist discovers a *lack*; (2) protagonist goes on a *quest*; (3) protagonist finds *helpers* and/or *opponents*; (4) protagonist is given *tests* of his mettle; (5) protagonist is *rewarded* and/or a *new lack* is discovered which causes the entire sequence to occur over again.[11]

The most valuable thing about Propp's effort was that it prompted folklorists around the world to see if their own national or ethnic tales fit into his system or, alternately, if they had to develop one of their own, similar to Propp's, but unique to their own study-group. And, crucially, Propp was taken up by early French Structuralists (he was sometimes called the first French Structuralist, a description that would not have been welcomed in Stalin's USSR). The Structuralists attempted in several ways to produce a grammar that would encompass all narrative: fictional and historical. The approach that is most useful for our present purposes[12] found sharp and economical expression in the English language in the work of Gerald Prince. In 1982 he published *Narratology: The Form and Functioning of Narrative* which built upon the base of the Formalists, Structuralists, and linguistic experts (especially the early work of Noam Chomsky).[13] This was a remarkable book whose clarity and quiet tone masked its massive ambition: to lay the foundation for a narratology that was not plot-based but worked independently of plot and, therefore, was the transformative engine of plot formation, in the same way that deep grammar is the engine that transforms our phonetic utterances into meaningful sentences.

Although Prince's work is applicable to both fictive and real events, here we will use historical events of our own choice since, ultimately, genealogy is a form of historical writing. Prince would say that the following is not a narrative:

'Jack Johnson is a champion boxer.'

Nothing happens there. It is simply a statement of condition and therefore is not a narrative. However, if one says:

'Jack Johnson, the champion boxer, threw a fight,'

then one has a narrative. "Narrative is the representation of at least two real or fictive events or situations *in a time sequence*, neither of which presupposes or entails the other.[14] The sample sentence meets those criteria, since being a champion boxer does not necessarily entail throwing a fight, and throwing a fight is not solely a prerogative of champions among boxers.

This example of a minimal narrative leads to Prince's definition of *kernel* narratives. These are narratives that meet the above condition and which contain only one modification of the original state of things. Thus:

'Jack Johnson was blackmailed by corrupt promoters and he threw a fight'

is a kernel narrative. The following is not, because it involves two changes of condition:

'Jack Johnson was blackmailed and he threw a fight and he started drinking'

is actually two kernel narratives, not one.

What Prince does with kernel narratives is to develop a grammar: that is, a set of formulas that show the various way under which "X" can become "Y." He presents rules that work irrespective of plot. In his grammar of kernel narratives, the formula for:

'Jack Johnson was cheated and he turned to drink'

is the same as

'Cinderella was beaten and she cried.'

Prince provides, in the form of symbolic logic, seventeen explicit formulas and a single implicit one that cover any simple plot sequence that occurs over time. (The one unstated rule is that there can be no null entity: that is, "X" and "not-X" cannot exist simultaneously.) There is no profit in going further with this matter – Prince develops a second set of rules that deal with complex (that is, non-kernel) narratives – but they are of wider reference than we require immediately. The point we can transport to genealogical narratives is that we should be looking for the kernel narrative that is specific to genealogy. I think there is one and that it operates under very restricted terms, so one does not need Prince's full seventeen grammatical rules of kernel-narratives, fictional and historical, to deal with genealogy.

Crucially, Prince does not stop with matters of grammar. He emphasizes that narratives can be fully understood only if one takes into account the intentions (usually discerned circumstantially or inferentially) of the narrator. That is refreshing, given that authorial intent has been a casualty of post-structuralist critical theory. Not only does locution count, but so does perlocution. And in genealogical work, deictic directions are often critical:

'*Here* lies Jack Johnson'

is about as terminally demonstrative as one can get. Such matters are within the ken of authorial intent.

Further, Prince argues that no narrative makes sense without considering the recipient of the story (the "narratee" is his word.) Hence the way the narrative is actually interpreted is as consequential an issue as is the question of how the author intends it to be interpreted. Effectively, every reader or listener rewrites the narrative at least a little bit. The degree and character of the rewriting is dependent upon matters external to the narrative (the personality and personal circumstances of the recipient) and also on how the reader or listener interprets the context that is implied by any narrative. For example, the brief kernel narrative of Jack Johnson's downfall means something different to someone who knows the history of slavery and of its aftermath in the USA and to someone who does not. Moreover, because every narrative is, at least to a small degree, part of the autobiography of the narrator (a person who spent time composing it and who had some reason for doing so), how the reader or listener intuits that bit of autobiography is consequential.

Hence, if Prince's work is our guide in looking for a kernel narrative in genealogy, we should recognize that each genealogical story has a narrator's intention behind it, and should understand that a single genealogy will legitimately be heard differently by different auditors.

Fundamental to the usefulness of narratology as done by Gerald Prince and his associates is the fact that it is not chic. There has been a massive amount of theorizing about narrative in the past half century in the form of postmodernism, postcolonialism, deconstructionism, and cultural studies, and structurally rigorous analyses have largely lost favour. Amidst discussions of power relationships, covert ideologies, and cultural imperialisms, the sort of narratology that has as its twinned bases French structuralism and transformative linguistics is not so much disproved, as disapproved of. Certainly there are present-day structuralists who can both fight their corner well and find accommodation on some points of contention with their opponents,[15] but their work is often regarded with the same quizzical attitude one imagines that Bill Gates holds towards a typewriter: dated, useful in the old days, but devoid of modern application.[16]

Particularly courageous is Prince's use of the words "fictive" (or "fictional") and "real" in relation to narrative, and his making it clear that any complex narrative can have both qualities in it. (Indeed, I

would suggest, complex narratives almost always will have both.) In
particular, the idea that a story can be about something real is a tonic
since, among most critical theorists, everything in the world is said to
be "constructed," by which usually is meant: unreal in large part.
Granted, one never captures fully the real. Anyone who has ever
tried to describe a sunset or to teach anything to a Sunday School
class knows that. However, there are degrees of approximation to reality and, ultimately, something is there. By that I mean that life,
death, love, hate, and the Grand Canyon are things that are there,
even if no one can encompass all their aspects. In examining the
character of genealogical narrative, we will be dealing with stories
that often are fictional, at least in part, but which frequently deal
with considerable accuracy, verifiability, and plausibility, with birth,
reproduction, and death. Real things indeed.

With the preceding material on general narratology as a source
of useful analogy, look at the following kernel genealogical narrative shown in figure 4.1.

Simple, is it not? The kernel genealogical narrative is that a man
and woman procreated and produced a child who survived. (The
"senior" after John Teskey's name means that he had at least one
surviving son who had a name identical to his, save that he was
"junior.") However, there is a bit more to it than that, for the typical
kernel narrative of genealogy (such as we have here) has several
parts, all of which are useful, but each of which is not absolutely
necessary. The kernel narrative is built like an atom. (1) The nucleus – the one item without which there can be no genealogy – is
that a woman gave birth to a child who lived. This is a bit hard on
men, but the fact is that, for the purposes of genealogy, so long as
one has a line from mother-to-offspring in each kernel narrative,
one has a story. (2) However, most kernel narratives give us the
satellite fact that there was a specific male involved, who was the putative father of the child. Indeed, given that most cultures are male-
dominated, the male is usually given top billing (as in our example,
where one learns only the wife's first name), even though there is
no way to be absolutely sure that he is actually the father of the
child. Many genealogical chains are so bent by males that they entirely leave out the name of the mother. However, in that case there
is an invisible nucleus – An Unnamed Woman – around whom that
kernel narrative revolves, no less real for being unseen. And this
hints at something important that we will observe in detail later:

Figure 4.1
A kernel genealogical narrative

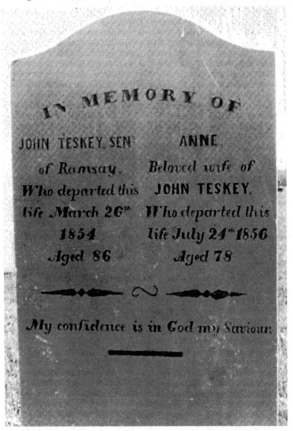

that most genealogies are male-dominated and are dictated by cultural desires rather than by biological reality: if a culture wants accuracy, it will trace descent through the female line only. The male line is just wishful thinking. (3) Usually, a less central portion of the kernel genealogical narrative concerns the birth and death date of the male and female whom the culture declares are the joint parents of the child. And (4) sometimes there is information about the life of the individuals who are designated as offspring of the female-male partnership: when they were born and died. For example, if the children have devoted a memorial to their parents, they often place their own names on the marker in a subordinate place. That information, though, is not central.

In the grammar of this relatively simple kernel genealogical narrative, everything hinges on a single yes/no question: (1) does a female successfully produce at least one child who survives? If "yes," one has a genealogical kernel story; if "no," one merely has an adventitious tendril of biography that is part of the previous generation's kernel narrative. Then (2) one determines if a specific male was recognized by the specific society as the father. Again, either there is someone or there is not. And (3) finally, one asks for the birth and death dates of all the individuals involved, parents and children. These three basic queries could all be drawn as part of a logic-tree or expressed in terms of symbolic logic, but they are too obvious to need that degree of polishing.

Remember that Gerald Prince suggested that even the most minimal of narratives implies both a narrator and a narratee (the reader or listener) and small kernels of genealogical narrative are no exception. Thus, in our example of the Teskey tombstone, some individual or group of people acting together (this obviously was not a multiple-narrator project) told a brief story that they wanted their immediate neighbours and later generations to read. Clearly, the narrator wished to say that the family had done well (the stone cost money), that the Teskeys had been a tight family ("beloved wife"), and that they had been god-fearing people. Fair enough, but a century-and-a-half later, a cynical reader might suggest that John Teskey was a bully (why had his wife's full name disappeared?) and a bit of a religious humbug. Then, again, a contextually savvy reader might see this as a document in the larger story of a fascinating cultural group, the Irish Palatines. These people, persecuted Protestants who originated mostly in the German states in the seventeenth century, fled to Ireland in the eighteenth century, and in the late eighteenth-and-early nineteenth centuries, many of them made their way to the New World. They were a complex, virtually invisible ethnic group, German Protestant in origin and economic values, oddly Hiberno-Teutonic in their use of the English language and, in this case, Upper Canadian in their ultimate settlement. In actual fact, the Teskeys were one of three Palatine families who were granted free passage to Upper Canada under Peter Robinson's 1823 scheme of emigration from Ireland to the Canadas. Given that they had to carve a life out of what to Europeans was a raw wilderness, they had done well to persevere. Their memorial stone should be read as a monument to people who had acted, in the context of their situation, heroically. This modern reading is confirmed by the fact that the family built a mill and the site of the village that grew up around it was for a time called Teskeyville.[17]

The basic atom, the genealogical kernel narrative, is not terribly complicated. Where the complexity arises, as we will see in the next chapter, is when these atoms are formed into molecules. That is an interesting business indeed.

5 *The Grammars of Genealogical Ascent*

One of the most memorable scenes, among many, written by the preternaturally prolific "Moliere"(Jean-Baptiste Poquelin) involves a discussion between a bourgeois gentleman and a philosophy professor. The professor tries to explain the difference between verse and prose to the gentleman, who finally gets it: "for more than forty years I have spoken prose, without even knowing it," the newly enlightened gent exalts (*The Bourgeois Gentleman*, Act II, Scene VI). This has resonance in our discussion, for there are millions of genealogists in the world and most of them research and write within a finite number of very tight grammars, but they are not much aware of the strictures under which they work or the structures through which they operate. There is no shame in that: "whoever discovered water, you can be sure it wasn't a fish," as Marshall McLuhan observed. But it sometimes is useful to comprehend the medium in which one operates.

Of the millions of genealogists in the world, most are amateurs in the sense that they earn their daily living doing something other than genealogy. But many of them are amazingly adept. Often they take on being genealogists as part of their social and cultural responsibility. One finds designated rememberers in every Polynesian society, in sub-Sahara African groups, among First Nations in North America, and in everyday "European" families throughout Europe and North and South America. Depending on the culture to which they belong, they operate according to differing assumptions about the rules of genealogical ascent, but all of them are in the business of creating complex molecules from the atoms that are the "kernel narratives" of genealogical grammar, as discussed in chapter 4.

Whether or not there is a human cultural universal – something that every extant human culture engages in beyond the physical universals of breathing, eating, drinking, and reproducing – is impossible to say. However, in my view the two most likely cultural universals are these: (1) trying to find a god or gods, if these are in some way admirable or, alternately, trying to avoid being found by the gods, if they are an ill-tempered lot; and (2) preserving a sense of lineage, either of oneself or of one's social group – call it a family, tribe, clan, or nation, depending on the individual circumstance.

Why this suggestion that lineage remembrance is nearly a human universal? Simple observation, actually: but that statement is hardly a convincing argument, and presenting 100 or 500 cases still would not establish anything more than familiarity. However, as instantiation, a single case may make my point, for it is located at the very limit of the human cultural spectrum as far as the practice of lineage preservation is concerned. This is an early-contact story from what is now Angola and like all such stories must be redacted. The material concerns a group called the "Jaga" who invaded the highlands of central Angola in the 1500s and 1600s. They had contact with Europeans. About 1600, an English seaman called Andrew Battell was taken prisoner and lived with the Jaga for some years. He reported that they were the ultimate Spartan war-tribe. He said that the Jaga on their march southward operated by strict military necessity: they killed all the children born to their tribe (infants are not helpful to an advancing army) and they recruited new warriors from among the adolescents of the tribes they conquered. Battell reported that in a camp of several thousand Jaga, only slightly more than a dozen senior warriors were of the original Jaga stock and that all the other fighters were forced recruits. This sounds preposterous, but there is independent circumstantial confirmation. In the late 1670s, after the Jaga had settled down and become the overlords of a vast kingdom, they were visited by an Italian named Cadornega. He found that the Jaga, though now no longer a mobile army, maintained a practice that we can recognize as being a residue of their Spartan period: all babies born within their camp were put to death. However, now, those infants born to mothers who went outside the camp to give birth were allowed to live. Thus, in evolving from being a fully military society to being a ruling culture, the Jaga moved from universal to selective infanticide.[1] The point, for our purposes, is that despite killing their own children, the Jaga kept a very tight and successful sense of cultural identity. They won long wars and this required a sense of commonality. Moreover, they were able to cease being a massive Spartan phalanx and to assert a continuing identity as a settled tribe. Indeed, their sense of kin identity was preserved even when the Jaga later merged with another tribe. This was possible only because they established a sense of lineage that was (for a time) independent of biological reproduction. Genealogy continued (admittedly in a strange way), even though biology was temporarily discontinued.

When genealogists operate, they use a limited number of grammars. Why are grammars necessary? Cannot lineages be made up spontaneously? Indeed, as an individual, you can declare any lineage that appeals to you for yourself or for your subject of study. But almost all cultures lay down rules for the lines that they will accept as valid: there is no sense in tracing your own line from your great-grandmother in a society that says lines from male antecedents are all that count. One has to play within the local rules. The existence of strict grammars is necessary for two reasons that are essentially literary in nature: first, because most lineages of consequence are complex narratives, covering hundreds of individual human stories; and, second, because almost all long genealogies are multi-author narratives. A final narrator in each generation gives shape to the lineage narrative, but does so with material from earlier generations. Yes, this material is often modified a bit to fit "modern" circumstances (a matter we will discuss in detail later); but respect for the earlier material must be evinced, even if the material is tinkered with. If genealogy-making is as close to being a cultural universal as anything can be, and if a genealogical lineage is a complicated multi-narrator product, then each society needs a grammar that makes the genealogy comprehensible to each succeeding generation. And a good grammar of genealogy not only provides a useable past (including, often, a set of origin myths), but it helps resolve tensions and contradictions in the everyday culture.

When, below, I suggest that there are no more than four grammars of genealogy, some preparatory matters should be made clear. First, these specific grammars are presented as *Ideal Types*, in the sense that Max Weber coined the term. That is, models that show in pure terms the characteristics of a given system, isolated from the real world. These are patterns toward which the various systems of grammar would migrate, if all the static electricity and whirl of everyday economic and social change did not mess up the details. Second, in the real world (as distinct from the realm of Ideal Types), every genealogical grammar is in transition. The evolution may be slow, but the rules of how one is allowed to connect the kernel genealogical narrative of one generation to its predecessors is modified over time. There are, for example, well-documented cases of matrilineal societies changing to double-descent cultures over no more than 100 years' time. Most alterations, however, are accretions, occurring slowly, like the growth of a coral reef. So one of the abilities demonstrated by the most skilled genealogists (and, alas, only by the most skilled) is to recognize that every generational paradigm usually changes a micron or two from one generation to another and to understand that despite individual terms staying the same, the grammar of the system often redefines the meaning of what appears on the surface to be an unchanging vocabulary. The easiest way to prove this to yourself is to take the terms "cousin" and "uncle" and trace them through several generations of any of the genealogical grammars that I will present below. The terms just will not hold still.

Third, although this opinion earns the disapproval of both the Church of Jesus Christ of Latter-day Saints and of the most severe of the French structuralists, I am not yet convinced that there can be a single Unified Grammar of Genealogical Narrative. My reservations are not based on any deep epistemological conviction, but on the mundane fact that none of the ones I have seen so far actually works. That is all: I am open to being convinced, but (to refer to the two leading scriptures on this matter) neither the writings of Claude Levi-Strauss nor of Joseph Smith, Jr. covers the real world very well, elegant though each may be in theory. And, therefore, fourth, although it is necessary for each genealogist to be aware of the variant possible grammars into which his or her work will fit, it is imperative that an empirical and inferential awareness be always present: that is, good genealogists do not force the data to fit the pattern but amend the pattern when they encounter strong data.[2]

Now, to terms. The study of human lineage systems is a Tower of Babel and we need a common set of terms for our discussion. No, I do not propose to be like Humpty Dumpty in *Through the Looking Glass* (1871) who declared that "When I use a word, it means just what I choose it to mean – neither more nor less."[3] Instead, as we work through the various grammars of genealogical narrative, I will suggest a compromise vocabulary between the conflicting

forces that, over time, have used varying terms for a single phenomenon and single words to blanket quite distinct phenomena. The
conflicting forces are the Mormons, genealogists in general, historical geneticists, historical demographers, and anthropologists. (I
am lumping together anthropologists, ethnographers, and ethnol-
ogists, while being fully aware that over the generations they have
fought with each other over the job specifications for each category.) All the various forces are produced by individuals who are
good-faith practitioners of their own discipline or sub-field within
their discipline. But if they cannot agree on something so basic as
what to call the human adult pair-bond, then we are in trouble; let
alone when they begin developing their own terms for various family members and for generational interconnections.

So my practice is, if at all possible, to use Mormon terms, for
their work is the source of our present exercise. Thus, the man and
woman who produce a child can be called a "couple," despite the
fact that in many cultures they are hardly that. In fact, with slightly
raised eyebrows we will even accept the Mormon practice, when
dealing with patrilineal societies, of calling a married woman whose
own name is not known, "Mrs So and So." That's what the LDS
computer does.

On the other hand, the Mormon use of "pedigree" to refer to human genealogical lines is to be avoided. The demographers, geneticists, and anthropologists are here correct: thoroughbred horses
and show dogs have pedigrees. But humans are not the product of
controlled breeding programs. In human societies we have "lines"
or "lineages," never pedigrees.

A set of words that also is to be avoided, except under very narrow circumstances, is "patriarchal" and "matriarchal." These are
perfectly good words, but not here. They carry connotations of
power relationships that can be confusing – and the power relationships can be spelled out better with other terms: for we need
to protect two terms: "patrilineal" and "matrilineal." These are
central to genealogical narratives, for they deal with lineage. To
whence someone traces his or her origins is a matter that is not
determined solely by power relationships: there are many male-
dominated societies in which a person's lineage is traced solely
through the female line. A perfectly good set of terms, "patrinomial" and "matrinomial," refers to certain naming grammars that
record lineage.

Other terms in our compromise vocabulary will become clear as we move along, but I must thump the pulpit very hard on one word. It is a noun that implies action: a coded verb, really. In our examination of the grammars of genealogical narrative, we must think primarily of lines of genealogical *ascent*, not descent. I say primarily: sometimes "descent" is descriptively necessary. But what we must continually remember is that, from the standpoint of genealogical research, lines of intergenerational connection run upward. The diagrams of Ideal Types of genealogical grammars which we shall view should be read from the bottom up, not the other way around. Yes, it would be nice to be God and look at things from the top down, but that is not our present calling. And false omniscience (which letting ourselves think we can look from the top downward certainly is) leads to one's postulating paradigms and then forcing the data into them.

Instead, this is our stance: every gold-standard genealogist should assume a posture that gives him or her a crick in the neck. In tracing individual lines that ascend upward, the genealogist is looking up into a rich but highly ambiguous and often confusing mass of material. It is as verdant, promising, and complex as the canopy of a rain forest. The patterns that exist are often outlined by only the occasional shaft of sunlight. If one is lazy or susceptible to preconceptions, one will not see the pattern that is actually there, but a pattern that is projected from below by one's own imagination. Observing and chronicling the lines of genealogical ascent in a self-disciplined fashion are often frustrating activities: frequently intellectually demanding and only long-term in their production of results. Most first-line practitioners, though, think it is worth the crick in the neck and the occasional twinge in the lower back.

———

From roughly the end of World War II until the early 1970s, the social sciences were on an imperial mission. Within each of the several disciplines, mega-projects arose whose goal was to unite into a Single Unified System each sub-discipline, so that eventually there could be a true science of human society. Those heady days came to an end with reduced funding and, more importantly, the rise of critical theories that called into question the validity, morality, and possibility of such efforts. (Curiously, the field of economics was the one social scientific discipline that did not shatter, or at least become tattered, during the last quarter of the twentieth century; this was largely a product of many of that field's major practitioners having been found useful to the expanding political and religious right wing.) Now, although many of the big-ambition social scientific projects of the mid-twentieth century lie abandoned and stripped like the rows of old cargo hulls on the strands of South India, their structural skeletons still are of value.

One thinks, for instance, of the extraordinarily ambitious work of George Peter Murdock who, in a series of efforts that began in the 1940s, produced in 1967 an *Ethnographic Atlas* that attempted to contain all of the most significant variables for all of the cultures that have existed since approximately the year 1500.[4] This magnificently immodest proposal is deeply headache-making to deal with, for its heart consists of sixty-four pages of tables that encapsulate in gnomic form eighty-nine major variables: everything from what was the material of the culture's dominant house-type, to whether or not the society knew how to build water craft, to linguistic affiliation, to the differentiation of economic roles according to gender. None of this is easy to work with, but for our purposes the useful aspect is that Murdock's material can be arranged in a way that efficiently communicates the overall pattern of genealogical grammars as they have existed worldwide over the past half-millennium. Murdock analyzed 863 societies, some large, many of them small; some expanding and robust, others aetiolating or now recently extinct. The size of the society is not here relevant, however, any more than is the size of a linguistic group: just as the existence of a given language is the key datum for a linguist, so the key fact for a genealogist is that a certain grammar of expressing genealogical ascent operates (or operated) even in a society of a few thousand people.

The simplest way to show Murdock's results is shown in Table 5.1. (The terms used are mine, and will be illustrated in just a moment):[5]

This tally of how-the-world works, expressed in terms of Ideal Types (no actual society fits absolutely perfectly into any category), provides a nice, clear agenda for us to follow.

So, first, the grammar of matrilineal ascent. It is productive to look at societies which arrange their immediate genealogies and often explain their ultimate origins in matrilineal terms, because this viewpoint breaks the usual perceptual set of European-heritage genealogists. (Just try to find a standard set of blank work sheets that

Table 5.1
Frequency of grammars of genealogical narrative according to
number of cultures using each system

Type	Number	% of Total
Unilineal		
Matrilineal	121	14.0
Patrilineal	401	46.5
Bilineal		
Standard Double	311	36.0
Variable Double	27	3.1
Insufficient information	3	0.4
Total	863	100.0

presupposes matrilineality.) A skeleton grammar of a matrilineal
line is extremely simple and is shown in Figure 5.1.[6]

Manifestly, the grammar demands that the kernel narrative be
connected between generations by a paradigm in which one's line
is traced through a female – one's mother and her mother and so
on. This simple matrilineal skeleton reminds us of a central matter
of all genealogy: although men (almost always) see themselves as
being in charge, the nucleus of the genealogical kernel is the
mother-child bond. Matrilineal systems take this fact and make it
the dominant link in the grammar that connects one generation to
the next. Like every genealogical grammar, this one depends for its
durability on two factors: some form of naming system that makes
memory possible, and also upon the strength of memory that characterizes the specific cultural group. For the purposes of dealing
with outside groups, matrilineality usually assumes a single matrinomial name. (It would not make sense to adopt a patrinomial
naming system, since the males are not part of the primary lineage
system.) This name operates as surnames do in present-day European cultures, and this "surname" may be a specific reference to a
common ancestress, or it may refer to a talisman or to a totem that
is held in common by all who are part of this matrilineal heritage.
(Sometimes these totemic "surnames" are a trifle unfortunate. In
the mid-twentieth century, the Ambo of what was then Northern
Rhodesia had names such as "the Loin Cloth family," "the Anus

Figure 5.1
Matrilineal lineage skeleton line

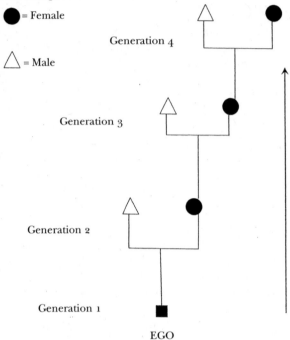

family," and "the Penis family" for their collective maternal lineages.[7] It must have made cashing cheques stressful.)

Until the second half of the twentieth century, most matrilineal cultures were dependent upon oral memory to preserve their genealogies. Most of these cultures were horticultural in their economic base and were found primarily in sub-Saharan Africa, parts of Polynesia and Melanesia, and among several First Nations groups in North America. How long did the oral memory run back? In the first half of the twentieth century, the Yao (of then-Nyasaland) traced each village (they were matrilocal) back to a founding ancestress. The genealogical lines of families in the village were counted clearly back five or six generations, but then became blurred.[8] A conspectus of the genealogies of sixty-four Ndembu villages (then on the border of the Congo and Northern Rhodesia) in the same time frame as the Yao data found that most lineages ascended for six generations, although one went for twelve. This was shallow by comparison with such matrilineal groups as the Hopi of the Americas and the Ashanti of Africa,[9] but I suspect that most present-day inhabitants of the urban First World would be hard-pressed to provide even a skeleton genealogical line of their own for six-to-twelve generations.

Mention of the Hopi – and by implication other major Amerindian groups that are, or were, matrilineal, such as the Navaho and the Iroquois – raises a point salient to the Mormon project. For certain theological reasons that were mentioned earlier (in chapter 2), the Church of Jesus Christ of Latter-day Saints has a distinct, albeit somewhat ambivalent, mission to the Native Americans. For the moment, suffice it to note that the LDS church wishes to integrate First Nations genealogy into its own genealogical system. This well may be impossible, but that is not here the point. The germane point is that there are more potentially valuable genealogical data available in historical sources concerning matrilineal cultures than one might at first think. This is because of the nature of European contact with indigenous groups. In many parts of the world, Europeans recorded social details – including genealogical references – that are now forgotten by members of the culture that once knew them. Worldwide, many indigenous groups that are so destabilized as to have lost most of the details of their cultural past, are now dependent upon European-produced memory aids such as books and tape recordings of previous generations. In fact, the contact literature with the western African slave-trading cultures, with some Polynesian groups, and with some North-American Amerindians permits pushing some lineages back into the eighteenth century and sometimes earlier.

It is not absolutely necessary that matrilineal societies be matrilocal, but most are. This matrilocality ties in with a number of secondary characteristics that the genealogist is apt to encounter. (I am not here arguing simple cause-and-effect, merely noting a constellation of characteristics that is genealogically relevant frequently exists.) For example, in most cases prohibitions on too-close inbreeding dictate that a man comes into the matrilocal village from outside. This is not romance: he is there for breeding purposes and typically he enters without status or prestige. He is known, to take the example of the Yao of Nyasaland, as a "billy-goat" or as a "chicken rooster," and though he is essential to the community (economically as well as reproductively), no one forgets why he acquired membership.[10] Generally in matrilocal societies, "divorce" is relatively easy, so one woman frequently has more than one "husband" in a lifetime. This

can either be labelled "serial monogamy" or, if she has more than
one husband at a time, "polyandry."

Because "plural marriage" is such a major issue in early Mormon
history (and such a major complication in the genealogical lines of
the LDS equivalent of *Mayflower* families), two clarifications are here
necessary. The first of these is that I will use *polyandry*, the term
adopted by most demographers and anthropologists for the practice
of females having more than one husband. However, instead of the
generally accepted technical term for the male equivalent – "poly-
gyny," – I will employ the term that Mormon history has pressed
upon the everyday vocabulary of non-anthropologists – *polygamy*. So,
although slightly wrong as technical terms, we can take polyandry
and polygamy to be the opposite sides of the same social coin.

Secondly, counter-intuitive as it may seem, *neither polyandry nor polygamy* change the genealogical grammar of the society in which it
occurs. Consider the effect on the skeleton genealogy of matrilineal societies of polyandry as shown in Figure 5.2. (For simplicity, we
will look only at Generation Two as being polyandrous.)

Obviously, social terminology becomes very complicated when
someone has not just full-brothers and sisters, but half-brothers and -
sisters by one's mother and her second and third husbands. (This is
a situation not completely unknown in present-day industrialized societies.) And the relationship of a person to a half-sibling's father
(who is not the same as her or his own) is complex socially and genealogically. More confusing is what happened in a real-life situation
wherein polyandry was not limited to a single generation, but in
which our subject's grandmother and great-grandmother were also
polyandrous, and they too had children by each of their various marriages. It is very hard to untangle genealogically. Nevertheless, neither polyandry nor polygamy are in themselves grammars of
genealogical narrative. Instead, they work *within* any given genealogical grammar. They do not change the rules of how lines of genealogical ascent are determined. They follow whatever grammar they
may be encased in – but they certainly make life difficult for someone who is trying to trace the full family tree, side-branches and all,
in a culture in which there have been four of five generations of plural marriages. Indeed, even one or two generations of plural marriages that occurred four or five generation in the past will make the
resultant full-family genealogy as challenging as unlocking the Double Helix. (The classic case of plural marriage driving genealogists

Figure 5.2
Polyandry in a matrilineal genealogy

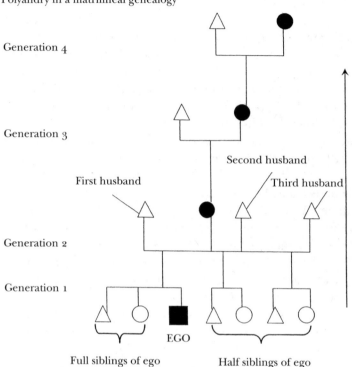

Generation 4

Generation 3

Second husband

First husband

Third husband

Generation 2

Generation 1

EGO

Full siblings of ego   Half siblings of ego

nearly barmy arises from the Mormon patriarch Brigham Young's having had twenty-seven wives, nineteen of whom had children: fifty-three offspring in all. He died in 1877 and the Church of Jesus Christ of Latter-day Saints officially abandoned polygamy in the 1890s, so, at most, two generations of polygamy were involved in the Brigham Young family. Yet, he had 301 grandchildren and Mormon genealogists had given up the full family genealogy after three generations of detail. Their effort though, was revived by the introduction of the computer.)[11]

If the argument that polyandry and polygamy operate within the basic genealogical grammars – and are not in themselves independent genealogical grammars – needs exemplification, the Ashanti of Ghana will help. In the early and mid-twentieth century, the Ashanti were strongly matrilineal in a very complicated way. The husband and wife usually kept separate residences and the children were strictly the property of the wife's kinship group. Break-ups of marital partnerships were frequent and, therefore, women often were serial monogamists. The interesting point is that the vulnerability of the male in the social structure (he was always a kinship-guest in his wife's lineage), meant that men could make themselves guests in several matrilineages – that is, they could be polygamous in a society that was organized on matrilineal lines. Indeed, paradoxical as it seems, the matrilineal social structure pushed them in that direction. Mind you, a male was expected to pull his weight economically in each of his marriages. (One is reminded of the saying common in another matrilineal society, the Bemba of then-Northern Rhodesia, that "a man is a granary on the veranda, but a daughter is a granary by the doorway.")[12] So, only the most economically able males had more than one wife. The prize for economic efficiency and for domestic diplomacy goes to the Ashanti husband of six women who one Christmas (the Ashanti were Christianized) gave to each of his six wives a phonograph and, no fool he, six identical sets of vinyl records.[13] Manifestly, polygamy in the Ashanti world required a circumspect approach to all the culture's rules, including domestic diplomacy.

Among the most salient lessons that matrilineal societies bring to our attention is the relative weaknesses of biological determinates of genealogy and the demonstrable primacy of social determinants. Adult males in matrilineal societies are a fairly mobile entity; they move about between their own mother's kinship locale and that of their wife or wives. Conversely, women may have several successive husbands. In this situation, it is very hard to tell who the biological father of a new infant is. Of course, to be virtually 100 percent certain has only become possible within the last decade or so, and we are here discussing past populations: this is genealogy, after all. So, determining the father of the child was a social, not a bio-genetic matter. The mid-twentieth century Yao, for example, operated on the principle that if a baby was born without puerperal complications, it was the offspring of the man with whom the woman was at that time living; if there were difficulties in that respect, the woman was kept in mid-labour until the pain forced her to confess who the "real" father was.[14] The value of such mid-birth confessions cannot have been great. The best definition of what "father" means in genealogical terms comes from David M. Schneider's ethnographic work on matrilineal societies. His definition of "father" actually holds for all grammars of genealogical narrative. "The *father* of the child, for present purposes, is that person who is married to the child's mother at that time during the child's early life when the child is formally affiliated according to some descent principle."[15] This formal affiliation is a cultural decision, determined and ratified by the society in which the infant lives, and biological fatherhood may be accurately ascribed or it may not: the decision is primarily a social one and biology is secondary, albeit consequential.

Probably most genealogists will accept the idea that fatherhood is a social matter, but they are apt to resist the correlate: so too is motherhood. As Schneider says, "the woman who has primary responsibility for the early care of the infant and child is its *mother*."[16] By this he means that whoever has responsibility for bringing up an infant is designated as its mother. Usually this is the female who gives birth, but women often have died in child-birth. Epidemics and natural disasters have robbed many children of biological mothers, and young women sometimes abandon their infant and levant. Often these children are raised by kin. In our own society, it is a not-rare story for a person to reach adulthood and then to be told that the person who has been his or her mother is, in biological terms, actually an aunt or grandmother. Hence, although the probability of the socially defined "mother" being the biological mother is much higher than for the socially defined "father" being the biological father, the jury that decides the case (meaning the society in which the child is raised) makes the decision on social grounds: what will be best for the child and what will help keep the fabric of society from sundering.

In most societies, marriage or its equivalent is employed to protect children. As one of the last century's greatest social observers, A. R. Radcliffe-Brown argued: "Marriage is a social arrangement by which a child is given a legitimate position in the society, determined by parenthood *in the social sense*."[17]

I place this point about the socially determined nature of mother and fatherhood in the midst of our discussion of matrilineal societies because it is easier to assimilate if viewed within a society whose genealogical grammar is quite different from that of most readers of this book. The point is universal, however. Although genealogical narratives all appear to deal confidently with biology, in fact none of them do so with certainty. (No, not even your own family line.) That is why our conceiving of genealogical narratives as being created according to a limited number of grammars is fundamental. It is the virtue of these grammars that (a) they easily link one generation to another and (b) allow the linkage to occur irrespective of the actual individuals involved. Change the names and the structure of the narrative is the same. *Genealogy, then, is the collection of certain socially approved stories that are arranged according to one of a limited number of possible patterns.* These are not narratives about what "actually" happened, but are narratives that some group of people believed had happened or wished actually had occurred.

To return directly to matrilineal societies, the hub characteristic of such cultures is that in the Ideal Type of this system, the male (the "father") has no rights over the children: the mother and her kinship do.[18] Yet there are a large number of circumstances in which someone has "male rights" over children. The "father" may be around the village, but that is irrelevant: the exercise of the central male rights (such as ritual induction into adulthood) is vested in the matrilineal kinship. So, who exercises these rights in a classic matrilineal situation? Answer: *cherchez l'oncle.* That is, in a matilineality, the senior (however defined) *brother* of the wife assumes the powers that are usually exercised in other social structures by the "father" of the child. The only trouble with this practice is that often the uncle is not immediately available, as he well may have married into another matrilineality located a distance from the home of mother and child. That said, there is one situation wherein the uncle-principle is seen clearly – namely, in the genealogical line of the headmanship of a matrilineality. (Males usually have held the chieftanships, although in First Nations groups in the twentieth century, women increasingly assumed chieftanships.) Given that a matrilineality usually needed a headman, the lead-male of the ranking hereditary line was either exempted from having to marry outside the matrilinealship or, more often, permitted to bring in an outside wife (or wives) into the matrilocale. Note, though, that his son did not inherit the headmanship. That stayed in the matrilineal line and, upon the headman's demise, went to the ranking male in the leading female line (see Figure 5.3). And, in some matrilineal cultures, the headman could be fired (to use a modern term) by his own mother or by her mother. Thus, in the mid-twentieth century, the ever-alert critic Edmund Wilson encountered an Iroquois high-steel worker who had recently been deprived of the headship of his own Iroquois clan by his grandmother.[19]

Manifestly, if one wanted to drive conventionally trained genealogists to tears, the matrilineal genealogical narrative is perfect, for it

Figure 5.3
Hereditary passage of headmanship in a simple matrilineal society

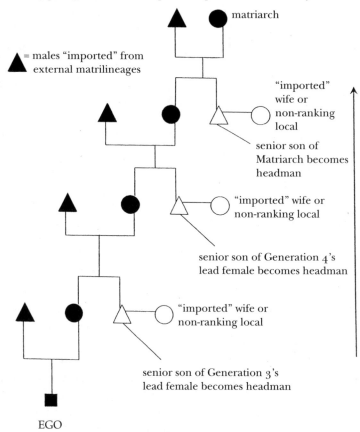

does not fit on the standard-issue genealogical forms. Granted, the basic grammar is simple. But in the matrilineal genealogical narrative, males are real trouble. They are like participle phrases in an English-language sentence: grammatically correct right where they are, but devilishly hard to diagram. The problem with men is threefold. First, and easiest to deal with, the headmanship follows a matrilineal line as diagrammed in Figure 5.3. Second, even outside the headmanship, uncles need to be accounted for in any serious genealogy. They frequently act as quasi-fathers and therefore for each generation one should document not only the socially defined father (from outside the matrilineality), but also the uncle who is the quasi-father within the matrilineality. Third, and, most vexing of all, males who marry into the matrilineality and become fathers of children that belong to the matrilineality, have genealogies of their own – however, these are not found locally, but in the separate matrilineal line to which these males belong for their entire lifetime. (Why bother learning this? Because in North American genealogical work, one needs to be able to deal with intermarriage of individuals of European and of First Nations backgrounds, and many of the aboriginal groups were matrilineal; because several Polynesian matrilineal Pacific Island groups have intermarried into the North American grid and also into various European cultures; and because the physics of black kinship systems cannot be understood without reference to matrilineality in many African origin-groups.)

Finally, one does not wish to leave the discussion of matrilineality as a genealogical grammar with either of two misconceptions. Do not, first, feel sorry for all the poor dear males who lived in such a culture. They may have been locked out of certain positions of prestige and limited in what property they could inherit in the matrilineal world into which they married, but they still were able to do what males have traditionally done in most societies: boss their own wives around, work a bit, drink home-brew, and strut. Further, in some of these matrilineal arrangements, young unmarried men had an automatic social insurance policy: their matrilineal grandparents (whose own sons would have moved away to another matrilocale village) provided them with food ("garden rights") in return for a little help in planting and harvesting.[20]

And, second, do not make the romantic assumption that cultures that arranged their lives in a matrilineal pattern were necessarily any nicer than those that did not place women in the key lineage positions. Some of the most warlike of North American Amerindians were matrilineal. The clearest case in my judgment, however, is that of the Fante "states" in the old Gold Coast (now Ghana) of west Africa. The Fante were a congerie of matrilineal clans that had migrated from the forest belt between the Black Volta and the Comoe River and had reached the Gold Coast sometime between the late 1200s and the late 1400s. They grew slowly until the early 1700s when they expanded powerfully, due to trade with Europeans. Trade? The Fante held slaves for their own use, so it was no great step to develop a trade in human bodies. In return for gunpowder, weapons, iron bars, lead, and rum, they provided European slavers with gold, ivory, and, most profitably, with men, women, and children who had been captured inland. The Fante were as clever at cheating the Europeans as the slavers were at short-changing the Fante: the Fante may have received watered rum, but the slave traders often received sickly slaves who had been fed-up and rubbed with lime juice to give them a healthy glow.[21] Today, scattered around the globe, are several million individuals whose ancestors passed through the hands of the less-than-kindly Fante matrilinealities.[22]

———

After engaging the mental contortions that the unfamiliarities of matrilineal societies present for most genealogists, it is almost relaxing to deal with cultures that tie generation-after-generation of genealogical kernel narratives together through patrilineal grammar and that usually employ patrinomial vocabulary for personal names. The schematic Ideal Type shown in Figure 5.4 is simplicity itself.

That simplicity hides a trap. Despite the schematic rendering of the Ideal Type of the patrilineal grammar of inter-generational narrative as being a left-handed version of the right-handed matrilineal model we saw earlier, it is not a symmetrical opposite. This is because of the invisible rule that seems to have run through virtually all human societies through most of recorded history: men try to rule, and usually have. The father of the patriarchal family (however those words are defined) "gains complete rights over the possession of his own children."[23] Under matrilineal grammars, he had few, or no, rights over them; his wife's matrilineal kinship group had those rights. Well, is this not simply a mirror-opposite situation? No. Recall that in the Ideal Type of matrilineal arrangements, the brother of the wife (in other words the uncle of a child) exercised the key male role (counselling, sponsorship of ritual initiation, protection of family inheritance) with regard to children, especially males. Had we examined a full set of genealogies for a matrilineal group – with all the siblings and all the uncles represented – the resulting diagram would have looked like the circuit diagrams for pre-transistor radios: just barely comprehensible. In contrast, the patrilineal system is very simple. Only one male is necessary in each generation to fulfill all male parental duties, including ritual and inheritance obligations.

Although women undeniably exist in a patrilineal system, in practice a form of cultural amnesia usually wipes women out of existence

Figure 5.4
Patrilineal lineage skeleton line

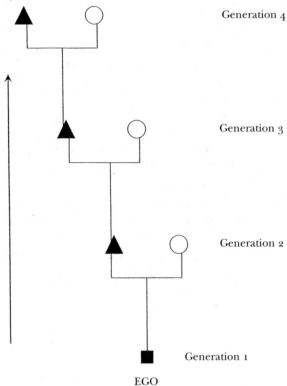

Generation 4

Generation 3

Generation 2

Generation 1

EGO

in patrilineal genealogies, except for a few heroic or particularly virtuous females who are held up for admiration. One way that especially virtuous females have been memorialized is in their being
presented as god-like in having the ability to give birth without requiring sexual intercourse. This occurs in the genealogical legends
of the patrilineal Sesuto of southern Africa[24] and in first-century
Christianity, in which an ancient male line is traced up to the point at
which a miraculous female gives birth without having carnal relations with a man.[25]

The reverse side of the coin, though, has been much more common. Thus, in what was a culturally diagnostic act, the Lifu of the
Loyalty Islands recorded a genealogical origin-myth in which the
three founding fathers of the society were born of three separate
males and a bird, a lizard, and a snake. An early twentieth-century
observer caught accurately the Lifu's view of women and lineage:

"and, indeed, who was she, a woman, to be handed down to poster-ity?"[26] In most of Asia, up to mid-twentieth century (when the Cultural Revolution made genealogical patterns very fraught mat-ters indeed), in theory patrilineal genealogies ran back more than 100 generations. In more realistic terms, they were reliable for about twenty-five generations' distance. There is probably some di-luted accuracy in earlier claims: but exactly what is hard to deter-mine.[27] The Koreans adopted the Chinese patrilineal system in the late fourteenth century.[28]

In Europe the one full-bore tribal society that survived into the twentieth century was the Gheg of northern Albania, a group that was patrilineal with a vengeance. In the early twentieth century, the Gheg had reasonable male genealogies that went back to the late 1500s and putative lines that ran back to the 1300s. Three related so-cial conditions kept their genealogical memory so acute. They were physically isolated; they lived in large extended families – fifty to sev-enty members was not uncommon; and they regulated their most important social relationships according to a code of family honour. Thus, lineage and large (almost military) patrilineal households and a ruthless code of blood-vengeance were interwoven. One does not wish to stereotype a group, but one notes an incident in the Otto-man period in which two dogs fighting near a boundary line between two sheep runs resulted in eighteen bystanders being killed and a feud ignited that lasted for years. And there are many similar cases, all relating to lineage honour. The observation of Ndoc Gjeloshi, who was part of a band who tried to assassinate King Zog in 1931, has an authoritative ring: "When an Albanian has not got himself in hand, he has a revolver in it."[29]

For better or worse, it is agreed by most present-day observers that *unilineal* societies–both matrilineal and patrilineal – are in de-cline. If, indeed, this is the case, it is all the more reason for geneal-ogists to pay attention to unilineal cultures, for even if they are not the wave of the future, they are the form in which the past was orga-nized for roughly (very roughly) half the world's population before the advent of the industrial revolution.

The reason that matrilinealities should decline is fairly obvious. They work best in horticultural societies in which there is no great economic advantage to either men or women being in charge of the community resources. One nice, albeit overly simple, observation concerning several Bantu-speaking cultures is that they tended to be

matrilineal until cattle-breeding and -herding came in. Those activities give the advantage to males: they do not have to take time off to
give birth and they are not required to carry nursing children with
them. "When cows came in, many matriarchal societies went out," is
the formulation.[30] But even without the move to elementary cash ag-
riculture (which cattle-herding usually implies), matrilineal systems
are fragile. To prosper they require a virtually homeostatic world. The
complicated arrangements with uncles, brothers, and husbands have
been vulnerable to any rapid change in the economic rules, especially
the mercantile invasion from Europe and urban America, whereby individuals were encouraged to act for their own self-benefit even if that
meant rejecting the old obligations of community responsibility. And,
additionally, matrilineal systems have been more apt to be hurt by the
spread of Christianity, at least until very recently. In its most aggressive
form, Christianity has put forward a male-dominated norm and a view
of family relations that are antithetical to traditional matrilineal practices. As one mildly ironic, mid-twentieth century observer noted regarding the Ashanti: "Persistently the literature and teachings of the
Europeans encourage the Ashanti to maximize their attentions to the
immediate family ... and to minimize the interests in the extended
family and lineage ... This family and religious emphasis is 'natural'
for Europeans who, after all, were not taught when they pray to say,
'Our Mother's Brother who art in heaven.'"[31] Rather more sombrely,
a mid-twentieth century conspectus of matrilineality stated, "in sum,
all non-extractive subsistence types except 'dominant horticulture'
tend to select against matrilineality."[32]

Patrilinealities also are located in quite narrow ecological
niches in the economic structure. Nevertheless, they are not so
strongly ideologically disadvantaged as are those matrilineal systems that have been attacked at their base-of-belief by Christianity. Still, patrilineal systems have the great disadvantage of
requiring a self-duplicating economic and social system if they are
to prosper. That is, they need an economic matrix that does not
provide excessive individual freedom and a social environment in
which rules of both exogamy and patrilineal descent can be enforced. Although not as vulnerable to mercantile and industrial
change as are matrilineal systems, the patrilinealities have had difficulty coping with the swift changes and loosening of social discipline that follow a technological revolution. Despite the great

strength of their cultural traditions, most have, or will, wilt or morph into a *bilineal* genealogical system.[33]

———

Bilineal systems are patterns of genealogical narration that have the potential to link clearly generations on both the male and female sides. For the purposes of defining grammars of genealogical ascent, we can reduce the myriad variations of double systems to two: Standard Double and Variable Double. (In each case, we are of course discussing an Ideal Type.)

The Ideal Type of the Standard Double lineage, shown in Figure 5.5, is a grammar that most persons of European heritage are familiar with from infancy. To put it succinctly, it is the same schematic as holds for Wimbledon or for the U.S. Tennis Open in their classic format.

This grammar of linking generation-to-past-generation is sometimes called the "English system,"[34] but that is a bit misleading: first, because Standard Double Ascent is a world-circling form of inter-generational narration. And, second, the term "English system" usually implies a set of naming practices that involves (a) permanent surnames for each individual and (b) usually the female's taking the male's surname upon marriage. That both conditions "a" and "b" are unnecessary for there to be a successful Standard Double genealogy is shown easily by reference to the Swedish system as it existed amongst the bulk of the population until the early twentieth century. Although each person's Double antecedents were carefully curated in excellent parish records (some of which run back to the seventeenth century), before the 1870s only the gentry and aristocracy were permitted permanent surnames. And only in 1900 did surnames become compulsory for the entire population of Sweden and its residual empire. Before then, the common people mostly used patronymics – that is, names derived from their father's first name. Thus, Åke, the son of a man with the Christian name of Herman, became Åke Hermansson, and his son Per became Per Åkesson, and so on down the generations. Moreover, most women below the gentry level kept a form of their father's name after marriage: Carin, the daughter of Ohle was called Carin Olsdotter and she kept that name. Manifestly, therefore, a Standard Double genealogy is not dependent upon the "English system" of names. (Like so many things from the Old World, the English naming system was imposed on several million migrants as a result of

Figure 5.5
Standard double genealogical line skeleton line

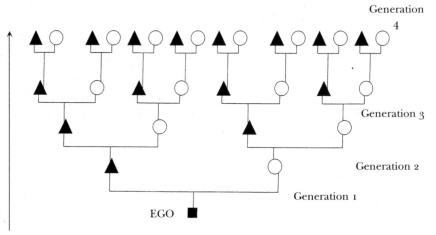

their move to North America; most probably, the majority of migrants who arrived in North America from 1815–1900 had their names altered by immigration officials – or changed the names themselves at the prospect of having to deal with those officials. Wives became "Mrs. Male Name" and the surnames that were assumed in immigration records became permanent, albeit malleable of spelling.)

(An aside: it is more than a little naively ethnocentric to think of the Linnean orderliness of the first-name/surname system as being the best answer to specification of individual identity. Take the twenty-first century case of the Mongolians. They were prohibited from having surnames by the Communists in the 1920s. Having finally become fed-up with identity confusion, in 1997 the government brought in a law requiring surnames. This was largely ignored by the everyday people until 2004 when an identity card was introduced and this required a last name. The result was that 90 per cent of the population of 2.5 million persons decided to use "Khan" as a surname. And, to make things worse, among the remaining 10 percent, it was common practice to find several siblings each of whom chose a different last name. "Try to have all relatives use the same name," an expert on Mongolian names wearily suggested.)[35]

Of course, a bilineal genealogical system depends no more, and no less, on written memory than does a unilineal one. In Double systems we find, as in patrilineal and matrilineal ones, prodigious feats of memory. One of the most impressive to me, largely because of the way in which it was recorded and documented, is that of the Iban of the island of Bornea, which is today split between Malaysia, Brunei, and Indonesia. In the middle of the last century, Benedict Sandin, an Iban with a twenty-five generation oral genealogy of his own family, began collecting material for the definitive record of the Iban people. He worked entirely with oral material until the late colonial period, when some written records began to emerge. Before that era, he collected orally the main genealogies of an aggressive, migratory people that run back in most cases fifteen to thirty generations. These lines are so long that they go crisply back into what one of his post-graduate assistants later called "proto-history." That is, the genealogies record a population expansion and migration that is unaccounted for in the usual archival sources. Crucially, this oral material was still intact late in the colonial period (and early in the era of decolonization) and it was collected according to then-prevailing standards of British and American ethnographic documentation: which were not at all soft. (One wishes that present-day anthropologists would cease bad-mouthing their predecessors; at their best, the late-day-in-the-empire anthropologists had high standards, were not condescending or disruptive towards the people they studied, and, as in this case, gave the indigene a vehicle for preserving fragile cultural memories that otherwise would not have survived modernization intact.) Most of Sandin's thirty-two primary genealogical lines of the Iban run back farther in the direct male line than does that of the British royal family, which has had some very ropey moments and the occasional queen when the male line has failed.[36]

Male line? Are we not dealing with a system of Double lineage? Indeed: and here the Iban oral genealogies, as recent and fresh and fulsome as any on earth, illustrate two signal points. The first of these is that although women are remembered, they are usually the victims of cultural amnesia. In Double systems it is a huge burden to carry all one's ancestors in one's head, so almost always males are privileged and used as trace-routes for the lineage; in contrast, females are remembered for a few generations in their own right and then disappear in the rising mist. The women who find place in the highest levels of genealogy are there most times as consorts of the males through whom the primary tracing of the lineage is done. There are exceptions, and this is the second point. In Double systems, if the male line runs out, genealogical ascent can take place for one or two generations through a female, then the male line can again resume. This feature of Standard Double systems allows memory chains to stretch much longer than in unilineal systems, wherein a break in the gender line means that the line comes to a dead end.

These two characteristics inhere to one of the world's most impressive orally based genealogical systems, the *whakapapa* of the Maori of New Zealand (Aotearoa.) The truly impressive thing about the whakapapa is not simply their length (which is indeed impressive), but the breadth of genealogical knowledge within the community. This at present is motivated to some degree by the economic incentive of land-claims cases being adjudicated under the Waitangi Tribunal set up in 1975. However, the genealogical lattice that runs through Maori culture was preserved prior to, and remains largely independent of, juridical matters. To put it simply, Maori society, as much as any modernized culture on earth, is obsessed with lineage. And, most strikingly, this concern with lineage is an inclusive one. In contrast, for example, to "Status Indians," or "Treaty Indians," in North America, wherein genealogy is used as a means of exclusion of those whose "blood" is in some way wrong, admission to the Maori genealogical network requires only one verifiable Maori ancestor. That said, there are arguments as between variously sized kinship groups (especially the *hapu*, sub-tribe, and *iwi* tribe, which are territorially as well as genealogically based units) concerning who owns what, or did so in the past.

The whakapapa that resonate today all trace back to a small number of large double-hulled canoes in which the ancestors of the present Maori population arrived (probably) in the early twelfth century on the islands of what is now New Zealand. The canoes are the climax point of the genealogies of the highest prestige, a handful of *Mayflower* lines. Everything about that arrival is open to argument: the date, the number of canoes (8 to 10 are the most common numbers), whether or not the canoes were part of a fleet or independent vessels, and where their point of origin was. Like most Polynesian peoples, the Maori point to an over-the-horizon mythic origin – *Hawaiki* (not to be confused with Hawai'i.) Wherever Hawaiki was for the Maori, the final leg of their journey had to have been prodigious: at least 3,000 kilometres, much farther than European navigators were capable of sailing until the fifteenth century.[37]

At some point between the present and the origin-canoes, the ancestors in all lineages become archetypes rather than actual genealogical figures. They are not so much fictive beings as real entities that are moved around in the past to make political and familial alliances in the present possible.[38] Where in the past that happens with each canoe-lineage, no one wishes to venture: there is not much of a career to be made in Maori culture by telling a large number of people that their treasured whakapapa have been twisted about; and it would be no comfort to suggest that they probably have not been played with any more than those of other long-line cultures.

Instead of frowning about what is not there (not a great deal of precision back beyond the 1600s or so) it is best to look at what is there: memory lines (however derived) that run back twenty-five to thirty generations in the best cases. Most of these were stabilized by having been written down in the nineteenth century. (Of course there are variant versions of almost everything, but that is the way with important things in any culture.) These memory lines mostly run through males but, as in almost all Standard Double systems, the female line is used to patch up weak spots in the male ascent pattern. Because of the fact that the Maori discovered and colonized an empty land and because there is general agreement that the eight-to-ten *Mayflower* vessels came from the same place (albeit not necessarily together) and arrived within a generation of each other, it does not matter so much that pieces of ancient lineage may have been moved about from one whakapapa to another: at least not from the communal perspective. Given that there was no previous indigenous population to encapsulate, and given shared origins of the Maori, the ten (or so) main whakapapa twist around each other like a very well-braided rope. This is anchored clearly at two ends – the present and the arrival of the origin-canoes – and should be considered before roughly 1600 to be *in*accurate as individual genealogy but completely creditable as collective genealogy. It says when and how we, the Maori, arrived on history's horizon, and that the cultural line to the present is unbroken.[39]

Implicitly, in looking at the Iban and the Maori, I have been instantiating the possibilities of the Standard Double system: it is adaptable, durable, and contains large pockets of memory. Given that implicit praise, a warning here is necessary: that system is

excellent as a lineage agent, but it can be used genealogically
only if the society with which one is dealing employed it: this system must *not* be applied retroactively and by main force to a culture that did not use it. Why is such an elementary warning
necessary? Any competent historian would take the necessity for
such respect for the context of historical evidence as axiomatic.
Because of the Latter-day Saints, actually.

If you enter any aspect of the Mormon genealogical system –
from blank genealogy forms to computer-generated lineages – you
will discover that it runs on the Standard Double system. Is this
ethnocentric imperialism? Probably, but there is a potential intellectual justification for the practice. This is the very clear
argument that all human beings have a biological mother and a
biological father and that, therefore, humans should be traced
in the same way one traces the breeding roots of Secretariat or
Red Rum.

Fairly compelling: except ... except that this ignores the point
that I argued earlier: that the various grammars of genealogical
narrative, while based on biology (real or imagined or asserted)
are narratives that are constructed according to the way a culture
wishes to portray itself to itself. And the specific biological "facts"
that are recorded in lineages are those that fit within the local
grammar. Recall that men are often declared to be fathers in
many matrilineages on the basis of their living with a child's
mother, and that the number of patrilineages that drop out
women altogether is large. (And, as I will argue in a later appendix, the level of biological indeterminancy even in the strict Standard Double system as it has existed in European nations is much
higher than is usually admitted; that, though, is not here the central issue).

The point is elementary, but adamantine: one cannot retroactively impose the Standard Double system on cultures that did not
employ it. In compressing the myriad genealogical systems of humanity into four basic genealogical grammars, I have gone farther
than many ethnographers would approve; but I think this is being
done without injury to the historical context of the individual cultures. What one cannot engage in, however, is further resolution
through the elimination of all forms of lineage outside of Standard Double genealogy. Such an Orwellian compression can only

occur by the replacement of the varied meanings and nuances that culture gives to the generational narratives of humanity with the protocols of stock breeding.

———

Among the cultures that stand out, like shards of shale, against the attempt to make Standard Double lineage the only one humanity is permitted, some of the most intriguing are those of Variable Double genealogies. In the case of the Yako of Nigeria, descent is double but the valence as between lines varies. In the usual Yako arrangments, fixed assets (to use accounting terminology) follow the male line and variable (that is, portable) assets run in the female line.[40] This, however, is not Standard Double descent: it is much less rigid than it looks. As any economist will suggest, it is possible in most cases to convert fixed assets to variable and vice versa. So, actually, this double genealogy is renegotiated in each generation, with the possibilities being anything between, say, 1 percent to 99 percent of the family wealth being placed in fixed assets and, conversely between, say, 1 per cent to 99 percent being placed in variable. There is thus no way of knowing in advance which of the two lines, male or female, will be on the top of the chart in any given generation. Hence, Variable Double.

The other form of Variable Double that may drive genealogists to despair involves, instead of changing valances as between the two lines of the Double genealogy system, a seemingly complete freedom of choice, generation by generation. Each generation in such an arrangement can choose to follow either the male line or the female, but can select only one. Thus, one will see a genealogical skeleton that looks to be patrilineal for a few generations and then will become matrilineal, and then will oscillate back and forth.[41] This is not a weird form of unilineal descent but rather Variable Double: in each generation the sibling-cohort is aware of the possibility of selecting either the female or male line in their own genealogy. So, in each generation both male and female genealogical narratives are available, as in all Double systems. In this case, instead of a range of 1 percent – 99 percent, as between male and female valences, the choice is always between 0 percent/100 percent and 100 percent/0 percent. This is truly a Variable Double form of genealogy.

———

Earlier, I suggested that polygamy and polyandry are not grammars of genealogical narrative. Rather, they are complications – like a flutter of adjectives in an otherwise standard-grammar sentence – that complicate our diagrams, but do not change the fundamental underlying structures. One can have polyandry or polygamy in any of the four major genealogical narratives.

Similarly, we should note that adoption does not in any way comprise a genealogical grammar of its own. Readers of classical history in the Roman period know that adoption was frequently used to fill in an otherwise failing heirship in a patrilineal system. Social ascription of position, not biology, determined genealogy. In some societies, adoption has been very common and was based on a purely social definition of motherhood: among the people of Arosi, on San Cristoval in the Solomon Islands, adoption at birth was extremely common and the first woman to cut the umbilical cord of a new-born child and to shave its head became the mother.[42] More revealing, because it occurred frequently in the first half of the twentieth century and involved large populations and is therefore more deeply documented, was the practice of adoption within the Chinese and the Korean middle and upper classes. These were patrilineal cultures and therein the lurking question for any couple was, "what happens if we do not have a son?" Three possible answers: (a) adopt a son; (b) provide the husband with a concubine who would bear a son who would be treated as a legitimate heir; and (c) if there were a daughter in the family, bring in a son-in-law and make the first male child of that marriage the family's heir. Among the Chinese, the two preferred options were concubinage or adoption, although the third was sometimes chosen. In the case of adoption, the upper classes insisted that the adopted son be a close relative, preferably the son of a brother. Once adoption was complete, the new male heir was transferred genealogically from one family to another and that was that. Because the Korean upper classes frowned upon the concubine route (in contrast to Chinese society, in Korean culture full legitimacy was not granted to the children of anyone but the primary wife) and also because the imported-male route offended against strict Confucian precepts, they were forced along the path of adoption. As in the case of Chinese upper-class adoptions, a brother's son was the preferred source of the male link in the family chain. (One footnote: among the peasantry of south and central

China, who were also patrilineal, adoption was the preferred way of continuing a family line, but they usually chose to buy a boy from a child-broker who brought the infant or young lad from a good distance away from the new hearth.)[43]

Obviously, in none of these cases does the adoption of a male heir change the genealogical narrative. Indeed, its purpose is exactly the opposite: to allow the narrative to continue uninterrupted. How does one treat adoptions genealogically? At the risk of repetition, one has to chant: the answer is "the way the society one is dealing with treated them." Usually this means that we will not even know about the adoption. Documentation exists for a few upper class adoptions in societies worldwide, but little is known about the overwhelming number of occurrences. Mostly, adoptions have been informal: such as the case of a man taking over his slain brother's children; or of picking up a feral child, the victim of orphaning by war or epidemic; or of grandparents raising the child of a young mother who ran away. In European and North American societies, most adoptions were informal until the twentieth century, and then for most of that century they took place under a cloak of confidentiality that was designed to make the adopted child juridically indistinguishable from a biological child of the same family. Only very recently have adoption protocols become more open in western cultures, but worldwide it is still mostly very difficult to document in specific cases – and it is for the specific case that genealogy exists.

I would be surprised if 0.1 percent of all male adoptions worldwide in the past three centuries have left any print on the historical record, and would be astounded if more than 0.001 percent of all female adoptions had produced any trustworthy record.

Still, genealogists will encounter indications of adoption and besides placing the adopted person exactly where the given society wished it placed as a link in the culture's genealogical narratives, what should their response be? It probably is worth recognizing that by manufacturing and curating information on a specific adoption, the given culture has told the genealogist that it was conscious of adoption as a volitional social act. Therefore, the genealogist may wish to find one of the origin points of that social transaction, and this will be with the biological parents of the child who was adopted. If the genealogist wishes to trace the biological family, that is done within the genealogical protocols of the specific culture. However, at some point, perhaps after a generation or two, this "biological" investigation will be allowed to blur away. The reason is simple: since adoption is a social act – and genealogy is a social construct that overlies biology – at some moment the genealogist will begin to feel that it is profitless to follow very far a "blood" line whose sole reason for being of interest is its putative biological accuracy, and whose primary distinguishing characteristic is that it is *not* consonant with the way the society actually arranged its economic and genealogical inheritance.

Having argued that both plural spouses and adoption fit within the genealogical grammar of whatever society the practices are found, I now must admit to being very tentative about three other matters. They flummox me.

The first of these is the practice of group marriage, or *Punaluan* marriage. Admittedly, it has been rare in the historical era of human existence, but still some reputable anthropologists list it as a major marriage type, albeit one that now may be extinct. However, it was documented in the first half of the nineteenth century by the pioneering scholar of vernacular marriage, Lewis Henry Morgan. His seminal work, published in 1877,[44] led to the most famous discussion of this phenomenon in Frederick Engels, *The Origin of the Family, Private Property and the State* (1884). The practice was found in Hawai'i and involved two forms. In one, a group of sisters (either biological sisters or collateral female relatives) held in common a group of husbands and all children of the "family" were brothers and sisters of each other. (The chief rule-of-exclusion was that no biological brothers of the founding sisters could be included.) The wives called each other *punalua*, meaning partner or close companion. The other form was the male counterpart. A group of brothers became conjointly the husbands of several women (none of whom could be a biological sister of the men) and the children of the joint marriage were all brothers and sisters to each other.[45] Now, whether or not group marriage has been very rare or merely unusual in human societies is unimportant. It existed and, as far as I can see, it existed outside the lines of the four basic genealogical grammars. Try this experiment: diagram, say, a four-man, four-woman group marriage with, say, sixteen children. Then, assume that pattern held for the previous generation. Diagram that. Get a stiff drink. Give up. The task is very difficult because of the myriad possible connections, but is actually made impossible because of the ambiguity. Whereas all of the four basic genealogical narratives are unambiguous (albeit sometimes complicated) at the point of generational transfer – that is, lineage tracing from younger generations to older – everything here is fuzzy to the point of being indecipherable. The grammars that we have surveyed earlier depend upon a clear and agreed (although often biologically spurious) definition of parentage and of off-spring. And of who is parent to whom. That basic set of datum points is impossible to determine in the case of group marriage. What we cannot know, we cannot show. Thus the diagrams are forever blank.

Next, take the matter of fosterage, and, as a specific case, the practice in pre-Norman and late medieval Ireland of fosterage among the upper classes. Irish fosterage involved a child (most often, but not always, a male) being sent by his parents to the home of a social equal (or, if possible, a social better) to be reared. This could occur at any time from late infancy (rare) to ages five to ten. The foster parents were responsible for the child's education into the mid-teens, when the young person returned to his original family. Fosterage produced life-long cross-family (and often cross-clan) alliances and these in three primary forms. One was the bond between the foster children and their foster parents. The second was the alliance formed between children raised by the foster parents: these would include both the adults' own biological children who were themselves not fostered out, and the foster children. As in some sense the children of one set of parents, the foster children and the biological children who were reared together were as the children of one womb. Third, the original parents and the foster parents of a child became in some way kin to each other. In a fragmented and warlike society, the practice of fosterage was an eirenic and binding influence. One did not easily let loose the dogs of war upon one's own biological family or one's biological siblings and neither did one do so upon one's foster parents or foster brothers and sisters; and one was less apt to visit violence upon any foster kin than upon complete strangers.[46]

The practice of fosterage is cited frequently in the record of historical times and is retrospected into early Irish mythology. Figure 5.6 shows a slightly revised version of Cu Chulainn's fosterage genealogy, as presented by Professor T. M. Charles-Edwards.[47]

It looks simple enough and seems to work according to the rules of early Irish genealogical narrative. But, consider the realities: fosterage produced a new set of social affinities that were as real as

Figure 5.6
Ancient irish fosterage

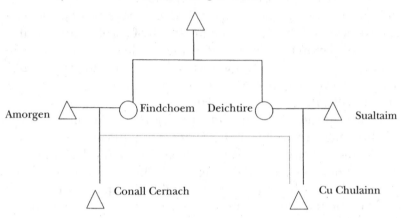

those of the primary parentage. Cu Chulainn and Conall Cernach were now brothers in the sense of being bound by the same rules as were biological brothers. (They happened to be cousins, but in fact the bond would have been just as strong if they were genetically unrelated; it was fosterage and shared childhood that produced the bond, not genetics.) Moreover, because of the unity-in-fosterage of the two boys, the two fathers, Amorgen and Sualtaim, became close kin to each other, much closer in alliance than when they were merely brothers-in-law.

Why is that a problem? Because the fosterage genealogies become a doppelganger for the primary genealogies. The fosterages leave a second genealogical narrative that, like a palimpsest beneath a medieval manuscript, is almost invisible but is palpably present. What appear to us to be *ghost-genealogies* were, in medieval Ireland, as determinative of social relationships as were the much better-recorded primary genealogies. So, if we are to have any sense of reality as historians, we should deal with the historically formative matter of fosterage narratives with the same attention to detail as we do when examining the primary family narratives. This would mean (to use the example of Cu Chulainn) that we trace his genealogy in the male and female lines, not just through Sualtaim and Deichtire but also through Amorgen and Findchoem. Thus, everyone who is fostered effectively has two genealogies, each reflective of the social reality of parentage as decreed in the early Irish family system. How far back does one take each aristocrat's double genealogy? I do not know, but one thing is certain: that high up the genealogical tree of aristocrats who were fostered, one will find more aristocrats who were fostered, and further up, even more. Each time that occurs a set of ghost genealogies is created, and a set of non-biological kinship relationships among other family members from both sides is also formed. To take a simplistic illustration of what this means: if, in each generation an aristocratic family practised fosterage only once (and, actually, multiple cases were common), an individual fostered in Generation One would be found to have eight different genealogies by the time we ascended merely to Generation Three: and eight kinship networks as well.

Diagrammatically, this is as difficult to capture clearly as is multi-dimensional space. And, as yet, we do not possess a vocabulary or a set of descriptive tools that allows us to depict this situation, much less analyze it. Nevertheless, the Irish aristocrats of the medieval era lived within a world in which multiple genealogical narratives determined some of the most basic limits on their behaviour: such as whom they could honourably try to kill. Or not.

I am not quite as through-othered by a similar case that also produces ghost-genealogies. This is the matter of gay or lesbian marriages (or if that makes you uncomfortable: partnerships, long-term relationships: whatever.) These are neither simply recent, solely "western," nor socially pathological. They are historically frequent if usually not very well documented, at least until recently. The following is an excerpt from oral material collected from the Azande people of central Africa in the late 1920s and the 1930s under the direction of Professor E. E. Evans-Pritchard:

> This is about how men married boys when Gbudwe was lord of his domains. In those days, if a man had relations with the wife of another the husband killed him or cut off his hands and his genitals. So for that reason a man used to marry a boy to have orgasms between his thighs, which quieted his desire for a woman. If this boy was a good wife to the husband five spears might be paid for him, and for another as many as ten might be paid.
> A husband who was liberal to his in-laws, they would later give him a woman, saying that if good for a boy, how much better for a woman; so if he married a girl his in-laws
> would greatly profit, so they gave him a [girl] wife.[47]

Clearly there is a lot going on here – a complex social matrix wherein the usual male-female genealogy eventually takes centre stage, but in which a ghost-genealogy was produced by gay marriage.

Now, it might be possible to escape from the complexity of this matrix by arguing that the ghost-genealogy in this case would be a palimpsest, but at least it would be a single one, unlike the multiple ghost-genealogies that come from Irish fosterage. Perhaps. And, further, one might make a plausible argument that gay and lesbian marriages are not very genealogically complicated, as they all come to a dead end; so one traces them just the same way one does a childless heterosexual marriage in whatever genealogical grammar the given culture employs. Maybe.

But what one cannot force into a safe corner is the fact that gay and lesbian marriages actually produce children: not solely biologically, but often through adoption, fosterage, surrogate womb rental, or (in our own time) *in vitro* fertilization. The result is a family that is defined not by biology (no matter what, at least one of the two parents in a gay/lesbian marriage, is not a biological parent) but by societal convention. Obviously, this societal decision begs many deep and controversial questions of theology and apologetics, but that is the prerogative of the specific culture. My suggestion is that such partnerships be placed in the same genealogical grammar that the society which enhulls these marriages employs. Yes, it will look strange to see a genealogical diagram that shows for parentage two triangles or two circles, but is that really an insuperable problem?

To some, yes, most notably the Roman Catholic church, the Protestant right-wing denominations, and, alas, the Church of Jesus Christ of Latter-day Saints. The climax of the Mormons' genealogically based liturgies involved the "sealing" for eternity of a married couple. No gay or lesbian partnerships need apply. And, indeed, one cannot record a gay or a lesbian family unit on the Mormon genealogical forms without using an acetylene cutting torch and a high voltage arc welder. Such families will not fit into the Mormon computer program and, effectively, evidence of their existence is elided in the LDS data base. Individual historians and genealogists, therefore, have to repair this severe deficit any way they can in their own work. This inevitably involves a good deal of hard labour that really should not be necessary. However, that is the price to be paid for refusing to obliterate the empirically verifiable practices of certain cultural groups by the application of a universal hermeneutical fiat.

One of the most skilled and influential of historians to practice in the twentieth century, E.P. Thompson, wrote a book with a perfect title, *The Poverty of Theory.*[49] Perfect because it fit his argument about the weakness of structural Marxism and perfect because it is portable. It is a phrase that should haunt anyone who proposes a big-system approach to human genealogical narratives. Certainly it haunts me in proposing that four genealogical narratives cover almost all (but not quite all) human cultures. Certainly, it should, but apparently, does not haunt the compilers of the Church of Jesus Christ of Latter-day Saints' genealogical data base: for, as I noted, they force everything into the grammar of Standard Double genealogical grammar only by breaking apart historical realities and making all family systems retrospectively fit with the Mormon model. Just as it is uncivilized to break open ancient tombs and to disturb the relics of the occupants, so it is disrespectful, and ultimately truth-destroying, to rearrange the lineaments of the families of the dead to suit an ideological template.

Yet, are there not in the world of ethnography or anthropology theoreticians who are much brighter than any of us and who put forward successful single-cloth systems of human genealogy? Brighter, certainly; successful, no.

Of the many attempts to seize the golden ring, the Grand Unified Theory of Human Kinship (and thus of human genealogy), the effort that comes closest to being successful of which I am aware was that of Claude Levi-Strauss. This came in the heyday and high times of French Structuralism. In the late 1940s, Levi-Strauss published a volume which, when translated rather late in the day, in 1969, was entitled *The Elementary Structures of Kinship.*[50] This was followed in 1958 by volume 1 of *Structural Anthropology* (as it was called in its 1968 translation)[51] and by volume 2, published in 1973 and translated in 1977.[52] These are not recreational reads, but they are immensely stimulating. In particular, *The Elementary Structures of Kinship* allows one to watch a truly fine mind grapple with a massive intellectual anaconda.

Levi-Strauss's main methodological conceit is that kinship systems are based less in empirical reality than in the modelling of reality by those who are within the system. To put it another way: in the jural definition of kinship, biology is merely an adjuvant to the social definition of kinship. The law that rules is that of the mind. It has been noted by a critic that an explanation of kinship that views it as an intellectual model proposed and adopted by a given culture has the problem of not producing testable hypotheses.[53] If that is the case, then orthodox social scientists will have a hard time accepting it, for hypothesis-testing is the mode of affirmation in the social sciences. However, historians (and presumably the sub-set called genealogists) will have less trouble with it, for we rarely produce testable hypotheses. Instead, we model the past, employing narrative and inductive and deductive logic. And that is what Levi-Strauss does.

The Elementary Structures of Kinship is worth examining primarily to see a beautiful mind at work; and the book itself is physically compelling for, when words fail Levi-Strauss, he turns to diagramming kinship structures. Many of his schematics are quite impenetrable and they are really aesthetic presentations rather than academic formulations. One encounters, for example, a diagram of Murngin (Australian) kinship nomenclature that could be used as a template for a classic Persian carpet, so intricate is it. Like the best carpets, this design is virtually impossible to understand fully unless one is part of the system that produced it.[54]

Still, it is clear what Levi-Strauss is modeling, even if the details of his formulations frequently produce a moiré effect. All of his models depend on one basic assertion of empirical reality and upon one asserted restriction on human behaviour. The basic assertion of empirical reality is that all human kinship systems depend on the "communication" of females. This does not mean talk. It means that there is "a practically universal fact of human societies. For a man to obtain a wife, she must be directly or indirectly given to him by another man ..."[55] Notice that women are worth "obtaining," in Levi-Strauss's kinship models, for their reproductive capacity and thus are valuable commodities. He would have taken as a case-in-point the Kalinga of the Philippines who in the mid-twentieth century still were practising infant-betrothal:

> Almost every Kalinga child is engaged to be married when quite small. The boy must always be the elder, if only by a day or two. Conditional engagements are often made before the girl is born. I [the ethnographer R. F. Baron], recently asked the mother of a two-month-old girl baby whether the child was engaged yet.

"No," she answered, "We received a proposal when she was two days old, but *she* wouldn't consider it."[56]

That is how, at its most basic level, the communication-of-women works.

Levi-Strauss's restriction upon human kinship behaviour was that, given that all societies have an incest taboo, the circulation of women, though it can take many forms, must not involve parallel-cousin marriages. *Cross-cousin* marriages, yes, *parallel-cousin*, no. Parallel-cousin marriages "cannot take place without upsetting the exchange process."[57] What does he mean by this? He means that his universal model of kinship systems could encapsulate the case of marriage of the children of adult siblings (that is, children who were first cousins) *if* the two adult siblings were of different sexes. Thus the term "cross-cousins." However, Levi-Strauss's modelling will not permit a marriage (and the attendant circulation of females) to take place if the first cousins are the children of adults siblings of the same sex as each other. Here he is particularly influenced by the classic work of J.G. Frazer that in part focuses on aboriginal kinship in central Australia.[58] And, Levi-Strauss makes a very effective rhetorical point by summarizing Frazer's reading of the sacred text of the Komati, an Indian trading clan:

> It concerns the solemn sacrifice of one hundred and two *gotra*, who prefer to throw themselves into the flames rather than allow the indescribably beautiful Vasavambika to make a marriage calculated to save the kingdom but contrary to the sacred rule of the *menarikam* (marriage between sister's son and brother's daughter [a specific form of cross-cousin alliance]). The one hundred and two *gotra*, with Vasavambika at their head, marched proudly toward one hundred and three fire-pits, but not before making their children promise to give their "daughters in marriage to sons of their father's sisters even though the young men should be black-skinned, plain, blind of one eye, senseless, of vicious habits, and though their horoscopes should not agree, and the omens be inauspicious."[59]

That is a nicely told story and it is apt to lead us to take our eye off the ball. So, at the risk of being Philistine, let me remind us of our need to keep a baleful eye open. Remember, it does not matter why Levi-Strauss could not fit parallel cousins into his modelling.[60] Here he has made a statement of expected-fact that allows us to check his model against empirical data. In essence, he has said that alliances that yield parallel-cousin marriages cannot be formed under his universal model. That provides a point of evaluation. And, when one checks the ethnographic literature against his model, one immense problem immediately arises. There are cultures (several in the Middle East and North Africa: the Berbers and also the Basseri of southern Persia, for example) that within the period of historical documentation practised parallel-cousin marriage as one of their culture's preferred forms.[61] That simple observation bring us to an elementary matter of proof and disproof. If someone says that all geese are white, one has to find only one black goose to prove the assertion inaccurate. Similarly, if there is even one culture (and there are indeed several) that effects marriage alliances and the exchange of females among parallel cousins, then Levi-Strauss's universal model is inadequate.

The other matter that is fundamental to Levi-Strauss's universal model is his belief that females are exchanged as being items of positive value. (Here forgive the heartless language, but Levi-Strauss's theoretical position forces one to employ it.) His view is suitable enough for many – perhaps most – cultures that have existed over the time of human civilization, for there is a real-world indication of this: the fact that what anthropologists call *bride-price* or *bride-wealth* is widespread. This is the payment by a male (or a male and his kin) to the parents or kin of a female, in return for which the children of the woman come under the control of the male or of his kin. It could be called "womb price," for that is what it is. The practice makes sense in a socio-economic situation in which children are required either as labour or as heirs and in which they are hard to come by.

Fine. What this (and most anthropological discussion of kinship, not just Levi-Strauss's) cannot handle is the frequency in western cultures of the opposite condition: the requirement that the parents of a woman pay a dowry to induce a male to take her away. In this situation, a young woman is manifestly not a wonderful item to have on your hands (just read your Jane Austen), and clearly she has a negative value. Whyever else would her parents pay to off-load her? And why would a potential husband require an endowment to accept her?

The idea of "communicating" females really has no robustness in this situation, although one can twist and reconfigure Levi-Strauss so as almost to cover the situation. But here Ockham's Razor intervenes with ruthless directness. Given that the simplest explanation of a given situation is the most robust, then the explanation that arises from neo-classical economics is the most useful. Instead of drawing baroque kinship charts, one can explain the difference between places where there is bride-price and where there is dowry in terms of cost-benefit relationships and in terms of supply-and-demand. In some social-economic arrangements, "acquiring" a female and a womb will provide more benefit than cost (hence bride-price), and in others it will be the opposite (therefore, dowry required.) In any case, Levi-Strauss's primary axiom, that all societies "communicate" young women as things of positive value is disproved.

With a sense of sadness, one leaves Levi-Strauss. If he could not put it all together in One Big System, then we are unlikely to be able to do so. We look back on him, however, with a sense of having learned something. Which is: that, just like the simplistic Standard Double system of the Mormons, the complexities of this most so-phisticated of French Structuralists, has a jussive character that is coercive in its comprehensiveness and inconsistent with much of what can be accepted (however gingerly) as empirical, statistical, and historical reality.

6   A Big Imperial Engine

Near the end of his life (1903–1966), Frank O'Connor, one of twentieth-century Ireland's finest writers, reflected on his lifetime both as a writer and as a very wide and shrewd reader. These lectures, collected as *The Backward Look*,[1] were a genealogical text of an unusual sort. When O'Connor looked backwards, it was no casual glance: he searched out his own authorial antecedents in a chain that ran back, robust and durable, into pre-Christian times. In examining the roots of the Irish literary tradition of which he was himself a link, O'Connor employed the concept of *primary literature*, and it is an idea useful to an understanding of the cultural power of genealogies.

To O'Connor, primary literatures were those that had their roots in strong oral traditions; which dealt with fundamental human problems of origin and demise, life and death; and which were catalzyed into strong bodies of written literature when they encountered cultural systems (especially religious ones) that engaged in fixing in place the orally based material. He pointed to the early Hebrew and Greek instances as his chief exemplars of primary literatures and in the case of Ireland to the material that emerged when Celtic oral traditions encountered Christian written traditions.

In the discussion that follows, I hope to illustrate four points. (Note that word: illustrate. I do not think that there is any way in verbal logic to prove beyond dispute the suggestions that I am making.) The first of these is that genealogical narratives (as they have been defined in the two previous chapters) often take a form that deserves to be denominated as literature. The best genealogies are artful and achieve the status of consciously crafted art.

Second, the most powerful genealogical narratives form seminal patterns that are adapted not only by the framers of other genealogical narratives but by those artists who are engaged in the creation of related cultural goods: legends and, especially, origin-myths. Thus, in reflecting upon the power of the genealogical narrative found in the book of Genesis, Jacob Neusner, the leading scholar of Rabbinic Judaism in the first six centuries of the Common Era, has used the term "generative," and this is apposite on a cross-cultural basis.[2] A generative set of genealogical concepts helps to explain to any group of people who they are and why they are a distinct collectivity. Often it traces the group's genealogy back to a tribal god from whom they all are said to descend.

Third, we must recognize that genealogical narratives exist on an intellectual street where traffic runs both ways. That is, they are not completely independent variables as far as cultural formation is concerned. They are influenced by other concepts. The form and substance of genealogical narratives are in part determined by the legends and the mythologized historical events by which a group defines itself. For example, one finds that among the Visigoths it was common for past leaders to be removed from the strictly human genealogical chain and converted into demigods.[3] Hence, as between any culture's set of genealogical narratives and its collection of basic mythologies, it is best to think of there being *mutually interactive generative feedback*. To put it simply: really strong genealogical narratives determine in large part the nature of a culture's gods; and the character of a culture's gods determines in considerable part the sort of genealogical narratives a society will adopt. It is a feedback wheel that spins very fast until, for those within the specific culture, it achieves a blurred simplicity that makes the central assertions about the culture's creation a single, believable entity.

Fourth, and crucially, certain genealogical narratives are extremely imperialistic. This is an aspect of their generative power that is pervasive. Ultimately, all attempts at explaining this phenomenon become merely descriptive restatements of the original fact. Still, I think that there is some robustness in the idea put forward by the evolutionary biologist Richard Dawkins in 1975 in his *The Selfish Gene*.[4] This was an attempt to interject into the study of human consciousness an argument similar to that which Dawkins was making in his study of human genetics: show that there are certain ideational units within the human brain that are "replicators" and which seem to act selfishly in the sense of actively trying to reproduce themselves. This idea, that there is a *meme* (spellings vary), a unit of human consciousness that, when considered on its own is a unit of cultural inheritance, has its difficulties. (Such as: is the meme being put forward as a "real" entity like a gene, or merely as a fruitful analogy? how big is a meme? the size of the Roman Catholic Church or of the first three lines of "Row, Row, Row Your Boat"?) These matters have been argued by some fine minds.[5] What we can assimilate here is the conclusion to one of their implied theorems: namely, that there are certain bursts of ideas that are inherently more attractive (for whatever reason) to human beings than are others. Within the human consciousness, certain constructions are (to use my own vocabulary) imperialistic. They take over. Certain genealogical narratives are one such meme.

Lest all of this become unbearably abstract, I think my four suggestions are instantiated in a trivial, but revealing case. This is the worship, born of mythology, genealogy, and mimetically articulated self-interest, of the figure of John Frum (variant: John Prum). This occurs on the island of Tanna in the Vanuatu complex in the south Pacific. (On older maps the islands are called the New Hebrides.) John Frum was an American trader or a renegade of some sort (no one is sure), who arrived on the island in the 1930s, did a great deal of trading, and made the islanders' lives a bit better. Then, in the early 1940s, he left the island, promising to return some day: in doing this, he resembled a fairly common god-figure in world mythology, one that promises to come again. After he left, the islanders were peripherally affected by the war in the Pacific, and they noted that good things came down from the sky under specific circumstances. They therefore built mock wharves and airstrips, including one landing field that had a replica airplane on it and landing lights made of pitch torches, for night arrivals. This was physical mimesis at its clearest. Where the picture becomes really intriguing is that the islanders subsequently melded their to-come-again demi-god, John Frum, with the practice of their cargo cult, and they did so through the mode of genealogical narrative. This merging occurred in 1971 when Queen Elizabeth II and the Duke of Edinburgh visted the Vanuatu complex and the local chief concluded that His Royal Highness was the reincarnation of their missing saviour-god. (From an ideational perspective, reincarnation is the ultimate form of direct genealogical descent.) Thus, the islanders took to worshipping the Duke of Edinburgh. To his credit the British Resident Commissioner, upon hearing of this admirable practice, wrote to the Duke and acquired a votive icon and a sacred text for the worshippers: an autographed picture of His Royal Highness and a letter that encouraged them to cling to their precious cultural heritage.[6] ·

———

Anyone who has survived Hebrew school or Sunday school knows that there are large portions of the Tanakh that are no fun, and among these are the genealogies. (Although it is somewhat insulting, for reasons of expository convenience I will continue to employ the commonly used designation of the Tanakh as the "Old Testament.")[7] The spine of the Old Testament is a unified and compelling narrative. Elsewhere, in *Surpassing Wonder: The Invention of the Bible and the Talmuds*,[8] I have defined and discussed that spine under the term the *Primary Unity* of the Hebrew Bible. This is a narrative that runs from the creation of Adam (or, perhaps, even before that moment)[9] down to the destruction of the First Temple and the Babylonian captivity of the followers of Yahweh in c.586 BCE. It is a compelling story, combining several origin myths, several gods, war and plunder and sin and punishment. The text that we have, Genesis-Kings in the Hebrew scriptures (that is, Genesis, Exodus, Leviticus, Numbers, Deuteronomy, Joshua, Judges, Samuel and Kings) is comprised of multiple shards and fragments that may date in origin in a few instances to as early as c.1000 BCE. These disparate fragments were woven together into a single narrative unity in the first half of the 500s BCE. The story this Primary Unity tells is that of the origin of the Hebrew people and, indeed, of the entire human race.

That a narrative so hubristic, so self-vaunting, really works (and whether or not you believe in it on a faith basis, the Genesis-Kings tale is as good a bit of storytelling as mankind has yet created), is because of the interaction of the amazing figure, the colossal prepotent imp Yahweh and the genealogical scaffolding that permits him to cast pith and derision upon all the worldly figures that scurry beneath him.

Concerning the Primary Unity of the Old Testament and the genealogy that makes the big story possible, we must be clear about two matters. The first of these is that, although Genesis-Kings presents itself as an historical narrative, there is no way to check any of the significant details of that narrative. The wishful evocations of old-school "biblical archeology" aside, the Old Testament's tales are remarkably sparse of independent confirmation, and this is reported not as condemnation but as admiration. Yet it is a direction as to how one must read the big story and its subsidiary tales: as works of art, and high art indeed. There is something historical behind the art, but what it is remains highly speculative. The genealogical sections are skilled literature in ways that I shall suggest in just a moment. Secondly, as far as the mainline details of the genealogical system of the Old Testament are concerned, it is a Standard Double system that strongly privileges males, but sometimes records the female side of the ladder of genealogical ascent. Although it can be an intriguing sidebar, it matters not a whit that behind the final redaction of the Primary Unity in the sixth century BCE one can see indications of earlier practices such as polygamy (see Genesis 29:17–28 and 2 Samuel 3:2–5, but remember the point that polygamy works within the grammar of any genealogical system); it matters fundamentally not at all that the classic form of the Yahweh-faith permitted a man to marry and also to keep concubines (See 2 Samuel 3:7 and 5:13, 1 Kings 11:1–3, and note that concubinage operates genealogically like polygamy, although usually second-status polygamy); and do not waste any time on the lubricious matter of "Levirate marriage," the requirement that a man had to marry his brother's widow, even if that meant a plural marriage resulted (Genesis 38:6–10; Deuteronomy 25:5), since one still is dealing with a Standard Double genealogy, albeit in polygamous form.[10]

What really counts is how genealogical narrative in the Old Testament achieves a compelling literary character and thus makes believable a set of stories that otherwise would be merely fractuous tribal relics or flaccid tales told around a dying fire.

The genealogies that are woven through the first nine books of the Old Testament (and which are amplified in 1 and 2 Chronicles) are variants of the basic Standard Double form (women are included but mostly they are elided as being of secondary importance). The genealogies serve a variety of purposes: back-stopping origin-myths, creating definitions of nationhood, pin-pointing of tribal origins within the polity of ancient Israel, locating the speciation points of all the world's non-Hebrew peoples, confirming the regnal lists of the kings of Israel and of Judah and the partial succession lists of Yahwist high priests. Genealogical narrative is central to each of these activities because genealogy is justification and is honorific. As Harold Bloom has remarked (in relation to Tractate Aboth in the Rabbinic literature), "the prestige of origins is a universal phenomenon."[11] The Old Testament is unusual among ancient near-eastern literatures, however, in having at least twenty-five full genealogies, whereas elsewhere one has only the Mesopotamian king lists and the history of the Amorites and these do not come close to the Hebrew attainments.[12]

The Old Testament genealogies are artistic in nature by virtue of their being a massive metaphor. They account for human life, religious practices, and dynastic and geo-political events "through a metaphor of biological propagation."[13] Thus, world history necessarily becomes a form of family history. This is a metaphorical framework so strong that the biblical tales could not be told in any other way: if the stories jumped out of the framework of genealogical narrative they would not be biblical. It is as simple as that: the covenant between Yahweh and his people is between an imperious god and an imperial sperm bank. As Yahweh promises Abraham, "I will make thee exceeding fruitful, and I will make nations of thee and kings shall come out of thee" (Genesis 17:6).

The basic biological metaphor that undergirds the Old Testament is not a brittle item; quite the contrary, it has a ductility that permits it to meld with a variety of mythological and historical demands. For example, the two versions of the creation of the male and female ur-parents of the human race that are found in the first two chapters of Genesis both work because of their extreme simplicity as genealogical narrative: a Standard Double couple is created and within a moment (by the start of chapter four of Genesis) they are producing descendants that spread out like a genetic umbrella. The early genealogy of humanity as it descends from Adam and Eve is given in such a matter-of-fact tone that its very flatness implicitly says "we're just reading you the news." And that flatness of tone makes it infinitely easier to accept the extraordinary claims for the starting point of this genealogy: the Hebrew equivalent of the Big Bang, which was Yahweh playing about in the mud and producing Adam, a name that is a pun upon the words for human and for soil.

Genealogies do not, however, just spill out in the Hebrew Bible. In a consciously artful fashion, ten generations are reported between the creation of Adam and Noah of the Great Flood. (Genesis

5:1–32). These are nicely balanced by a genealogical skein of ten generations that run from the immediate post-Flood (from Shem) down to Terah, the last of the pre-patriarchs (Genesis 11:10–26). Elegant symmetry here, but there is more: whereas the average lifespan in the pre-Flood era was a bit over 857 years (for males; women are not included), that of the first ten of the post-Flood generations was just under 300 years.[14] Implicitly, in the gradual reduction of lifespans towards a normal (meaning believable) human level, the genealogist is helping the narrator of the story to give cues to his audience on how the creation tale and its subsequent biological descent should be received: with seriousness, certainly, but with the recognition that religious truth and biological literalness are not the same thing. The diminishing age of the men in the first twenty biblical generations tells the listener that as things came closer to the present, the content of the stories is coming closer to the ordinary.

When the so-called pre-Exodus "patriarchs" are reached – Abraham, Isaac, Jacob, Joseph – their average lifespan is down to less than 150 years.[15] This was still in the demigod range, but more realistic than in the immediate post-Flood stories. These ambitiously long life spans, however, were not those of normal people and that raises the question that has forever puzzled the hearers and readers of the patriarchal tales: are they intended to be taken as archetypal stories or as historical reports? Since there is no independent evidence that the Children of Israel ever spent a moment of their collective history in Egypt (just show us one clear piece of archeological evidence, please or, for that matter, get a band of competent experts to agree on the route out of Egypt) it is hard to take the narratives at face value. This is just what the genealogical "record" would also imply in associating the Exodus with the patriarchs who lived for a century and a half: demigods.

Thus, the genealogies of the "Twelve Tribes"[16] through which Yahweh performed his side of the covenant with the descendants of Adam are interwoven into the Old Testament so as to be the trellis upon which scores of tales of "primary literature" are hung. As a result, it is easy to miss another artistic function of biblical genealogical narratives: when necessary, a deft genealogist skilfully papers over cracks in a tale that otherwise would distract the audience. A clear case is in the story of the twin brothers Esau (the elder twin) and Jacob, the first-born sons of Isaac (son of Abraham) and his wife, Rebecca. In one of the most memorable embodiments of what moral choice means in everyday life, Esau exchanges his birthright (which is nothing less than Yahweh's blessing, handed on to him through the genealogical chain that runs back to Adam) for some bread, something to drink, and a bowl of lentils. (Genesis 25:27–34). The tale is made richer by the black embroidery of several strands of deceit and trickery within the family of Isaac. A truly dark and far from simplistic lesson, but it lacks one element a successful folk tale should have: all the loose ends should be tied up, and one big one is left dangling by the biblical narrators: what happened to Esau once he was out of the divine line of genealogy? Nine chapters later (chapter 36) a gimcrack genealogical narrative bales out the storyteller. Six separate genealogies are cobbled together to give the subsequent line of descent from Esau.[17] This lineage is used to explain the founding of the kingdom of Edom (near the Gulf of Aquiba), a perpetual enemy of the Chosen People and thus an illustration that rejecting Yahweh's blessing makes one an enemy of His people.

In one other instance, a very large one indeed, we can see the skilful genealogist turn a stuttering aporia on the part of the textual narrator into tranquilizing amnesia. This occurs through the form of the regnal lists. These are actually genealogies *manqué*. That is, the king-lists that are so prominent in the latter parts of the Primary Unity in the Old Testament are not always genealogical in being a record of father-to-offspring inheritance. They are imitation genealogies, however, in defining the passage of power from one king to another, reign after reign. Mostly this is done in the book of Kings. There a set of regnal lists covers the period from c.928 BCE to 722/721 BCE, an era in which there was no such thing as a single House of Israel but rather two rival kingdoms. One of these, in the south, centred on Jerusalem and consisted of the tribes of Judah and Benjamin and of one half of the former tribe of Joseph, which now was split into sub-tribes, Manasseh, which allied with Judah and with Benjamin, and Ephraim, which did not. Usually the southern monarchy is called the kingdom of *Judah*. The other, the northern kingdom, was that of Israel. Two centuries of rival kings and rival kingdoms testified to a fundamental split in the Hebrew polity.[18] This rivalry came to an end in 722/21 BCE, however, when the Assyrian empire totally destroyed and scattered the people of Israel. (It is from this event that we receive the term "Ten Lost Tribes of Israel," which, to be accurate should be the "9-plus Lost Tribes," since remnants of other tribes stayed with Benjamin and Judah.)

Now, we know from reading the Hebrew scriptures that the story of the "children of Israel" does not stop in 722 but continues in an unbroken story line until the Babylonian captivity in the 580s BCE. How do the author-editors of the Genesis-Kings narrative keep everything together? After all, it appears that the covenant granted by Yahweh first to Adam and then to Abraham has been voided.

Two brilliant moves are employed and for using them the final redactor of Genesis-Kings deserves the All-Time Nobel Prize for Literature, History, Religion, and Genealogy. The first of these moves is that, despite what the main historical narrative says, he simply refuses to let Israel disappear! Even though the scriptures' writers believed that the Israelites deserved what they got (they had built altars to idols and had worshipped them; 2 Kings 17:7–12), the redactor of the subsequent narrative continues to associate the religious heritage of Israel with that of Judah. The promises made by Yahweh to Israel are assimilated into the history of Judah. The kingdom of Judah now becomes the kingdom of Israel, even while being under the kings of Judah. (It is of course from the name Judah that the world received the term Jewish.) By assimilating into the books of Genesis-Kings the history of Israel, the Judaean final redactor of the story achieves a smooth and irreversible feat of cultural imperialism. He subsumes into the history of Judah all the desirable aspects of the history of its ancient rival Israel, and at the same time (via regnal lists) make it clear that Judah ruled from 722 BCE onwards. In conceptual terms, Israel continues to exist, but as a conceptual colony of Judah.

There is more and this second, related move also involves the king-lists. For not only does the final redactor of the Primary Unity of the Hebrew scriptures imperialize for Judah the history of Israel in material that follows the Assyrian destruction of Israel, he *pre*dates the superiority of Judah over Israel to an era that antecedes all those regnal lists of the "split kingdom." He does this by suggesting something for which there is no evidence save the text itself: that there once was a united kingdom in Eretz Israel and that it was at its zenith under a Judahite, namely King David. Granted, King David is the most fully formed figure in the entire Hebrew Bible and he is probably the first human being of whom we have a biography. But one can accept the textured reality of his greatness without necessarily buying as fact that he ruled a monolithic kingdom encompassing both Israel and Judah. Perhaps he did, perhaps not. The indisputable textual fact is that Judah is made prepotent over Israel on both moral and political scales by the king lists (King Saul-King David-King Solomon-and then bifurcation) and by an insertion of a phrase into the death-speech of the patriarch Jacob giving his son Judah genealogical priority over everyone: "thy father's children shall bow down before thee" (Genesis 49:8).

The kingdom of Judah wins big.

But not by exterminating the memory of Israel, but by assimilating it. This astoundingly brilliant act of cultural imperialism in the scriptural text, like so much in the Hebrew Bible, is made possible by the melding of sharp story-telling decisions to rich genealogical narratives. In this case, the genealogical narratives are not biological but are tropes of biological narratives: regnal lists which function like father-to-son biological succession, by virtue of their being part of a divine succession of power from the ultimate king, Yahweh, through King David and then down through history. Anyone interested in the history of the Christian religion would do well to pay attention to the accession to cultural hegemony of Judah and of its icon King David, for David is posited as one of the forefathers of Yeshua of Nazareth.

One of the most vexed questions of western history is one that I here state and then refuse to engage. It is: how pure an act was the literary establishment and maintenance of the Davidic line? That is, did the author-editors of the core text of the Hebrew Bible participate collectively in what can be called a "performative utterance" – the creation of the object about which they wrote and which had no concrete corresponding object in empirical reality?[19] Or were they writing about biological and regnal succession in the real world? In my view, that question as it affects the Davidic line misses the point entirely. The text itself is so strong, so rich in structure and detail, that it is a real entity in either case: whether it is a performative creation or reportage of actual events, or anything in between.

At the risk of trivializing what is a matter of belief about eternal destiny for some people, one notes a story that illustrates the ubiquitous influence of the entire Genesis-Kings narrative. It comes from E. Stuart Bates's grappling in the 1930s with the genre of autobiography:

What constitutes authenticity, *i.e.*, what we may accept and what we must reject, is the most difficult problem of all. We must reconcile ourselves to being deceived at times; like the miner who knew one J. P. Beckworth and thought he was listening to Beckworth's autobiography being read out – tall stories of Red Indians and frontier life, with the author in the limelight – in a mining camp, when the reader had really got hold of the Bible by mistake and had started on the story of Samson and the foxes. "That'll do," he called; "I'd know that story for one of Jim's anywhere."[20]

Anywhere: just the right word when we transfer it back to the biblical genealogies. With epic immodesty, the compilers of the ancient Hebrew genealogies assert that the lineages they define are everywhere and anywhere. When, in Genesis chapter 10, Noah lands on dryish land after the conclusion of the Great Flood, he is confronted with a world that is empty. He produces children and grandchildren by the platoon, and these are the progenitors of all the lineages of the world. Seventy to seventy-two persons (interpretations vary) are involved in the *Table of Nations* and from at least the mid-sixth century BCE onwards there has been a non-stop industry in figuring out which groups in the earth's subsequent population are descended from which of these Noahic-derived figures. Most readers of the Old Testament know of Shem, Ham, and Japheth, but after that they glaze over. So many names, such ambiguous clues. Still, this genealogical cornucopia is the first-known effort at a comprehensive human ethnography: by the vehicle of genealogical narrative, it is an attempt to classify the entire population of the then-known world.[21]

Whether you accept this *Table of Nations* as the practical starting point of all human genealogical study (as did, for example, the authorities of apartheid South Africa), or find it to be an astonishing, but fictive, cultural artifact is your own choice. What one cannot do is ignore it: the *Table of Nations* and the genealogical narratives in which it is entrained, are the most powerfully subsumptive cultural engine since (I would hazard) the invention of the written word.

––––––

Amongst the many partially justifiable complaints that modern Jews have about Christianity is that the Christian writers stole much of the Old Testament when they were writing the "New" and, worse than that, tried to steal the covenant with Yahweh as well. Anyone who has attended a Christian communion service of a traditional denomination will recognize that when the chalice is passed, the words that the Gospel of Matthew ascribes to Yeshua of Nazareth at his Last Supper are employed: "This is my blood of the New Covenant which is shed for many for the remission of sins" (Matthew 26:28; see also 1 Corinthians 11:25). This is no small claim, and it is the foundation of most later Christian theology: the assertion that the covenant Yahweh had made with the Chosen People was now taken from the followers of the ancient Yahweh-faith and entrusted to the followers of the new Yeshua-faith. This massive theological *putsch* is of course a claim to interrupt and permanently void the genealogical claims of the Chosen People, for their covenant was expressed as a function of a metaphorical genealogical connection that ran all the way back to Adam.

Indeed, the entire New Testament (which is equally accurately translated "New Covenant") is a rewriting of the Old Testament. As I have argued elsewhere, there is scarcely an item in the New Testament that is not derived from the Hebrew scriptures or from parabiblical texts of the late Second Temple era and this runs from tiny resonances of detail to the entire structural organization of the new Christian text.[22] To take a single example, note the simple matter of the Twelve Disciples. No more obvious claim could be made to replace the genealogical pre-eminence of the Twelve Tribes with the adherents of the new Yeshua faith.[23] Also, note that from the earliest Christian writings (Paul's letters) onward, Yeshua of Nazareth becomes the Son of God. This is a direct competitive strike at the only other son of Yahweh, Adam. In fact, in two of Paul's letters (Romans 5:12–21 and 1 Corinthians 15:21–22, 45–49) the First Adam, through whom death and sin entered humanity, is contrasted with the Second Adam who overcomes both sin and death.

Yes, the Christians stole the main items of the Yahweh faith, and well worth stealing they were.

So, the complaint is in part correct, but things are a bit more complicated than simple felony. This is because of the nature of genealogical narrative, as embedded in the massively powerful piece of primary literature that is the text of Genesis-Kings. The genealogical mode of thought is so strong that the chroniclers of the new Yeshua-faith *had no alternative but to continue to think in that idiom and to present Yeshua of Nazareth in genealogical terms.*

In one of the twentieth century's most significant works of literary criticism, Harold Bloom developed a theory of poetics under the title *The Anxiety of Influence* (1973).[24] Bloom's apperceptions translate easily from poetical practice to genealogical narrative. He suggests that among "strong" texts (and the two sets of scriptures, Hebrew and Christian, are nothing if not strong), a new text comes into being as a result of *misprision*, by which he means a "strong misreading" of the older text (or texts.) That is, the older strong text has imperial power over its descendant text, but at the same time the new strong text grapples powerfully with its progenitor and succeeds in some degree in breaking away. In the following statement, I am replacing Bloom's reference to strong poetry with the concept of strong genealogical narrative: "Genealogical history ... is held to be indistinguishable from genealogical influence, since strong genealogical narrators make that history by misreading one another so as to clear imaginative space for themselves."[25] And, "the meaning of a genealogical narrative can only be another genealogical narrative."[26]

That works. It recognizes that the Christians were indeed up to a bit of thievery, but that the imperial power of the Old Testament was so great that, if the Yeshua-followers were to create a new religious text, it had to involve appropriation and revision of large portions of the old text. The basic material of the new faith's narrative had to be emplotted as a purposive misreading of the genealogical metaphor that underlies the Old Testament. There was no other way.

But wrestling with a strong forebear is an uncertain and dangerous business and that is indicated in Bloom's recognition of the "anxiety" inevitably involved. This anxiety is most clearly shown in the early Christian texts when, in the Gospels of Matthew and of Luke, the writers put forward two incompatible genealogies of Yeshua of Nazareth.

Matthew's version of the genealogy of Yeshua of Nazareth is more confident and elegant than is Luke's. In the Gospel of Matthew (1:1–16), Yeshua's descent in the male line (four women are included in the genealogies, although the linkages that count are all male) employs the principles of symmetry and of magic numbers that we observed in Genesis (5: 1–32 and 11:10–26), where there are ten generations from the creation of Adam to the Great Flood and ten from the Great Flood to the earliest of the patriarchs. The author-editors of Matthew begin with the first patriarch, Abraham, the father of the faithful, and have Yeshua's ancestry divided neatly into three segments of fourteen persons each (that is, the magic number seven being doubled, a nice inside move: a quiet claim of superiority). The first set of the three sets of fourteen runs from the patriarch Abraham to King David; the second from David until the Babylonian captivity; and the third from the captivity until the birth of Yeshua of Nazareth. The primary point of the whole chain is to make it clear that Yeshau of Nazareth was a direct heir of King David, the iconic figure for the Judaean polity that had swallowed up the religious inheritance of long-gone Israel. To maintain the degree of neatness that a divinely arranged genealogy requires, the author-editors of Matthew had to cheat. They dropped out the names of three of the kings of Judah and one co-regent in the era between King David and the Baylonian captivity. Also, their final list of fourteen is clearly a work of artifice for the similar list in Luke contains the names of nineteen leading figures of Judah.

The author-editors of the Gospel of Luke provide a markedly different genealogy for Yeshua of Nazareth, although its purpose is the same as Matthew's: to lift the mantle of divine authority as defined by the genealogical covenant between Yahweh and the ancient Hebrews, and now worn by the kingdom of Judah, and drape it around the shoulders of Yeshua of Nazareth. Luke's effort (3:23–38) is both more ambiguous than Matthew's and sharply incompatible with it. Luke's ambition is such that he traces Yeshua all the way back to Adam "the son of God." He does this in a non-biblical style, however. Whereas all the classical lineages of the Hebrew scriptures are genealogies of descent (they start from Adam and cascade downward), Luke runs the line upward: it starts with Yeshua and ends with Adam. From its very beginning, Luke's genealogy of Yeshua clashes with Matthew's: Joseph the carpenter is the son of Heli in Luke (3:23) and the son of a man called Jacob in Matthew (1:16). In fact, after the figure of King David (proceeding chronologically downward), the two lineages agree only on two figures, plus Joseph the carpenter and Yeshua. (That Christian interpreters have often suggested that there is no incompatibility, since the two compilers "had different tasks," is a form of special pleading that is also self-destructive: different tasks yield different "facts.")

Heightened anxiety here: two-fold. First, the early Christian writers were trying to show the legitimacy of the divine genealogical line of Adam-David-Yeshua. That is dictated by the biological metaphor upon which the Old Testament is based and which any Judaean religion of the later Second Temple era had to honour. They could have gotten away with either Luke's line or Matthew's, but not both. The two invalidate each other. And, second, an even bigger problem makes the author-editors of Matthew and of Luke very twitchy: why in the world would each present to believers a genealogical line, articulated through the male line and which has as its primary focus of reference Joseph the carpenter? Why do that and then implicitly tell the faithful that this was not a valid genealogy because Joseph the carpenter was not the father of Yeshua of Nazareth and, indeed, that Yeshua was the product of a Virgin Conception? (Matthew 1:18–25; Luke 1:26–38). The unavoidable conclusion is that under the anxiety of influence – the pressure of having to work within the lines of ancient Hebrew genealogical narrative and having to overcome its imperialistic force with their own strong reading – the author-editors of these two gospels buckled. They lost control.

That is understandable, for the gospels of Matthew and of Luke were written in tough times for the early church, the late first century of the Common Era. Keeping the story of Yeshua in order in the chaotic years that follower the Destruction of 70 CE was no easy matter, for the centre of the faith – the temple on King David's mountain – was obliterated and the faithful of all forms of Judaean religion were scattered. But what is understandable in the chaos of the late first century is hard to fathom in the fourth and fifth centuries when the church fathers were defining the canon of the New Testament – what was in and what was out.

Given that the goal was to show that Yeshua of Nazareth was a direct heir of Yahweh, any of their three genealogical gambits would have succeeded if left to stand in the new Christian scriptures:

1 the genealogy in Matthew
2 the genealogy in Luke
3 the Virgin Conception that makes Yeshua a new Adam, a direct biological son of God.

Any single *one* works, but any two invalidate the whole enterprise.[27]

Why these New Testament texts were not straightened out by the early church authorities is a mystery that is beyond solution. What is certain is that these big wrinkles in the text did not preclude Christianity's becoming in the fourth century the religion of the

Roman Emperor and thence of the Roman Empire. As Christianity, riding on the historical ripples of the Roman Empire, became an imperial religion (remember from your school days the Holy Roman Empire), it overthrew the religious systems of several cultures.

————

The test case that is most revealing is that of ancient Ireland, for that culture was the toughest to crack. In this instance (which I think is representative of many other cases), it is notable that, although Yeshua of Nazareth and the holy mysteries surrounding his death and reported resurrection were adopted readily enough, the parts of the Christian message that had the most impact in forcing the Irish to re-orient their entire cultural compass were not the uniquely Christian elements but those that came from the Old Testament. Specifically: the ancient Hebrew genealogies.

The Irish case is richly confusing in detail, but unambiguous in its overall direction and unmatched in portent. Why is Ireland so important? It is historically pivotal because it is the only case that has the following characteristics: (1) Unlike every place else of any size in the Indo-European world, save most of the Indian sub-continent, it was not successfully invaded by imperial Rome. This means that the fundamental social order – the original pre-Roman structure, including family life and therefore genealogies – was not warped by the pressure of the Roman legal and governmental apparatus. (2) The battalions of missionaries, priests, abbots, and bishops who were the agents of the Christian church's cultural conquest of Ireland (which began spottily in the fourth century, was nearly complete in the ninth, then battered the Irish church into tight Roman shape in the eleventh) encountered for the first time in their collective experience a culture that was unbroken. No Roman armies had softened up the Irish. (3) The culture the Christian colporteurs encountered was highly self-conscious, with its own rich mythology, highly developed genealogies, and sharply articulate professional remembrancers who were paid to recall and to revise history, myth, and genealogy, all of which were intertwining genres.

Now, if you are an historian, your heart sings when you hear something like that, for historians live in constant jealousy of the scientific professions wherein practitioners have the luxury of conducting experiments. We never do: we just take what is left to us in the empty rooms of human ruins and try to make sense of

the shards that lie there in the dust. But, occasionally, the shards
of time are arranged in a natural experiment and this is one of
those moments. Because: here, in the Irish case, we have an experiment that answers two closely related questions that we would
have set up in experimental laboratories if only we could. These
are, first, would Christianity have done very well if, unlike the case
in most of Europe, it had not been dealing with societies that already had been beaten up pretty thoroughly by Roman armies
and chained by Roman law? Could the Christian faith take over a
strong country primarily by cultural means and without an army
preceding it? And, secondly, if the Christians were victorious in
overcoming an intact, unbowed society, what parts of the Christian
toolkit would be most useful in subsuming that alien culture? Ah:
Ireland, the great experiment.[28]

I claim no expertise in early Irish history, but my long-ago good fortune was to have as my mentor Professor John V. Kelleher (1916–
2004), who was not only the founding figure of Irish studies in the
American academy but also one of the world's truly great genealogists
– although he would have rejected both the praise and the job description. John Kelleher is relevant here because in the late 1950s he
immersed himself in a project that became too big for him to control:
to collect the Irish annals, regnal lists, pre-and post-Christian mythologies and redact them for several layers of editorial emendation, for
the euhemerization of Irish gods and the interpolation of Christian
and Hebrew figures, and then do as complete a population conspectus of early Ireland as was possible. But there was more. John was not
interested in counting heads. In his basement study, three of the four
walls were covered with books and the fourth with large black binders. In those binders were genealogical charts that linked together the
entire data-set of the early Irish material, or at least tried heroically to
do so. These binders, full of fold-out charts, held nothing less than a
potential history of the family social structure of early Ireland. Publicly, John would not explain where all this work was headed, but in
private he admitted he was on to the Big One. He was trying to crack
the nature of the Indo-European family before it was affected either
by classical civilization (meaning Roman culture and its Greek acces-
sories) or by the Semitic rules of family structure and of genealogical
narrative that Christianity enforced upon the Indo-European world.

John Kelleher married this ambition – big, sensible, but just-
barely doable – to his own excessively high academic standards.

John could never accept the concept that social scientists live with – namely, that there are outliers in any large data-set: anomalies whose existence one recognizes, but then ignores in presenting a generalized model. He just could not bring himself to do that. Everything, every name, every anomaly had to fit. So, many, many times the following happened, and I here paraphrase the explanation he gave to me a score of times. He said, "Don, it's all like a house of cards. I get the whole pyramid made, and then I check one last tag of some misbegotten bastard's ancestry, and pull out that card and the whole damned pile falls down. And I start again." Finally, in his late seventies, he stopped starting again and passed the whole collection on to a ranking scholar in Ireland, with the hope that a new mind could make sense out of this old midden.

Since I talked or exchanged letters with John Kelleher at least once a month from the late sixties until his death (we chatted more about ancient Irish genealogy than I wished and less than he would have liked), I still hear his voice and I try to keep up – at a very amateur level – with the recent material: and the progress made in the last twenty years is impressive indeed. Still, I think we should continue to let the conversational voice of the great Harvard scholar (as resonated through another friend's persiflage) break through the academic mien. When I was a postgraduate student, Professor Kelleher and I had lunch often and one time he brought a set of letters and postcards that he had received from a fictional person (a mythological figure in an Irish sort of a way) named "Bucko Donahue." These were written by John's friend Edwin O'Connor, the twentieth century's most talented novelist of the Irish-Catholic Americans. O'Connor used the figure of a Bahamian black (who, not-so-incidentally, was the ex-slave of Bernard Baruch and who had been educated in Latin by the Christian Brothers) to peck away at John for his devotion to the ancient Irish sources, especially the Irish annals. Anyway, Bucko Donahue was said to be the only expert on the Irish Annals and one missive John showed me said this: "It's all cod, you know, this work you're doing ... I reject the Annals *in toto* for two reasons. First, it was all swiped from the Jews. Second, it's all crap anyway."[29] That was Edwin O'Connor's voicing of what were John Kelleher's doubts, and they were made to bounce off his countervailing conviction, that the Irish sources were the richest genealogies in premodern Europe. Both the convictions and the doubts should be shared by anyone who works with the Irish material: empirically rich beyond facile rejection, disconcertingly creative beyond literal acceptance. In fact, it was the rampant creativeness of parts of the Irish corpus of ancient history, monarchy, and genealogy that made John respect it so much that he despaired. Collectively, the texts of ancient Irish history in his view were a reintegration of pre- and post-Christian material. "The corpus could never be presented wholly apart from *Lebor Gabála* [The Book of the Invasions of Ireland] on the one hand and the annals and regnal lists on the other, which is but another way of observing that all Irish history and prehistory was ideally intended, and to a considerable degree actually composed, as one self-consistent body of information."[30]

Since we can accept as common knowledge that Ireland was indeed Christianized without the necessity of the country's being thumped by Rome's once-imperial legions, we can take that part of the Irish-based experiment as resolved: yes, Christianty was indeed strong, imperially strong. But what about the other half of the experimental query? What part of the Christian toolkit would be prepotent in this venture, this subsumation of a proud, vigorous, previously unbroken culture? Here, after his first decade of swimming in the sea of Irish sources, is John Kelleher's answer and it deserves quotation at length:

> If (let us say, in the sixth or seventh century) one were given the job of inventing a prehistory for the newly Christianized Irish people which would place them satisfactorily in the framework of universal history they had learned from the Bible and from Isidore [of Seville], something very much like *Lebor Gabála* would be an obvious first step. This would connect them ancestrally to the most appropriate forefather, Japheth son of Noah, would account for their existence during many centuries, and would at last bring them to Ireland, their destined home.[31]

What then?

The next step would be to account for the then present-day Irish by constructing pedigrees which would link them, group by group, according to their known kinships and alliances, to the original immigrants. Such a scheme need not be elaborate, but it ought to be clear and consistent. Each stock should have a collective name derived from an early eponym. The eponymous ancestors of the major existing groups of that stock should come later – say, about eight   generations before the beginning of the Christian period in Ireland – should be contemporaneous with similar figues in other lines, and extending from each of them to the present there should be a *croeb coibneasa*, a branching of relationships which would adequately account for the known structure of the tribal-federation or kindred-group.[32]

And that is exactly what happened. Between the first hesitant introduction of Christianity in the late third or early fourth century, until the completion of Roman Christian conquest in the twelfth, the Irish built up a body of texts. We would not call them scriptures, but they acted the same way holy texts do: they explained origins, retold big myths, enclosed and protected genealogical narratives, and did this in a manner necessarily consonant with the Old Testament. At the risk of great simplification, these texts were: (1) *The Book of the Invasions of Ireland*;[33] four major annalistic records (and many minor ones), *The Annals of Clonmacnoise, The Annals of Innishfallen, The Annals of Tigernach, and The Annals of Ulster*;[34] lengthy myths and legends recorded by Christian writers,[35] and myriad accounts of saints' lives.[36] Taken together, these and scores of related secondary items take the Irish from Adam to Noah, through various pre-Celtic inhabitants of Ireland, through Celts from Spain, and right through half the petty kings of Ireland up to the Norman invasion. The material is complicated and often contradictory, but it is not a mess, because in its central elements it operates by Old Testament rules. Granted, Jesus gets his time in court, but if one were first reading this material with an innocent eye, one would conclude that King David and Finn MacCool belonged to the same social club and that Yeshua of Nazareth was only a guest member.

That is the main transaction – the imperialization of early Irish culture by the Semitic mythology and genealogical narrative of the Old Testament – and the rest is mere detail. Still, some of the details require attention, since they cast light on the mode, mood, and moment of this extraordinary process. Irish society undeniably was culturally imperialized but, paradoxically, it was energized and entered a period of its history (say, from 500–900 CE) when it was the most culturally dynamic society in the Indo-European world.

The mid-wives of the entire process were poets, at least if one accepts the suggestion of Charles Dunn and Morton Bloomfield that in ancient societies poets not only worked in verse forms but also in narrative.[37] They were professional remembrancers and many of their early genealogies were in verse form (verse has a mnemonic structure that narrative lacks and is easier to preserve in a world where writing is not the primary form of memory). However, whether in verse or narrative, whether speaking from memory or reading from texts created by Christian scribes, the Irish poets presented genealogies in a self-consciously literary fashion – which relates, of course, to the discussion of genealogy as a literary form and as a set of pre-configured narrative structures that we engaged in chapter five. This was primary literature at its most basic, and Dunn and Bloomfield are in no way exaggerating when they describe the words of these early remembrancers as "in a very strong sense magical."[38]

What is hard to grasp is the sheer size of the Irish project as it integrated its genealogies and mythologies into a coherent corpus under the umbrella of Old Testament rubrics, while employing the writing system that the Irish had acquired from Rome and from Roman Christianity. As has recently (2003) been noted in a first-time translation of the five-volume, seventeenth-century *The Great Book of Irish Genealogies*, Ireland, up to the Norman conquest had both the most extensive vernacular literature in Europe and the largest genealogical corpus of any country in western Europe: encompassing 12,000 persons by the twelfth century.[39] All this material was kneaded into a mould that, while contradictory in internal details, took the Irish back to Japheth, Noah, and Adam.

Inevitably, this heritage (rather like any aristocratic lineage, except more so) contained an implicit arrogance. The *Lebor Gabála* makes the Irish a second Chosen People and the island of Ireland therefore becomes a second Promised Land.[40] As late as the mid-seventeenth century, Geoffrey Keating's *Foras Feasa ar Éirinn* accepted the *Lebor Gabála*'s king-list that included two of the Hebrew scriptures' most prestigious figures: Enoch, who reportedly did not die, and Methuselah, the person who allegedly lived longest in human history.[41] Our sort of people, indeed, the lineage says with puffed chest.

The trade-off the Irish were required to make for this reflected Semitic glory was that they had to tug the forelock concerning some of their earlier mythological and genealogical beliefs. One simple rule was that the old gods – Lug, the Sun God, for example

– had to be tamed. This was done by complete censorship or by turning gods into ordinary names in genealogical lists or, more interestingly, letting the gods remain as what we would today call super-heroes: big figures, but not divine ones, at least not in the way the Christian scribes wrote them into the script; how demotic audiences interpreted the Christianized tales was another matter altogether, one suspects. Take, for example, the god Nuadu of whom there are archeological evidences of a cult in pre-Chrstian Ireland. In The Book of the Invasions of Ireland he become Nuadu of the Silver Hand. He was the king of the Tuatha Dé Danann in the years before they invaded Ireland, and he lost his arm in battle. After seven years (a magical biblical number) his stump healed and he had his arm replaced with one of silver, completely functional and possessing the full strength of a human hand in each finger and each joint.[42] That would work in a modern comic book: a god had become a super-hero.

Obviously, in fitting the big contours of their national genealogy into ancient Hebrew patterns, the Irish were bowing respectfully to their superiors. (That's what one did in an aristocratic world; bow before those who were more powerful than oneself.) But what is easy to miss is that the corpus of Irish origins also contains a number of grace notes, moments like those instants in a court dance when the courtier smoothly reaffirms the superiority of the king without interrupting the overall pattern of the dance. Two small examples: the super-hero Cu Chulainn (a euhemerized god if ever there was one) is made to prophesy the birth of Christ. And, earlier in time, one of the most learned of the predecessors of the Gaels was sent to the children of Israel in order to learn Hebrew.[43]

None of what we are observing affects the accuracy, or non-accuracy, of the Irish genealogical narratives once they are past the mythological era. "Genealogies were used from an early period in Ireland to support claims to power and territory, and therefore the forging of pedigrees to accord with changing political relationships and circumstances became something of a minor industry, akin to the forging of charters in other countries." Thus, the genealogical authority, Nollaig O'Muraile. "Because of this, one cannot say that because a pedigree dates from a particular period it is to be deemed either reliable or unreliable ... Whether early or late, it may be a wholly accurate record of a particular line of descent, it may be entirely fabricated, or – as often happens – a mixture of the two."[44]

Seemingly, one extreme – that of massive fabrication and inaccuracy – occurs in the genealogical narratives of Irish saints. Here, one case will do, that of St Brigit, who is virtually the patroness-saint of Ireland and who came close to being ranked ahead of St Patrick. Unlike Patrick the Briton, who had a specific origin as a human being (the traditional date for his coming to Ireland is 432), Brigit had the advantage of being a Celtic goddess. Indeed, if "Cormac's Glossary," a ninth-century guide to early Irish history is correct, there were three Celtic goddesses named Brigit, each of them the daughter of the Celtic god Dagda, the "Good God."[45] Whoever "St Brigit" might have been (*The Annals of Ulster* have her being born 452–456 and dying 523–525), this Christian figure, an abbess, most likely, picked up an aura from the lineage of the ancient Celtic gods. Her supernatural penumbra was not to be referred to aloud by Christian priests and scribes but it had resonance with the laity, who knew full well that she was not just a Christian saint but a Celtic goddess.

The rivalry between the wraiths of St Patrick and St Brigit for Number One status in the Irish pantheon is revealing for genealogical scholars, because of the evidentiary clash of their respective partisans in the seventh and early eighth centuries. This contest was between the southern Uí Neill of Ulster and the Leinster dynasty of the Uí Dunlainge. In geographic terms, the struggle was between Armagh (which had a wobbly association with St Patrick) and Kildare (which had a strong association with St Brigit). Of course the two dynasties, the Uí Neill and the Uí Dunlainge, were engaged in a larger contest for territory in the Irish midlands. The intellectual weapons with which they fought included several lives of St. Patrick and three lives of St Brigit. Unlike St Patrick (who has no Irish lineage), Brigit's genealogy could be played with. A splendidly rich line was created that showed her to be the descendant of several midland kings, not bad for a former slave girl.[46] Tied to this, her hagiography includes miracles. Ultimately, probably in the early eighth century, a compromise was brokered between the two secular dynasties (the Uí Neill let the Uí Dunlainge back away with honour) and the spiritual side of the compromise was that St Patrick became the patron saint and Armagh Ireland's holy hub, while St Brigit became an honorary consort of Patrick: some hagiographies have the two of them being buried in the same grave.[47]

Whether you prefer Brigit as a goddess or saint, at least her hagiographical and genealogical narrative illustrates Francis John

Byrne's incisive summary that "genealogically, relationships can be altered to suit political circumstances."[48]

One twelfth-century Irish chronicler pointedly listed six specific techniques used for re-configuring Irish genealogies to suit the circumstances of the moment.[49] Undoubtedly, a good deal of the Irish historical material is both old and accurate and, considering that this is the largest genealogical trove in early medieval Europe, that is splendid: if only there were some way of knowing exactly what is solid and what is not. At the most basic level, we encounter a Standard Double set of lineages, one that strongly privileges males. This underlying pattern can be accurate and revealing, but the details often are a mire of misdirection. As John Kelleher once observed, "So extensive was the revision of historical evidence that we have, I would say, about as much chance of recovering the whole truth about early Christian Ireland as a historian five hundred years from now would have if he were trying to reconstruct the history of Russia in the twentieth century from broken sets of editions of the Soviet Encyclopedia. Not that the historian's task would be quite hopeless. Eighty or ninety percent of the information in the encyclopedias would be sound enough. In the Annals too, we shall find that most of the information, at least from the early seventh century on, is reliable ... It will, however, be a long while before we shall be able to say with confidence what is reliable and what has been tampered with or falsified."[50]

And, alas, we are left with an even bigger mystery: what, dear Lord, did the Irish genealogical narrative look like before it was bent beyond immediate recognition by the forces of the great Semitic genealogical engine?

This question – the Big One that eventually was beyond even John Kelleher's efforts – will, for a full response, require a degree of technical expertise and of mental ability that almost surpasses comprehension. I suspect that the result will be to show a pre-Christian Irish genealogical system that is as different from the Standard Double genealogy of the Adam-and-Eve variety as quantum mechanics is distant from Newtonian physics.

This guess (I would not even label it a speculation; just a guess) is based on two verifiable observations, each of which points to a pre-biblical conception of genealogy that is head-shakingly complex. First, as I discussed in chapter five, the practice of fosterage in pre-Norman (and certainly in pre-Christian) Ireland produced an immensely complex network of fosterage-based ghost-genealogies that were as binding as were the "biological" ones, and equally complex. A set of genealogical narratives that would encompass both the usual "biological" and the ghost-genealogies would be possible only in a society that defined the family in some corporate form that is not within our own ken.

Secondly, that there was in pre-Christian Ireland indeed such a sense of corporate family, different in concept, composition, and rules than the usual Standard Double family (no matter how extended and complicated), is indicated by some marks that one finds in the post-fourth century regnal lists, left like smears on a looking-glass. If one views with an innocent eye any verified set of king-successions (such as are found in vol. 9 of *A New History of Ireland* (Oxford: Oxford University Press, 1984), one is apt to be struck by a simple fact: that in all the kingly lines (and Ireland had scores simultaneously) the ratio of kings-to-time is too high by modern standards and the regnal successions frequently do not follow father-to-son lines. Yet, the successions have something to do with genealogy. John Kelleher spent a lot of his life cracking this and he (and others) found that the kingship system followed that of a corporate family. Because there were several branches in each corporate family, because each branch was eligible for four generations (and then it dropped down into the commonality), and because successions usually went to older men and rarely to minors, the result was the seemingly too-large stack of kings. Fine, but retrospect that explanation backwards into vernacular society in pre-Christian times: it appears that the Irish family unit was not based on an individual man, or upon a man-and-a-woman, but on some unit whose substance we cannot see, whose borders we cannot define, and whose regulations we cannot intuit.

Not yet. The day will come.

7   Resistance, Submission, Subversion

When we viewed the case of the Irish early medieval genealogies, there was not much evidence of direct resistance by the keepers of the pre-Christian Irish material to the adoption of the Old Testament biological metaphor as the dominant mode for the understanding of the Irish world. That is not to say that there was not a vigorous *Kulturkampf*, but the records were all written by the winners. Indeed, the Irish case is especially biased evidentiarily because the pre-Christian Irish had only the most awkward form of writing: certainly nothing to rival the flowing power of church Latin. And all the surviving records were either written by clerics or by Christian laymen who had been trained by the Christian clergy. That it is profitable for present-day scholars to search the vast Irish trove of Christianized material for pre-Christian traces is a result of two ancient practices. One was that the Christian scribes collected and recorded (however inaccurately) pre-Christian material rather like Victorian missionaries collected stories from the Dark Continent. Secondly, for impercipient reasons, a good deal of pre-Christian material was both recorded and, sometimes, encoded in the genealogical registers.

At this point we leave Ireland and pose a large question: in practice, what has been the spectrum of response to that massive cultural siege engine, the Old Testament's genealogical system? Obviously, one response has been to submit to it. But, even in instances of apparent submission, either direct resistance or subtle subversion has been employed. To illustrate the range of resistant behaviour, we observe three cultures. One is medieval Iceland, a pagan society that accepted a veneer of Christianity; another is Rabbinic Judaism and the new rules for marriage introduced by the early medieval Rabbis; the third is the Roman Catholic church and its creation of the Petrine spiritual genealogy.

———

We will keep the Icelandic case brief, although the material is so rich that many scholarly lives have usefully been spent on it. The Icelandic material is of course situated in a larger literature of Norse mythology, history, and genealogy, However, since Iceland was the last full-blown culture to be hived off of the Nordic stem, it was also the culture that produced the most self-consciously artful set of interrelated sagas, the most clear genealogies and, most importantly, the first real author and certainly the first one of real genius in the Nordic region: Snorri Sturluson (1179–1241; spellings and dating vary slightly).

Christianity came relatively late to the Scandinavian countries, which is to say that reading and writing arrived late as well. Hence, in the period when the Irish Christian scribes were recording their version of Irish genealogies and origin-tales, the Nordic genealogies were kept only orally and the mythology was preserved both by word-of-mouth and by carvings and engravings that memorialized key motifs in the main tales. The year 1000 CE is the traditional date for the conversion to Christianity of Iceland and if scholars enjoy arguing about whether it was really 999, or 1000, one cannot begrudge them their fun.

The key point is that Iceland became a cultural lead-sector in the Nordic world. This occurred, first, because Iceland was quite quick off the mark in converting. Denmark had Christianized in the mid 900s, Norway about the same time as Iceland, and Sweden later. However, because Iceland was such a small society numerically, the penetration of Christianity throughout the culture occurred much more quickly than in those other nations. Secondly, Iceland had only been seriously settled from the last quarter of the ninth century, so the populace could (and did) maintain an accurate oral tradition of their family genealogies until, through the intervention of Christianity, they were recorded in written form. These genealogies existed coterminously with a sharp memory of general Nordic mythology as shared in large part with the other Norse cultures. Thus, thirdly, Iceland had an advantage in the cultural sweepstakes over the other Nordic nations in that it was relatively easy for it to throw up an educated elite who had mastered both reading and writing and who had lived in a society in which settler genealogy and sagas were organically intertwined in everyday life. Hence, it was Icelanders who become the premier paid remembrancers of the Norse aristocracy. The best of these was Snorri Sturluson who, among other things, produced a life of St Olaf of Norway and a biography of an Icelandic poet-warrior, and also a record of the kings of Norway and Sweden from the earliest times through the twelfth century. Some of this was puffery, but in fact it was also high art.[1] Grasping Snorri's personality is impossible for he comes from a world for which we have at present few cognate figures: a large and ambitious landholder in southern Iceland, a courtier to Norwegian royalty, a major political figure in his own country and, apparently, a fearsomely ill-tempered man whom you really did not wish to have sit at your table. Beyond that, he was a disciplined and erudite genius in prose, poetry, and poetics.

Snorri's monumental work, *The Prose Edda*, is (despite its title) in part about the theory of Nordic poetry and a thesaurus of figures of speech and of characters' names, but that is not what is central to our present purpose. What counts here is that Snorri assembled in one package a coherent corpus of work, parallel to the *Lebor Gabála* in Irish mytho-genealogical writing but much smoother and more believable. He melds together a small bit of Christian piety with the largest collection of Norse mythology assembled in the Middle Ages, incorporates the genealogies of the ancient Norse gods, and joins these to sagas and genealogies that date from the settlement of Iceland and which were part of an oral tradition that was close enough in time to the actual events to be fundamentally factual, albeit not necessarily precise in every detail.

Robert Kellog has demonstrated that the structure of the individual sagas in Icelandic history is constructed around genealogies that are so specific that they can be charted simply by using the narrative as a guide; and, conversely, to read the narratives sensibly one must credit (however temporarily) the genealogies that underlie the stories.[2]

In essence, Storri freezes at one moment a belief system of an entire culture that was actually changing quite quickly. His *Edda* shows an Icelandic culture that is extremely proud in a familial way. The ancient Norse mythological stories and the sagas of the Norse explorers and settlers are interwoven with local family tales and of course with details of lineages. The result is surprisingly comforting, if tales of monumental violence can be that, for the whole corpus is articulated in a tone that affirms our-people-can-handle-it. This tone is just the opposite of hysteria and more than one observer has noted that Snorri unfurls his stories – some of which are truly outlandish – as if they are history.[3] And, in his gentle passages, Snorri can be charming: how can one resist King Dag of Denmark who "was so wise a man that he understood the song of the birds."[4]

Snorri was a Christian, or at least a shrewd enough courtier to bow his head before the Hebrew genealogies, however briefly. He composed a prologue to the first major section of his *Edda* (entitled "The Deluding of Glyfi," a mythical king over Sweden), an opening which has the tone of a denial-of-liability-statement one receives from lawyers for insurance companies. He is about to endorse the ancient Norse gods and their genealogies but does not plan on being charged as a heretic under the rubrics of the new Christian religion. So his first sentence pays ritual respect to the Hebrew Bible: "In the beginning Almighty God created heaven and earth and everything that goes with them and, last of all, two human beings, Adam and Eve, from whom have come families. Their progeny multiplied and spread over all the world."[5] He then escapes smoothly and swiftly sideways by jumping up a ramp of pseudo-anthropology. He explains that after Noah's flood the population grew so large and their settlements so spread out that the great majority of humankind left off paying homage to Yahweh and boycotted all reference to him. Soon, they developed their own religion, one based upon the material world, but reflectively so: Snorri does not condemn it. Instead, he slides gracefully into telling us about the "Aesir," Nordic gods who come from Asgard, an otherworld found vaguely in Asia and also, according to other Norse versions, where Valhalla and the palaces of various gods are located. Once he has a locale and a broad description of world geography defined, Snorri drops any pretence of Christian piety and gives us the real goods: god stories, genealogies, the works.

Clearly this is an act of cultural resistance to the imperial might of the ancient Hebrew model as enforced through Christianity. That is interesting in itself, but I think Snorri is much cleverer than that: he is, I suspect, engaged in a massive subversion of the Hebrew-Christian genealogical program.

Instead of an intricate textual argument, we can demonstrate how extraordinarily successful Snorri was by a simple two-fold process.

First, I am highlighting certain names that are found in Snorri's narrative. (For the moment the colourful adventures of these figures can be set aside.)

> In the northern part of the world he [Thor] met and married a prophetess called Sibyl whom we call Sif ... [Several generations later] was born *Godolf,* his son [was] *Finn,* his son Friallaf whom we call *Fridleif;* he had a son named Voden whom we call *Odin;* he was a man famed for his wisdom and every kind of accomplishment. His wife was called Frigida, whom we call *Frigg.*

> Odin, and also his wife had the gift of prophecy, and by means of this magic he discovered that his name would be famous in the northern part of the world and honoured above that of all kings ... Then Odin set off on his journey north and coming to the land called [Jutland] took possession of everything he wanted in that country. He appointed his son *Skjold* to govern there; his son was *Fridleif;* from thence has come the family known as Skjoldungar; they are kings of Denmark ...[6]

This highlighted list does not require much parsing. They are Nordic gods and demi-gods (some of whom we pay respect to weekly: on Wednesday, Odin's Day, and Friday, Frigg's day). Snorri and other writers have a wonderful compilation of their acts.

Now for the second part of our demonstration. Ask: could anyone really be taken in by what Snorri was doing? The easiest way to check this – and also to help us towards one of our ultimate purposes, a calibration of the usefulness of the Latter-day Saints data base – is to take the world's largest and technically most advanced collection of genealogical information and see how those highlighted names are comprehended.

One can enter the LDS data base at a huge variety of points, but for our purposes it is best to take a well-documented and historically significant person as our starting point. This will be the alleged Ur-father of the Scottish clan Donald, Somerled of Argyll, king of the Isles. (One necessarily says alleged, but he probably is the real item.)[7] He is credited with driving the Norse from the western seaboard and western isles of Scotland in the mid-twelfth century, and he undoubtedly had secondary Celtic roots, probably Irish. Here, however, the salient matter is his Norse heritage: one enters the LDS data bank and follows the most probable of many of his allegedly possible lines (excluding several that are biologically impossible, such as a child's being born before his or her parents, or having children born to couples who are over 100 years of age; items of that sort.) Two things become very clear. Up to a point Somerled's genealogy, which within two generations becomes tightly linked to Scottish dwellers of Norse background and within nine generations is solidly back in Norway, is fundamentally accurate in this sense: recent genetic studies have shown that Clan Donald's DNA carries a marker distinctive of Norse descent.[8] This is lovely, for it suggests that the Norse genealogies going back to 800 or so are accurate in general outline, albeit not beyond question in detail, and that the LDS are employing those genealogies appropriately.

The problem comes when one traces Somerled farther back, as far as the massive LDS computer, which has ingested all of Norse genealogy. There one finds Snorri's revenge. By way of Frodi, a legendary third-century king of Denmark, the line passed to *Fridleif Skjoldsson* and then to *Skjold*, king of the Danes, figures we know from Snorri's prologue. (Incidentally, the Mormon genealogies have picked up from elsewhere in Snorri's writings that Skjold was married to Gefion, a mythological figure who at one time had mated with giants to produce sons who were useful as massive draught-oxen.)[9] And who were the parents of Skjold? The computer tells us that it was *Odin*, the one-eyed Norse god of wisdom and of a good deal more, and *Frigg*, the less-than-faithful queen consort of Odin. These are all reported as being real people, with dating and locales; Odin, for instance is registered as being born in 215 and being "Of Asgard, Asia or East Europe," which was the Norse home of the gods. The Mormon genealogies go back father yet, to Odin's grandfather *Froethalaf* [var: *Fridleif*], whom we saw as Odin's father in Snorri's prologue. Then back to *Finn*, reportedly born about 130, and finally to Finn's grandfather *Godwulf* who was entered as Finn's father in Snorri's prologue. That is a fairly long lineage for Somerled, king of the Isles: from the mid-twelfth century in western Scotland to an "ancestor" born about 80CE and hailing from Asgard.

What Snorri Sturluson, with a little help from his friends, has done is marvelous. Out of disparate pieces of oral literature, genealogies, and family pieties, he created a monumental piece of literature. The spine of this self-conscious literature (and Snorri, remember, was Scandinavia's first theoretician of poetics) was a steel chain comprised of links of genealogical narrative. This chain was a line of resistance to the cultural imperialism of the ancient Hebrew system of genealogical thought that was enforced throughout most of Europe by the Christian church. Snorri bowed momentarily before the book of Genesis and then set up an alternative scheme of human descent through which the entire aristocracy of the Norse world was descended. Resistance, certainly.

Yet, Snorri's greater achievement was his counter-imperialism. He did not just resist; he subverted.

That is why the demonstration of the Mormon's great computer's being directed by Snorri's prose more than eight centuries after it was written is so compelling. Here the Mormon computer is merely a metonym. Snorri was effective centuries before the invention of printed books, much less computers, for he did not baldly reject the Hebrew-Christian genealogical engine but.used the energy that engine provided to power an entirely antithetical set of human lineages and to preserve pagan gods and alternative origin-myths. Anyone who was committed to the Hebrew genealogical system in its literal sense (until the twentieth century, most Christian and Jewish clerics) was a natural mark for his flat-voiced, factual-sounding, quietly seductive product.

To change our metaphor. Snorri's material was adopted so easily by the LDS genealogical system because it fit. For many Mormons, Scandanavian mythology has been an acknowledged (if muted) part of their heritage. Snorri had tailored a glove that would fit perfectly onto the hand of anyone who was committed to accepting the ancient Hebrew system of lineages; its threads started with Adam and went through Noah and, implicitly, joined on to the Table of Nations. That glove, though, was cut by Snorri to fit the left hand. When the Mormons (and again, they are representative of a long line of western thought) put on the glove they placed it on their right hand. That way it still fit perfectly – provided the glove was turned inside out.

And that is what Snorri, subversive genius that he was, accomplished. He turned the Old Testament genealogical system inside out and used it to preserve a congerie of genealogical narratives, origin-myths, pagan gods and sagas that were deeply alien to the Hebrew and Christian way of thought. The crowning point of this masterpiece of subversion is that the very people who were trying to imperialize the pagan Norse cultures out of existence are found in the end to be proudly displaying Snorri's seamless glove as if it were part of their own culture's everyday habiliment.[10]

———

One of the United Kingdom's most distinguished scientists, Steve Jones, professor of Genetics at the Galton Laboratory, University College, London, says that Judaism is "the most genetic of all religions."[11] He is close to being right.

Not quite right, though, since there are some faiths that have been somewhat more rigorous in their genetic record-keeping or in their lineage limitation for membership. On the genetic-record front, the present-day Jewish pool of knowledge is actually quite shallow and in comparison to some groups – especially the Latter-day Saints – is minuscule. In considerable degree this is because both written and oral records of Jewish genealogy took a terrible beating in a century of persecution of Ashkenazim that ran from the Russian Pogroms through the Holocaust. But even before that, other major persecutions (such as those of the Sephardim in the fifteenth and sixteenth centuries) reduced familial knowledge and, in fact, a series of displacements running back to the two disastrous wars with Rome in the first and second centuries of the Common Era scattered Jewish communities and destroyed memory and records of most lineages. Naturally there are exceptions to every generalization – the Rothschilds and similarly privileged families have long lineages and so do the most famous Sages of Blessed Memory, but they are the rare exceptions. At present it is usually difficult to put together a Jewish family tree that is documentarily verifiable and longer than four generations: unless there has been significant intermarriage with non-Jews whose existence kept the family in the record system of the non-Jewish world.

If, alternately, one takes Jones's "most genetic of all religions" to mean that in the era of verifiable history, Jews have been more rigorous in their genetic requirements for membership than any other group, this simply is not true. In recent centuries, one has needed only to have been born of a Jewish mother to satisfy the genetic requirement of Judaism. This is positively *louche* when compared with certain branches of Coptic and Ethiopic Christianity. Indeed, even some bands of Quakers have been more rigorous, demanding that one be born of Quakers on both sides of the ledger, thus becoming "birth-right Quakers."

And, if being "genetic" means that Jews have refused new in-
comers on genetic grounds, than why has there been such a centuries-long debate about the requirements for conversion to Judaism? The whole matter of Jewish genetic exclusivity was pretty
much put to rest by the Maccabeans who, in the Second Temple
era conquered Galilee. They "Judaized" it by giving the Galileans
the choice of two knives: they could either be circumcised or have
their throats slit.[12] Quite a lot of new genetic material was swiftly
incorporated into the Jewish community.[13]

Where Steve Jones is on the right track is that among significantly
sized and culturally important ethno-religious groups (the Jews today are roughly 13 million persons and certainly are among the
most historically compelling of cultural groups), the modern Jews
have thought, argued, and produced more articulate reflection on
the relationship between group membership and family lineage
than has any other group dealing with a comparable issue. And this
material is reasonably transparent, at least if one is willing to look at
the Jewish scriptures, Rabbinic texts, and halachic decisions. Moreover, all this material has indeed had something to do with real-
world behaviour, not least in keeping the question of what the
proper genetic/genealogical threshold should be for membership
in the group at the forefront of everyday consciousness.

Notice, that here I am dancing away from the question of whether
modern Judaism is a religious faith, an ethnic group, or both; that is
for the members to decide and what their decision is depends in large
part on how strictly the group members observe the unique genetic/
genealogical requirements that I will describe in just a moment.

Nevertheless, at this point we need to agree on what we are talking about: modern Judaism, meaning *Rabbinic Judaism.* This is not
the same thing as the ancient Yahweh-faith, although it, like Christianity, has tendrils that reach back to that faith and to its Temple;
and, like Christianity, it claims to be the only true heir of that earlier faith. Also, like Christianity, Judaism has multiple "denominations" (although that word is not used very often). Almost all of
these, except the tiniest splinter groups, would fit within the following historical description. (And, I confidently assure you, not a single one of the multiple modern Judaisms will accept fully any
summary of their collective history; still, read on.)

Rabbinic Judaism has an ideological horizon line that stretches
back to Adam, but a specific beginning point that is much later and

much more precise. This is the Destruction of 70 CE, when a massive Roman army finally overwhelmed the citadel of the Yahweh-faith – Jerusalem – and nearly cleared it to the ground.[14] Thus, the "Second Temple," that of Solomon being the First Temple,[15] where the covenant between Yahweh and the people of Judah (who had claimed the mantle of Israel) was daily enacted, disappeared. It had been the epicentre of their religious universe, the literal House of God, and without it the practice of the Yahweh-faith was impossible. Something had to be invented to fill the void and this was begun with the surviving leaders of the Pharisees withdrawing to Yavneh to begin a holy academy. The need for a new revelation was made all the more imperative when the Judahites who had remained in Eretz Israel backed a rising by a Messiah named Bar Kochba and another war with Rome followed, that of 132–135 CE. This time after an arduous Roman victory, Jerusalem, the holy city, was literally levelled and most of the Chosen People were dispersed throughout the Middle East and, indeed, farther. It was not until c.200 CE that the first document in the construction of a substitute for the old Yahweh-faith was created by the Rabbis – who now took the place of the former priests of Yahweh's temple; and not until the sixth or seventh century that an entire religious system, Rabbinic Judaism, was stabilized. Rabbinic Judaism not only replaced the former Yahweh-faith but it also changed many of the rules. Yet, all the while the Rabbis admitted to doing nothing new, just reinterpreting Torah more accurately.[16]

Among the most basic changes was the way that the fundamental biological metaphor that underlay the scriptures of the ancient Yahweh-faith was made operational. In the Rabbinic era, (meaning from late antiquity to the present) the genetic/genealogical terms on which the standard definition of Jewishness is based became markedly different from that required of the Chosen People under the covenant of the Yahweh-faith.

In a crisp and prescient essay on Rabbinic Judaism, Meir Soloveichik has noted that "to speak of descent ... itself implies a remarkable assumption: that Jewishness can be a matter of descent, rather than belief; that the foundation of Jewish identity is genealogy rather than theology ... In this respect Judaism differs fundamentally from Christianity, in which participation is essentially a matter of faith, rather than descent."[17] He quotes approvingly the Christian theologian R. Kendall Soulen. "Most Jews are members of the

Chosen People by birth, and the privileges and obligations of the
Covenant fall to them accordingly. Christians, on the other hand,
understand themselves as a fellowship that can be entered only
through repentance and rebirth into the messianic community ...
Hence, no one can be born a Christian."[18] Soloveichik concludes
in a lapidary phrase that *Christianity then, is a faith, while Judaism is
also a family* (italics mine).[19]

By this point in our discussion, observers should be either curious
or, if devout, edgy or borderline livid: does this argument, which is
included in a chapter of examples of the subversion or resistance to
the genealogical imperialism of the ancient Hebrew faith, actually
mean to suggest that the Rabbis radically revised the most fundamental rule of the ancient faith – namely, the Abrahamic definition
of the relationship between the seminal and the salvatory? Yes, and
they did so with good reason.

To demonstrate this change in the genetic/genealogical rules, a
simple historical exercise is here employed. (It is simple in historical method, albeit potentially endlessly pilpulistic in apologetic resistance.) First, one asks, what is the most reasonable interpretation
of the rules concerning the relationship of a person's birth and his
or her being one of the Chosen People as defined in the books of
Genesis-Kings in the Tanakh and most particularly in the first five
volumes, the so-called Books of Moses? Second, one asks what is the
rule concerning birth and Judaism that has operated from late medieval times to the present day? Thirdly, given that there is a
marked difference between the ancient rule and the present practice, how and why do the differences arise? Easy enough to answer,
seemingly, but so too is pulling the pin from a hand grenade.[20]

In the books that form the Primary Unity of the Hebrew scriptures (Genesis-through Kings, as arranged in the Jewish canon),
the genealogical narrative is simplicity itself: which is one reason
that this Semitic model has had such an overpowering influence in
many other cultures as the articulation of the desirable norm in genealogical matters. It is the Standard Double narrative. That is:
family membership is traced through both parents. The male side
of the genealogical tree usually is privileged and normally is better
recorded than is the female side. According to the Hebrew scriptures, the paradigm of all humanity is that of Adam and Eve. Eve is
subordinate to Adam (symbolically, clearly: she is made from his
rib), but both of them are recorded as being the parents of Cain

and Abel, and thus ultimately of the whole human race. That is simple enough and no subsequent authority, either of the Yahweh-faith
or of Rabbinic Judaism questions it: for determining who is family,
both parents count.

But what happens, as the human race expands, when, after the covenant between Yahweh and Abraham, a person marries outside the
tribe? The answer in the Hebrew scriptures is clear. Several instances
show that the female is incorporated into the tribe (or, if you prefer,
religion) of the male and without any necessity of conversion (which,
as either a concept or a liturgical practice, did not seem to exist until
late Second Temple times). When the first census of the Chosen People was conducted by Moses, the people were assembled "and they
declared their pedigrees after their families, by the house of their
fathers …"(Numbers 1:18). That is, membership in the covenantal
people was defined according to who one's father was. This is just
what one would expect in a Standard Double genealogy which privileges men. "Judah married a Canaanite, Joseph an Egyptian, Moses a
Midianite and an Ethiopian, David a Philistine, and Solomon women
of every description," is Shaye J.D. Cohen's succinct summary of the
most salient examples.[21] In none of these cases is there any suggestion that the off-spring of the union was anything but a member of
Yahweh's covenanted people.[22]

The reverse side of the coin – the fate of Israelite women who
married non-Hebrew men – is unspoken. The Hebrew scriptures
have no concern in recording their stories and the most likely explanation is simply that they became members of whatever group
their husband was joined to: the same principle as ruled when non-
Israelite women married Israelites. There is only a single instance
in the Primary Unity (Genesis-Kings) in the Hebrew scriptures of a
marriage of an Israelite woman and a Gentile man that yielded an
Israelite child (Leviticus 24:10–23) The case is remembered only
because the Israelite offspring of the Israelite mother blasphemed
the Almighty and as punishment Moses had him stoned to death.
Apparently, the Leviticus passage is meant to show that the Israelite
son of a Hebrew mother and a Gentile man could be an inherent
danger to the faith.

Later (that is, post-70 CE) Rabbinic commentators on the Hebrew
scriptures focus not so much upon the case law (which is quite clear
in its implications) but upon the monition of Deuteronomy 7:3–4
that declares:

Neitcher shalt thou make marriages with them; thy daughter
thou shalt not give unto his son, nor his daughter shalt thou take
unto thy son.
For they will turn thy son away from following me ..."[23]

Notice that this is ethnically specific. The context (see Deuteronomy 7:1) makes it clear that it applies to the Canaanites and to six
other powerful nations and this at the time when the Chosen People were conquereing Eretz Israel. The prohibition, slightly altered, is also found in Exodus 34:11–17. Still, this is far from a
universal banning of mixed marriages. For example, the Egyptians,
the most powerful civilization in the world of the ancient Israelites,
are not mentioned: this is a marching order for the conquest of the
Promised Land, not a universal commandment.

Somewhat confusing, but understandable, is the fact that Deuteronomy 7:4 and Exodus 34:16 each give the same explanation for
the no-intermarriage rule – that bad girls will lead good boys astray
– but no parallel warning about foreign gigolos seducing from the
faith the daughters of Israel. That is no surprise, given our knowledge of the instances of intermarriage that form the case law of
Genesis-Kings: the ancient Hebrews cared a lot more about the fate
of their sons than of their daughters: hardly worth mentioning the
females' fate.

Thus, if one is intent on reading these two intermarriage pro-
scriptions non-contextually – by universalizing them to forbid all intermarriage with non-Jewish groups – then one has three problems:
they warn against intermarriage, while giving no example of the
penalties to impose when it occurs; they prohibit both male and female Israelites from intermarriage, yet give no indication of bad results when females stray (and thus, the alleged universality of the
monition is negated); and, thirdly, in any case the universalization
of the conquest-of-Canaan's marching orders do not tell whether
or not the offspring of those misguided sons who marry non-
Hebrew women were members of the Chosen People – although
the cases of Joseph, Moses, David, and Solomon make it clear that
normatively they still were. Therefore, as far as providing a plinth
for a universal code of non-intermarriage, the power of the two
proof-texts is null. The case law (as inferred from several instances
of individual behaviour) overpowers the situation-specific rules for
the conquest of Canaan in any argument concerning precedent.

The narrative portion of Genesis-Kings makes it clear that at least until the time of the Babylonian captivity (c. 587/586 CE) the genealogical/genetic situation was as follows: (1) family membership was a function of both mother and father in the Standard Double arrangement; (2) males were privileged in terms of social position and inheritance of property (married women were in essence the property of their husbands): (3) when Israelite males married non-Israelite women, they and their offspring were enclosed in the covenant; their children were Israelites; and (4) it is highly probable, but not as certain as point "3" above, that when Hebrew women married outside the faith they normally became whatever their foreign husbands were.

Now the striking contrast. If one takes the Rabbinic rulings that have been predominant in the Jewish faith since at least 600 CE, one finds a rejection of the basic biblical pattern. The situation has been that (1) membership in any given family has been a function of both father and mother; each count in genealogies, but (2) that for birthright membership in the faith a person must have a Jewish mother. And (3) a person with a Jewish father, but a non-Jewish mother, is not accepted as immediately Jewish. There are of course caveats (such as being born of a Jewish mother and later embracing Christianity leads to exclusion). In the second half of the twentieth century a significant segment of North-American Jewry decided that having a Jewish father was as good as having a Jewish mother. Nevertheless, the overall picture is unambiguous: namely, that the founders of modern Judaism – the Rabbis of the first seven centuries of the Common Era – significantly amended the basic pattern of membership in the Chosen People as instanced in the founding documents of the ancient Yahweh-faith. The Rabbis did not change the rules of family formation, but did introduce the *Female Licence Principle*[24] as a requirement for birth-right membership in the people of the covenant. Immediate (non-conversional) licence to be a Jew came only of having been born of a Jewish mother. This change is a much more overt form of subversion of the grand imperialism of the genealogical narrative of the Hebrew scriptures than was that illustrated in our previous case, that of the Nordic Sagas, and it cries out for an answer – when and why did this arise?

One possibility is that the Female Licence Principle arose between the end of the Babylonian captivity (c.538 BCE) and the early Maccabean era of the middle of the second-century BCE. This is a time period reflected in the books of the Old Testament that are subsequent in composition to Genesis-Kings. For our purposes, the ones that are potentially valuable evidentiarily are Chronicles and Ezra-Nehemiah. A slight addition to case law is found in the first nine chapters of Chronicles, which is a genealogical list of hundreds of successions running from Adam down to King Saul and half a dozen generations after him. Women are occasionally mentioned, but in only three instances is succession amidst the Chosen People affected through the female link (1 Chronicles 2:16–17 and 2:34–35); and in one of these cases (2:34–35) a special note is made that this was necessary because the man in question had no sons, so he had his daughter marry an Egyptian servant or slave. Given that all the other cases in the long genealogical lists are male-to-male succession of membership, these three exceptions are certainly no indication of a change in genetic/genealogical policy. Quite the opposite.

More promising if one is keen to find an early origin of the Female Licence Principle is another text written in the same era as the Chronicles genealogies, the Book of Ezra (in this case roughly 405–430 BCE). The prophet-reformer Ezra represented the interests of the descendants of the religious elite of the Chosen People: those who had been taken into Babylonian captivity as against the position of the "remnant" (actually, probably the majority) who had been left behind.[25] Ezra's mission was to achieve control of the new Temple (Zerubbabel's Temple, which later is renovated by King Herod and becomes known as the Second Temple). He did this by denouncing the local religious leaders as corrupt, lazy, deficient, and given to intermarriage with non-Hebrews. On the matter of laxness among the priests and upon their intermarriage with foreigners he well may have been right: the prophet Malachi noted this same phenomenon (Mal. 1:6–14; 2:11). On the marriage matter, Ezra is reported to have learned that

… The people of Israel, and the priests and the Levites, have not separated themselves from the people of the lands, doing according to their abominations, even of the Canaanites, the Hittites, the Perizzites, the Jebusites, the Ammonites, the Moabites, the Egyptians, and the Amorites.

For they have taken of their daughters for themselves, and for their sons: so that the holy seed have mingled themselves with the people of those lands: yea, the hand of the princes and rulers hath been chief in this trespass. (Ezra 9:1–2)

Ezra issues a prohibition of this practice and makes all intermarriage a breach of the covenant:

> Now therefore give not your daughters unto their sons, neither take their daughters unto your sons, nor seek their peace or their wealth for ever: that ye may be strong and eat the good of the land, and leave it for an inheritance to your children for ever (Ezra 9:12).

The priests, Levites and ordinary people accept Ezra's demands and resolve to put away their "strange wives" (in the King James Bible's wonderfully archaic term for foreign wives) and, crucially, to exile the children formed of the physical union with such women. Thus, approximately 113 married women and their children were "put away," probably meaning they were sent back to their foreign parents: bad cess to them, as far as Ezra was concerned. (See Ezra 10:18–44.)

A memorable, although not a very gentle tale: but then Yahweh's commands rarely are cosy or comfortable. What does one make of this story in the context of our historical interest in the development of genealogical narratives? In the first place, we should recognize that this is a situationally specific story. Ezra has two interests: in general terms he desires the Israelite (really, "Judahite" or "Judahist" would be a more accurate term in this period) community to draw its general boundaries tighter and to get on with finishing the rebuilding of the Temple. He especially wishes to discredit and displace those of the local priestly class (both Aaronite and Levite) who were not descended from the religious elite that had been taken to captivity in Babylon more than a century earlier. That is why intermittently throughout the tale the shocking fact that priests and Levites had married foreign women keeps being mentioned.

Still, there is the second notable matter that relates to genealogy and gender: the text only talks about the extrusion of foreign women married to Hebrew men and of their children. Mixed marriages of Jewish women and foreign men are not mentioned, nor are the children of such unions. Why? Some scholars have claimed that this is because Ezra introduced what I have termed the Female Licence Principle. That, however, is a long reach and not very convincing, given that the text (Ezra 10:18–44) does not even mention Judahite women actually being married to foreign men. Further, the historical context provides an apposite explanation of why such mixed marriages are not mentioned: normally, such women would have already gone to live with their foreign husbands. In the case of the few who may have lived among the Chosen People along with their foreign husbands and resulting children, the husbands would not have been persons of any great consequence, especially not in the liturgical hierarchy: and, remember, Ezra was leading a reformation movement whose primary goal was to gain control of the Temple that was being rebuilt and of its religious personnel. Hence, one suspects that Hebrew women with foreign husbands were not mentioned simply because they were of no consequence in the context of Ezra's mission.

The real innovation in the Book of Ezra runs opposite to the gender-asymmetry that is embodied in the Female Licence Principle. The signal genealogical/genetic point in the text is the explicit extension (in Ezra 9:12, quoted above) of the prohibition on marrying outsiders to include both men and women equally: *give not your daughters unto their sons, neither take their daughters unto your sons.* Compare this to the earlier texts, Deuteronomy and Exodus, where the prohibition is phrased only in terms of not permitting Israelite sons to marry foreign girls. When that is done, the trajectory in ecclesiastical thinking is quite clear and it manifestly is on quite another path than that which would be followed in establishing that female-based mixed marriages would yield covenanted babies, but male-based ones would not.

Confirmation of the view that the Female Licence Principle arises only in Rabbinic times is found in the para-biblical documents that are produced in the later Second Temple era. Running from roughly 150 BCE until the Destruction of 70 CE, this was a remarkably rich period in religious thought and scores of luminous, sometimes lurid, texts were produced. Although these were not included in the canonical Hebrew scriptures, many of them were very splendid religious visions and even those texts that were merely prosaic are useful historical documents. In shorthand terms, these texts are referred to as the Pseudepigrapha and the Dead Sea Scrolls.

Simply put: there is affirmative evidence of a continued adhesion to assumptions of the gender-parity scheme that Ezra propounded for dealing with mixed marriages. And there is no mention of anything in the textual evidence (and that is the only sort that we have) for anything that could be construed as the Female Licence

Principle.[26] That leaves one with the choice of either inferring that the principle did not exist in Late Second Temple times or one has to make the smoke-blowing suggestion that although there is no evidence that the Female Licence Principle existed before the Destruction of the Temple, that does not prove that it did not exist.[27] This argument we reject on the basis of the chant of Jacob Neusner, uttered so effectively throughout his career in Second Temple and Rabbinic studies: "what we cannot show, we do not know."[28]

The only possibly indicative comment comes from a post-Second Temple writer who chronicled the earlier period: the fascinating turncoat, Flavius Josephus. (Joseph ben Mattathias was his Hebrew name.) Living in Roman-financed retirement, the one-time Jewish general compiled a narrative of the Roman-Jewish war, a history of the Jewish people, and his own memoir, plus occasional pieces on topics relating to Jewish issues. Although he indicated no acquaintance with anything like the Female Licence Principle, he at one point quotes a reference to Herod the Great as a "half-Jew," a term of opprobrium. This was allegedly said in a sledging speech by one of Herod's rivals and it was reported a century and a half after the event by Josephus, and well after the Destruction of Jerusalem and the Second Temple had destroyed the world of Herod the Great.[29] Given its provenance and the distance in time of the writer from any witnesses, it is not the type of item that possesses immediate credibility.

So why pay any attention to it? Only because it has been used rather desperately to suggest that Josephus was saying that the man who made the Second Temple into the world's largest religious edifice, who controlled the appointment of the highest levels of the Temple priesthood, and thus who had more influence over the practice of the faith of the Chosen People than any other single person in the Late Second Temple era was not really Jewish – and this because his mother had not been Jewish but an Arab. Therefore his female Jewish line was discontinuous and, since he had not formally converted, Herod had not met the requirement for Jewishness.[30] Somehow he was half-Jewish (which, incidentally, is not a category that any later Rabbinic commentator accepts as a possibility for any person).

A forced justification for the Female Licence Principle: yet, there is something here that merits attention. This is that Herod's family came from Idumea which is a region south of Jerusalem running down to the Negev desert. It is just south of the traditional strongholds of the tribe of Judah. In 129 BCE the Maccabeans conquered Idumea and, as they had done with the Galileans, gave them the choice of becoming Judahites or becoming dead: most males chose the knife of circumcision over the knife at their throats. They, their wives and children, became part of the kingdom of Judah. Herod's father was descended from one of the knife-edge Judahites and his mother was of a Nabattaean family.[31] So, when Josephus repeated that long-ago vilipending of Herod, he was not implying, much less saying directly, that Herod was not Jewish because his mother was Arab. In fact, Josephus was not even quoting a malicious delation that Herod the Great was half-Jewish, whatever that might mean. What Josephus was repeating, as Shaye Cohen has convincingly demonstrated, was that Herod was "half-Judean," which is an accurate statement of his genealogy.[32] That "Jewish" and "Judean" should be mis-equated in most translations of Josephus is understandable, for the word for Jewish comes from the word Judaean. I think that when Josephus was saying (if it is indeed an authentic quotation) that Herod was a half-Judaean, he was repeating a statement made by Herod's rivals, suggesting that, given his Idumean background, Herod was a hick-from-the-sticks. This is the same motif that emerges concerning Yeshua of Nazareth: that, being Galilean, he is not really the true polished Jerusalem item. The difference of course is that the New Testament writers use it to build up the picture of a virtuous outsider, one who certainly was Jewish, albeit with a bit of a twist.

So, at last, we arrive with probative clarity at the pivot of our examination of the most extraordinary instance of "de-colonization," in relation to the imperial power of the Old Testament genealogical system. The supreme irony is that it is the modern Jewish hermeneutical system (Rabbinic Judaism) that performs this massive jailbreak.

The Female Licence Principle first appears in prototype in the most mysterious text in the entire Judaeo-Christian library: the *Mishnah*. It is the founding document of modern Judaism, more important even than the scriptures, and few Christians have ever heard of it and not many more Jews have actually read it except mediated by layers and layers of later explanatory commentary. It must be encountered on its own, because it is miraculous in its origin and unprecedented in its configuration. The Mishnah appears in written form about 200 CE and it is the record of arguments about social and religious law that the Rabbis (who replace the old

Temple priests) have among themselves. The Rabbis most likely were the survivors of the Pharisees. In any case they were the leaders of a minority sect within later Second Temple Judaism who, after the Destruction, re-coalesce and argue "oral law." Their disputes are about the rules that must prevail in their new world, a world without the Temple and, indeed, without Jerusalem as a functional capital. They are concerned both with the religious practices that will connect their new world to the God they worshipped in the pre-Destruction era, and with the details of the social contract between each other and the Almighty. These disputations, at first preserved only orally, are written down about 200 CE when the Mishnah comes to a close. Among the difficulties in dealing with it (even for persons fully acquainted with the biblical and parabiblical texts of the pre-Destruction faith) is that the Mishnah is all law (*Halachah*), with virtually no narrative. Moreover, the Mishnah's points of law are asserted as being authoritative without their being directly dependent upon the Hebrew scriptures. That later generations of scholars will expend immense amounts of energy finding invisible ties to the ancient written texts is not here germane; the point is that the Mishnah has to be encountered directly on its own terms and this can be a disconcerting experience.[33]

As far as the mixed-marriage issue is concerned, the Mishnah shows that Rabbinical thought is radically different from earlier ideas and perspectives found in the Hebrew scriptures and Late Second Temple religious texts. For one thing, the Sages are willing to argue openly about mixed marriages. Moreover, they seem not only agitated, but slightly confused.

The prototype of the new rules on genealogy/genetics and membership in the Chosen People is found in three segments of text. Perplexingly, one of these instances is in principle and in practice incompatible with the other two. Ruling One (Ketubot 1:10) deals with a rape case. Who is a sanctioned spouse for a Jewish woman who is raped? "Ruled Rabbi Yohannan b. Nurri, If most of the men of the town marry off their daughters to the [Jewish] priesthood, lo, she may be married to the priesthood."[34] So, the right to form a family for a Jewish woman who is sexually attacked depends upon the ethnic composition of the neighbourhood she lives in. No matter who raped her and who is the genetic father of any resulting child, if she resides among priestly families, she can marry not just ordinary Jews but even the priestly elite and her children will be

Jewish. On this local-demography principle, a Jewish woman who lives among Gentiles and is raped by a Jewish male would not be eligible to marry a Jewish man. As to the eventual child of any union she might make with a Gentile, the fate of her offspring is not dealt with in this ruling. Whatever one thinks of the justice of this Halachah (doubtless, there is some spiritual meaning to it behind the advice to young women that, if you are sexually vulnerable, live in a good postal code), it assuredly does not assert female Jewish marital rights as a juridical principle. And that is critical: for the Female Licence Principle as it ultimately develops is a licence printed on two sides. One side gives Jewish women a licence to have progeny with Gentiles and still have their children automatically considered to be Jewish (this is not an aspect much talked-up in devotional circles, but it is clear enough). The other side requires that for a Jewish male to sire a son or daughter who is immediately Jewish (with no necessity for conversion), he must obtain a pre-marital licence in the form of affiancing himself to a woman who is Jewish.

Ruling Two in the Mishnah (Yebamot 7:5) also begins with the Sages worrying about the procreational product of rapists (and of idiots and of seducers), but, as is sometimes the case with Rabbinic disputations, it drops this issue and moves laterally into general matters. Two points of law emerge. The offspring of a Jewish father and either a Gentile or a slave is not Jewish. (Thus confirming a passing mention of this point in Yebamot 2:5, G.) And the offspring of a Jewish woman and a Gentile or a male slave is a *mamzer.* This is a very difficult concept. A mamzer is definitely not a legitimate Jew. But illegitimacy in the English common law sense of the term is too pale a concept. A mamzer can never lose its stain, can never be legitimated. In the Mishnah's system, a mamzer is a sort of a Jew, but one who cannot marry other Jews, at least not without reducing the subsequent offspring of that union to mamzer status. The closest parallel I can think of comes from the equine kingdom. A mare (noble creature) can mate with a male donkey (a beast of burden) and yield a mule. The mule is a lower-order beast and, crucially, it cannot reproduce. This is analogous to the position of the mamzer (to use the male form for both men and women.) Just as the mule remains an equid beast, albeit a degenerate one, so the mamzer is still a Jew, albeit of a permanently imperfect sort. And just as the mule cannot reproduce, so the mamzer cannot join with a legitimate Jew; hence, as far as the genetics of the Chosen People are concerned, the mamzer is as procreatively sterile as the mule. (Mamzers can marry other mamzers – Qiddushin 4:1:D – but for the purposes of the genetic requirements to be Jewish that is simply another form of sterility.)

Ruling Three in the Mishnah's meditations on aspects of intermarriage (Qiddushin 3:12) is the hub of the matter, for it yields a four-segment spectrum of genetics/genealogy in relation to group membership. The first is that when both parties of a valid betrothal are right-standing Jews, then the children of the marriage shall be Jewish. Within the flock, children shall follow the status of the male. (This is crucial in cases of priests and Levites, who have their own special eligibility requirements.) Secondly, if a liturgically valid betrothal takes place between Jewish persons, if either party is in some way impaired (for example a leper cannot be a priest) then "the offspring follows the status of the impaired party." (3:12, II, D.) And, thirdly, the Qiddushin passage declares (3:12, III, G) that in any situation when a woman has the right of betrothal to the right sort of man (broadly, a Jewish woman who would have the right to marry a Jewish man) if she marries a man whom it would not be proper for her to marry (a foreigner being a person of this sort) then "the offspring is a mamzer." Finally, if a woman has no right to marry any Jew (she is a slave or a Gentile), then the offspring of any union she shall make (including with a Jewish man) shall be either a slave or a Gentile. (3:12, IV, J.)

The power of the arguments in Qiddushin and in Yebamot (Rulings Two and Three), which make "tribal" membership contingent upon various genetic/genealogical rules, trump those of Case One, (Ketubot) where local demography was the guiding principle. That Rulings Two and Three prevail on the basis of their articulating a much broader band of applicable principles is not just a matter of secular logic but is confirmed by all subsequent Rabbinic commentators.

Manifestly, in the years 70–200 CE the intellectual elite of the survivors of the two Jerusalem disasters (70 and 132–135 CE) worried about mixed marriages and argued about intermarriage much more clearly than at any time in the history of the Chosen People. This makes sense: however spiritual the early Rabbis were, they lived in the real world. In that world, the former compact entity, the people of the Second Temple era in Eretz Israel, had become a *diaspora*. They were transformed from being a large majority in a Roman-recognized ethnarchy into a network of scattered minority groups living amidst Gentile nations.[35] Of course the Rabbis began to worry about intermarriage. A simple epidemiological model explains why: individual young people were more apt to make contact with non-Jews when the young Jews were only in small clusters than in the earlier period when the Jewish community, centred in Eretz Israel, was large enough to be self-enclosing. Significantly, in two of the three passages of the Mishnah that deal directly with intermarriage or with the progeny of intermarriage, the matter of rape is the opening point for the discussion. This is a diagnostic item: it documents a sharp sense of vulnerability among the early Rabbinic thinkers. As we have seen, this feeling of vulnerability led not just to consideration of female-based issues, but to a direct rejection of the practice that had predominated since the time of the patriarchs. Now, the offspring of Jewish males who took "strange wives" were declared to be Gentile.

That is one big step towards the eventual Rabbinic articulation of the Female Licence Principle, for it requires a Jewish man who wishes to have Jewish children to betroth himself to a Jewish woman. That is his marriage licence.

But the Rabbis had not yet written the other side of the licence, the half that makes the offspring of a Jewish woman and a Gentile man a full Jew. The Mishnah is unambiguous in its rulings that such a child is despoiled, a mamzer.

After c.200 CE, with the Mishnah brought to a close, the continuing task of the Rabbis was to explain exactly what this massive volume (more than 1,100 printed pages in a recent modern translation) meant. There was a lot to argue about. As a result, a series of commentaries slowly emerged and these gradually interpreted, refined, and, sometimes rewrote, this fundamental document of Rabbinic Judaism. The *Tosefta*, which can be thought of as the "First Talmud," meaning the first Rabbinic commentary on the Mishnah, was composed in Palestine in the period 250–350 CE.[36] Significantly, despite its expansive scope (it has three words for every one of the Mishnah's) the Tosefta deals with intermarriage only once. This is a curt endorsement of the Mishnah's ruling on Jewish women and intermarriage: "A Gentile, or a slave who had sexual relations with an Israelite girl, and she produced a son – the offsping is a mamzer" (Qiddushin, 4:16, A.). Apparently the Mishnah's rulings were adequate to hold the social network together at least into the mid-fourth century.

And the Mishnah's intermarriage code held throughout the fourth century. That this is the case is confirmed by an examination of the next major Talmud, called variously the *Yerushalmi*, the Talmud of the Land of Israel, the Palestinian Talmud, and the Jerusalem Talmud. It is a monumental work (in a recent translation it fills thirty-four volumes of text)[37] and was compiled by the Rabbis in, roughly, the period 325–400 CE. (It certainly was completed before the end of the Jerusalem patriarchate in 421.) It follows in sequence of creation the Tosefta, but speaks with its own staccato voice. The Jerusalem Talmud is not a smooth piece of work and it only comments on, roughly, the first two-thirds of the Mishnah, which is where most of the betrothal rules are contained. As far as the intermarriage rules are concerned, the Mishnah's ruling are confirmed and an example is given for each major principle (see Qiddushin 3:12). Piquancy and emphasis upon the Halachah that the offspring of a Jewish man and a Gentile woman is a Gentile, is provided by the case of a certain Jacob of Kepar. His status is undefined; he may have been a Rabbi or a secular elder. In any event, he visited the city of Tyre and when a group of Jewish people asked him if it was alright to circumcise the son of a Jewish man and an Aramaen woman on the Sabbath, he was inclined to let them do so, on the basis that the Hebrew scriptures made the child Jewish and, implicitly, that the scriptures outranked the Mishnah. One of the Rabbis, Haggai, heard of this and thundered, "Let him come and be flogged." Thereupon the two men argued, and Rabbi Haggai won on the explicit basis that a ruling in the Mishnah trumped the Hebrew Bible. So convincing was Rabbi Haggai's argument that Jacob of Kepar said "Carry out your flogging," for it was better, he thought, to be punished now than to make the same mistake in the future. (Qiddushin 3:12, IX G-Q.)

At the same time as the Yerushalmi was being composed, a separate Talmud – usually called *the* Talmud – was being compiled in "Babylon," south of present-day Baghdad and its environs. This amazing document is called the *Bavli*, or the Babylonian Talmud, and is effectively the Talmud of the diaspora. Despite its immense size – it is a small library, two-and-half million words in length – the Babylonian Talmud is a comfortable, livable book, almost fatherly in tone. About one third of the Bavli is fable or short narrative and this cushions the legal portions which, like all the other commentaries, focus on the Mishnah. A reasonable estimate is that the Babylonian Talmud was completed roughly by 600 CE, for it certainly was done before the rise of Islam. The Bavli is undoubtedly the most formative document in modern Judaism, more important even than the Mishnah and even the scriptures.[38]

Given the context in which the Bavli was written, one would expect it to differ from the Tosefta, the Jerusalem Talmud, and also from the Mishnah in its concerns. Unlike those texts, the Babylonian Talmud was not composed by Sages who were merely aware of the diaspora, but rather by men who were actually part of the dispersal. Because of that simple geographic fact and also because the Babylonian Talmud was still being worked on in the seventh century (it never was entirely completed), the Babylonian Sages had a better and more accurate view of what secular developments meant for them: these being the fourth century conversion of the Roman Empire to Christianity, the death in battle in 363 of the Emperor Julian who had promised a rebuilding of the Temple in Jerusalem, the extinction in the 420s of the last bit of independent Jewish rule in Palestine, the harassment of the Theodosian Code of 439 and the increasing discomfort and sporadic persecution of Jews in the Middle East and southern Europe.[39] The Babylonian Rabbis did not refer directly to these matters; they revised many religious rules, but almost always argued from precedents in ancient scriptures or in oral law and gave no hint that expediency also was involved. Yet they knew what was going on in the outside world and they made exactly the changes one would have expected them to make, given the increasing vulnerability of the myriad Jewish communities.

Their alteration of the rules of intermarriage is demonstrative of their tactical shrewdness. In a long debate about who is and who is not damaged goods, the Mishnah's ruling that the child of a Jewish woman and a Gentile man is a mamzer is dramatically reversed. The way this is accomplished is not through strength of logic but through employment of the prestige of origin: it is asserted that Rabbi Judah the Prince, who is credited with being the final editor of the Mishnah, had ruled that such a child was fully legitimate. (The odd fact that he had not included the ruling in the Mishnah, but rather an opposite ruling, is not mentioned.) Morever, it is also asserted that "Rav," Rabbi Abba, former student of Rabbi Judah the Prince and founder of the premier academy in Babylon, had followed the Prince's ruling and had declared a child of a Jewish

mother and Gentile father to be fully Jewish.[40] This opinion wins because it is declared to have a better pedigree than the opposing view.
Thus the full Female Licence Principle came into being. The
date is impossible to determine, but sometime between 450 and
550 is a sensible estimate. The signal point is that this principle was
adaptive for Jewish life in the diaspora (where most Jews lived) and
therefore it was honoured in practice. Adaptive? The stipulation
that if a Jewish man did not marry a Jewish wife, his children would
not be Jewish was a strong disincentive for young Jewish men to
marry outside the group. Keeping men in the fold was critical for
diaspora communities as all the most important liturgical obligations of the faith were carried out by males. And, in any case, in medieval and early modern times, maintaining a vital male core to any
group was the key to viability for the group.

Fine: but how did the decision to accept as fully legitimate Jews
the children of unions of Jewish women and Gentile men benefit
diaspora Jewry? It did so by its recognition that women are vulnerable in diaspora communities to sexual predation of all sorts, and often this would be by Gentiles. If one makes an outcast the child of
every such instance of sexual exploitation, then both the Jewish
woman and the child have been punished for events for which the
woman well may be an innocent victim and the child certainly is.
Bluntly, albeit anachronistically, how many times do Cossacks have
to rape and pillage their way through a shtetl for a community to
realize that punishing the female victims of brutal rapacity was
hardly sensible? Not many.

Moreover, a hard-eyed genetic realism lies behind the new ruling.
The Female Licence Principle, by requiring that all legitimate Jewish
children must have a Jewish mother, but not necessarily a Jewish father, is a recognition of a fact that few lineage-conscious societies are
able to thole. This is simply that there never has been any certainty
about paternity (at least not until DNA testing began in the last decade of the twentieth century), but there is near-certainty about maternity. The only biological fact that can be stated with complete
confidence concerning a child born of a marriage of a Jewish man
and a Jewish woman is that the child's mother is Jewish. And that is
exactly the same thing one can state of a child born of a marriage of
a Gentile man and a Jewish woman. Therefore to draw a sharp distinction made little logical sense and even less tactical sense. If one of
your goals is to have enough males to keep communities viable, both

socially and liturgically, then the best tactics are (a) to scare your young men into marrying within the fold, and (b) to admit as members the offspring of Jewish women by foreign men, for half of their children will be males. This is a harsh calculus, but the Rabbis faced harsh realities.

The amendments to the Hebrew scriptures' genealogical/genetic requirement for group membership that were effected by the Rabbis of the first seven centuries of the Common Era are immensely revealing. The Rabbis did not change the basic pattern of tracing lineages through both parents (the Standard Double system). Nor, in matters of inheritance, property rights, and right-of-participation in devotional practices did they cease to privilege males. But they added an additional genetic/genealogical requirement for birthright group membership. This maternal requirement is the sort one finds in most matrilineal societies, but almost never in a bilineal one. The Rabbis were subverting the Old Testament system by process of amendment. The law-subtle Rabbis shared little with a tale-weaver such as Snorri Sturluson except this: they accomplished their subversion without giving away by a trace of a smile or a twitch of the lips that they knew full well what they were doing.

―――

If genealogical narratives are generative concepts that a group employs to explain its origin and to justify its existence; and if, as we saw in chapter six, the genealogical narratives contained in the Hebrew scriptures have proved to be so strong that they can justifiably be said to have operated as an *imperium* of the mind, then they are very difficult for any culture to reject entirely, once they have been introduced into that society's ideational kitbag. They are ideas that eat other ideas, and this all the more easily because the ancient Hebrew constructs often provide a new, dramatic, emotionally satisfying mythological explanation for social patterns that the society in question already is practising, but has not yet mythologized very well. Yet, as we have also seen, resistance to the Hebrew scriptures' generative pattern is also possible, either through subversion (the Nordic case) or through amendment (the instance of Rabbinic Judaism.)

A third form of resistance is the Judo-technique. This involves embracing the basic biological metaphor that undergirds the genealogical narrative of the Hebrew scriptures, but doing so in such a way that one uses its energy to further its rejection. The instance we have to hand is the Roman Catholic church's theory of Papal succession. (From now on I shall usually say "Catholic church," and I hope persons who are Catholic, but not Roman Catholic will forgive me.)

Make no mistake: the ancient Hebrew metaphor, the one that began with Adam and was articulated in the covenant with Abraham, was not seminal in the merely literary sense. It was seminal in the sense of semen, and what counted was sperm count. In contrast, the Catholic concept of Papal succession is totally non-biological. Indeed, in its final form, it rejects with horror the idea of procreation for its higher clergy, much less biological succession to its highest office. Yet, it runs off the energy of the ancient Hebrew covenant.

Here we recall how early Christianity, through two somewhat banjaxed, but artful, lineages (in Luke and Matthew, composed sometime between 70 CE and 90 CE), established a genealogical narrative for Yeshua of Nazareth that ran back to King David and to Abraham and (in the case of the Gospel of Luke) back to Adam. In the strict sense, these narratives failed as they hit a big roadblock, aside from technical flaws in each. To the extent that the Virgin Conception was part of the story of Yeshua of Nazareth (it seems to have become accepted after 70 CE, although how quickly and widely is impossible to say), the biological lineages crashed, because the male line had nothing to do with Yeshua's birth and the female line was inoperative as well. Whatever animated the life in Miriam's womb was itself beyond genealogy.

Yet, in a larger sense, the Yeshua-lineage succeeds: flaws aside, it clearly communicates the assertion that Yeshua of Nazareth was a direct heir of Yahweh. In doing that, it also indicates the opening for another way of deflecting the full force of the ancient Hebrew generative genealogies: through the replacement of reproduction with mere contact. In Luke and Matthew's lineages, Yeshua is the heir of David and Abraham not by blood but by some form of social, as distinct from biological, contact.

The specific tool that the Catholic church has employed is the trope, and this in both of that implement's major senses. A trope is a figure of speech that uses a concept in a way other than its strictly proper form. And a trope is a distinctive cadence that indicates a termination and change of mode or melody in Gregorian chant. Each meaning fits what happens with the cascade of one Pope after another in the enduring, continually altering plainsong that is Papal succession.

When this Papal trope arose is impossible to determine. Certainly before the Destruction of 70 CE Jerusalem, not Rome, was the centre of the world of the Yeshua-faith. This is hardly surprising, for what later was called Christianity was merely one of the two dozen or more sects of the Judahist faith that swirled around the Second Temple. Jerusalem was the hub of that religious world, no less for the Yeshua-faith than for any of the other sects – Awakeners, and Knockers and Sadducees and Pharisees and on and on.[41] Whoever ran the Jerusalem branch of the Yeshua-faith was the most influential figure in the embryonic Christian religion, and this was Yacov, the ascetic, reserved, authoritative brother of Yeshua of Nazareth.

Both the centrality of Jerusalem and the seniority of Yacov are clearly demonstrated by the behaviour of Paul: three years after his conversion, Paul went to Jerusalem and there he stayed with Peter for fifteen days; the only other apostolic figure he met at that time was Yacov, Yeshua's brother. (Galatians 1:18–19.) One surmises that in more than a fortnight of intensive discussion with Peter, the apostle must have tutored Paul in the basic acts and sayings of Yeshua as he knew them. Further, Paul probably was being examined not only on his own character, but on his knowledge and ideology. The audience with Yacov, direct heir to the headship of the Yeshua-faith, has the appearance of a doctoral candidate being assessed by a stern External Examiner. Manifestly, Paul passed the examination and was free to go about his mission. Further, fourteen years later, when Paul wishes a licence to preach to the Gentiles, he appears at the "Jerusalem Conference" (between 47 and 50 CE; the date is disputed) headed by Yacov: see Galatians 2:9; cf Acts 15:13–20 where it is Yacov who gives judgement in favour of preaching to Gentiles. The price of this concession is that Paul has to spend a portion of the rest of his life raising money for "the poor" in the Jerusalem church that Yacov heads (Galatians 2:10). This is as close to an expression of feudal homage as one gets in the ancient Near East.

Crucial to an appreciation of the difficulties that the invention of the Papal tradition would have to overcome is the clear documentation that Peter, as well as Paul, recognized the authority of Yacov: when Yacov orders Peter to stop eating with Gentiles, he does so. (Galatians 2:12.)

One of history's great unknowns is how the Yeshua-faith would have developed if the great Destruction of 70 CE had not happened.

Jaroslav Pelikan, one of the world's leading church historians, reminds us that Irenaeus in the second century had called Jerusalem
"the church from which every church took its start, the capital city of
the citizens of the New Covenant." And Pelikan adds his own note that
in the central community of embryonic Christianity, Yacov, brother of
Yeshau, "was a kind of caliph."[42] Whether the caliphate would have
been passed on to other members of Yeshua's family and their descendants, or to others, is anybody's guess. Certainly a Jewish-dominated
"Papacy," with its headquarters in Jerusalem, would have been a very
different organization from the one that eventually evolved.

In any event, the three leading figures of the second-generation
(c.30–69 CE) of the Yeshua-faith, Yacov, Peter, and Paul, all were
martyred in the 60s, Yacov in Jerusalem and Peter and Paul in
Rome.[43] Then in 70 CE the centre of the religious world that they
and all the others of the Yeshua-faith had lived in was destroyed, as
if hit by a meteor. The evolution of the Yeshua-faith into a separate
religion became not only possible, but actual.

Whereas for Yeshua-followers (as for all Judahist religious
groups), there had been a single world-hub, now for the embryonic
Christian faith there were two rival poles: Rome, where a large
Jewish diaspora community lived, and Antioch-on-the-Orontes,
an early Syrian missionary centre. Antioch was associated with missionary work by both Paul and Peter and was where by tradition
the term "Christian" was first used to denominate the disciples of
Paul and Barnabas. (Acts 11:26.) Yet, in the contest between the
two cities, Rome eventually won. The creation of the Papacy was simultaneously one of the levers for Rome's elevation over other
Christian missions after 70 CE and, in its final form, the Papacy was
the laurel crown of Roman victory.

The first stage of Rome's victory was probably a two-pronged affair, and these were only fortuitously interrelated.[44] The tradition
that Paul and Peter had been martyred in Rome in the 60s (probably an accurate tradition, although it is puzzling that neither
Paul's nor Peter's martyrdom is mentioned in the Acts of the
Apostles) spread among the widely dispersed congregations of
the Yeshua-faith after 70 CE. This was the period wherein they
evolved into what we can recognize historically (and what the con-
gregants self-recognized) was a religion separate from Judaism. As
far as the eventual hegemony of Rome is concerned, the intriguing note is that Rome's early claim to special sanctity (albeit not

authority) was based on both Paul's and Peter's having shed their saintly blood there.[45] How long this claim to contact-authority being based on the two early martyrs lasted is indeterminate, but a half century after 70 CE is a sensible guess.

Simultaneously, something very strange was happening at Antioch. The Gospel of Matthew was being composed, and its effect was to heighten the prestige of Peter over that of Paul. This is pivotal because before the three Synoptic Gospels (Mark, Luke and Matthew) were written (after the Destruction, in the period 70 to about 90 CE, at latest), the only documents of the Yeshua-faith that have survived made Paul the star and Peter a somewhat ambiguous, though still very significant, character. These documents are of course the seven authentic letters of Paul.[46] They are unique in the Christian canon, for they are the only portions of the Christian scriptures that undoubtedly were written before the massive Destruction of 70 CE, and thus they are the only contemporary documentation of the nature of the Yeshua-faith before it was transformed by the destruction of Jerusalem and of the Second Temple. Moreover, they are also the only documents in the Christian canon (the New Testament) of which we know the name of the author. (The epistles ascribed to Peter, James, and John are almost certainly pseudepigraphic and the apostolic names on the spines of the Four Gospels have no attestation before the mid-second century; they are given apostolic designations in order to provide them with greater authority: and the "Revelation of St John" is a clearly spurious attribution.) Thus, to the extent that Paul's letters were circulated among the members of the Yeshua-faith (and what early Christians were reading immediately after 70 CE is a forever-mystery), they carried this message: (1) that, as already discussed, in the three-and-half decades after the Crucifixion of Yeshua of Nazareth, his brother Yacov was accepted as the rightful head of the emerging faith; (2) that Paul was a star missionary, doing among Gentiles and among the Jews outside of Eretz Israel what Yeshua himself had done inside the Holy Land. Paul's self-evaluations were often remarkably immodest, such as, "Be ye followers of me, even as I also am of Christ"(1 Corinthians 11:1). Yet Paul himself recognized that as an authority figure he had a big handicap: as an apostle, he was a late-comer and, indeed had never set eyes on Yeshua of Nazareth; (3) and Peter is painted as an ambiguous figure. Paul usually grants him authority as the senior figure among the original apostles (see, for example,1 Corinthians 15:5).

Yet, he also presents Peter as being an instinctive rat: Peter had backed Paul against the hardline Jewish rigorists and then had double-crossed him (Galatians 2: 11–14). And, in the Pauline letters, Peter was a free-loader: like the brothers and sisters of Yeshua of Nazareth, Peter did missionary work on the church's money and took along his family, whereas Paul had to travel alone and earn his own crust of bread, pay his own expenses, and take up a collection for the Jerusalem church (1 Corinthians 9:1–6).

So, Peter was not the automatic choice for the historical godfa-ther's role. That the early claims of Rome to special status were based upon Paul as much as upon Peter confirms that the early Roman Christian leaders understood this.

However, when the Gospel of Matthew was written (80–90 CE is a sensible estimate), it gave a position to Peter that is unmatched any-place else in the New Testament. This has the signal effect of over-coming the power of Paul's letters and the prior history that those letters imply. The key passage, of course, is the one that has been fought over virtually since it was first written – Matthew 16:18 – "And I say also unto thee, *That thou art Peter, and upon this rock I will build my church*, and the gates of hell shall not prevail against it." Whatever these words were intended to mean when they were put in the mouth of Yeshua of Nazareth by the writers of the Gospel of Matthew, there is no question that Matthew portrays Peter generally as the primary apostle and most-favoured heir of Yeshua. Therefore, as the Gospels emerge as the most prestigious part of the evolving Christian canon, it becomes obvious that Peter, rather than Paul, is the best icon to seize in the competition for prestige and power. Capture Peter and you win; Paul can be kept in the shadow, though not discarded.

This is what the church in Rome did, while, puzzlingly, Antioch (where the Gospel of Matthew probably was written) let their own grasp on Peter's prestige slip away. By the 150s, a letter of Polycarp, bishop of Smyrna, makes it clear that Rome had achieved recogni-tion as the leading Christian centre and thus the bishop of Rome was someone we would recognize as a Pope, albeit not of the same au-thority as later accrued.[47] The first authoritative list of Popes, run-ning from Peter through subsequent bishops of Rome (albeit without any dates), is found in a letter of Iranaeus, bishop of Lyon.[48] By roughly 200 CE, the bishop of Rome was the ranking figure in the Christian church, though he did not yet have line-authority over other bishops. The first attempt by a Pope to assert direct power over the other bishops was that of Pope Stephen I in 257. Significantly, this move, which only partially succeeded, involved the first known invocation of the claim that a Pope's authority stemmed directly from Matthew 16:18 and that Peter was both the necessary and sufficient conduit of Papal sanctity and authority.[49] Only with the conversion of the Roman Empire to Christianity in the fourth century did the bishop of Rome's title of "Pope" come to mean what it does at present: *the* authority figure and *the* heir of Yeshua of Nazareth.

In pious literature one finds lists of early Popes with suspiciously precise dates: Peter (32–67), Linus (67–76), Cletus (76–88), Clement I (88–97), Anacletus (97), Evaristus (97–105), and so on.[50] Until the mid second century, none of this can be authenticated by conventional historical means, but that is irrelevant.

For: this is a good genealogy because it works.

It takes the hand of Yahweh and has him mould humankind from the primeval mud of earth. Then the genealogy runs from Adam down to Abraham, where a dramatic seminal covenant is made, and then down to King David, who established the Kingdom of Judah and thus all subsequent Judahisms, and then down to Joseph, father of Yeshua of Nazareth. At that point the biological metaphor stops being biological: Yeshua of Nazareth is a descendant of Adam only by a contact-genealogy (through his father Joseph), and he is somehow simultaneously the offspring of Yahweh, by way of Miriam's womb. From that point, Yeshua touches (both spiritually and physically) Peter, who, it is said, touches Pope Linus, and then on to Pope Cletus, and on and on and on. Thus does the Almighty, who formed the first human with his own hands, place his hands on the shoulders of each successive Pope.

Today, if they have been baptized, the hundreds of millions of the world's Roman Catholics (are they a billion? Probably, but no one really knows) have had hands placed on them liturgically by a priest, who has been ordained by the hands of a bishop who has been consecrated to his see at the hands of either an archbishop or cardinal who has received his pallium from the hands of a Pope, and thus all Roman Catholics in the world partake of the line of succession from Yahweh to Adam and do so by physical touch.

This is the ultimate contact-genealogy. It is amazingly successful. And it is a stunningly brilliant pirating of the original biological metaphor of the Chosen People.

Resistance and subversion indeed.

PART THREE

The Saints Come Marching

8   *God's Massive Engine?*

So, what has God wrought?

Immediately one poses that question concerning the massive Mormon genealogy project, one wants to withdraw the query and to leave quickly without being so gauche as to even attempt an apology.

Like many professional historians, I have been helped immensely by the generosity of the Latter-day Saints.[1] In my case, my debt to them was incurred when I was writing a book entitled *The Irish in Ontario. A Study in Rural History*.[2] To complete the study I needed a comprehensive data base of a set of mid-Ontario land titles and their passage from generation to generation. My local county registrars office wanted a fortune (they were used to charging for lawyers' title searches) and I had no research grant. The local LDS ward came to my rescue and obtained a microfilm of everything the registrar had and for next to nothing. You will find similar acknowledgments in prefaces or in opening footnotes in scores of books, especially big-base social history studies. So, one does not want to hurt these generous people.

In the preceding four chapters on human genealogical narratives (and also in the technical appendices that follow the text) I have implied quite clearly the ways in which I think the Mormon project is badly off-kilter. Because I wish to move quickly to more positive matters – namely, how useful the LDS project may be even if one notes its problems – those problematic issues can be quickly listed. First, as a professional historian, I can make no judgement about the primary purpose of LDS genealogical activity, which is to move a dead person from one status in the celestial world to a higher realm. Historians can only adjudge what we see in this world, and even that should be done with a good deal of humility. Second, I disagree with the basic Mormon belief that human beings have person-specific biological pedigrees. The Mormon view is taken from the Hebrew scriptures and is a terrifically powerful concept: that God blesses the "seed" (more literally, the semen) of a specific group through a covenant with them. For them genealogy has to be considered primarily as a form of biological pedigree rather than of socially determined lineage. As I indicated earlier, the position of individuals in a genealogical narrative actually is determined as much by social custom as by biology. Further (as demonstrated in Appendix C) the biological inaccuracy in human lineages is so great as to render most full genealogies genetically invalid in half-a-dozen generations, even if the paper documentation is perfect – long before one gets back to Father Adam. Third, powerful as is the imperial force of the ancient Hebrew model of human descent that the Mormons employ, it is clear that there exist other forms of genealogical narrative. The LDS is demonstrably wrong in its base-belief that there is only a single grammar of genealogical narrative. The coercive character of this belief must be resisted, for it quashes the integrity of cultures that do not fit the story of their humanity into the procrustean template: and because the Mormon paradigm can be embraced only by rejecting empirical, statistical, and historical evidence for the existence of other, incompatible ways that human beings have kept track of their humanity.

Irreducible as those problems with the LDS genealogical system are, the church's activities are nevertheless among the most important approaches to human history at present in train. The world's largest data base on individual human lives scarcely can be ignored – though most professional historians manage to do so. Instead of walking past this monumental edifice with our eyes fixed on the ground, we should look up and at least ask, "how useful is the Mormon project – and to whom?"

That question produces answers that are often counter-intuitive and sometimes paradoxical. We shall see that a basic first evidentiary paradox characterizes LDS data. Namely: the data are *most* useful and most trustworthy for historians when they are used in the form that is *least* like the way the Church of Jesus Christ of Latter-day Saints employs them: as precise statements of individual familial relationships. That is, when used in their *primary source form* – microfilms of parish registers, land title books, sets of probate records, birth and mortality collations – the material is excellent. It is not perfect, but one can design research methods that allow operational questions of social or economic history to be asked and, often, confidently answered. Here the key is that large data bases in social and economic history do not have to be perfectly precise. In fact, they can have 20 or 30 percent error-rates and still be useful. There are numerous statistical ways to deal with outliers in any large data-set and also to compensate for any systematic biases in the collection of the original data. The church, in processing the primary material into genealogical form, incorporates all the biases and shortcomings of the original material, for genealogy requires treating as precise records that often are highly resistant to precision.

Before going into the welter of details this LDS genealogical precision entails, we have to prescind from our knowledge the point, made so well by Robert Alter, that the cascade of lineages upon which the "Saints" base all their work – those in the Tanakh – are self-conscious and artful literary compositions. They are employed at moments when they help to underline a mythological point, such as the injunction to go forth and multiply. And they serve as historical cover, giving a patina of plausibility to some fairly imaginative story-telling. As Alter argues, "surely part of the intention in using the genealogy [in the "Old Testament"] is to give the history the look of authentically archaic documentation."[3] Biblical lineages are compositional units, not historical lines. *Mutatis mutandis*, this is also the case for the myriad lines found in the Book of Mormon and in the other LDS scriptures, for they base themselves on the techniques and upon many of the characters in the Hebrew compositions. The inevitable melding of literary composition and of lineages is beautifully, if unconsciously, recognized in the church's The Pearl of Great Price, where the gift of reading and writing is given to human beings through their recorded lineages (Book of Moses, 6:6–7).

We can pretend we do not know any of this and instead look at the Mormon genealogical project the same way we would assess any large-scale socio-historical enterprise. The project is certainly big enough to warrant attention. Surprisingly, when one tries to find what replication studies show about the fundamental research design and the technical quality of the work, one finds that there are none.

Replication studies? To large-data studies of human behaviour, these are what disinterested auditing is to business and government: the guarantor, if conducted properly, that everything is kosher: no unpunished fraud, no uncorrected accounting errors, no attempt to mislead shareholders. The ethics of large-scale research on human subjects, dead or alive, requires researchers to make both their primary data and their analysis of those data available to other researchers to check. On large projects, especially those that have the robustness to become classics and to influence future work, there usually is an independent replication of a sample of the original study. (Think drug-safety studies as an analogous activity.) Now, as far as I can discover, there have been neither independent replication studies of LDS genealogical work, nor large in-house studies: minor in-house corrections, yes, but no evaluation of the validity of the entire enterprise. Perhaps I have missed them.

There exists a second possible sort of check, a kind of semi-replication study. This involves smaller data-sets than a full quantitative replication (in the Mormon case, even a sample would require a million or more datum points). In this sort of replication study, a small unit – a community for example – is examined and the replication work involves fact-checking everything that can be found about the original work, noting pieces of evidence that were overlooked in compiling the original data set and, crucially, noting matters of social context that determined the reading, or misreading, of the original data. The classic case of such a smaller replication study is Derek Freeman's *Margaret Mead and Samoa. The Making and Unmaking of an Anthropological Myth.*[4] Freeman revisited the data (and, indeed, some of the informants) who had given the twenty-three year-old American Margaret Mead the material for one of the most popular pieces of non-fiction published in the USA in the first half of the twentieth-century: *Coming of Age in Samoa* (1928). Further, he looked at criminal statistics, birth and death records, and at masses of material produced by early missionaries, material that Mead had simply ignored. He demonstrated clearly that her study was inaccurate from start to finish. Samoa was not some easy-going, sexually loose, non-violent, egalitarian paradise, free of the inhibitions of religious-based guilt (as Mead had it in her allegedly empirical academic study), but instead had a high rape rate, lots of violent crime, a complex hierarchical social structure, and a ubiquitous use of the sense of guilt and shame as a mode of social control: paradise not. Mead's initial assumptions and her refusal to put any given piece of data into a wider probative context had turned her study of family life into a novel. One shifts uneasily on one's chair and asks, well, would similar community replications, paying attention not just to genealogy but to context and to previously ignored data, make one suspect that the LDS church is writing a world narrative that is not a history but rather a massive and imaginative saga?

A third sort of replication work is not nearly so formal and is the most common sort in historical work. This consists of professional scholars going over each other's work, checking the footnotes, looking for fallacies and solipsisms, and for their having missed context or, most contentious of all, perhaps having stolen somebody else's research. For a good example of how awry professional historians can go before getting caught, see Jon Wiener's *Historians in Trouble: Plagiarism, Fraud, and Politics in the Ivory Tower.*[5] The trouble here is that few historians care much, if at all, about genealogy in the Mormon sense. So there is no equivalent of the constant footnote checking, day-by-day, assertion-by-assertion, that occurs (or should occur) in other historical areas.

What does exist is a scattered, bitchy, and virtually fugitive spattering of complaints about the inaccuracy of specific Mormon genealogical assertions. These are not systematic but are found in individual family genealogies or on genealogical net-sites and they are convincing in their individual cases. Yet, one does not know what to make of them for, simply put, everybody gets to make an error or two. No historian of any sort is perfect. We really need some kind of sense of what an "acceptable degree or error" is. What proportion of LDS genealogical assertions are credible?

As a simple test case of the way Mormon genealogical data was produced and affirmed in the first half of the twentieth century, the period in which the genealogical work became a serious and somewhat specialized church activity, note the LDS version of the founding of the main European monarchies. This was summarized at the church's international genealogical conference in October 1931 by Anthony W. Ivins, director of the Genealogical Society of Utah and First Counselor in the First presidency of the LDS church. First, he explained that the Assyrian conquest of 722 BCE resulted in all the ancient Hebrew tribes except Judah and Benjamin being carried away. These people, "Israel," scattered, but some of them did return to Palestine and they are recognized as being part of God's original covenant, as are their descendants. More important, though, was the other branch of this genealogical shrub, the tribes of Benjamin and, especially, of Judah. Zedekiah, the last king of Judah (who, incidentally was reigning when Lehi and his group are said to have left Jerusalem for America) had two daughters. According to President Ivins and the official narrative, they were saved from the Destruction of 587/6 by their great-grandfather, the prophet Jeremiah – who hid them in his cave. In a nice piece of genealogical storytelling, their great-grandfather took them down into Egypt where they went to the same place that later Joseph and Mary and the baby Jesus sought refuge (a site undisclosed in the Christian scriptures). Next, somehow, the ancient prophet and his two beautiful great-granddaughters took ship to Spain. There, the younger of the two married into the Spanish royal house and provided a genealogical link between the descendants of the biblical Joseph and the peoples of the western Mediterranean. The other of Jeremiah's great-granddaughters – named Tamar Tephi – accompanied the old man to Ireland where he "is referred to ... as Ollamh Fodhla (the old prophet) in their traditions and the songs which they still sing of him." So said the spiritual heir of Joseph Smith, rather to the surprise of Irish scholars. In any case, the genealogy continued because the beautiful Tamar Tephi married a certain Eochaidh who was said to reign as king over Ireland. Mind you, the Irish king had to agree to accept his bride's religion. The wonderful event, though, was that Eochaidh had a small chest (an ark, really) hitherto closed, and this he opened in front of the old prophet Jeremiah – who found that the documents inside corresponded with the laws set down by Moses. So, the law of Moses was established in Ireland, sometime in the middle sixth-century BCE. What a wonderful use of genealogy as a compositional entity! Just a few genealogical ties are enough to carry a story of epochal implications. And epochal it was, for Mormon genealogists carried this Irish connection forward, tracing "both the Tudor and Stuart lines of kings, from the present King George of England [this was 1931] directly back to the girl Tamar Tephi ... So the Lord has kept the royal blood of the house of Israel until today."[6]

    Thus, in the first half of the twentieth century, the genealogically adept among the "Saints" were able to trace the lineages of the leading European monarchies in a set of genealogical links that ran to a single point in the Tanakh, the appearance of Father Adam.

This is amazing story construction, but if presented as historical material it can only be judged as delusional. As history, and as the branch of history called genealogy, it is complete codswallop, as any Irish historian would be pleased to confirm concerning the Irish foundation of the present English monarchy.

Fortunately, we can disaggregate the Mormon genealogical efforts. This is done very easily. Seemingly, all that is necessary is to excise from judgement all stories that are not based on records that were formed independently of the faith-state that now affirms them. In practical terms, one simply needs to exclude any genealogical statement that claims to be before, roughly, the year 100 CE. That is the farthest conceivable stretch backwards that can be made from the present day, for that is when the earliest run of independent records is found, and even then the reliability of the material is very dicey.

———

There: just stop in time and the job is done.

Not really. The residual problem is that the *mode* in which Mormon genealogy operates cannot be totally corrected simply by eliding a good deal of the material on which the LDS church's genealogy machinery operates. Remember the basic point argued in chapters 4 through 7: that genealogical systems are similar to transformative grammars in that their underlying rules are so strong that their paradigms partially determine what is thought to be substantive. So cleansing the system of pieces of bad data does not make the system itself work any more accurately. (Here, again, we are talking about the great LDS venture on its own terms, as a genealogical system, not as a goldmine for secular historians who use it as a convenient source of primary records that can be used in non-genealogical ways.) Therefore, we need to turn to a brief consideration of the character of Mormon genealogical thought.

In a brilliant study entitled *All Abraham's Children: Changing Mormon Conceptions of Race and Lineage* (2003), Armand L. Mauss has demonstrated that the morphology of Mormon genealogical thought has been more malleable in its finer points than one might think. What the immediate followers of the Prophet believed and what later "Saints" embraced was never the same. And, further, Mauss makes it clear that behind the official church pronouncements there were always several layers of folk- and semi-official beliefs among Mormons that had a life of their own. However, in both of these realms, the trend, from 1830 to the present day has been (1) "the waxing and waning" of an Israelite identification constructed on their own behalf by the "Saints," and (2) a roughly parallel incremental articulation and later diminution (albeit not full renunciation) of the racist implications of the "Israelite" identity.[7]

Accepting the fact that at any given time one cannot quite pin down what the most-widely accepted Mormon beliefs were on the mechanics of genealogy, one can nevertheless ask with some profit: "What, at mid-twentieth century, did the genealogically-alert among the LDS community believe was the character of the operating system that plugged the divine Creation, through Father Adam, into their own personal histories and into the lives of the rest of the human race?" Mid-twentieth century is a good time to summarize matters because it is close to mid-way in the distinct period of LDS thought that runs from President Joseph F. Smith's revelation in 1918 concerning the necessity of preaching the gospel to the "Gentile" dead, and 1976, when that revelation was declared to be holy scripture and was included in The Doctrine and Covenants of the church. In this period, the great Mountain of Names was begun and the family history branch library system inaugurated. This era, 1918–76, is the period in which were laid the foundations of the massive present-day Mormon push for their singular history of the entire human race. My own reading of the mid-century situation is that most active LDS church members believed that their work was being directed by a Providence that would eventually confirm that the world's history was shaped not only by the Divine Hand, but resembled it.

By that I mean that in practice they believed that five groups descended from Father Adam, like the digits on a human hand. These were: (1) the descendants of Ham, a son of Noah, who (as discussed in Chapter Two) were the black peoples, who were inferior to the other peoples of the earth and, not incidentally, were barred from full priestly membership in the LDS church; (2) the Jews. They were descended from Shem, another of the sons of Noah. They had been scattered to the four corners of the earth, but they would at some future date be reintegrated into God's plan. Although the Mormons claimed themselves to be of the true Israel, they did not claim to supercede it, a different position than that held by most Christian denominations. Thus, as Armand Mauss establishes, the "Saints" did not engage in the more active and vile forms of anti-Semitism that occurred in some other Christian denominations;[8] (3) the Amerindians, who were also identified as being descended from Shem, and later from the eponymic tribal leader Manasseh. This is one of the sectors of Mormon genealogical belief that was covered most clearly by the Book of Mormon. Therein, Amerindian lineage is traced in loving detail – king by prophet by king – from the biblical Joseph down through the biblical Manasseh to the non-biblical Hebrew prophet Lehi, who emigrates with his family to America about 600 BCE and thus avoids the Destruction of 587/6 BCE. Thereafter, the genealogical foliage becomes so lush that one can scarcely read the family trees that are produced, especially because the Prophet had a rather small bank of names at his disposal. Hence, keeping the various representatives of ancient Israel straight in their TransAtlantic Promised Land is difficult. The key here is that eventually one side of the American genealogical tree sheared off (that of the descendants of Nephi, one of Lehi's sons) when they were wiped out, according to Mormon scriptures, in 421 CE. The other American branch, the descendants of Laman, another of Nephi's sons, was responsible for driving the Nephites into extinction. Called the "Lamanites," they were dark-skinned and were said to be the progenitors of the native peoples of the Americas. Their genealogy just peters out and, therefore, one of the challenges of Mormon genealogists has been to tie the present-day Amerindians to their alleged ancestors of the fifth century.[9]

And (4), the most curious digit of the Divine Hand concerned the descendants of another of the sons of Noah, namely, Japheth, who were said eventually to comprise the Gentile nations (in the usual sense of the word, not the theological sense). Since they were not part of the main divine line that came through Noah's son Shem, one would expect them to have been ignored as being second-rate, like the descendants of Ham. At least, that's what one would expect in logic. However, for the first century of the church's existence, most of the "Saints" came from these Gentile stocks (in the secular sense) and, besides, in the nineteenth and early twentieth centuries, it was well-known that certain of these groups, especially the British, the Scandanavians, and the Germans, were Very Superior People. And you can only be very superior if that is part of the divine plan. So the LDS church developed its own genealogical riff on the Aryan Myth. That is, in conflict with the biblical story, the Mormons posited that among the descendants of Japheth (the non-coloured "Gentile" peoples, in secular language) there were scattered remnants of the true tribe of Israel, descended from Shem through Joseph and through his son Ephraim. These true-Israel remnants were to be found in the English, Swedish, Germans, and associated northern European groups. Just as a primary mission field of the nineteenth- and early twentieth-century LDS proselytizers was to convert persons in Great Britain and northern Europe (a task they assayed with considerable success), so the task of genealogists was to document the lineages of these superior persons of WASP and north-European heritage.

Finally (5), the "Saints" for the most part believed that they themselves were *literally* the descendants of Ephraim, brother of Manasseh, and the foremost descendants of Shem, around whom all of Israel's tribes would eventually rally. In other words, they were the genetically prepotent of all the descendants of the ancient Hebrew patriarchs. That is an extraordinary concept and one has to ask, did most Mormons actually believe this? Armand Mauss suggests that in the 1830s it was ambiguous: first, whether this proposed lineage was a metaphor or an empirical statement; and second, if meant literally, it was unclear if it implied that the "Saints" as a group were descended from Ephraim or, instead, that each individual "Saint's" lineage was blood-pedigreed from Ephraim. However, in the century after the Prophet's early and ambiguous utterances, the dominant doctrine became that the LDS were literally the descendants of Ephraim and that they and their "blood" had been scattered among all those good north-European and "Anglo-Saxon" peoples.[10] Upon becoming a "Saint," each individual's bloodline was confirmed, albeit not specified in detail. This occurred in a Mormon ritual that I have not previously mentioned. After baptism a new member of the faith, having been called out as a presumptive member of the house of Israel, had that status confirmed in a ceremony called the *patriarchal blessing*. This ceremony provided the individual with an identification of the tribe of Israel to which he or she belonged and, usually, it was the tribe of Ephraim.[11]

Taken together, points "1" through "5" were the base genealogical narrative and its attendant genealogical grammar that dominated the LDS church as it was laying the foundations for its present-day move towards a universal human history. (Of course there were myriad other matters of detail, but these were the main tramlines.) So, was the Mormon genealogical enterprise characterized by a racism that was cut so deep into the bone and muscle of Mormon divinity that even if the wound healed, the scarring would be perniciously permanent?

From 1976 (when the mission-to-the-dead was declared to be scripture) to the present day is a new temporal page in Mormon genealogical work. The present-day, well-informed "Saint" probably would be surprised and embarrassed to learn the nature of what was held to be divine truth only a generation or two ago. At an official level (whatever folk-beliefs may be), the LDS church today (1) no longer literalizes the descent of individual members from Ephraim. A new "Saint," in receiving a tribal identity in the patriarchal blessing, now is merely being assigned a tribal identity by adoption, not the definition of his or her literal lineage;[12] (2) the implicit "British Israelism" – the idea of the Anglo-Saxons and the Nordic Europeans being flush with the blood of the Lost Tribes of Israel – has been quietly dropped;[13] (3) the bar to black priesthood was removed by divine revelation vouchsafed to the First Presidency in 1978; (4) the LDS church has tried to get along better with Jews (in, for example, stopping its baptizing of Holocaust victims), but there is a limit here to how far the "Saints" can go. After all, they still see themselves as being the truest (albeit not the only) form of the real Israel; (5) and, the idea that there is a connection between whiteness of skin and closeness to the Almighty, which had made for difficult relations with "brown" New World populations – the "Lamanites" – now is not much talked about. However, in the mission fieLDS of Latin and South America, it still is useful to tell potential converts that they are descended from the ancient Israelites. And particularly in Polynesia, where the indigenous cultures maintain long and highly prized genealogies, the literal belief in brown peoples' being part of an Israelite group can be tied into each indigenous culture's origin-myth. This is very helpful for conversional purposes.[14]

Each reader will have to make up his or her mind upon the extent to which the massive new Mormon genealogical machine – some more details of which will be discussed in a moment – has adequate safeguards so that the mechanism can be employed with confidence to deal with recording, recovering, and inter-relating information on all the families of humankind: not just those whose world was arranged like that of the "Anglo-Saxons" and European peoples.

When (as discussed in chapter 3) President Wilford Woodruff received his revelation in 1894 concerning the need to make genealogical work central to the activities of the Church of Jesus Christ of Latter-day Saints, he was not questioning the decree of Brigham Young that "there must be this chain in the holy priesthood. It must be welded together from the latest generation that lives on the earth back to Father Adam."[15] However, he was introducing a concern with accuracy that was brand new. Woodruff was concerned about the 13,000 "adoptions" whereby ordinary "Saints" had been genealogically sealed in the afterlife to church luminaries. He did not like people messing about with other people's genealogies, so he directed that sealings should be based upon family groups. And he introduced a sense of historical responsibility: to follow one's own progenitors "just as far back into the past as they can be followed *from existing records*; arrange a *complete and accurate record* of each family group in the lineage; and link up these groups into pedigrees"[16] [italics mine].

Those requirements are the beginning of Mormon genealogical quality control, at least in the era of verifiable records, and seem to mean that from their early modern period onward the Mormons were willing to play by the same rules as other genealogists and historians.[17]

Yet, as names of families and of their individual members flooded into Salt Lake City for recording and then to temples for baptism, endowment, and sealing, the real concern was not with accuracy (in the secular sense) but with *duplication*. Watch that word, for it, not historical error, is the bête noir of the church. The authorities had a fear (unexplained, at least publicly) of doing "temple-work" twice or more for the same individual. So, beginning in 1919, a simple system of ticking each name on the master genealogical record as it went forward for temple-work was introduced. The policy was not very effective and was abandoned in 1927. One Mormon accountant, Harry H. Russell, became so incensed at the time being wasted in duplicate work in the five temples that were then operating that he conducted a personal crusade for the indexing of all individuals who had had ordinances done for them. Thus was born in 1927 the Temple Records Index Bureau, which was essentially a giant card file of every person whose name was put forward for a votive ceremony.[18] This eliminated most duplication. But note what it did not control: the quality in terms of accuracy of the genealogical input that was sent forward for temple-work. Bad egg, good egg, as long as the name (and the dead human being to which it allegedly referred) had not been processed earlier: as a system of genealogical quality control this was curious.

An indirect form of quality control was that tried during the 1920s when the central genealogical library limited access by letting researchers work on only four surname lines at once and then only those of their own ancestors. This did not really work, because "Saints" anxious to save posthumously as many lost souls as possible made up spurious family groupings to cover the fact that they were actually transcribing the vital details – birth, marriage, death – of individuals with whom they had no family connection.[19]

That fact leads us to a recognition of two fundamental problems that lie at the base of the LDS genealogical program. The most basic of these – one that has yet to be successfully addressed – is that there has been for at least the past ninety years a desire for "Saints" to be involved in retro-saving as many souls as possible. Hence, temples need to have sufficient names available to keep the faithful occupied in performing ceremonies for the dead. These pressures have strongly militated against scrutinizing any given genealogical item too closely.

The second problem – one that eventually was successfully addressed – is that in logic there was no reason to restrict genealogical data to persons who could be identified with an existing Mormon family. President Woodruff's attempt to restrict research to an individual's own family was a practical approach to a particular problem, that of spiritual "adoptions," but as a long-term genealogical strategy, it was self-defeating, at least given the ambitions of the church. If one accepted the Mormon genealogical mission as being eventually to tie together all humankind, then one soon would hit a point-of-sharply-diminishing returns if only the names of individuals known to be direct ancestors of present-day Mormons were admitted to the church's data base. It would make more sense to store the unattached names and then, when more work was done, these names would fit into lineages. When a professional genealogist, a Mormon, pointed this out in 1935, he was sharply slapped down. The idea of *extracting* – watch that word, it is another important term of art – individual names of those not having a

Mormon familial connection, was rejected as "inconsistent with and contrary to the revealed word of the Lord on our responsibility in temple-work and the established policy of the church as to our responsibility."[20]

These two fundamental issues were pushed aside, even as the genealogical activity of the "Saints" kept growing during the 1930s and 40s. Fervent attempts were made to improve the quality of submissions to the genealogical register in terms of the spelling of names and the completeness of the information forms. In 1938 an unfortunately named Censor Committee was established to check for elementary completeness (full name, dates of birth and death, etc.) of the material various "Saints" sent in for temple-work: half of the submissions had to be rejected.[21] As for tying together their own families, Joseph Fielding Smith in 1943 estimated that "ninety-five percent of those working on their own lines bungle the records in compiling them, leading to confusion comparable to a tangled ball of string."[22] This shows an admirable awareness of a problem, but it is a secondary problem, really. The primary one – not ever directly addressed – was *how accurate were the widely scattered "Saints" when dealing with the primary records* from which they derived the family record sheets they sent to Utah for central processing?"

Human error, stemming from individual "Saints" cobbling together questionable lineages, compounded by the ever-increasing demand for names to be cleared for temple-work, led to a significant doctrinal change in the church and, as usual, it was accepted as a bit of progressive revelation and not as a repudiation of previous practice: which it definitely was. In the 1950s, the family catchment as the sole basis for genealogical collection and for temple-work was quietly set aside. Previous to 1952, no sheaf of family data could be accepted unless the "heir"– the oldest living, or dead member of the family – was designated by the individual submitter of the data. That stopped and instead the "heir" was designated, where necessary, from the Genealogical Society's now-extensive card-index. That took some of the pressure off the central authorities to provide temple-ready names for the ever-growing number of Mormon temples to work with.[23]

That was a half-step and had nothing directly to do with primary genealogical sources. The next was a big one, and it did improve data quality. Ever since the late 1930s, when microfilm had been shown to be a fast and reasonably permanent way of collecting large amounts of primary data – birth rolls, parish registers, birth, death, and marriage registrations, censuses of population, mortgage and tax records, probate records, and more – the church had been amassing a huge amount of raw historical data. Only in rare instances could this primary material be quickly linked to any one Mormon family. Yet, the names were those of real human beings who now were in the spirit world and needed proxy baptisms, endowments, and sealings if they were to have a full celestial blessing. Given the need for more names to keep membership morale up through participation in the rich liturgy of temple-work, the solution was to begin a *name extraction* program in 1961, which evolved into the "stake record extraction" program in 1978. The extraction business involved practices that earlier had been condemned: (a) recording genealogical data that had nothing to do with one's own family; (b) submitting single-person records rather than family-based sheets; and (c) putting forward the names of these individuals for temple-work, even though they had as yet no known connection to any LDS family.[24] This was a revolution: the Church of Jesus Christ of Latter-day Saints had gone from reconstructing humanity by a linear method – beginning with known Mormons and tracing them backwards to Father Adam – and now was using a shotgun approach for the reconstruction of the family: recording and baptizing everyone who had ever left a name and minimal personal information (such as birth or death date) on the earthly record.

Ironically, President Woodruff had been suspicious of random genealogical work because it was often wildly inaccurate. Yet the modern name-extraction program turns out to provide the most accurate data the LDS church possesses, at least if one uses accuracy in the secular sense. In the version of name-extraction that was farmed out to local wards, quality control was quite good. One person did a primary deciphering of the microfilm, then a second one did the same thing but without knowing what the first person had recorded. Then a supervisor (now computer-aided) compared the two and if there were differences, all three met to sort them out.[25] This did not mean that the name-extractors had the vaguest idea what the original records might mean in their historical context (try figuring out nineteenth-century Lowland Scottish family patterns from tenancy lists), but it at least makes probable that the transcription is true to the primary record upon which it is based. In the present century, the double-checking is done by computers: useful, but less rigorous than having two or three pairs of eyes go over the same material.

(Parenthetically, the one big drawback of the name-extraction revolution in Mormon genealogical methods requires mention: that it really irritates a lot of people. Many non-Mormons find impious, intrusive, or arrogant the "Saints" digging up their ancestors, as it were, and baptizing them as Mormons. This practice is especially offensive to Jews, who certainly have a right to be sensitive about Christian treatment of their heritage. Some Jews could not care less, seeing Mormonism as a bizarre superstition. Others see it as an evil one. "Baptism is the second ugliest word in the English language to a Jew," says Jewish activist and genealogist Gary Mokotoff: "The first is gassed. The third is raped."[26] As a result of pressure from a group of Holocaust survivors, aided by Senator Hillary Clinton, in 1995 the LDS church promised to stop their policy of baptizing posthumously victims of the Nazi death camps. With Orrin Hatch, senator from Utah, brokering the deal, the church also agreed to take all Holocaust victims and all deceased Jews who have no Mormon descendants off the church's International Genealogical Index, which registers persons for whom at least baptism has been performed, and perhaps other ordinances. Whether or not the celestial baptism is (or even can be) undone is a matter beyond mortal discourse. It is not clear whether LDS officials have kept their word; in any case, it is impossible for the central authorities to know whether or not a name submitted by a private individual reflects any Jewish heritage, so the question actually is moot.)

Now, the key conclusion that follows from the Mormons' introduction of their name-extraction program, with its wide base of sources and its high level of accuracy of transcription of historical records, is the historians' second evidentiary paradox when dealing with LDS data. (The first, remember, was that the LDS data are most useful and most trustworthy to historians when they are used in the form least compatible with Mormon purposes in collecting the data in the first place: that is, using them to answer historians' questions about large historical groups, rather than about individuals.) The second evidentiary paradox is this: if you really insist on using the LDS material as a genealogical source, it is most likely to be accurate (in the sense of being true to primary records) if you are *not* Mormon and have *not* had Mormon ancestors. This follows unavoidably from what we have discussed already: (a) the original data bank of the Genealogical

Society was built up mostly from submissions from "Saints" who dealt with their own ancestral families. Many had a Stakhanovite notion that in submitting as many names as fast as possible they would save the most souls. From the late 1920s onward, "duplication" of temple-work was practically controlled for, but not the actual quality (or, reality, to use a cutting term) of the original submission. And (b) since name-extraction began in 1962, more of the names have been drawn from a wider variety of primary sources, composed of persons who, at the time of the data-extraction program inception, had no known connection with the LDS church or with the genealogies of Mormons, either alive or dead; and the data concerning the persons in the name-extraction programs were recorded very carefully. Therefore it follows (to put it quantitatively), at present the less apt you are to be a Mormon, the more accurate your genealogy as derived from Mormon data bases is likely to be.

———

Because the Church of Jesus Christ of Latter-day Saints believes in progressive revelation (God has not spoken just once, but keeps on speaking) one must not periodize their thought and practice too tightly: it evolves. Nevertheless, it is fair to see the period from 1918 to 1976 as a distinct, if loosely boundaried area in their practice of genealogy. If, in 1894, President Woodruff had tried to effect some damage control as far as errors were concerned (he required Mormons to work on their own family chains only) it was the revelation of 1918 to President Joseph F. Smith of the potential for doing missionary work among the dead that distinctly energized genealogical work: one had to know the dead in order to evangelize them. By 1976, the 1918 revelation was declared to be holy scripture (it becomes The Doctrine and Covenants, section 138). Thus, the foundation and first courses of the Mormons' genealogical ziggurat were in place: the great mountain depository of primary data, a quickly growing, paper-based system that interlocked genealogical and liturgical records, and a relatively new, exponentially expanding pool of information on non-Mormon individuals.

Yet, the church was heading for trouble. As always, it was having horrific problems with "duplication": holy ordinances were sometimes inadvertently performed over and over for the same individual. More importantly, the church was faced with a frequent shortage of names. In order to make the liturgical rites conducted in the various temples continue smoothly, more and more names of as yet unsaved dead persons were needed. This was a long-standing problem. It had begun to be noticed in the 1940s[27] and became more acute as the number of living Mormons increased.

Then, in the last quarter of the twentieth century, a technical breakthrough, combined with a massive growth and alternation in the character of the LDS constituency, were permitted to effect a radical alternation in Mormon liturgical practice. All this had a direct effect on matters of genealogy.

In fact, these phenomena were part of a single self-spinning system of change. In describing them separately, one should not obviate the fact that they really were a synergistic system and no aspect was independent of any other.

First, membership worldwide grew immensely. In 1950 there were 1.1 million Mormons in the world. In 1975 the number was roughly 4 million[28] and the curve was still sharply rising. In 1994, membership was approximately 9 million, and by 2004 it had risen to more than 12 million[29] and was still increasing. Second, in the later 1990s, the church reached the point where most of its membership was outside the United States.[30] This was a radical cultural shift from the 1960s when most of the membership was in Utah and contiguous states. In some degree, the success of the church outside of the United States was a reflection of the prestige and, increasingly, the imperial power of the USA in the second half of the twentieth century. More directly consequent were factors internal to the LDS church itself: a redirection of foreign missions to non-European areas and the sacred revelation in 1978 that black-skinned people were eligible to become full-privilege "Saints."

Thirdly, these quantitative and cultural changes in LDS membership were accompanied (and accelerated) by a transformation in liturgical practice as sharp as that which occurred in the Roman Catholic church in the same period. In the Mormon case, while participation on the local level continued to be important, as Kathleen Flake notes, the "primary indica" of church membership became participation in temple worship.[31] Cathedrals (an appropriate term for Mormon temples, but one the LDS church avoids) had been few before mid-twentieth century: eight temples in 1950, all in the US and western Canada.[32] The number was forty-seven in 1994 and 123 by the end of 2004.[33] The majority of new temples from the mid-1990s onward were built outside the Mormon belt in the western states and prairie Canada; indeed, most were outside North America.

That in the latter decades of the twentieth century and in the early years of the twenty-first century the number of temples grew even faster than did Mormon church membership indicates that the focus of Mormon liturgies was changing. The temples now became more central. The pivotal liturgical prerequisite was a supply of the names of specific dead persons so "Saints" could vicariously carry out for them the temple ceremonies of baptism, sealing, and endowment. The reader will notice that the system has at this point spun upside-down: whereas the nineteenth-century causality was that one needed "Saints" to engage in liturgical acts in order to save the dead, now the twenty-first century situation is that one needs the dead in order to permit "Saints" to perform these rituals. And, since these temple rituals are increasingly the centrepiece of the faith, the pressures on the genealogical section of the church is immense.

All of the preceding developments forced the LDS church into the front edge of computer development for genealogical work and, conversely, it was the investment of resources and ingenuity in vast name-spewing computers that made possible the church's later-twentieth-century transformation.

Because present-day "Saints" are so conservative socially, it is easy to make a big mistake: to assume that they are conservative technologically. Just the opposite is true. As a by-product of the hyper-optimism that enhues all aspects of Mormon belief – faith in progressive revelation, belief that few humans ever go to Perdition, and the doctrine that all believers can become gods in the afterlife – technology is seen as something to be enthusiastically embraced. Technological change, as produced by the God-given talents of humankind, has the power to make the world better and better and better. From the early twentieth century onward, many of the LDS elite have been fascinated with practical science. Thus it was fully in character with the faith that many of the brightest young Mormon minds were at the front of several sectors of the computer revolution. Most importantly in the present context, they took the lead in developing complex name-recognition, storage, and linkage programs that, when employed in LDS genealogical work, promised not only to make life in the present world better but to improve the after-life condition of millions of souls.

The Mormon computer revolution occurred so rapidly (and still is occurring) that even the best-intended descriptions of it by LDS scholars are confusing. Basically, from 1969 through 1991, five generations of new computer systems were introduced. When combined with new genealogical practices at the ward level, the entire system turned into a massive intellectual engine. Today it contains about 1 billion searchable names and another billion in raw form[34] which eventually will be searchable. Yet this achievement is only the beginning of the Department's quest to identify, as nearly as possible, "all the people who have ever lived."[35]

Such a powerful engine. Such a generous accompanying set of new policies allowing outsiders free access and permitting non-Mormons to submit their ancestors' names to the LDS data base. The computer data base, it should be understood, has its origins in three tributaries. The first is all the old material collected by hand on index cards; the second is the continually growing body of material "extracted" from primary sources. Much of this still comes in directly from ward-based "Saints," often working as part of a local collective project on, say, one particular parish register. (Eventually, much of this extraction will be done by computer and printed out digitally, but the authorities do not want to talk much about this as yet.) And, thirdly, there is "submitted" material. In the old days (meaning before the 1970s) this material came almost entirely from church members whose identity and sources, such as they were, were revealed to other genealogists. Now, most of it comes in over the Internet from anyone at all, and since 1991 privacy legislation and church policy have made it hard to find out who and where the material comes from. (More on that in a moment.)

The form the massive data base is arranged in is appropriate for most Mormons today, but is headed for some cultural difficulties. The data are arranged according to the classical model of the European patrilineal family. This fits with LDS church doctrine of what a family should be: Dad at the head, even in multiple-wife families, lifetime marriage being the form of male-female bond, and children clearly identifiable as to their maternal and paternal parentage. The basic Mormon population in, say, 1900, was mostly of British Isles extraction, with Scandinavian and German additions. This followed from the point of origin of the original "Saints" (New England and the northern tier or frontier states) and from a large migration from Great Britain, especially from the city of Liverpool and surrounding areas of Lancashire where early Mormon missionaries had concentrated their work. Also, many old Mormon families prized their intermarriage with Scandinavian families who had converted in the Old Country and migrated to Utah. This had the practical effect of leading Mormon genealogists to embrace Scandinavian mythology and to build linkages between their historical ancestors and figures who clearly were mythic Nordic entities. As late as the 1960s, the majority of Mormons lived in Utah and came from the same ethnic background as a century previously, so the unconscious acceptance of white European family structure as the norm for the world made sense, as did the concentration of energy primarily upon collecting British, Irish, German, and Scandinavian data and with filling the library with European books. In practical terms, if one looks up an individual in the LDS data base – say, of a person of whom you are writing a biography – you will find if you are lucky, a lovely "pedigree chart" (the LDS church's term). It is a visual reification of the church's white-European cultural assumptions. It is set sideways, and in the centre is the person (referred to as "ego" in anthropological kin-studies) you are interested in. That person's parents are then shown in a forked diagram (with the male *always* closer to the top of the page) and then another set of forked diagrams for the grandparents. And so on backwards, sometimes for dozens of generations. These pedigrees are good about preserving female names when they are available, but when they are not, the women are simply declared to be – for example – "Mrs Merfyn Ap Rhodri," whether or not there is evidence of marriage or whether or not the use of the term "Mrs" is historically appropriate: in the example that I just gave, it was not, for the case comes from Wales in the ninth century. This sort of thing is not fatal, so long as one is aware of it and one is dealing with a British-Isles or European-based family history. Appropriate correction is easy enough, and the data base can produce some marvelous suggestions that can serve as the basis for direct primary historical work.

Where the present Mormon system is marching into a conundrum the size of the Everglades is elsewhere. Since the beginning of the twenty-first century, more "Saints" live outside the USA than within, and the cultural assumptions that underlie the present system of recording and organizing data often do not hold. Indeed, even within the USA there are problems. For example, consider the

LDS church's desire to reunite genealogically with the descendants of the so-called Lamanites – the Amerindians. Even if the "Saints" do unearth enough data to trace most Native Americans back to the early fifth century when the Lamanites wiped out the Nephites (a decidedly unpromising task), the fact is that their model of continuity is not going to work: several of the major Amerindian groups were matrilineal. And so too were several Polynesian societies and African groups. As the church expands rapidly in Latin America, Polynesia, and Africa, it will increasingly embrace new "Saints" who, whatever their family pattern today, did not meld with the Mormon template as recently as two or three generations ago. Their genealogies will not fit the basic European charts. And matrilinealities are easy as compared to double-descent systems; and what in the world are the LDS genealogists going to do with the ancient Chinese descent system? If anybody can ever solve such problems, and merge the answers with all the existing European charts, surely it will be the Mormons, but I would be happier if they were not so confident before they start about exactly where all the work will lead: back to Father Adam, in 4004 BCE, give or take a year or two.

It is no secret that professional genealogists (by which I mean people who make a living producing pedigrees on a client-pays basis and, often, by lecturing on genealogy) have long had a love-hate relationship with the Mormons. They deride the LDS church's work (the motto, "never endorse a competitor," holds whatever the product), and at the same time they often use Mormon sources to key their own research. The biggest complaint about LDS genealogical work that is not mere cheap-shotting is that most of the Mormon data are from voluntary submissions. Tracings from old family Bibles and sheaves of family records arranged according to the "heirship system," were the basis of the church's original genealogical card index. And today hundreds of thousands of computer submissions of individual names are made annually by the general public (mostly, still by LDS members, but increasingly by others).

In contrast, an organization such as the New England Genealogical Society, which has its own for-fee data base, is proud that it contains no information contributed by the general public but rather all material is derived from scholarly sources.[36] That is excellent and is certainly a rational choice of method for operating a genealogical system. However, merely damning the general public and disparaging their voluntarily submitted data rather misses the point (aside from unfairly implying that the general public has no access to scholarly sources and that private data bases are necessarily the product of high competence in scholarly activity). It misses the point because evaluating the difference between the two systems (assuming each works equally well in its own way) is a question of what one wants to do with the data. What story do you want, a tight and narrow one or a broad and loose one? The material recorded in the front and back of all those old family Bibles and copies of the Book of Mormon that made it to Utah would never be found or substantiated in a million years by the usual modes of scholarly documentation – much less the oral material from grandparents that served as the basis for the first few years of family lineage sheets. Much of the genealogy of New England (and a fair bit of that of the United Kingdom) ties into this early material, yet most of it would not make it into the front door of a probate court: the form in which it survives is a set of derived records, not originals. So, at some point one asks, "Do I want to take the high road and get 100 percent accuracy and almost no results – or 30 percent accuracy and a lot of hits?" Thirty percent of something is a lot more than 100 percent of nothing. Take your pick. And then do your own verification.

Instead of damning all voluntary submission programs, let us look at how the LDS church tries to keep its voluntary submissions on track at the present time. Their online help could hardly be better. They provide researchers with blank forms designed to record all pertinent details of ancestors found in most of the western European, English, Scottish, Irish, Canadian, and United States censuses and the most common form of church records. These work-sheets include places to record exactly where each item is found and thus are potentially useful to future researchers who want to get quickly to a proper take-off point for their own work. They are the sort of data-record sheets a professional historian would use if he or she were constructing a large-sample history project.

Then the procedure goes wobbly: at present, when transmitting the material to the central LDS genealogical authorities, there is no provision for providing citations for where the primary material on which the names and dates are found is located![37] The church authorities are interested only in checking that no previous temple-work has been done for the people involved – the "duplication" problem they have so long worried about. If no duplication is found and unless there is something preposterous in the information submitted (such as someone living for 200 years or being born at the North Pole), the material is sent out to a temple for proxy baptism and subsequent endowment and sealing. Thus, although the voluntary submissions often (I think, usually) are basically accurate, they cannot ever be checked in a large sample replication study. So, the final answer to the question that I posed early in this chapter: "what do replication studies show about the fundamental research design and the technical quality of the work?" is that one will never know, as the basic record collection process precludes wide-scale replication.

Yet, individual genealogists now-and-again are able to check specific items. This is fairly hard work, but in material submitted before 1991 (when privacy codes started to require limiting some parts of the data base to LDS members), the name and address of the submitter(s) was often provided and one could write to that person. On some items a microfilm number was given. Almost always, however, that item turns out not to be a primary source but rather a microfilm record of a register of church ordinances performed, sealings being the ones which required – and thus provide – the most genealogical information. And, with experience, one comes to know from the microfilm batch number if the information comes from an individual or from the more rigorous "extraction" method. Unfortunately, items submitted after 1991 are now nearly impossible for non-Mormons to check for origin, a pity, as at present, patron-submitted items are roughly half the new names being added to the data base.[38] Members of the church have a registration number and a password derived from their confirmation date, so they often can learn the names of post-1991 submitters.

Millions of names are coming in each year and "in 1987 submission policies permitted the clearance [for temple ordinances] of people with incomplete names, estimated dates, and places of birth or marriage unknown; this change meant that virtually any person known to have lived could be cleared for ordinance work."[39] After liturgical entry, these persons would be listed in the International Genealogical Index without any realistic chance of outsiders doing source verification.

Still, there is all that "extracted" material that has been taken from primary sources. It comprises about half the material in the present data base[40] and that proportion is apt to remain stable even as the base expands. As I mentioned earlier, on "extracted" material the quality checks are very good at the level of data entry. Where they are weak is at the level of historical context. Names and associated births, marriages, and deaths are easy to mangle unless one knows the precise historical context, which few extractors (and even fewer computers) understand. Here is one example from St. Margaret's Bay, Nova Scotia, which was the subject of litigation early in the twenty-first century. (The case itself is covered under lawyer privilege, so I will not identify the families involved or the precise locale.) As often happens, a land ownership dispute rested on a genealogical chain, this one running back to the mid-nineteenth century. It should have been easy to resolve, for the Mormons had microfilmed all the local censuses and then some ward, as its genealogical project, had dutifully alphabetized everything. All the material was useless, however, because this area had only a few family names and generation-after-generation the families had used only a limited number of first names. Hence, to tell who somebody actually was, one needed not just two names and to know an event or two – birth, marriage, death – but also where the individual lived. Not having formal street numbers, one could only figure out who-was-who and who-was-parent-to-whom by knowing what road they lived on and who their neighbours were: that's how the census takers worked; they walked from house to house and down mile after mile of concession roads. When the Mormons alphabetized things, not only did they get everything wrong (lumping together two or three persons who had the same name), they then provided the locals with a lovely set of microfilms which the locals accepted gratefully and then let their original records go to ruin.

The area where the name-extraction program is most apt to be accurate (within the limits of some very dodgy primary data) is in the period before, roughly, 1500, and also on subjects involving royalty. Those are the areas that attract the greatest number of nutcases among genealogists and the church has wisely fenced them out. The instructions to those who are doing such work are unambiguous. Information about royalty or persons who lived before AD 1500 is difficult to verify. "Before preparing the names of such people for [church] ordinances, write or call the Family History Department, Medieval Families Unit ... The Medieval Families Unit will help you determine whether your information is correct."[41] Effectively, this is the one genealogical sector where the LDS authorities provide a qualitative check on material and do so at the level of adjudging how good the original sources are.

How good are these judges? Quite expert, I suspect, but one needs to be a broad-based medievalist to render an opinion with any authority. In the only area where I have a small knowledge, the genealogical patterns of pre-Norman Ireland, I ran a simple experiment. This consisted of comparing a representative line of the kings of Leinster from Donncuan (reigned 1014–16) backwards to Ailill (reigned 527-?) and then compared this to the most recent scholarly statements of that line.[42] This is a tough area of scholarship, for the Irish annals are awkwardly arranged and also were tinkered with as various families rose or fell. Still, once one deals with problems of orthography (approved spellings of ancient Irish names keep changing) and of fictitious females in the genealogy (every king had to have a Mrs King, for reasons of LDS family ideology), the Mormon material was consonant with the best recent scholarship: impressively so.[43]

The one place where the experts of the Medieval Families Unit seem to go wrong consistently is at the start of many lines. Inevitably, these are almost all royal or aristocratic lines since the rulers were the ones who paid for professional memory-keepers to memorialize their ancestry. Most of the historical sources (if such they are) for this material lie in collections of ancient oral material that were written down, in the usual case, after the introduction of Christianity. In the early written sources of Ireland, Wales, Scotland, Scandinavia, Iceland, and Germany, genealogy and mythology mixed together. In virtually every case, a monarch traced his own roots back to a pre-Christian god. When Christianity became dominant, in each of these places the keepers of the records scrambled to rid the pedigrees of pagan elements. They did this by euhemerising the gods: turning the old gods in the aristocratic genealogies into recognizable (if often oversized) human beings. The Mormon genealogists miss this in many cases and in others, where the gods have not been humanized, the genealogists often do the euhemerising for themselves. Thus, for example, if one looks up the LDS pedigree of the (probably mythical) Skjold, king of the Danes (allegedly born c. 237) one finds him married to Gefion and having Odin as a father and Frigg as a mother, all these being north-European gods. His parents, Odin and Frigg, are reported as living in "Asgard, Asia, or Eastern Europe." Asgard of course is the Scandinavian heaven where several deities live and where Valhalla is located. King Skjold's line is eventually traced back to Godwulf who was supposedly born about the year 80 CE. Without trying very hard, one can find several hundred examples of this sort of thing in the Mormon pedigrees. I think the problem here is that even among their experts in early medieval history, the credulity of the "Saints" concerning god-figures follows directly from the habits of mind formed by their immersion in the Mormon scriptures. If one can accept The Book of Mormon, The Pearl of Great Price, and The Doctrine and Covenants without flinching at the largely fictive and polytheistic nature of the material, one is programmed to accept the multiple god-figures of early European genealogies without noticing that one is dealing with something unusual and inappropriate to modern historical practice.

Finally, how well does the LDS machinery merge all the name-extraction material and all the submissions by LDS church members and by the general public? Because the data storage and search engines that the Mormons employ are evolving so rapidly, it is profitless to describe in detail what one finds in the data bank. However, almost certainly the data bank will continue to store just two basic categories of data (however many separate sub-sections or categories appear on the computer menu). These are information on dead persons (1) for whom church ordinances have yet to be performed and (2) the names and details of persons for whom temple-work has been at least partially accomplished. This second file is called the International Genealogical Index and usually (but not always) is the place one is most apt to find a lineage for any given person. However, one must remember that this genealogical usage is a secondary employment of the IGI. "The primary purpose of the IGI, however, from the [Genealogical] Department's perspective, continued to be as an index to ordinances."[44] If the record of a liturgical act is later found to clash with new genealogical data, the ordinances prevail. The celestial realm is forever.

Granting that, one finds some impressively long genealogies in the International Genealogical Index and the other files. Perhaps they are true to primary records, perhaps not. In most cases they are beyond verification, as I have explained earlier. However, when one encounters a "pedigree" of any length, the key check that can easily be performed is based on simple common sense. If, as is sometimes the case, a woman is reported as having a child at an age over 100 years, or if a person is credited with being a sire or a dam at age two, torch the lineage from that point. And, be particularly wary if you find an especially desirable ancestor in your own "pedigree": *Mayflower* figures or the like. Take one *Mayflower* example, that of the enigmatic Peter Brown (or Browne). Said to have been the ship's carpenter, he was one of the signers of the *Mayflower* compact. He is an ancestor prized by a certain type of snob and a battle of pamphlets and articles has raged over his poorly recorded body for at least a century. The point is: note how someone keen on having Brown sealed into his or her Mormon line in heaven chronicled the successive generations of his lineage (I am beginning with the early material, and including only the male parent and his birth, death, and locations):

- Christopher Browne. Born about 1482, of Swan Hall, Hawkendon, Suffolk. Died 3 July 1538, Hawkedon, Suffolk.
- Thomas Browne. Born about 1533, Swan Hall, Hawkendon, Suffolk. Died December, 1590, Swan Hall, Hawkedon, Suffolk.
- Peter Brown. Born 1596/98, of Hawkendon, Suffolk. Died 4 October 1633, Plymouth, Massachusetts.
- Edward Brown. Born 9 September 1586, of Inkburrow Parish, Worcestershire. Died after 1610, Inkburrow Parish, Worcestershire.
- Nicholas Brown. Born 1601, of Inkburrow Parish, Worcestershire. Died 16 Nov. 1694, Reading, Middlesex, Massachusetts.

The obvious point here is that even if the sketchy details of Peter Brown's lineage are right – and Peter Brown's having been born a half dozen years after the death of his father is noteworthy – there is no way that he was the father of Edward Brown of Worcestershire, since Edward (gen. 4) was born a dozen or so years before the birth of Peter (gen.3). That someone keen to have a *Mayflower* ancestor intercalated Peter Brown into the line of Edward Brown of Worcestershire is clear. What is not so clear is how even the most enthusiastic of soulsavers (in the old days of the human checking of "pedigrees" for temple-work) or even the most rudimentary of computer programs could let slip through the plonking great impossibility of a lineage having someone's being born before his own father's birth. Or, for that matter, how in the world did Peter Brown come to be born so long after the death of his putative father? Such errors can be found scores of times in even a couple of hundred searches down some of the longer LDS "pedigree" lines.

Since so many errors are now sealed forever in the celestial sphere, it is perhaps supererogatory to recall one important point about genealogical lines. Unlike wide-lens social historical studies, which can stand a certain degree of error and correct for it quantitatively, there is no statistical technique for correcting an error in a lineage. If an error enters a genealogical line, then at that point either (a) the line must stop dead in its tracks until new and correct information can be found or (b) everything that follows from that point is in error. Anyone who can find a full Mormon "pedigree" that runs from the present back to, say, 100 CE that does not contain at least one of these rudimentary errors (never mind lack of adhesion to primary sources) is witnessing a miracle. Yet, all of us, "Saints" and "Gentiles" alike, are being built into one massive narrative, an all-encompassing story of the human race.

Enjoy the process – but never forget that it is a really good story, nothing more, nothing less.

APPENDICES

APPENDIX A

The Poverty of Terminology

It is very hard to think clearly about something for which one has inadequate words and only blurred pictures. To discuss genealogy rationally, we require tools that have intellectual adhesion and thus will permit our mental grasp of the matter. That is no different from any other subject of considered debate. Some (but not all) matters of genealogy require a technical vocabulary. In particular, terms for family and for multi-generational relationships are crucial for collecting information on kinship and for providing an agreed and denotative vocabulary for the various relationships of individuals within a lineage and within a kinship structure.

At present, it appears that, in the English-speaking world, our collective language is deficient in that (a) there is no agreed term for many basic relationships in lineage and kin systems and (b) there are some terms that simultaneously cover two distinct phenomena.

This poverty of language seems to be increasing. The general society from which most readers of this book spring – European-derived cultures – has been losing its vocabulary for lineage matters for at least a century, and this affects genealogists: they must learn semi-archaic vocabularies and must try to employ them as a means of communication without sounding as if they just stepped off a time-machine.

Today, in the twenty-first century, I think one would find that less than half the adult members of North American or European societies could go beyond their grandparents and their grandparents' descendants in filling out a lineage-kinship diagram of their own. This would most commonly include the possibility of the following:

- Ego;
- parents of Ego;
- brothers and sisters of Ego;
- brothers of Ego's father and brothers of mother ("uncles" of Ego);
- sisters of Ego's mother and sisters of father ("aunts" of Ego);
- Ego, expressed as son of his father's brother and his wife
  and of his father's sister and her husband ("nephew")
- Ego, expressed as daughter of her father's brother and his
  wife and of her father's sister and her husband ("niece")
- all grandchildren (not siblings) of the same grandparents
  ("cousins")

That, I suspect, is about as far as most people could go in either personal kinship or in theory. It is not very far, high, or wide, and reflects the predominance of the nuclear family, the high degree of physical mobility that reduces kinship consciousness, and the frequency of divorce which truncates the trains of lineage and kinship knowledge.

Let me guess (and this is only speculation based upon reading and archival work) that in, say, 1950, the general consciousness in the same cultures would have gone back a generation farther. That is, in addition to the terms and relationships mentioned above, most people would have understood the concepts of, and had personal examples of, the following:

- "first cousins" as a refinement of the term "cousins," above;
- "second cousins" for great-grandchildren of the same grandparents other than siblings;
- "first cousin once removed" for two persons, one of whom is the grandchild and the other a great-grandchild of the same ancestral couple;
- sisters and brothers of Ego's grandparents would be called "great aunts" and "great uncles."

This is a considerably richer palette than predominates in our own day. Still, in the mid-twentieth century, it would have been only the family historian in most lineages who could map out matters as far and as wide as all the kinship of their own great-great grandparents:

with its rich array of "third cousins" (everyone with the same great-great grandparents), "second cousins, once removed" (two persons, one of whom was the great-grandchild, the other the great-great grandchild of the same ancestral couple) and so on.

Even though it would be nice to have this five-generation conceptual framework wired into the everyday vocabulary of the English-speaking world, it would not be an adequate set of terms even within that five-generation frame: too frequently it calls different things by the same word, either by blurring gender or, more frequently, by failing to distinguish what side of the family the lineage category is on. (For example, "aunt" covers both sides of the family and includes both "blood" relations and married-ins.)

Most of these matters were handled better in European lineage systems, but these were flattened out with the massive migration to North America and the dominance of English-language culture. If we step back to, roughly, 1900, we can take the Swedish system as an example of a more precisely articulated language. The following were the primary relationships of Ego for three generations up and then for two down. First, ascending the potential genealogical tree:

- Ego had a *far* (father) and a *mor* (mother);
- Ego had a *farfar* (paternal grandfather), a *farmor* (paternal grandmother), a *morfar* (maternal grandfather) and a *mormor* (maternal grandmother);
- Ego had a *farbror* (paternal uncle) and a *faster* (paternal aunt) and a *morbror* (maternal uncle) and a *moster* (maternal aunt);
- If Ego's four uncles and aunts were married, their spouses were given honorific titles. These were the same as blood titles, but were understood to have quotation marks around them: thus, respectively, "*faster*," "*farbror*," "*moster*," and "*morbror*";
- Ego and the children of his uncles and aunts were cousins (sing. *kusin*) without distinction as to gender and a second cousin was a *syssling* or a *nåstkusin*;
- Ego had a *svåger* (brother-in-law) and a *svågerska* (sister-in-law).

Now, for two generations downwards the lineage terms were as follows:

- The husband of Ego's daughter was his *svårson* (son-in-law) and the wife of his son was his *svårdotter* (daughter-in-law);

– Ego's grandchildren could be called his *barnbarn* (children of his children) but usually they were differentiated: *dotterson* and *dotterdotter* on his daughter's side and *sonson* and *sondotter* on his son's side.

– The children of Ego's brother and sister were nephews and nieces but these were differentiated; *systerson* was his nephew on his sister's side and *systerdotter* his niece on the same side, while *brorson* was his nephew on his brother's side and *brorsdotter* was his niece on that side.

This system is not perfect. The failure to differentiate the gender of cousins is confusing and that is not trivial. (Just ask the parents of some teen-ager who wants to have his cousin come for a sleep-over.) Also, the honorific titles for uncles and aunts slur the distinction between "blood" relatives and those who marry-in. The key point, however, is that this Swedish system illustrates that it is not too difficult to employ lineage terms that are more accurate than those at present employed in everyday English speech.

It is curious that the English vernacular did not develop a fuller set of denotative terms for lineage relationships than it actually did. This was not because of any failure to be aware of the relationships, just an inexplicable poverty of language. That this is the case is easily established if one looks into most editions of the *Book of Common Prayer* of the Church of England as it was published before the revisions of 1928. (See Appendix B.) In it one will find a set of sixteenth-century distinctions, by which the church defined the "degrees" of relationship wherein marriage was not permissible. There were thirty of these for men and thirty for women. They included as compound nouns such things as "wife's father's sister," "son's daughter" and "brother's son's wife." Clearly the culture of later sixteenth- through nineteenth-century England was cognizant of fine lineage distinctions (otherwise the prohibitions on marriage within these rubrics would have been gibberish to parishioners), and yet no set of words for most of the sixty terms emerged in general usage. Curious, that, and impoverishing to subsequent generations.

One looks with envy at the Kalinga of the Philippines who had a rich (although not absolutely perfect) set of terms covering both gender and side-of-family running from Ego's children through Ego's great-grandparents. Everything through third cousins (meaning everyone descended from Ego's eight pairs of great-great-grandparents) could be easily diagrammed and then a sharp boundary was drawn: anyone beyond Ego's third cousins was outside Ego's kinship circle. Thus each individual had both a sharp definition of in-out as far of kinship was concerned and a precise knowledge of each position within the kinship circle.[1] The ability to obtain lineage preciseness by sloughing off the periphery of the kinship circle is something members of present-day European-derived cultures might covet. I mean, really, what does one call the sister-in-law of one's brother-in-law and why should anyone have to worry about it? (Hint: consider avoiding large family weddings.) Mind you, one could argue that the matter of terminology is not fundamental and the argument is correct, but not entirely satisfying. This is because, as we have seen in the text, almost all human lineage systems operate according to four basic grammars. So, the words one uses for kinship terms are secondary: just as formative grammars in linguistics hold, despite fashions in the use of words; and just as fundamental linguistic grammars can be expressed symbolically, irrespective of word-styles; so the narratives of lineage can be traced diagrammatically in each of the four fundamental lineage systems, no matter what words the people within the system employed, or did not know how to employ.

Still, accurate and culturally specific terms within each grammar would be very helpful for several practical reasons. First, within our own culture (broadly, western European in origin) it would help us to be able to communicate with each other. Secondly, before we can adequately translate family terms from other cultures (especially those not embracing the Standard Double genealogical grammar), we need our own vocabulary to be well anchored.

Thirdly, within each of the four basic grammars of genealogical narrative we should pay respectful attention to the terminology of each individual society. Of course we need to know what their words mean (or meant) on a case-specific basis. There is another, more pervasive, matter. The richness or paucity of a culture's lineage vocabulary is both indicative of, and in part determinative of, its *genealogical horizon*. Within any of the four genealogical grammars, it is possible to have a culture with a rich vocabulary and a *wide lineage* perspective; another can have few words and a *narrow lineage* view of itself. This matter of the genealogical horizon is one of the most important matters in determining any culture's self-concept and it is no less salient for usually going unremarked by social and cultural historians.

The fourth reason for paying close attention to the lineage terminology of cultures other than our own is simply that each culture
uses words in a way that is its own. To charge into cultures distant
from our own (whether distant geographically, or in terms of their
values, or distant in historical time) and to read their genealogies
and their stories of kinship matters as if we automatically know
what the words mean is vandalism. In particular, the easy reflex
when faced with a complex and alien genealogical system, which is
to declare that it really is the same as the Standard Double system
of western Europe, is nothing short of Fascism of the mind.

Granted, many of the words and practices of cultures other than
ours can demand immense patience and sometimes deep scholarly
ingenuity to crack. Here are just a few examples.

Father Pierre de Charlevoix, a Jesuit priest, made an heroic voyage from the St Lawrence Basin to the Gulf of Mexico in the 1720s.
He closely observed several Amerindian groups. These were unilineal clans. His general observation was that the members of these
groups never used personal names in polite conversation among
themselves, but referred to the people they were talking to by kin-
terms. When these were absent or unknown, they used the terms
brother, uncle, nephew, or cousin, depending on age, degree of in-
timacy, and relative social status of the individuals involved.[2]

Note that the term "uncle" is very slippery and in many societies is
used at some moments in a literal genealogical sense and at others as
a term of affection or deference. The word translated as "cousin" is
often extremely nebulous, meaning everything from friend to a kins-
person of the same generation other than a sibling, to a concept
identical with the European term. All these terminological matters
are time-specific, culture-specific, and context-specific. So too are the
most basic parental terms, especially "father." The meaning of "father" in a matrilineal society often has nothing to do with biology
and sometimes is so immaterial as to go unrecorded. The cultural
universe, and thus the universe of genealogical meaning, is not ho-
mogenous and thus every instance of lineage terminology requires
that we attempt a respectful translation, however imperfect that inevitably will be.

The problematic matter of variant genealogical vocabularies over-
laps with the vexed matter of naming systems. The "English" system
of fixed last names is relatively recent: roughly 500–800 years for

most of the population of England (but not Wales, highland Scotland or Ireland). And for most of Europe it was only within the last two centuries that the bulk of the population adopted fixed surnames. At least, however, personal names and some other identifier (occupational, locations, patronymics) were used even before the adoption of permanent surnames. Consider, though, the problem of tracing lineages in societies that avoided the usage of personal names. For example, among the Lufa of the Loyalty Group, adult women were almost never referred to except as the "Mother of so-and-so," meaning her son. "I have heard of a woman addressed as 'Mother of Xupa' even after her son Xupa had been dead for some years," reported an early twentieth-century observer.[3] That sort of nomenclature has been very common historically in patrilinealities and in bilineal cultures in which male dominance is very tight. A less opaque naming system was practised by the Rossel Islanders of Papua New Guinea in the early twentieth century. They observed bilineal genealogy, whereby the husband was frequently referred to as "the man of" his wife and the wife was called "the woman of" her husband.[4] That was readily charted genealogically. More confusing was the practice of the matrilineal Tlinglit of what is now British Columbia and Alaska. In the second half of the nineteenth century they were observed to give a person three names, applied at different stages of life: first a birth name of a maternal ancestor (potentially confusing that), then in young adulthood a new name, one from the father's family. And then, when a son was born, the man or woman became "the father [or mother] of so-and-so." The rule of successive names was fixed, so that "a highly regarded chief in Sitka who had no son ... was called after his dog, the father of such-and-such a dog."[5]

Still, in chronicling many cultures one has to be grateful to be given access to any personal names and to any clear lineage information. Imagine the difficulty of adjudging the accuracy of a nineteenth- or early twentieth-century Fijian genealogy. Brothers and sisters were prohibited from speaking each other's names. Thus the threat uttered in a blind rage by the daughter of Thakombau, a provincial king: "I will swear the most dreadful of oaths. I will mention the name of my brother."[6] And, we should also be grateful when lineage terms are explicit in meaning. Among the Lifu of the Loyalty Islands women called their own children and their nieces and nephews "my sons and my daughters" and one could only sort out the most basic genealogical facts by inquiring directly if a certain woman had given birth to a specific individual.[7]

As an object lesson in just how stressful accurately interpreting the lineage patterns of non-European societies can be for westerners, one observes C.E. Fox, an early ethnographer of the Solomon Islands, trying in the early twentieth century to figure out the genealogical system of the people of San Cristoval in the eastern Solomons. In this bilineal society (Variable Double), he encountered a complex pattern of adoption. One form was mutual-adoption by which individuals formally exchange names with each other and then become the other person: in the sense of each person taking on all the other person's property rights and also the other's kinship circle, including spouse, while shedding his or her own kin. Another form of adoption occurred when an individual wished to memorialize a member of his own lineage and therefore gave a family name to a young person. In this case it was not a mere remembrance of the name, but an actual ascription to the young person of the previous person's genealogy position and kin network: "A man named Mono wished to remember his own father Sutagera, who had lately died, and bought [note: bought] a boy from twenty miles away. This boy was then called Sutagera and took his status, becoming Waiau's [his adoptive brother's] grandfather, though younger than Waiau. Mono's brother [the adopted boy's new uncle] and Mono himself [his new father] alway called this young boy *Mama* (grandfather) … Later on he married a girl of about his own age, whom he called daughter and Waiau [adoptive sibling of the now-married lad] called mother.[8] Fairly complex: the sort of transaction that would leave nothing but false genealogical trails even if these matters were regularly recorded, which they were not. Moreover, a third form of adoption was practised on San Cristoval: a person, such as a foreigner, could be inducted into the culture by a local person giving him his name and all of the local's kinship references. This happened to the ethnographer Fox twice. First, he was adopted (in the island sense of sharing identity) by a Bauro man. "I was received into his place in the society of the village, called all the people in it by the terms used by him, and was called by the terms they gave him."[9] Later, Fox was adopted by an Amwean man. "I found that not only was I now Amwea, but Amwea people everywhere gave me food as a matter of course, and if I wanted a native bag or limebox they were made for me without any payment being asked."[10]

This level of acceptance made the ethnographer happy, but one detects in his report a degree of uneasiness. One suspects that he is not quite sure that he is not being laughed at: Pacific island societies had a marvelous record of ridiculing contact Europeans, especially missionaries and ethnographers, by teaching them a false vocabulary that often was obscene and included a set of kinship terms that was a parody of the real thing. I think that Fox was hearing the real thing, but one can never be completely sure. In any case, he remained intellectually blocked by encountering fluid lineage identities that moved about independently of biological "facts." Perhaps wisely, he did not try to crack the full genealogical code, but wrote down whatever definitions and mini-diagrams he could acquire and then staggered back home with his notebooks full and his honour satisfied.

As I have argued in the text (chapter 5), it is not at present possible to reduce the grammars of genealogical narrative to fewer than four, and even then there are a few loose ends (notably the ripely confusing matter of group marriages and their resulting progeny). Unhappily, this not a matter of historical complexity that can somehow be resolved by asking modern-day anthropologists to produce a Grand Unified Theory of kinship in the present and then retrospect it into the past: no single system works fully in the present and, *mutatis mutandis*, none will work in engaging the past.

What holds true for the grammar of genealogy – no single system encompasses all humankind – holds virtually logarithmically for the bundles of lineage terminology within the world's myriad cultures. Although we can boil the world's genealogical grammars down to four, I think we would be hard-pressed to reduce the world's systems of lineage vocabulary down to a mere four hundred. I have heard serious Latter-day Saint genealogists suggest that only when the Millennium arrives will the problems of variant genealogical systems and multiple incompatible terminologies be solved.

Perhaps they are right. For the moment, as far as terminology is concerned, a modest goal is that genealogists read widely in the social, cultural, and economic literature regarding any community with which they are dealing. Thus they will be more apt to crack alien (in terms of time and place) sets of genealogical data and they can then translate this information into the vocabulary of the present-day historical profession. At that point, they will cease to be the most under-appreciated members of the community of historians and be recognized for what they should be: foundation practitioners of our craft.

APPENDIX B

Inbreeding and Incest

Initially, we must recognize that all human reproduction is a form of inbreeding. This follows from our being a single species that (assuming historical geneticists to be correct) emerged by genetic divergence rather than by confluence. It was not necessary (or even likely) that the ur-mother of the human species and the ur-father were even acquainted with each other. Each of them is simply the first possessor of the human X or the Y chromosome whose genetic descendants have survived, while other, competing versions have not. How far we must go backwards in time to find the first human male with whom we share a genetic linkage and how far (probably much earlier) the first female, is a matter of continuing debate and the answers will certainly be revised time and time again within the next few years.

Despite this uncertainty, two exercises may illustrate signal aspects of the human in-breeding situation. First, recall here the exercise in chapter one in which we found that, without interbreeding you probably would have over one million ancestors if your family umbrella were traced back to the time of Christopher Columbus. By the time of Yeshua of Nazareth, "6" followed by 23 zeros would be the required number, much more than the population of the earth. That is a useful indication of the complexity of creating a world genealogy as the Church of Latter-day Saints is intending to do. Here, continue to play with zeros, but turn the way of thinking on its head. By what number would one need to multiply our own existence (starting with "Ego") to get back to the two founding personages of our distinct human genetics? Whether the dates are 60,000 years ago or 200,000, the number by which we need to multiply Ego to get back there is 1.0 with a whole line of zeroes to the right of the decimal point and then a final "1." That indicates the degree of inbreeding in the human family, considering just the X and Y chromosomes.[1]

Yet, though inbreeding can produce great variance (some of it highly adaptive) and can also yield hideous heritable characteristics ("defects"), it is impressive how behavioural patterns can limit the genetic volatility of inbreeding in quite small populations. Here, the second exhibit is by way of analogy: to the remarkable behaviour of the Greater Horseshoe Bat, found in England. Genetic researchers have discovered that the male Greater Horseshoe will mate with whatever female will let him, but that the female can say "no," and she does so in a way that encourages inbreeding but at the same time limits the genetic closeness of that inbreeding. Female Greater Horseshoes will mate with their mother's or even their grandmother's partner, but only after those other females have switched partners – and even then they will never mate with their own fathers. This produces some wonderfully complex families – individuals have a life span of about thirty years – such as females who are half-aunts if looked at from the side of maternal genetics, but are sisters if viewed from their father's side.[2] The point is, that even in a small population (as the human race once was), and even with a long lifespan and with fairly frequent couplings, a behavioural pattern can emerge that permits a lot of inbreeding but limits those forms that are most apt to be genetically deleterious.

Humanity has done just that. Of necessity, it has always inbred, but with a certain genteel discretion usually being socially enforced.

One of the things that Everybody Knows is that getting closer than genteel discretion specifies causes great problems. One of the common pieces of wisdom floating about North American genealogical circles is that marriage of first cousins can lead to horrible genetic defects. The exhibits most frequently instanced are the descendants of sects of central European (mostly German) Protestant religious radicals of the sixteenth and seventeenth centuries. They settled in North America under the names of Mennonites, Amish, and (the most inbred of them all) Hutterites. These groups have practised cousin-marriage over long periods of time and are afflicted with a number of diseases that, if not singular, are singularly transparent to diagnosis because the illnesses are concentrated in relatively small populations.[3] A strongly argued counter-current to what Everybody Knows is the view that grants, yes, multi-generational first-cousin marriages within a small population are genetically trouble, but that first-cousin marriage in larger populations (where the same families will not be inbreeding over and over again) is only a small risk factor, and second-cousin marriages are virtually risk free (with certain rare exceptions). Considering how deeply ingrained the first-cousin issue is, one is surprised to learn that the first wide-base study of the issue that meets scientific (and social scientific) standards of evidence was not conducted until after World War II, as part of the assessment of that war's interaction with human medical problems. The population studied was that of Japan which, until roughly the mid-1960s, had one of the highest rates of cousin-marriage in the world. (4–5 percent). And it was found that inbreeding as practised within the Japanese population structure had no statistically significant genetic effects on mortality (the keystone variable).[4] What genetic impacts were detectable did not exceed the variations in mortality occurring randomly in other population groups. Other studies have produced similar results, but the question is very much an open one and the entire issue is much more complex than its simple statement in terms of Mendelian inheritance patterns initially suggests.

When one enters the centuries-long literature on inbreeding, one is discouraged to find that very little intellectual evolution has occurred in the development of a denotative vocabulary. One has to be a word-detective before one can decipher what any given author is talking about. When dealing with degrees of human biological relationships, since Roman times a basic distinction has been drawn in many western societies between *consanguinity*, relationship by descent from a common ancestor and *affinity*, relationship through marriage. (The Roman upper classes had some shaded connotations concerning consanguinity, but they are here irrelevant.) The problem is that the concept of consanguinity has bounced around. Today, it is sometimes used by geneticists and investigators of heritable diseases to mean (a) persons descended from a common ancestor; (b) by some researchers to refer to all biological second cousins or closer relatives; and (c) by others to carry a vague, but undefined, imputation that various human relationships are somewhat too close biologically to be entirely free of worry.

Against this definitional fuzziness has arisen a century-long attempt to develop precise mathematical descriptors of degrees of inbreeding. The most commonly used method is to define a "coefficient of inbreeding" based on some fairly simple assumptions about genetic sharing among relatives. Thus, a parent and child (who are said to share one-half of the same genes) have a coefficient of 0.5. By the same reasoning, siblings are assigned a coefficient of 0.25, grandparents and their grandchildren and also aunts-uncles and their nephews-nieces 0.1250, first cousins 0.0625, second cousins 0.0156, and so on. (A related method, assigning a "coefficient of kinship," works the same way except that it calculates relationships one generation later than does the coefficient of inbreeding.) This numerical approach has a usefulness for large-population studies, for it allows one to generalize with precision about how inbred, say, the Hutterites are when considered as a distinct population. And, at a gross level, analysis of incidence of some genetically-linked problems can be conducted.

But, admirable as the numerical precision seems, its use is limited. At its heart, when used medically is the assumption, accepted for several centuries before genetic theory was in existence, that there was a direct and causal relationship between closeness of family relationships and various medical problems or physical defects. Trouble is, the nice straight-line relationships that the mathematical coefficients use, do not work so well in real life. Apparently, human genetics does not operate like simple arithmetic. As-yet unknown thresholds and combinations of genetic factors break the mathematical mode. Thus, since the mid-nineteenth century, it has been documented that certain defects related to inbreeding are triggered more frequently in second- and third-cousins than in first.[5] (Note that these are specific genetic defects and not the keystone mortality-effect that was mentioned earlier in the large post-World War II Japanese study.)

For family historians to read and interpret appropriately the medical and genetic literature on population groups, an understanding of the coefficient of inbreeding is valuable as background work, but it rarely helps in the evidentiary chase that is genealogical work. Basically, none of the coefficients can be calculated until after the genealogical tracing is completed. So, by definition, one provides genealogical information to the geneticist, but receives no genealogical information in return (medical information, perhaps, but that is a different matter). In the case of any individual family history there is no gain in knowing that first cousins once removed (under European-derived family systems) have a coefficient of inbreeding of 0.0312, when one can obtain that number only after one has determined that the two individuals involved are indeed first cousins once removed.

Ultimately, in the context of the field of family history, the general issue of inbreeding comes down to a single question: given that all human beings are genetically inbred, do we have sufficiently accurate records to define that genealogical matrix?

In most instances, no, but the Mormon data base is improving our odds immensely.

"All societies have incest taboos," is something most first-year anthropology students have in their lecture notes. If, to be probatively cautious, we say "almost all human cultures, both now and in the past, have had taboos, or at least inhibitions on sexual reproduction with primary kin," then we have a sensible statement of what seems to approach a universal law of human societies.[6]

Yet, this universal law turns out not to be constructed of tempered titanium, but of very flexible plastic. The definition of the primary kin who are off-limits to each other has varied hugely as between cultures and also over time within cultures.

Take some historical examples. Brother-sister marriages were frequently practised by ancient Egyptian royalty. In the Middle Kingdom era (beginning c.2000 BCE), the pattern spread to the aristocracy and later to the upper and genteel classes. In the time of Rome's first- and second-century administration of Egypt, household censuses of substantial citizens indicated that at least one-third of the families who had marriagable children contained at least one brother-sister marriage.[7] Undoubtedly the most famous (and, to William Shakespeare, John Dryden and George Bernard Shaw, inspirational) practitioner of sibling marriage was the first-century BCE monarch Cleopatra VII. She was herself the product of eleven preceding generations of incest (by modern European-derived standards) and she married first, one of her younger brothers, Ptolemy XIII and, after his murder, another brother, Ptolemy XIV. None of this diminished what history records as a notably successful extra-marital sex life or the ability to bear children conceived with the various men in her life.

This pattern of permitting (actually, encouraging) brother-sister marriages among the upper reaches of society was also characteristic of some of the ancient Greek city-states and, indeed, after the rise of Alexander of Macedon it became the rule among Greek royalty. After Alexander, two-thirds of the royal marriages in the unified Greek-Macedonian royal family were between full siblings. This only came to a complete close through a Roman law of 212 CE.[8]

Why would any self-defined population group practise such tight inbreeding? The reasons hold not just for brother-sister marriages but for other forms of primary family inbreeding: (1) because the population (however defined, socially, religiously, ethnically) is small; (2) the members of the group desire to prevent themselves from being polluted (in a religious, ethnic, or social-class sense) by outsiders; and also (3) to bond more closely among themselves.

Observing such reproductive strategies may seem repugnant to present-day observers; however, one should reflect that even if these ancient cultures had possessed present-day knowledge of the genetic risks, their own assessment of the risk-benefit ratio might have been that the risk was well worth taking. This must be accepted as a genuine possibility because we have no way of directly knowing what the utility-function was in any ancient culture, and can only infer what it might have been from observing that culture's behavioural patterns.

Where ancient patterns and ancient decisions of risk-benefit most affect modern thought is when one starts thumbing the Hebrew Bible. This Semitic text provides the blueprint for western genealogical narratives, but in its reporting of early events (and some later ones) it is candid and contradicts what later is taken to be "proper, Bible-based behaviour." This occurs because the ukase that any reproductive act is permissible if the group is threatened with biological extinction is clearly exemplified. For instance, take the case of Lot (the nephew of Abraham) and his two daughters. The two women became convinced that their branch of the Chosen People was about to die out, so they took turns getting their father drunk and having intercourse with him. The results were two children, one of whom was the progenitor of the Moabites, the other of the Ammonites, destined to be Israel's neighbours and frequent enemies, but occasional benefactors. The noteworthy point about this origin-myth (it explains where Israel's awkward neighbours came from) is that the tale does not indicate any punishment for the two daughters (and not for Lot, who was drunk at the time). The daughters' actions are reported as not turning out all that well, but are presented as being understandable under what the women believed to be the circumstances (Genesis 19: 30–38).

This tolerance would seem also to cover the case of the patriarch Abraham's marrying his half-sister Sarah: the pair shared a father but had different mothers (Genesis 20:12). However, such relationships had to be consensual. The negative pattern-case in the Hebrew scriptures is that of one of King David's sons, Amnon, who rapes his virgin sister and then has her thrown out of the palace. This so incenses one of her other brothers, Absalom, that he carefully plots and accomplishes the assassination of Amnon. Yet, this despatching of Amnon is a double-bladed knife: for, although Amnon deserved punishment (why did not King David do something? one would like to know), Absalom's slaying of his rapist-brother was held to be reprehensible, rather than an act of justice and Absalom had to flee into the wilderness (2 Samuel 13: 1–39).

Where this rather plastic set of precedents on brother-sister sexual congress becomes deeply unsettling to later readers, both Jewish and Christian, is in one of the later books of the Tanakh, the Song of Solomon, sometimes known as the Song of Songs. How it came to be accepted in both the Jewish and the Christian canons is both a holy mystery and embarrassing to many. The Song is a lovely long licentious poem and good fun to read with a bottle of wine and a nice fire, and therefore has had to be explained away by generation after generation of apologists. Christians have read the book parabolically as being about the relationship of Christ and his church and Jews have interpreted it as being about the relationship of the Chosen People and their God. Fine. But in either case there remains the fascinating point that the original Hebrew text unambiguously uses the word "sister" in many highly charged phrases, such as "how fair is thy love, my sister, my spouse!" (4:10). The Hebrew term is actually tighter than the English translation: It is "sister-of-me" and it is unambiguous. Yet, so embarrassing is the familial picture here implied, that the Jewish Publication Society's recent translation of the Tanakh (1985), consciously theologizes it out of existence, and makes the scripture read "how sweet is your love, my own, my bride!" (4:10). No: it is sister-of-me. For the purposes of our present discussion, it makes no difference whether one decides to read this text as an erotic poem or as a spiritual allegory. In either case, the base-metaphor is that of a man who has a hard-on for his sister. And, whether the author of the text intended it as high-art, bawdy literature or as a theological parable, the fact is that he wrote for an audience that accepted as possible (albeit not necessarily desirable) the occurrence of brother-sister sexual love. The book's becoming canonical in the Hebrew scriptures indicates that the concept of such an incestuous relationship was suitable as a mode of conveying a holy message.

For those who take the genealogical narratives of the Old Testament not just as being scriptures, but as Scripture, other reports of primary-family inbreeding are nearly as unsettling. The genealogical lists in Genesis indicate that Nahor, one of three brothers that included the patriarch Abraham, married his niece, daughter of the third brother, Haran (Genesis 11:27–29). In the genetic converse, we later are told that the woman who bore Moses and Aaron was the product of the union of a woman, Jochebed, and her nephew Amran (Exodus 6:20). That three of the most fundamental figures in the genealogical narrative of the Chosen People (Abraham, Moses and Aaron) are members of families that practised aunt-nephew inbreeding confirms the rule we observed earlier: if necessary, do anything to continue the tribe and to obviate the need for introducing allegedly impure blood lines from outside the group. And this is not a matter of mere antiquarian interest. Certain Orthodox Jewish sects still condone aunt-nephew and uncle-niece marriages. Although this is illegal in almost all parts of the United States, the state of Rhode Island has a special exemption in its incest code that allows Jews to marry within these otherwise-prohibited degrees of consanguinity.[9] (And, to break out of the Jewish-derived tradition for a brief moment, one notes that among Hindus of Southern India, uncle-niece marriages, far from being avoided, are the preferred form of union.)[10]

The imperative of keeping a population intact by limiting the instances when outsiders might enter the tribe explains a practice that to observers in modern western societies seems strange: the requirement in the Hebrew scriptures (and its continuance to the present day by some strict Jewish sects) for Levirite marriages. Like so many matters of biblical law, this involves a bit of nimble legalism. The fundamental ruling text of the Hebrew scriptures prohibits marriage between a man and his sister-in-law (Leviticus 18:16 and 20:21). But then, in seeming contradiction, occurs the case of Onan whose tribal leader, Judah, commanded him to make a child with the wife of his dead brother and to raise the child as the dead brother's son. Onan refused and instead of having full intercourse with the woman, ejaculated on the ground. This "displeased the Lord: wherefore he slew him also" (Genesis 38:10). Apparently Yahweh demanded that men breed with their sisters-in-law in certain circumstances. The Rabbinical way out of this was fairly simple: a man can (indeed, must) have sex with his dead brother's wife only if that marriage was childless. This is a clear and clearly reasonable way of reconciling the conflicting texts and Levirite marriage became compulsory in Judaism and customary under Islam. It remains a discreet practice of minority sects within both those faiths, albeit tempered in most jurisdictions by the existence of secular statutes against bigamy.[11]

Anyone who has read much English history has encountered the at-first puzzling topic of long and vitriolic public debate: the so-called Deceased-Wife's-Sister-Question. It was, in fact, a small intellectual wave that was resonant of the big splash of the promulgation of the Levitical code 1,500 to 2,000 years earlier. Although the Levitical case-law cited above dealt with the circumstances when a man could (indeed, should) marry his sister-in-law on his brother's side, there of course was another sister-in-law in many families: the sister of the man's wife. If a man's wife died, was his (presumably unmarried) sister-in-law fair game? Leviticus 18:14 said "no," and so did the medieval Catholic church and later the Church of England. Yet, although marrying a deceased wife's sister was not acceptable under the ecclesiastical law of the Church of England (nor was the less-common female counterpart, the deceased-husband's-brother's- marriage), the marriage itself was valid under civil law, unless specifically voided by civil action, which it usually was not.

In a very Jane Austen-ish way, this became a mote in the eye of increasingly-evangelical English middling and gentry classes: for it was not uncommon that the only sympathetic female a man knew outside his own wife was her unmarried sister, who among gentlefolk often was a dependent who helped around the house and lived a useful spinsterhood. In many instances, she was the natural source of affection for a recent widower. In a just-pre Victorian statute that was quintessentially Victorian in its prim and inexplicable respectability, Lord Lyndhurst's act of 1835 made such a marriage null and void under civil law.[12] (Incidentally, Lyndhurst, who eventually became Lord Chancellor, had been a radical lawyer in his youth and was the son of the American portrait painter John Singleton Copley.) It took nearly a century of bickering between bishops, law lords, proto-feminists, and political liberals before the Deceased-Wife's-Sister's-Act was repealed in 1907.[13] In a feminist counterpart, the Deceased-Brother's Wife's-Act of 1921 gave parallel civil rights to widows.[14] The Church of England still disapproved, however, but this attitude was increasingly irrelevant to English society in general.

Of all the matters that show incest taboos to be flexible and culturally relative, marriage of "blood" cousins is the most revealing, not least because it tells as much about a specific society's values and mythology as it does about its understanding of biological heredity. (This discussion excludes affineal cousins – that is, cousins-by-marriage – who have rarely been included on tables of prohibited partners.) Discussion of cousin-marriages (especially first-cousin marriage) is a somewhat tense issue for American readers, because, from the mid-nineteenth century onwards, US lawmakers have been more opposed to first-cousin marriages than have been those of any other country in the English-speaking world. This reflects, perhaps, some deep knowledge of hereditary patterns on the part of the US population, or, alternately, some primal fear. Or both. Still, it is perhaps salient that two fairly smart and well-informed individuals each married his first cousin: Charles Darwin and Albert Einstein.

If one goes back to the base text of the Judaeo-Christian tradition, especially to Leviticus chapter 18 wherein the degrees of taboo inbreeding are defined, the prohibitions are simple. Table B.1 indicates what was banned under Levitical rulings.

The nuances and potential ambiguities of these rules were teased out in later Rabbinical interpretations. The key points, however, are first, that (by definition) the determination of affineal relationships that were taboo was solely cultural, not biological. These were sexual relationships that were not genetically threatening but which nevertheless were considered to upset the social order. The related second fact is that cousin-marriages, consanguineal or affineal, were not on the forbidden list.

Take that second observation as implying a crucial question: why would a group that was manifestly very concerned with the regulation of the proper degrees of kinship, permit cousin-marriage – and, indeed, by reducing the various alternatives to cousin-marriage – implicitly encourage it? The answer is a general one and it covers not just

Table B.1
Prohibited marriages according to Leviticus 18

A man was forbidden to marry:	
Consanguineal relations:	*Affineal relations:*
1 Father's sister	1 Father's brother's wife
2 Mother's sister	2 Mother's brother's wife
3 Mother	3 Father's wife [=stepmother]
4 Sister	4 Wife's sister
5 Son's daughter	5 Brother's wife (Levirite exemption)
6 Daughter's daughter	6 Stepdaughter
	7 Son's wife
	8 Stepson's daughter
	9 Stepdaughter's daughter

Note: the only explicit prohibition applicable to a female was the taboo on incest with her father; however, the implied range of prohibited degrees probably was parallel to the male list.

ancient Israel. Cousin-marriages actually are potentially extremely beneficial to a tribe or clan. (We are here talking about "blood-cousins.") Because: (1) the inbreeding that follows from frequent first-cousin marriages produces strong familial and tribal loyalties; (2) cousin-marriages are economically beneficial to a family or clan by reducing the potential number of separate blood lines that are heirs to any given body of property; (3) and in certain sub-sets (such as hereditary priesthoods, like the Cohens), this form of inbreeding helps to keep the sacralized males "unblemished."[15]

Thus, first-cousin marriage became the preferred form of marriage in several Middle Eastern cultures, most of which are now Islamic. (However, cousin-marriage among Jews of Middle Eastern heritage – often called "Oriental Jews" within the Jewish community – is also a positive form of sexual partnership;[16] as it is also for indigenous Christians in the Middle East.)[17] Thus, to take two examples, a 1986 study of about 4,500 patients and staff in Baghdad hospitals showed that 46 percent had married a first or second cousin.[18] A recent study has estimated that between 50 and 60 percent of the marriages within the half-million strong Pakistani-derived community in Great Britain are with first or second cousins.[19] We require more work on populations that intentionally inbreed this way (on the top of the to-be-done list is the crucial case of the Cohens, an hereditary Jewish priesthood that has maintained a specific genetic marker for 3,000 years or more).[20] In their present configuration, most of these cousin-preferring groups are modernized, reasonably sophisticated about the risk and the benefits of inbreeding, and they make a rational choice in doing so. This is not the choice most Europeans – and certainly not most Americans – approve of, but it is not a crazy decision. It fits their world.[21]

When one turns from the basic Semitic rules as found in Leviticus to those of the Christian churches (and, especially for our purposes, those of the main denominations in the English-speaking world), things go all different. The Roman empire in its glory days had no impediments to cousin-marriage, although it had more prohibited decrees of relationships than had the Semitic groups. Still, it was only in the late days of Empire, after Rome officially converted to Christianity, that Theodosius I in 384/385 CE forbade first-cousin marriages. Even then, dispensations were often given; and in 405, first-cousin marriages were again made licit in the eastern portion of the empire.[22] Still, something was going on relating to the western (Roman) version of Christianity: after the empire had well and truly tumbled, one finds the council of Agde (506 CE) prohibiting all first- and second-cousin marriages. As the Catholic church came to replace the old Roman state in regulating marriage (which is to say, in controlling the rules for reproduction), the prohibitions grew continually until in the eleventh century the table of prohibited degrees went all the way out to the seventh degree. The church excluded from marriage, for reasons of being improperly consanguineous, all first, second, and third cousins, aunts, uncles, plus affines running all the way out to husband's-wife-mother-sister, and of course a deceased-wife's sister; The church even invented the new category of "spiritual kin" which meant, for example, that godparents and godchildren, though having neither a biological nor an affineal relationship, could not marry. Also, legal (as opposed to customal) adoption, which had been common under Roman law, became extremely difficult and for all except the very rich virtually impossible.[23]

Why this switch? No single answer suffices, but one has to accept that the Roman church, like any organization, had to use whatever tools came to hand to guarantee its own survival and, later, prosperity. As the Roman empire crumbled, the church shrewdly recognized that acquiring power over family law would further not only its spiritual mission (for example, Christian baptism became the functional replacement for Roman citizenship) but would also further its temporal one of building places of worship and spiritual retreat that glorified the Almighty. Professor Jack Goody has argued convincingly that by eroding the rights of kin (as previously defined under Roman and Semitic law) the church was able to interpose itself in property matters. Thus widows who could not find a suitable husband under the increasingly arcane rules of the church had their property threatened; this led to conspicuous, albeit coerced, charity. Similarly, aristocrats and royalty who now were forced to bow to the church's definition of the legitimacy, or illegitimacy, of their heirship, required either dispensations (expensive) or retroactive corrections of family lineages (even more pricey). Taken together, the Roman church did very well out of the family-law franchise.[24]

The extent of Roman Catholic prohibitions on sexual unions became relevant to what was eventually to become the English-speaking world by virtue of the Protestant Reformation in the peculiar form that it assumed in England. The English Reformation was singularly contorted as between biblical Protestantism and the heritage of apostolic Catholicism. Keen Protestants noted that there was no biblical prohibition on the marriage of cousins, yet Henry VIII's claim to have legally rid himself of his first wife, Catherine of Aragon, was based on her being the widow of Henry's late brother and upon the Henrician claim that she had not been granted a proper dispensation by the Catholic church for her marriage to the English king; hence the marriage was dissoluble. In short, both the civil and the ecclesiastical establishment of England had a large investment in keeping many of the old Catholic standards in place.[25]

As far as English reproductive law was concerned, the practical compromise was a set of incest taboos that, while considerably less fulsome than those of the Roman Catholic church of the same period, was nevertheless markedly more extensive than the biblical template as found in the Book of Leviticus. In 1563, Michael Parker, archbishop of Canterbury (appt. 1559) published a Table of Kindred and Affinity that followed John Calvin's view that marriage is forbidden between any two persons who are related as nearly as any pair mentioned in Leviticus 18; this in contrast to

Martin Luther's interpretation that only those relationships explicitly mentioned in Leviticus were forbidden.[26] From 1603 onwards, the Table of Kindred and Affinity had the status of Anglican canon law and was printed in most editions of the Book of Common Prayer. Expressed in the form of civil law categories (the Prayer Book's list was a bit hard to follow)[27] the forbidden relationships were as detailed in Table B.2.

Given how well articulated the Table of Kindred and Affinity was, it is striking that first- and second-cousins are not mentioned. In a kin-conscious culture this was certainly not an oversight. Manifestly, cousin-marriages were an approved form of union. This Church of England Table acquires its power neither through being biologically logical (it certainly is not) nor in its being as full-blown as it might have been concerning affineal relationships. The Table's power comes from its being a codification of the social consensus of the English people of the time about the boundaries of familial relationships.

During the late nineteenth and the twentieth centuries, the Church of England's Table of Kindred and Affinity was reduced in the number of relationships it proscribed.[28] So too was the number of relationships specified in the civil incest statutes of most states of the USA.[29] Nevertheless, the contrast on cousin-marriages between developments in the United States and England is very strange and leads us back to the main point being instanced here in several ways: that incest has mostly been a social designation rather than a description of a biological relationship.

Here is the litmus item. Although the USA did not have an established church, the definition of prohibited degrees of kinship and affinity followed the Church of England model until the beginning of the American Civil War. No state prohibited the marriage of cousins as incestuous. Then, in 1861, soon after it joined the Union, Kansas became the first state to prohibit such marriages. Of the twelve states that joined the Union between 1860 and 1900, eight introduced laws that defined first-cousin marriage as unacceptable, and four of the states previously in the Union brought in similar statutes.[30] What explains this clear change in the way that cousin-marriages were viewed? The most convincing answer comes from Martin Ottenheimer who asks, in effect, "what, of a potentially relevant causal nature, was occurring in the United States in the last four decades of the nineteenth century?" The answer is as causally robust as it is easy to state: massive immigration of non-English speaking groups. Recall here that cousin-marriage is a very effective strategy for small populations

Table B.2
Prohibited marriages according to the English Book of Common Prayer, 1761

*A man was forbidden
to marry:*

Consanguineal relations:	*Affineal relations:*
1 Grandmother	1 Wife's grandmother
2 Grandfather's wife	2 Father's brother's wife
3 Father's sister	3 Mother's brother's wife
4 Mother's sister	4 Wife's father's sister
5 Mother	5 Wife's mother's sister
6 Daughter	6 Stepmother
7 Sister	7 Wife's mother
8 Son's daughter	8 Wife's daughter [=stepdaughter]
9 Daughter's daughter	9 Son's wife
10 Brother's daughter	10 Wife's sister
11 Sister's daughter	11 Brother's wife
	12 Son's son's wife
	13 Daughter's son's wife
	14 Wife's son's daughter [=stepson's daughter]
	15 Wife's daughter's daughter [=stepdaughter's daughter]
	16 Brother's son's wife
	17 Sister's son's wife.
	18 Wife's brother's daughter
	19 Wife's sister's daughter

Note: The table of forbidden relationships for women was exactly as for men, save that the gender specifications were the mirror opposite (in gender terms) of the male prohibitions.

to keep themselves separate from larger groups. That is exactly why it was necessary to prohibit first-cousin marriages: to promote the more rapid transformation into "real Americans" of all those strange foreigners.[31] (The use of the public school system to break down immigrant language groups was a parallel exercise of the same era.)

Significantly, much of this nationalistic social engineering was clothed in talk of the biological danger of inbreeding and today most Americans are convinced that first-cousin marriage has been scientifically proven to be disastrous. As of the mid-1990s, thirty-one American states forbade first-cousin unions.

If there is significant genetic evidence that the children of first-cousin marriages are at a high degree of risk (admittedly a value-term) then it is hard to explain why at present not a single European country (including England) has a prohibition on cousin-marriage.[32] There well may be good reasons for a society to discourage generation-after-generation of first-cousin inbreeding. Yet only in the USA is first-cousin marriage of all kinds generally regarded as a great genetic risk, the anaconda in the chandelier that terrifies an otherwise remarkably sexually undisciplined population.

———

Family historians and professional genealogists need to approach inbreeding and especially incest with unembarrassed resolve. Inbreeding is a human constant: without it, our species would not exist.

Incest will usually be encountered by lineage historians in two forms and each of them should be highlighted explicitly in notes to whatever the genealogical narrative is being developed. One form consists of reproductive alliances reported in the narrative that may at present be unacceptable, but were quite proper in the past. (For American genealogists, the whole matter of first-cousin marriage is the obvious case.) The second form is sexual partnerships that at present are acceptable (such as marriage with a deceased-wife's sister) but were not approved in most parts of the English-speaking world until the twentieth century. Necessarily, these sorts of matters should be noted, for the societal context of a marriage (especially whether or not it was considered incestuous) is crucial to interpreting the meaning of the social narrative that is a family lineage.

As for the forms of incest that usually (but not universally) have been considered too vile to speak their own name, there are three. None leaves much of a record. "My reading of the situation," reports Robin Fox, one of the twentieth century's leading observers of kinship relations, "is that father-daughter is easily the most common, brother-sister variable but not so common, and mother-son rare or non-existent."[33] Should any of these items appear on the societal record, the family historian has only one path to follow: tell the story clearly.

APPENDIX C

False-Paternity

Launcelot, servant of Shylock in Shakespeare's *The Merchant of Venice*, had a sense of humour that was distinctly seventeenth-century, as well it should have been. He encountered his own nearly blind father who was looking for Shylock's house so that he could find his son. Launcelot decided to have some fun with the old man and told him that Launcelot was dead. Some fun, eh? Much wailing and comedy ensue and then Launcelot confesses who he is. Out of it all, Shakespeare has Launcelot utter a phrase that should haunt all genealogists: "It is a wise father that knows his own child." (Act II, Scene 2.)

If one insists upon understanding genealogical narratives as matters of pedigree (that is, of pure biology), rather than of lineage (socially mediated versions of familial succession that may or may not have anything to do with biology), then shrewd genealogists become highly nervous: even one false link in the genealogical chain renders all previous links invalid. And there is no way of correcting for hidden errors. This is in sharp contrast to research in social and economic history in which there are techniques for detecting and correcting errors in a given data set. Here, take a simple example. There is no doubt that census records frequently contain errors. If you are an economic historian and are doing work on, say, age-profiles and migration to North America, one will find that the nineteenth-century censuses of the British Isles, various European states, of the United States and its territories, and of British North America all are obviously full of errors, for the phenomenon of "age-heaping" is manifest. That is, in any given census, way too many people report their age in a figure that ends in zero – 30, 40, 50, etc. In any normal population the numbers should be nearly (but not quite) equal in each age category – age 30, 31, 32, etc. Because large-sample historical investigations operate on the basis of redundancy in their data base (thus the loss or error in any single piece does not cripple the research project), the economic historian can invoke standard statistical methods of correcting for age-heaping. Once this is done, the historian can use the data with confidence and thus complete the research study. Hence, both self-diagnosis of error and correction have occurred.

Contrast this to the genealogist: he or she simply has no way of knowing what data are lost, much less being able to correct for that loss. For example, the misrepresentation in official records of the English spelling of a European name can render it unrecognizable and thus a genealogical narrative comes to a blind alley. Moreover, it is very hard to guard against the throwing up of the genealogical equivalent of what the medical profession terms "false positives."

For example, the same US and British North American censuses that have lost so many European names through orthographic error have also created a melange of false-positive genealogical links by simplifying European names into a misleading pattern: Smith, Miller, and similar family names are well-known problems, but actually any one of the 100 most common names in North America is trouble. Given that most nineteenth-century censuses are now computer-searchable, if a researcher is following one of the more common names, it is easy to find someone with the "right" family name and a fair approximation of confirmatory details. And the censuses (depending upon the year and the jurisdiction) will often point to country-of-origin. So, swiftly, the descendants of Per Robersson from Sweden become the descendants of Peter Robinson from Ireland and indeed the researcher finds a nicely documented genealogical trail on the far side of the ocean: all biologically and socially false, alas.

The weakest-link vulnerability of any genealogical chain is rather worse than that, however. *Even if* each link is an exact and accurate fit with the various sources of contemporary information, there remains this hideously unsettling spectre: the strong possibility of false-paternity in any genealogical umbrella of more than three or four generations. (I will here concentrate on Standard Double genealogies, but the basic point holds for all forms of genealogical narrative.) False-paternity breaks the bond of genealogical narrative and biological pedigree. This will not upset anyone who understands genealogical narratives as being cultural artifacts, but it hits a nerve with most consumers of genealogy.

Within English and US medical circles, a good deal of literature has been building since about 1950 on *false-paternity* or, if you prefer, *non-paternal births*. This phenomenon can be given a complex technical definition, but the basic meaning of "non-paternal birth" and of "false-paternity" is simple: the situation in which a child is socially identified as being the offspring of a man who is not the biological father. This can occur either intentionally (through the man's being purposively deceived) or accidentally (sometimes a pregnant woman guesses wrongly about which one of her sexual partners is the father of a child). It excludes cases of formal adoption.

If we collect the literature up to the year 2000 or even 2005, we have a useful body of old-fashioned data. It is old-fashioned in the sense that most of the data were derived before the advent of DNA testing. Indeed, we do not as yet have any large-base study of non-paternal births using DNA, despite DNA testing being done routinely in individual cases of disputed paternity since, roughly, the beginning of the twenty-first century.

In the summer of 2005 a research team from Liverpool's John Moores University published a summary of the false-paternity studies that focussed on the public health consequences of the phenomenon.[1] Unfortunately, the study, which was simply a review of the available literature, was couched in a way that was easily misread by newspaper columnists looking for a quick story. What came out in the headlines was that one in twenty-five children was being raised by some poor man who mistakenly thought he was the child's father.[2]

Actually, the real conclusion of the study (which was the equivalent in medical science of an historiographic essay in the field of history: a summary of what everyone had said previously, not an original piece of work) was buried in the article. Twice in the piece, the real conclusion was stated: that there has not been in the English-speaking world (or any place else for that matter) a well-designed, wide-based population survey on false-paternity. *None.* But there have been a lot of small studies that illustrate the likely boundaries of possibility. That is a sensible set of conclusions, but hardly apt to put anyone's name in lights and so the

John Moores University's team presented their review of the existing literature in a way that was news-catching.

This would not be worth our attention except that the matter of false-paternity is central to our adjudging the dangers to genealogical "accuracy" of non-paternal births, at least if accuracy is defined in a strictly biological manner. Follow what the John Moores group did. They first engaged in a very responsible assessment of each item in the literature. Two and sometimes three independent assessments of each item in the literature on non-paternal births were conducted and the specific item was either accepted as creditable or rejected. Then, the accepted body of material was split into two groups: those studies whose data base was cases in which false-paternity was already suspected before data collection began (such as data required for legal cases involving paternity) and those in which the material on false-paternity was generated as a by-product of another procedure (such as prophylactic genetic screening for heritable diseases.) Because of self-selected bias, the selection of data in the former category considerably overstates the prevalence of non-paternal births (in the usual case, there was some social reason, such as marital infidelity, that led to the individual case's being examined); and in the latter category, the data probably slightly under-represented the degree of false-paternity, as individuals who are aware of the possibility of false-paternity being revealed inadvertently in the procedure may refuse to participate). Fine so far – the two categories should not be mixed. And, sound, also, the decision to pay the bulk of attention to the non-adversarially generated data.

Then the whole exercise went spongy. All the research studies that were based on data coming as a by-product of some medical screening for something other than false-paternity were placed in a row, from lowest reported incidence to highest. Then the *median* – the middle point in the row – was presented as an approximation of the most likely correct point of incidence! This was judged to be 3.7 percent of all births, but because the by-product data tended to underestimate false-paternity, this median was rounded up to *4 percent* for presentation purposes. That figure was suggested as a replacement for the *10 percent* incidence that was the minimum level generally accepted as conventional wisdom in medical and genetic teaching in England.[3] It is also the number most frequently taught in US medical schools.[4]

Consider what this method of summarizing the state-of-research means. A simple little study that included two dozen cases was given equal value with a sophisticated one that may have had several hundred datum points. This principle of splitting the difference between studies without regard for the robustness of each is akin to defining Aristotle's Golden Mean as being halfway between right and wrong. Further, astoundingly, the Liverpool John Moores group arranged on the same scale items from widely different socioeconomic groups and widely varying cultural and ethnic configurations and did so without attempts at equilibration. About half the studies were conducted in the United Kingdom and the USA, but the Moores' computer included the Yanomama tribe in Venezuela and newborns in Nuevo Leon, Mexico.

Hence, we must temper the Moores group's self-vaunting epidemiology with modest historiography. Here, we accept as a starting point, one that is in parts equally obvious and crucial, that *there is as yet no creditable broad-base, wide-sample study of non-paternal births.* Then we highlight the more intriguing items of evidence. These indicate (though they do not determine) the boundaries within which a trustworthy study would provide results. The range is quite extraordinary and varies greatly according to social, geographic, and situational factors.

At one extreme, a very early and ingenious study conducted in West Isleworth, a village in southeastern England, by a specialist obstetrician, E.E. Philip, indicated that 30 percent of the children he delivered could not be the offspring of the man who was named as father.[5] Philip analyzed the blood types of 200–300 births and found that at least that proportion were non-paternal births. Actually, however, that was the minimum possibility, because blood testing as it was done at that time understated false-paternity by between 66 percent and 100 percent.[6] A reasonable correction according to medical specialists would be about 50 percent. Now, the problems with this study are obvious, but they do not merit ignoring completely: the data were collected by a practising clinician and not reported in the style now required in the medical literature. The cases for the study all involved girls who were pregnant before marriage or, in the vocabulary of the time, "in trouble." The probability is that the girls were more apt to be socio-economically disadvantaged than was the general population. And in almost all cases these would have been first pregnancies. Those facts are relevant because a convincing number of studies show that the socially disadvantaged are more apt to produce non-paternal children than is the general population.[7] Further, if a US study conducted in Michigan is representative of the US and the UK, a woman's first and her last children are more apt to be non-paternal than are those in the middle of the birth order.[8] In sum, one does not need to throw out the results, but should note that it probably is a very unusual population segment that produces a 50 percent rate of false-paternity.

At the other extreme, a calculation of multi-generational false-paternity by the Oxford geneticist Bryan Sykes came up with a rate of 1.3 percent over the past 700 years for males bearing the surname Sykes.[9] We can take this as nearly the bottom limit of probability. It comes close to the 1.4 percent found in a study of Michigan white people who obtained blood screening for certain fatal pediatric diseases.[10] At this end of the probability spectrum one has the same problem of unrepresentativeness as at the other extreme. In this instance, first, it has to be noted that any group of males which kept the same surname alive and (as in the case of these particular Yorkshire Sykeses) lived in the same area for seven centuries is a very highly selected group indeed. Secondly, the white cohort that comprised the Michigan study may have been a relatively privileged socioeconomic group which, in the medicine-for-cash system of the USA, was able to gain access to what at the time (the late 1950s and early 1960s) was an advanced medical technology. That this well may be the case is shown by a Michigan study conducted among rural white people, as reported in 1984. It found a 10 percent false-paternity rate.[11] (Incidentally, under the blood testing methods of the time, both the 1.4 percent and the 10 percent figures would require doubling to counteract the non-detection rate.)

The fascinating point about the various studies is that they are all different from each other in terms of sampling technique and, in some cases, in methods of determining or inferring false-paternity. Thus, one can arrive at virtually any conclusion, depending upon which study one favours. The seventeen studies used by the Liverpool John Moores University team to yield a 4 percent guesstimate actually followed a template set down by the behavioural ecologists R. Robin Baker and Mark A. Beltis in 1995. Baker and Beltis referenced as reliable nine studies (all of which were done by blood groups), they mixed cultures from around the world, and they then produced a median number for non-paternal births of 9 percent.[12] This has the advantage of being close to the 10 percent/10-plus percent taught in medical school genetics courses, but has no more inherent reliability than does the 4.0 percent of the John Moores project.

Until wide-sample DNA studies are done, the general false-paternity rate in the British Isles and North America from 1950–2005 can be taken to be almost anything the observer intuits it to be. In the examples that follow I will use 5 *percent*, but that is merely for heuristic purposes. It is a convenient figure for calculations, but if the "real" number turns out to be 4 percent or 10 percent, the arguments I make concerning the cumulative impact of false-paternity about genealogical narratives that are construed as biological pedigrees still will stand.[13]

———

Yet, some might say, why should family historians care? The various case studies were produced in the second half of the twentieth century and most genealogical narratives go back considerably farther than that. True, but human biology was the same in 1650 as in 1950. So, refusing to recognize the constant possibility of the false ascription of paternity in recorded lineages is willful blindness and false faith.

In response, someone wishing to cling to the biological accuracy of a long genealogical narrative could argue that the twentieth century was a seedy and promiscuous age and that in earlier eras virtue reigned. This would be found risible by most professional historians, but nevertheless, let us consider it to be a possibility. If we accept that premise, a series of self-cancelling arguments is derived. First, it would follow that there was less non-marital sex in, say, 1650 than in 1950. However, this would be cancelled by the fact that contraceptive knowledge and techniques were more advanced in 1950, so that any given act of "infidelity" would be less apt to produce a non-paternal birth in the latter era. Also, in more recent times, abortion has been more easily and safely available, thus reducing the incidence of modern false-paternity. Secondly, one might claim that the penalties for getting caught (that is, being publicly denounced as a fornicator or adulterer) were so much greater in an earlier age that there was less opportunity for non-marital sex. Again, possibly, but, equally, all the greater-danger argument may mean is that people formerly were more careful not to be spied out. Thirdly, whatever the penalties for being spied out, there was a background danger in earlier societies that made women more willing to commit adultery than one might think: namely, the penalty for being barren was great, often resulting in the annulment of a marriage and a subsequent life of economic and social marginality. Given that female barrenness is frequently the result of male infertility, then in this historical context the sensible course for a barren women was to at least try to conceive with a male other than her husband as sperm source. Fourthly, one might argue that families were much closer in the past, that extended families were common, and that travel outside a small geographic radius was not common. So, does that reduce the incidence of non-paternal births? Or does it merely draw a circle around the group that produces those births? To put it another way, did not the posited closeness of earlier-era families yield a higher rate of inbreeding and of incest than is at present the case? And inbreeding-incest is harder to detect both socially and biologically than is fornication or adultery with a stranger: in these tight-family situations, false-paternity is less apt to be caught by obvious differences from the family norm in size, and in physical appearance, especially skin, eye, and hair colour.

Therefore, the most reasonable conclusion is that there always has been a significant incidence of non-paternal births and there is no compelling reason to believe automatically that in the past the incidence was any less than in the present. With one caveat: this conclusion holds for the genealogical lineage of every family except your own. Hence, we can examine what false-paternity does to genealogical narratives in general without including any specific family in that generality.

The exercise proceeds in steps.

Step One. Making the fairly modest assumption of a *5 percent* false-paternity rate for purposes of illustration, initially we look at the least-damage assessment. For these purposes, we will make the simplifying assumption that only the "Y" line is part of the genealogical narrative and that there is only a single child, a male, in each generation. Thus, we are following the equivalent of the primogeniture line, which in western cultures generally has privileged the eldest male in each family. (Actually, in this illustrative case there is only one male, so he is automatically privileged.) The lineage of the eldest male has usually been the best-recorded.

If there is a 5 percent rate of inaccurate paternal ascription, the relationship of the genealogical lineage (the social narrative of the family) and the pedigree (that is, the biological narrative) is shown in Table C.1. Before starting, recall that, unlike the case in large scale quantitative historical investigations, genealogical "errors" are neither self-diagnosing nor easily correctable. Thus, when a line is broken biologically (that is, when it becomes inaccurate) every item in the biological pedigree that occurs from that point is invalidated, no matter how far and with what verisimilitude the narrative claims to ascend into past generations. All breaks are permanent. Table C.1 provides the percentage in each generation of *in*valid genealogies considered as biological pedigrees. (In case you are a gambler, do not confuse these percentages with the way that your bookie quotes the line on any given event. Bookies quote prices, not probabilities – the probabilities are up to you to figure out before betting. The percentages in Table C.1 and in subsequent tables are calculated on exactly 100 percent of the probability pool, neither more nor less.)[14]

In the illustration in table C.1 (and in the ones that follow) we have a set of predictions of the likelihood that the lineage contains a fatal error. This is not, however, an indication of where the error occurs. It could occur with equal likelihood in any generation, from Ego upwards. However, the collective probability is that (in this example) after Generation 13 the line has already been biologically broken somewhere, even though it may be well papered with documentation. So, if you were to place a bet at even-money, before Generation 14, bet on valid; from Generation 14 onward, bet on invalid. Then wait for the Almighty to determine if you really won the wager – because, remember, this is not a detectable error.

Whether the "real" societal proportion of false-paternal births is 2.5 percent or 10.0 percent or any other number, the curve will be fundamentally the same. That is, the probability of *in*validity will rise continually and will asymptotically approach, but never quite reach, infinity-to-one.

Here we encounter "Catch 22-A" of genealogical narratives. If one wishes to consider these narratives not to be socially constructed lineages but rather biologically-determined pedigrees, then one runs into one segment of the Law of Increasing Rubbish. Table C.1 makes that clear: the longer a genealogy is, the more apt it is to be broken biologically at some point. Of course, the break is not self-diagnosing, and the genealogy still rambles backward in time. Later generational ties may indeed be biologically accurate, but they are accurate for some other lineage than the one whose connection with the past has been severed by an inaccuracy. A

Table c.1
Biological validity of single-child male lineages, assuming a
5% incidence of false-paternity.

Number of generations	Probability that the lineage is invalid, expressed in percentages (rounded to nearest 0.1)
Ego = 1	5.00
2	9.75
3	14.3
4	18.6
5	22.6
6	26.5
7	30.2
8	33.7
9	37.0
10	40.1
11	43.1
12	46.0
13	48.7
14	51.2
15	53.7
16	56.0

short – say, three-generation – genealogy is less apt to be broken biologically by non-paternity than is one of fifteen generations.
Hence, the following ineluctable conclusion: in general, the longer
a genealogical narrative is, the higher the proportion of inaccurate
biological pedigree information it will contain, if the present generation is the reference point. That means not only a larger absolute amount of rubbish but a higher proportion of the data pool as
well. This situation holds even if the paper-proof standards are absolutely perfect. Knowledge of this fact is a good antidote against
being proud of what appears to be a long lineage.

   Step 2. Without being controversial, it is relevant to suggest that everyone has not only a biological father (as in Step 1), but a mother
as well. Since we are dealing with a Standard Double form of genealogical narrative, the female has to be taken into account. Nor is it

controversial to suggest that half the births wherein the father is falsely identified (from a biological point of view) will be those that produce girls. And girls become mothers and mothers become part of everyone's genealogy in the Standard Double system.

Here the effects are obvious. We will still assume that in the male line (the primogeniture line) there is only a single male child per generation. And in the maternal line, the only female we will trace is the mother of Ego. To limit the "damage" (if improved accuracy is such), we will assume that she is the descendent of a long line that only had male children (except for her) and that the 5 percent false-paternity rate holds for her lineage just as it does for the line of Ego's father. Table C.2 provides ratios in the same way as Table C.1.[15]

As in the case of Table C.1, the invalidity line curves towards 100.0 percent *im*probability, but never quite reaches that point. Table C.1, when compared with Table C.2, suggests something that will become even clearer when we reach Table C.3. This is the "Catch 22-B" of genealogical narratives and it is the second segment of the Law of Increasing Rubbish. It posits that the broader a genealogical narrative is – that is, the more it approximates the double-branching character of Standard Double genealogies – the "sooner" (that is, the nearer to Ego) it will likely have a non-detectable biological break somewhere in the lineage. The more information a genealogy contains about a family network, the higher the likelihood of an increase in the absolute amount of rubbish and also the greater the proportion of dreck in the narrative, considered from a biological viewpoint. This holds no matter how professionally the paper research is done.

To illustrate this point further, we turn to *Step 3*. Here we abandon the simplification of Table C.2 where for illustrative purposes it was shown what a 5 percent false-paternity rate would do to any given genealogical portfolio even if Ego had only two genealogical lines. Now, recall how the full genealogical umbrella is shaped in the Standard Double System. (It is found in the schematic in Figure 5.5, p. 106). Rather than concentrating on males, we need to recognize that in each generation there are two genitors. The number of persons in a skeleton genealogy (one that includes only direct forebears and not other relatives) doubles with each generation as the genealogical narrative climbs from Ego upwards. None of that is complex. The simplicity, however, masks the sharply debilitating character of false-paternity (of any

Table C.2
Biological validity of single-child male lineages in one male
and one female line (with ego in common), assuming a 5%
incidence of false-paternity.

Number of generations	Probability that at least one of the two lines in the lineage is invalid, expressed in percentages (rounded to nearest 0.1)
Ego = 1	5.00
2	14.3
3	22.6
4	30.2
5	37.0
6	43.1
7	48.7
8	53.7
9	58.2
10	62.3

level-of-incidence) when it is assessed within its proper perspective – namely, the entire ever-widening genealogical umbrella.

To catch the metastasizing-tumour character of this phenomenon, only a very uncomplicated model is necessary: (1) assume for the purposes of illustration that everyone in a genealogical umbrella has only a mother and a father (forget for a moment that there are brothers and sisters in most families); and (2) apply the 5 percent rate to everyone in each generation.[16] Table C.3 indicates how quickly even the most clearly documented genealogies fall apart as biological statements when they encounter the effects of false-paternity.

This says that no matter how precise and firmly documented the paper trail may be, with a 5 percent non-paternal birth rate a biological error is probable in all genealogies that go past Ego's grandparents. (Where, it must be emphasized, is indeterminate.) If the real false-paternity rate is 10 percent, it will become probable sooner (during, rather than after, the grandparents' generation); if 2.5 percent, later (during the generation of great-great grandparents). But in every case, Ego's genealogy will become biologically false at some stage and that will happen without the researcher of

Table c.3
Biological validity of single-child lineages in Standard Double genealogies
(with Ego in common), assuming a 5% incidence of false-paternity

Number of generations	Number of genealogical lineages	Probability that at least one of the lines in the lineage is invalid, expressed in percentages (rounded to nearest 0.1)
Ego= 1	1	5.00
2	2	14.3
3	4	30.2
4	8	53.7
5	16	79.6

the genealogy knowing either at what generation or through which individual member the biological break occurs. These are non-correctable errors, because (a) they are not self-diagnosing and (b) if the errors were known, they would not be in the lineage in the first place. Hence, eventually, every line in every genealogy is a false pedigree. That is yet another reason why I have been insisting during our several-sided examination of genealogical narratives that they are extremely valuable as social narratives but of peripheral value as statements of precise biological pedigree.

A useful plimsol line for judging the effect of false-paternity upon allegedly biological pedigrees is the classic Latter-day Saint requirement that adherents trace in full their own family lineage back four generations from themselves. If this is done, with only a 5 percent false-paternity rate, there is a 79.6 percent chance that at least one of the lines will be invalid. Even going back to one's great-grandparents yields a 53.7 percent chance of biological invalidity. And that is when only the main line of progenitors is considered.

If the present form of the argument concerning false-paternity needs any further confirmation, acquire one of the standard genealogical forms that has space for the spreading umbrella of Ego's ancestors, and pick up the ancillary sheets as well: the ones where ornaments are hung on the family tree. That is, the sheets that include Ego's siblings, those of his aunts, uncles, first cousins, and so on upwards and outward. These persons are not direct ancestors of Ego, but they become part of the usual family tree. Each of these individual ornaments has a chance of being the product of false-paternity (a 5 percent chance is the illustrative figure we have been using). Their false-paternity does not impact on the main line, but each instance adds a chance of biological error in the genealogy considered as a whole.[17] More information: therefore, more error.

Here, in summary of the effect of false-paternal births upon genealogical narratives when they are considered as biological pedigrees, we switch our metaphor from trees to lumber. Or, more specifically, to wooden constructions.

Among wooden constructions, one of the most compelling set of installations ever made were the Potemkin villages, allegedly created for Catherine the Great by Grigori Aleksandrovich Prince Potemkin. In 1787, Catherine made a regal tour of Ukraine and Crimea and Potemkin ran out of nice places for her to see. As she progressed, he took to adding fake parts to existing villages in the form of arresting details on homes or churches; false fronts were nailed onto decrepit shops, thin roofs of new straw were laid over rotting plaits on peasant cottages. Finally, on some of the river portions of Catherine's journey, he placed entire fake villages – mostly false fronts with a few three-dimensional pieces at the beginning and end of each "Potemkin village," so that everything was comforting, easy on the eye, and just the way the empress had imagined it should look.

Considered as statements of biological pedigree, genealogical narratives are like that. Most of them start out being pretty close to the real thing, but generation-by-generation as one continues up-river in time, they become more and more fake until, finally, almost all of them are no more real than the trompe l'oeil installations that Catherine the Great glimpsed in the distance from her slowly moving state barge.

APPENDIX D

False-Maternity

Although in the text we concluded that any culture that wants to have its genealogical lineages aligned as closely as possible with its biological lines of descent should use *maternal* succession as the primary mode of narrating genealogy, that must not obscure the fact that, indeed, there is such a thing as error in the maternal line. The trouble here is that I have been unable to find any empirical study of even the most minimal degree of competence that deals with this matter. All of the instantiation that I will mention below is purely anecdotal and should not be read as anything more than simply illustrative, a mere shadow of a social phenomenon that is yet to be assayed directly. Moreover, the anecdotal material that comes to hand (I am selecting merely a few pieces for purposes of discussion) is overwhelmingly from cases of false-maternity that have come to light: which is to say cases that, by virtue of their being discovered, are not really instances of true false-maternity: real cases go *un*discovered.

False maternal ascriptions may occur for a number of reasons. Cases of false-maternity for personal gain can occur. For instance, placing an infant into the bed of a woman who desperately needs to produce an heir is not unprecedented. The alleged-case with which the reader is most apt to be familiar is that of the Warming Pan Prince. This stems from the belief that a male infant was smuggled into the bedchamber of Mary of Modena at the end of a fake pregnancy, and that the child was then announced as the heir to King James II of England. Thus, the bairn was destined to become the Old Pretender in more ways than one, or so widespread folk-belief declared. Actually, the situation where well-engineered false-maternity is most apt to occur is in matriarchal cultures. There the need for a female child to carry on the line can be great. Unfortunately, most matriarchal cultures are in Africa or the Pacific islands, and to a lesser degree in First Nations groups in North America. They are not readily permeable for information on this issue.

Then there is a second motive for declarations of false maternity: to improve the lot of the child. The archetypal case comes from the Hebrew scriptures. There the text says that Moses, the founding figure to whom the basic theophany of the Chosen People was vouchsafed on Mount Sinai, did not spend his early years as a young Israelite but as the false-maternally ascribed son of an Egyptian princess. The story of how this came about – "Moses in the Bull-Rushes" (Exodus 2:1–10) – is a beloved tale in all three of the major modern religions that stem from the ancient Yahweh faith. Eventually, the false-maternity is revealed and Moses becomes the leader of the Exodus from Egyptian bondage, the signal metaphorical warranty that the blood Covenant with Yahweh is valid and provides salvation.

One should emphasize at this juncture that false-maternity is ethically neutral: it can be done for selfish or for unselfish reasons. In our own time, the necessity for false-maternity as a form of informal adoption is obvious to any reader of the newspapers: children in epidemics, earthquakes, wars, often are left orphans or with parents who are disabled and no longer able to care for them. The children pass sometimes to the care of relatives, sometimes to strangers, and whether the child is given a new family identity or is taught to maintain its own biological history is decided case-by-case according to local conditions. In a set of parallel situations, it is common to read of persons reared in either rural or urban poverty (more often the latter) in North America or the British Isles who discover in adulthood that their "mother" is actually a kindly aunt or their grandmother. Because false-maternity can be a major inconvenience to genealogists of certain individual lineages, they are apt to shove it aside, rather than face it as a possibility that must be dealt with and to do this for two reasons. One is that "false-maternity" has a pejorative ring. Emphatically, I repeat: it is morally neutral. If it makes dealing with false-maternity any easier, simply think of it as adoption without official records. Of course, whatever the motive, false-maternity produces a result that makes the genealogist's work desperately hard. Secondly, there is always the comforting objection of the lazy: "it did not happen much in the past." Actually, social historians who do intensive micro-histories of small communities over a long stretch of time frequently find instances of an infant moving from one family to another and being given a new lineage as part of that move. (Because such moves are statistically insignificant, they usually go unmentioned in research monographs.) Here, I speak from some experience, having done micro-histories of a parish in Ireland, a township in Ontario, and an island in the West Indies.[1] Indeed, I suspect that false-maternity was actually more common in the English-speaking world in the eighteenth, nineteenth, and early twentieth centuries than it is at present, because only into the twentieth century did most legal jurisdictions work out codes for the formalization and limitation of adoption that applied to the middle and working classes. (Royalty and the aristocracy had legal patterns for adoption set from the early Middle Ages onward.) And with formal rules came records that reduced the incidence of family arrangements that would make later genealogists mistake a maternal social lineage for a maternal biological lineage.

Given that at present there apparently exist no reliable studies of the general incidence of falsely-ascribed maternity in western societies, it is necessary to speculate about where the genealogist should be most alert for the phenomenon. Another way of putting the query is to ask what types of historical communities in western society are most apt to have yielded false-maternal records?

As in so many matters relating to genealogical narratives, most of the answers elicited by these probes are counter-intuitive.

First, I would suggest that false-maternity is most apt to have occurred (and to be extremely hard to detect) in historical communities that were highly "moral." By that, I mean societies that limited sexual relations as strictly as possible. The most transparent case of this is Ireland, from c.1850-c.1970. In those years, Ireland had the lowest rate of "illegitimate" births in the western world and a socio-religious code that punished harshly extra-marital sex. In the era of independence (from 1922 onward), the Irish government made illegal the publication of information on birth control and prevented the distribution of birth control devices. Thus, Ireland was one of two European countries where population reduction was actually achieved (France was the other, but by quite different means) and this would have occurred even without out-migration of many of the country's younger persons.[2] Now, in that situation, for a "girl" (as she was referred to in contemporary usage) to produce a child out-of-wedlock was a disaster. A common response was for the girl to head for England, usually London. There she would have the child and follow one of two paths. One alternative was to wait a decent interval, so that the bairn reached a size and age when its birth date could be fudged; if the girl had acquired a husband, then she could return home and the child would be accepted without scandal. The other choice was for the girl to live in poverty and try to rear the child by herself. With the advent of the British Welfare State, this Pregnant from Ireland problem ("PFI" was a standard social workers' category in the 1950s and '60s) was treated with some compassion and considerable practicality. This is the background of an extraordinarily revealing exchange during Question Time in the Irish parliament. Sean MacEntee, minster for health, confirmed that the London County Council had two officers permanently stationed in Ireland whose sole job was to trace the grandmothers of the "illegitimate" offspring of Irish girls in London and to transfer the children to the grandmother or to other "first-degree relatives."[3] There the story stops, except one realistically can suggest that the way the children were entered in English birth records and the way they were entered in Irish family Bibles was always potentially dissonant. After all, each step in a genealogical narrative provides opportunity for fiction, only some of which will eventually be unravelled by an assiduous later researcher.

Secondly, I suspect that polygamous communities are apt to have a higher incidence of false maternal ascription in their genealogies than are most monogamous communities. In small part this is because the welter of humanity involved in a polygamous society makes it easier to deceive the outside world about who is the biological mother of a child, if that deception should be necessary for some reason (such as the mother's being below the legal age for sexual congress). The more significant reason has to do with memory. It is hard enough for most people to maintain an accurate memory of their ancestors back to, say, their great-grandparents' generation, let alone to do so for a succession of families that had six or seven wives, all bearing children. Obviously, this issue is of considerable concern for historians of the social character of the Latter-day Saints. They face a particular problem because the records kept by polygamous families do not interface very well with governmental records. This holds both during the nineteenth century, when the main Mormon church practised polygamy, and in the twentieth and into the twenty-first century when Mormon fundamentalist break-off sects continue the practice, albeit illegally.

Thirdly, I think that false-maternity has probably been a small, but sharp, distorter of Jewish genealogical narratives at certain eras of crisis. Although the Jewish family system from early medieval times onward has been the Standard Double chronicle of genealogical ascent, it has had (as discussed in chapter 7) a unique secondary characteristic: the Female Licence Principle. This principle states that for a child to be a birth-right Jew, it must have a Jewish mother. This is genealogically and genetically prudent, but it puts individuals in the same bind that occurs in a matrilineal society: it is really important to have the right mother and the motive for false representation is increased. At moments of crisis (of which the Jewish people have had more than their fair share) and in their aftermath, genealogical narratives become garbled (Jewish records are notably fragmentary) and often individuals' assertions of who their mothers were has been accepted as the primary validation of their Jewishness. Fine, but given the sketchiness of Jewish genealogical records, what window is there on the configuration of the potential false-maternity problem? The only one I have encountered is a cloudy one, stemming from the massive migration of former-Soviet Jews to Israel during the 1990s: cloudy, but not opaque. In sketch form, the situation is as follows: (a) in the late 1980s the then-Soviet Union permitted self-defined Jews to emigrate in large numbers. The preferred destination of the emigrants was the USA, but the US blocked that (probably after consultation with Israeli authorities) and by default the overwhelming majority went to Israel. This wave of migration continued after the dissolution of the Soviet Union and continues to the present time; (b) anyone in the world who is halachicly Jewish – either having a Jewish mother or being a convert – has the right to settle in Israel: the so-called Right of Return. Also, under a law passed in 1970 anyone who had a Jewish parent or grandparent (of either gender) was allowed to settle in Israel and to bring along spouse and children. This was an intentional mirror-image of the Nazi law of Jewishness and was a valid piece of cultural self-assertion. However, it opened the door to severe problems in family genealogy, problems that were not taken very seriously until the former-Soviet aliyah began; (c) most of the former-Soviet citizens who claimed to be Jewish had little in the way of formal authentication of their Jewishness. Synagogues were scarce on the ground in the old USSR and had sketchy records; most former-Soviet Jews were ethnically Jewish, but not religiously observant; and the former Soviet state did not keep public records of individual religious affiliation (it was, after all, an officially atheistic state). Therefore, both an opportunity for false representation of Jewish heritage existed and a motive for providing that false representation: getting out of the crumbling Soviet empire and fetching up in a first-world economy; (d) taken as an arbitrary, but historically consistent era, the 1990s provide an intriguing picture. Between 1991 and 2000, approximately 785,00 persons from the former USSR migrated to Israel. According to the Orthodox rabbinate, about 10 percent of those who arrived in the early 1990s were not halachicly Jewish in that they did not have Jewish mothers. (This was permissible under the Grandparent Clause.) However, in the late 1990s the flow from the former USSR (mostly from Russia) was said by Israel's chief rabbi to be 70 percent halachicly non-Jewish. The Interior Ministry's estimates were lower than that, but still over 50 percent; (e) now, one could explain this phenomenon by suggesting that the "good" former-Soviet Jews came in the early 1990s, but that the late 1990s was a period of ethnic (but non-religious) Jewish migration and of outright fakery. There may be some validity in that suggestion, but an additional suggestion melds with it: that once the avidity of the Israel authorities for new immigrants became fully obvious, the former-Soviet migrants no longer bothered with cobbling up a genealogy that included a Jewish mother. They simply declared that they had a vaguely Jewish grandparent and, with a bit of coaching, gave the right answers to the officials of the Jewish Agency which sponsored most aliyah programs. Thus, it is plausible to suggest that the apparent high-halachic rate of the early 1990s was in part because the fakery was more carefully constructed in the early days, before the evidentiary looseness of the Israel authorities became clear; (f) now, why is this strange set of events significant? Because it alerts genealogists of Jewish families to a point easily overlooked (sometimes volitionally): not only must genealogists be aware of the widespread phenomenon of persons burying their own Jewish genealogical narratives during times of persecution, but of the opposite occurrence. False-maternity has been used both to hide Jewishness where it was halachicly present and to create it where in fact it did not exist.[4]

Finally, to keep false-maternity in perspective: as a phenomeon that runs through western cultures, false-maternity is certainly less powerful than is false-paternity as a silent destroyer of biological pedigrees. I would be surprised if the general false-maternity rate in English-speaking countries is more than one-fiftieth of the false-paternity rate. But much more than false-paternity, it is a phenomenon that spikes sharply in certain times of crisis or of social confusion and its affect is apt to be concentrated on quite sharply defined religious, ethnic, or economically vulnerable groups.

Genetics as Genealogical Evidence

Perhaps human geneticists will rescue genealogists from their perpetual confusion of noise with signal. Some day.

At present, the only sure thing about the field of human genetics is that much of whatever is accepted today will be passé in ten years. This is not only because of the spectacularly brilliant nature of some of the discoveries and the large-scale funding that such work attracts, but also because any field that starts from a small base of knowledge grows exponentially in its early years. A big discovery in human genetics can change the intellectual field quickly; in a large knowledge base – such as, say, Roman history – even the biggest discovery will shove thought only a few degrees on the compass one way or another. For our purposes, the modern genetic age can be thought of as beginning in early 2001, when the human genome was first fully read. (More accurately, it should be called the "genomes of humans," for each person's is unique, although the overall arrangement is nearly the same.)

For convenience, think of each human strand of genetic material as a very long novel, one that is included in the genes that comprise your forty-six chromosomes. This novel is written in a language made up of only four letters – and these letters are used about 3,000 million times in the nearly interminable volume. Fortunately, the novel is divided into paragraphs, called "haplotypes." These paragraphs were identified and in 2005 placed into a binder that has an accurate table-of-contents and a standard index: the haplotype map – "Hap Map." Most of the paragraphs do nothing – they are like padding in an airport novel – but even the paragraphs that just lie there on the page are useful for historical purposes: for this horrendously long novel was printed on an old-fashioned cold-type press by a bunch of journeymen and shop stewards who belonged to one of the old English printers' unions. They took endless tea and smoke breaks and as long as the presses did not break down, just kept feeding them more paper and bundling up the final copies and shipping them to someplace they had never heard of. Trouble was, bits of the old lead type broke after a few years and bits and pieces migrated from one spot in the text to another. Sometimes these hiccups produced obvious smudges; other times, letters actually fell from one sheet of lead type and landed in a slot in a second sheet. Once or twice, the printing presses' gears skipped and moved an entire palette of paragraphs into the wrong place in the novel. So, the novel changed over time. Not a lot, but a careful observer could sort out the instances of change. If very intelligent and very lucky, the observer would find the key to the morgue where the older editions of the novel were kept, and then with this information, and with heavy logic, could work out the sequence in which the changes had occurred. Essentially, geneticists have been doing what bibliographers do with variorum editions of ancient texts that have been copied over and over.

In practical terms, three sorts of human geneticists are on call. First, there are those who specialize in short-range matters. These matters involve dealing with two or three successive generations in the usual instance and engage a single family or set of relatives. The obvious instance springs from the whole menu of medical conditions that are hereditary or are influenced sharply by heritable genetic factors. This medical use of genetic histories is not new, but it is newly precise.[1] A less comfortable usage is the now-extremely precise employment of human genetics to determine individual biological heredity. This is a slightly queasy issue, because it is mostly done when non-paternal births are suspected and is usually associated with marital breakdown and messy law suits. However, a secondary market is for families that are deeply obsessive about their own bloodlines. In this brave new millennium, they can begin to keep high-probability proofs of each new generation's biological pedigree. One can imagine royal lines doing this, albeit covertly, and also persons who believe human society started with the *Mayflower* or similar foundation event. Further, assuming

that grandparents are willing to be genetically tested, it is possible
for some families to build their attested genetic bloodline back as
far as the middle of the twentieth century. One hopes that the enthusiasm for family biological pedigrees stops with the living, but
in theory nothing except good taste and legality precludes digging
up the family cemetery. (Incidentally, for the sake of clarity, note
that genetic tests do not prove an affirmative case about parenthood, but rather show that the possibility of random results yield-
ing the same genetic product is so small as to be negligible.)

In sharp contrast to the short-range focus of medical and foren-
sic geneticists, another band takes an extremely long-range perspective and deals with the character and chronology of the
differentiation of human beings from our nearest animal relatives
and then studies the spread and further differentiation, reintegration, migration and, in general, the collective swirl of our human
genetic evolution. The field is necessarily speculative, but strongly
evidence-based.[2]

Between the long- and the short-view human geneticists are found
those that are attempting to relate the long-view information (on, for
example, national and ethnic groups) to individuals. This is immensely entertaining (in the best sense of being an enjoyable intellectual game) and it is naturally of great interest to family historians.
But before looking at how geneticists and genealogists can interact
profitably, it is well to heed a caution or two or three. For instance,
anyone dealing with a DNA search into his or her own background
should be aware (just as in a conventional genealogical search) that
research may turn up things one does not want to know. That is why
British genealogists have lobbied for psychotherapy to be available at
public cost for persons who make unpleasant discoveries while doing
conventional research on their own genealogical narrative.[3] If one
has strong racial or ethnic prejudices, results of a genetic test can be
sharply traumatic if, perhaps, morally improving.

Equally, one does not wish to reify a set of archaic racial concepts
– used to justify racism – by taking race to be a real scientific categorization of fundamental human differences.

The other caution (besides the usual consumer warnings in dealing with service-for-profit consultancies) is that it is easy for two big
sorts of errors to occur in relating genetic and genealogical data in
family history. Obviously, it is possible for family historians to reify
general genetic statements – such as those regarding the relationship

between ethnic groups – and make them apply to specific familial situations. The more worrisome one (because it is rarely considered a
possibility) is that geneticists will misinterpret the social meaning of
their data and will explain to genealogists certain truths that are not
true at all. I will present an example of such a case in a moment.

At present (key phrase, that) the history contained in the human
genetic code that can be related directly to narratives of human life
since human speech (and thus oral records) began and, more help-
fully, since human forms of leaving permanent records (cave paintings and incised monuments and, later, writing) evolved is limited
to only two versions of the long novel, out of the forty-six possibilities provided by the human chromosomes. That there are only two
is surprising. The problem is that the majority of chromosomes,
constituting the forty-four main "nuclear" chromosomes, although
themselves separable into distinctly definable entities, are themselves each the product of the combination in their previous generation of two separate strains of DNA, very similar to each other, but
not identical. And, each of these is the product of a similar recom-
bination of two DNA strands passing on one version of themselves
to the next generation. Even if one could trace each side backwards
in time, by the era of Roman civilization one would have several bil-
lion-trillion cases of ancestors to document (most of them popping
up several times, as genetic lines crossed and re-crossed). Dealing
with this is far beyond the technical ability of geneticists, let along
genealogists. And even this is to avoid the troubling matter that if
we could trace the genetic history of each of these forty-four
strands of nuclear DNA, the results would not be the same for any
two strands of the family tree, since re-combinations and mutations
(polymorphisms) occur independently in each sequence. Each of
the strands of DNA would have a different family tree.

Fortunately, in two strange additional cases things become man-
ageable. Two sources of information, one in the female line and one
in the male, act differently than do the other chromosomes and they
have a potential relationship to documentary sources in human historical records. The first, and at present less useful of the two is an associate of the "X" chromosome; or, more precisely, "mDNA"
or"mtDNa," meaning mitochondrial DNA. It is a specialized piece of
the DNA and associated proteins that in functional form women pass
only to the next generation of women. Mother to daughter. No re-
combination occurs in the genetic replication process, unlike the

case of the main nuclear chromosomes. This mtDNA is shorter (about one-four-thousandth of a "normal" genetic sequence) and it mutates about ten times faster. Those are useful characteristics: no random recombinations involved; simpler to sequence; and more notches on the time-stick of history than for most other parts of the human genetic machinery. Why then is its usage limited? For documentary, rather than genetic reasons: human societies have kept very few long-term records of female-to-female ancestry. And the genetic work is still at such a low level of resolution that one cannot gain anything from a specific mtDNA sample except very general information on ethnic background: useful, but usually not very satisfying.

That admitted, the mtDNA still tells an intriguing story. This has been most popularly presented by Bryan Sykes, professor of genetics in the Institute of Molecular Medicine, Oxford University and founding proprietor of Oxford Ancestors, the sort of entrepreneurial spin-off that university administrators dream about. Between 1991 and 2001, Sykes, using well-preserved ancient Alpine corpses (5,000 or so years old) and modern genetic samples, traced the origin of European mtDNA to seven "ancestral mothers," who were said to be the seven direct maternal ancestors of all modern Europeans, 650 million of them. To each of the seven ancestors, Sykes gave a *sitz-im-leben* fictional (but highly plausible) background, an heuristic personality (he was writing for a popular audience) and sexy names: Ursala, Xenia, Helena, Velda, Tara, Katrine, and Jasmine. The mitDNA analysis was not controversial (albeit certainly open to questions of technical competence like any other scientific procedure). Essentially he drew an MtDNA family tree, using the variorum editions of mtDNA to pinpoint where branchings took place.

According to Sykes, the "oldest" of these ancestral European mothers originated in Greece about 45,000 years ago, the youngest in Syria 10,000 years in the past. Assuming that the science is good, Sykes's family tree provides a narrative of ethnic evolution: these datings are just within the ken of most of our imaginations. He later expanded his analysis worldwide to identify a total of thirty-three "clan-mothers" who were joined in a complex family tree to "mitochondrial Eve," the name that had been accepted since the late 1980s for the first woman to provide genetic roots for present-day *Homo sapiens* and she came from Africa.[4]

This and similar work in long-term genetics interfaces with the emotional needs of everyday people when, for a fee, a sample of

DNA (a cheek swab will do) is sent, along with a cheque for a few hundred dollars, to one of the several services that will track down your mtDNA (both men and women can apply; mtDNA in men just lies around as non-operational gene-junk). From Professor Sykes's service you will receive your miDNA sequence, an indication of which clan-mother(s) you are descended from, a nice set of certificates and, for an extra fee, the gemstone most closely associated with your clan-mother.[5] Sykes states that his service, Oxford Ancestors Ltd. "has become the world's leading provider of DNA-based services for use in personal ancestry research."[6] This and similar services can purvey vague confirmation of old family stories; if the family tale is that your ancestor brought back a Chinese concubine from the Opium Wars, the right bit of mtDNA might indicate that this was plausible. It can provide genetic surprises, non-specific, but still eyebrow-lifting: "pure white" people are frequently amazed at the proportion of African-origin mtDNA they have, and allegedly "pure indigenous peoples" often have a surprisingly large amount of European mtDNA in their genetic make-up. At present (important term) none of these results should be confused with, or even conflated with, genealogical lineages. The error-rate is too high, the degree of specificity too low in the genetic work and, on the genealogical side, it is an extremely rare female line that is long enough and evidentiarily strong enough to push back to even the most recent break-points in the ethno-genetic record.

So, finally, we turn to men. But first a parenthesis that you should feel free to skip.

(For purists, I need here to make the point that even if we had the precise generation-by-generation genetic sequence for a specific woman stretching all the way back to Mitochondrial Eve – something we will never have – even then we would *not* have the genetic history of the human race, or even of half the human race. We would have *only* the history of mtDNA. Each of the other forty-five chromosomes (including Y, the male evidentiary counterpart in the sequencing exercise to mtDNA) would have an entirely different set of ancestors. Recall that earlier we discovered that the DNA of the forty-four main nuclear chromosomes was impossible to unscramble in terms of their family trees at even the grossest level because of their recombinant activities. Through hundreds of generations of randomness, each acquired a different ancestral story. Of course, making this point may seem a bit precious, but purists correctly demand its articulation so as to keep the whole genetic-sequencing business in perspective: necessary because it is an industry that sometimes mistakes itself for a theology. This industry sequences only two genes that relate directly to the way that human culture records its own existence – namely, through cultural characteristics that are a function of the female and the male chromosomes. More practically, the point about the unique history of each strand of DNA is worth making because we need to become accustomed to the fact that the human story told when we look at the Y-chromosome need not intersect with the historical sequence of the mtDNA family tree, except for the modern-day male who provides the sample. It may or it may not intersect earlier, depending on the specific case. But the two sources of historical information may involve ancestors that lived at different times and in different places and "met" only in the present generation.)

The Y-chromosome, the one that determines maleness, is, like mtDNA, somewhat of a freak. Save for a tiny bit (called a pseudoautosomal region at the end of each Y-chromosome that is screened out in tracing historical genetic lineages), the Y-chromosome is not recombinant. That is, Y-chromosomal DNA is passed directly from father to son, on and on, in a form that varies, if at all, only in the tiniest details. The Y-chromosome is the most accessible version of the really long novel that we referred to earlier. Its vices are that it is very long indeed, and thus it was initially technically difficult to unstack its sequence of variation. And Y-genetic lineages are more vulnerable to going extinct, and thus to be lost from the genetic tree, than are mtDNA lineages. This is because (a) some males do a lot more mating than do others and thus block less sexually aggressive genetic lineages from reproducing themselves; and (b) because, while an aggressive male can monopolize any number of females (through keeping their wombs occupied with his genetic material) the females cannot monopolize the males in a similar manner. So, males block out each others' genetic lines much more often than females block each others'. The result is that Y-chromosomal DNA is more vulnerable to lineage extinction than is mtDNA.[7]

These biological drawbacks are more than compensated for by a simple social fact: overwhelmingly, the really long-line genealogical narratives that humanity possesses privilege the male line. Not only through genealogical narratives, but through the preservation of surnames in the male line for the last 800 years or so in European societies and, through the maintenance of clan, tribe, and ethnic borders by the force of male dominance. Thus, a rich array of social markers is avalable. These have the potential of being integrated with information on Y-chromosome lines to produce meta-narratives that encompass both genetics and culturally-determined memory systems.

———

But it is not a foolproof business.

A story follows as an example of the complexity behind an apparently simple instance of the integration of genetic and genealogical information. This tale is intended to illustrate, first, that the melding yields an immense potential for enrichment of knowledge in both information systems, genetic and genealogical. Second, that genealogists, while being extremely respectful of historical geneticists when the scientists are doing their laboratory work, should be wary of geneticists when they begin to make pronouncements on matters of social history: experts often become disoriented when they wander away from home. Third, genealogists should be especially watchful of the way in which denotative terms may be quietly given quite new meanings by historical geneticists. In the example below, the neon matter of the concept of false-paternity will again appear and it will become clear that a minced redefinition of the term in genetic work is not only directly misleading but in this instance masks the existence of the single least-discussed issue in genealogical narratives: in-breeding and its narrowest case, incest.

Here is the story and it involves no straw man, but the prestigious Oxford professor of genetics who was mentioned a moment ago, Bryan Sykes. He has a spark-emitting intellect and possesses the ability to tell a story really well. In the mid-1990s, he ran into a big-time drug company executive, Sir Richard Sykes, and the Oxford professor wondered if perhaps the two men were distant relatives. There was no genealogical paper trail on this matter, but Bryan Sykes set off on an intriguing intellectual journey: to find out not only if he and Sir Richard were related, but whether or not the various Sykeses in England were related to each other in the male line. This he did by obtaining cheek swabs of men with the surname of Sykes (he acquired forty-eight such samples) and also by searching out the family historian of the Sykes family. This dual approach was canny, for most of England's surnames became fixed in the male line quite early – by the thirteenth century in many places – so a decent run of name-preserving males could be compared with Y-chromosome data. When Professor Sykes put together the information from his collection of Sykes Y-chromosome DNA with the best documented information on the origin of the main Sykes family, he found these fascinating conjunctions: that, although they were unacquainted with each other, the genetically related cohort of men bearing the Sykes name pointed to a shared point of origin, that the documentary history of the Sykes family argued for an origin of the name in Yorkshire in the thirteenth century, and that there was even an individual on ancient manorial rolls who, if not the actual genetic founding father, was not far down the line from the founder. Nice detective work, and Sykes told the story, first, in the peer-assessed *American Journal of Human Genetics*[8] and then in a best-selling work of popularization concerning the Y-chromosome, *Adam's Curse: A Future Without Men.*[9]

The danger of this twice-told tale is that its artistic merit (it is a beautifully constructed detective story) will lead family genealogists, keen and hopeful that Sykes's mode of approach will work for his or her own families, to miss the points where the author, like any good story teller, overemphasizes some matters and understates others, not mendaciously, but as a form of art. One of these is the hardly crippling way that the story is framed so that one has the proximate mystery (a gaggle of Englishmen of today who bear the same surname) and the distant solution (in a damp, fog-shrouded parish in Yorkshire) and one has blessed little in between in the way of documented connections. Skilled magic-realist writers often do this: remove the middle ground, and it is something that a lot of family historians would love to be able to do: jump their narrative from today to a long time ago, and quickly. The science here may be good but, as we shall see, the biological and the social stories involving the Sykes line are potentially divergent.

Crucially, Professor Sykes makes a statement that is apt to find its way into the literature on the question of non-paternity as a fundamental "fact." This is the assertion that in the long-running saga of the Sykes Y-chromosome there was only a 1.3 percent false-paternity rate. This rate is extremely low and Sykes says that even it may be an overstatement.[10] The number needs to be dealt with because it is apt to be grabbed by genealogists who wince when they encounter the 10/ 10 percent-plus rate that is used in present-day medical and genetics education, and who recognize what even a rate of half that figure means: that social lineage and biological pedigree quickly separate. "Put it another way," Professor Sykes suggests concerning his 1.3 percent rate, "it means that ninety-nine percent of Mrs Sykeses have been very well behaved, or very lucky, for the last seven hundred years."[11]

Does it indeed?

Actually, only if one misses this point: that Sykes does not in fact compute a false-paternity rate, but rather something quite different. He has a logic tree that works as follows. (1) The Y-chromosomal DNA of half the sample is identical or nearly so. (2) However, although the other half of the sample comes from men who bear the Sykes surname, this half varies greatly and is distinguished solely by having nothing in common with the other half; it is therefore a deviant phenomenon that requires explanation. (3) There is at present no genetic technique that will allow men in this Don't-Know-from-Where category to be identified as to their origin. (4) Nevertheless, instead of labelling this half of the results as an unexplained mystery and focussing on the half for which there is Sykes-signature evidence, Professor Sykes dismisses the possibility (with, I think, some plausibility) that there was any reason for lots of people in England to take up the name "Sykes" autonomously. "Sykes" is not a toponymic. There have been no national heroes named "Sykes" whose name would be widely adopted as homage. And there is an actual thirteenth century figure, Henri del Sike, who held land in the isolated rhinns of Yorkshire. (I have made his argument a bit stronger here than it is in his own formulation.) This means (5) that the Don't-Know-from-Where Sykes in the sample are silently incorporated into the overall gene pool of persons who were originally of Sykes origin and then are declared to be false-paternal deviants from the original genetic line. In other words, they are magically transformed from being men of mysterious and unknown genetic origin who bear the Sykes surname into men who were originally (say in 1300) Sykes whose genes somehow became adulterated, diluted and polluted by non-Sykes Y-chromosomal material. Therefore (6), to explain this deviation from the pure-Sykes norm, this half of the Y-chromosomal sample are declared to be nasty little bastards (well, not in so many words, but the tone is unmistakable). Or, to be polite about it, the Don't-Know-from-Where lot are declared to be the result of non-paternal births among Sykes women and that is announced in the context of Professor Sykes's fulsome praise of his female ancestors' otherwise virtuous behaviour.

The caution signs here concerning too enthusiastically merging genetics and genealogy are manifest, but there is quite a bit more to the problem than these obvious surface flaws. *Even* if one permits Professor Sykes the artistically subtle sleight-of-hand of turning his analysis-resistant data (half of his sample) into a data base for calculating deviation from the Sykeses thirteenth-century genitor's genetic signature, the exercise is *still* invalid and fundamentally erroneous. For Professor Sykes has conflated two incommensurate and incompatible forms of analysis.[12]

Recall here what the concept of false-paternity (or its equivalent term, non-paternal births) means. In simplest terms, it is the circumstance of a man rearing a son or daughter whom he believes is his own biological offspring, but who is not. (Only sons count in Sykes's calculation, but that does not affect his overall results.) False-paternity is a phenomenon that is defined on a generation-by-generation basis. In our own time, that is what all those false-paternity suits are about and what all the false-paternity studies in the medical literature deal with: a tightly specific one-generation failure of genetic transmission, kept veiled by some form of deceit or failure of information transfer. As such, it is a valid concept and has operational practicality, no small virtue. Now, we saw in Appendix C that if one proceeds as a genealogist, and ascends the genealogical narrative generation-by-generation, one can calculate the probability (it is only a probability, not a certainty) of the effect of any rate of false-paternity upon the biological accuracy of a genealogical narrative. Note the method: generation-by-generation tracing. What one cannot validly do, however, is start at any given point, then skip to some place generations downward (twenty-three in Sykes's case) and note that a certain proportion of the children deviate from the original paternal pattern, and then collapse the cause of that deviation into a single percentage. Why? Because in mashing a specifically generation-by-generation concept into an undifferentiated multi-generational lump, one gets the interplay of social narrative and of genetics wrong. Very, very wrong.

Given that one is here presuming to question an Oxford professor of genetics, let us be absolutely clear about what Sykes is asserting. First, and less importantly, he is saying that those persons with the Sykes surname who do not have the Sykes genetic signature are, by virtue of circumstantial argument, to be defined as false-paternal Sykeses. That is questionable, but let the assertion stand: it is this group that provides the 50 percent false-paternity total. Secondly, crucially, the other half – men with the Sykes surname who possess the Sykes chromosomal signature – are therefore defined as being universally the product of true paternity, as defined genetically. This is a very precise statement and the precision of its meaning follows from the employment of the concept of false-paternity (a generation by-generation statement) to implicitly posit that false-paternity is confined only to the Sykes men who bear the Sykes surname but who do not bear the male genetic signature. (Professor Sykes introduces the term "illegitimacy rate" as the major explanatory component of non-paternity; the other component being non-recorded adoptions.)[13]

So, it is now clear that the Sykeses' alleged 1.3 percent non-paternity rate is actually an assertion of the following proposition: that in the "true" portion of the Sykeses line the passage of the Sykeses' Y-chromosome from one generation to the next was always through the known and accurately acknowledged sexual union of a specific male Sykes with a female who then produced a son with the Sykes surname: were the situation any different, the child would be a non-paternal birth and therefore not be in Professor Sykes's true-Sykes category.

Neither society nor genetics works this way. Any number of false-paternal births could be (and probably are) included in the genetic line of males that Professor Sykes exalts as having been born by all those virtuous Sykes wives. Please. Look at the genetics at even the lowest level.

First, and so obvious that one apologizes to the reader, consider the case that could have occurred in the foundation generation, which we will take to be the thirteenth century for the Sykes family. Remember that we have no ancient DNA samples. The body of Henry del Sike has not been preserved as far as we know. So, to take a plausible case, what if one of del Sike's acquaintances from a not-too-distant parish in Lancashire, say one of the Kenyons of the Parish of Winwick (renamed Newchurch Kenyon after the Reformation), got a leg over the otherwise virtuous "Mrs Sikes." The line of descent would be as found in Figure E.1. All the subsequent men (at least those whose mothers had been "virtuous") would carry the Y-chromosome of the Kenyons, a family stretching well back into Norman France and

Figure E.1
Genetic effect of simple false-paternity

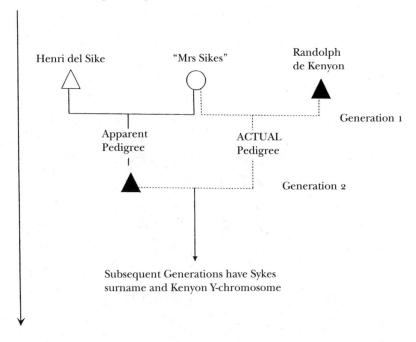

would carry no Y-chromosome of the Sykeses, and yet would bear the Sykes surname. In other words, early in the line, false-paternity is not only undetectable, but it has massive genetic effects.

Much more interesting is a phenomenon that could occur any place in the family line: the matter of self-concealing false-paternity. Say that a Sykes women cheats on her husband with the dextrous Mr. Qwerty. So, a child is born with the Surname Sykes and the Qwerty Y-chromosome. Now in the next generation, this Sykes Jr. marries and his wife cheats on him. If the dalliance is with a Sykes (not necessarily a close one, just one with the genetic line to the family's Y-chromosome) the male child in generation 3 has both the surname of Sykes and the Sykes male chromosome. Yet, the process is that, with three generations involved, there has been 100 percent false-paternal births, while the surname has stayed the same. And, even if we had DNA tests of the Y-chromosome of Generation 1 and Generation 3 (but not of Generation 2; the middle ground is usually missing, remember) the tests would show 100 percent fidelity to the Y-chromosomal transmission of the Sykeses.

Figure E.2
False-paternity and its genetic erasure in the Y-chromosome line

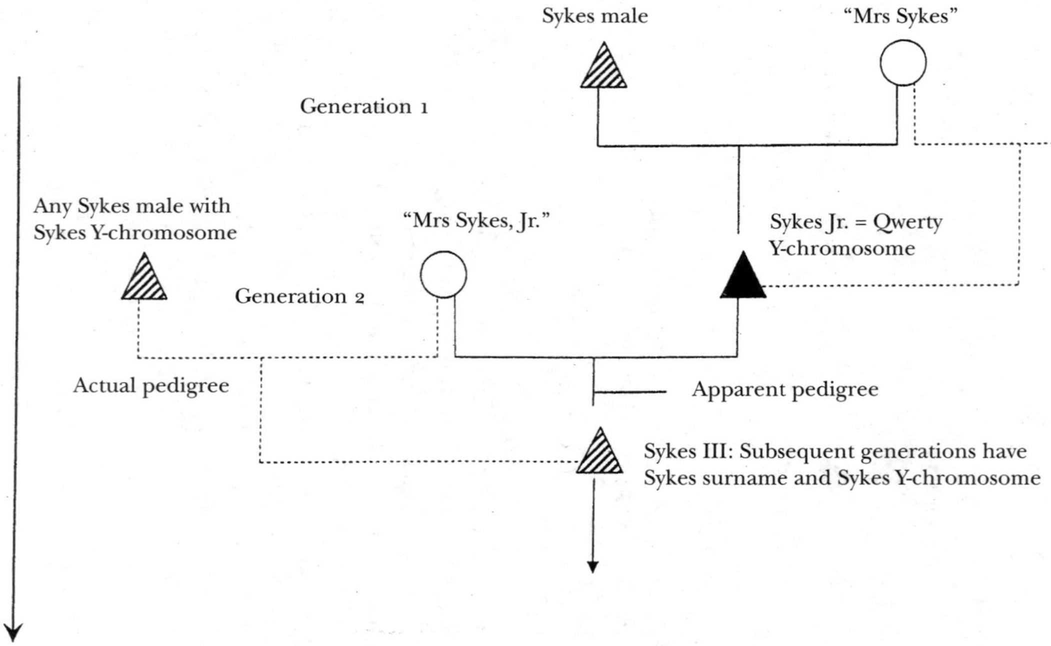

This is illustrated schematically in Figure E.2, and is not as unlikely an occurrence as it may sound. Consider that this family, until the advent of the railway train in the mid-nineteenth century, lived in a world in which most social contacts were limited to a radius of five miles or less and in which the most common social interactions were with people of their own extended family. So this silent, unrecorded, and (to our present-day eyes) undetectable aspect of false-paternity and its erasure from the genetic record (the Y-chromosome line) always was possible. Such an erasure would go undetected even if (in the ideal and rarely achievable case) we had a Y-chromosome sample of the founding father of the genetic pedigree (which almost no family has) and a sample of the present-day bearers of his Y-chromosomal signature. The missing middle ground occurs under even the most ideal circumstances and precludes establishing how much false-paternity was involved in passing the Y-chromosome from the urgenitor to present day descendants. This is yet another way of stating that genetic inheritance and genealogical narratives are not the same thing and should be conflated only rarely and then with the greatest degree of caution.

Those two heuristic examples prepare us to engage what is the real deep-dish problem with Professor Sykes's conceptualization of the relationship of genealogy and genetics as exemplified in the fundamental issue of false-paternity. This is the ubiquitous matter of inbreeding and the often-unmentionable form of inbreeding that is defined in societal terms as incest. For the moment, stay with non-incestuous inbreeding. Here, for the sake of simplicity, accept as fact that in the English-speaking world, first-cousin marriages have at times been socially acceptable, at other times not, and usually they have been frowned on but not considered to be incestuous. (In some other cultures, notably Middle Eastern, they are the preferred form of marriage: on these matters, see Appendix B.) Table E.1 provides an indication of some (only some) of the possible forms of (non-incestuous) extra-marital inbreeding that could occur and would produce non-paternal births; and yet these events in the lineages of the individual men would not be detectable by the analysis of a bundle of samples of Y-chromosome material from the present-day descendants of those men who, generations earlier, had been born via false-paternity. (More specifically: not detected by the form of Y-chromosome DNA analysis of present-day populations that are employed by the various family pedigree services.)

Table E.1
Possible non-incestuous extra-marital relationships that would preserve
the Y-chromosome line through non-paternal births.

Assumptions (1) of a common male ancestor ("Sykes 1") for all male philanderers and cuckolds and (2) that all women in this illustration who bear non-paternal children are married to some other Sykeses: they are all "Mrs Sykes," whatever generation they are in.

Direct male descent	In-married females
Gen. 1. "Sykes 1"	"Mrs Sykes 1"
Gen. 2. "Sykes 2"	"Mrs Sykes 2"
Gen. 3. "Sykes 3"	"Mrs Sykes 3" can have non-detectable non-paternal offspring with "Sykes 3's"
	(1) first cousins
	(2) father's blood uncles
Gen. 4. "Sykes 4"	"Mrs Sykes 4" can have non-detectable non-paternal offspring with "Sykes 4's"
	(1) first cousins
	(2) first cousins once removed
	(3) second cousins
	(4) father's blood uncles
	(5) grandfather's blood uncles
Gen. 5. "Sykes 5"	"Mrs Sykes 5" can have non-detectable non-paternal offspring with "Sykes 5's"
	(1) first cousins
	(2) first cousins once removed
	(3) first cousins twice removed
	(4) second cousins
	(5) second cousins once removed
	(6) third cousins
	(7) father's blood uncles
	(8) grandfather's blood uncles

Actually, the possibilities for far-past false-paternities that are not
detected by collective Y-chromosome analysis of present-day descendants of the earlier non-paternal births are much richer than
the table indicates. In part this is because I have not included the
more distant forms of extended-family sexuality. In larger part,

however, the full richness of possibilities for non-incestuous false-paternal births is understated because the figure identified as "Sykes 1" is meant to be a generationally mobile symbol, not the ur-genitor of the Sykes pedigree. That is, he has a Sykes father, and a grandfather, and a spreading cousinship (and beyond) and in his locale there were men with the Sykes name and the Sykes Y-chromosome who are not even on the chart. A whole back-of-beyond parish could have such people as a major genetic component of the male population. Further, the phenomenon that is caught in Table E.1 is a repeatable one. It could (and I suspect did) occur several times. There was nothing to keep it from being a continuous and rolling social (and, ultimately, genetic) configuration from the fourteenth well into the twentieth century. Without being at all facetious or disrespectful, I would suggest that when various academic and commercial studies come up with a ratio for "fidelity" – a generational percentage of alleged non-paternal births or, to put it in positive form, the incidence of Y-preserving true paternal-births over several generations – they are quite possibly letting social misprision destroy the real meaning of their data. They may be reporting a figure that is (perhaps) an indicator not of marital fidelity but of family inbreeding. If we were to have several dozen studies similar to Professor Sykes's, a range of levels of Y-chromosomal preservation in various lineages could be defined and a pattern discerned. This index-of-inbreeding would be evidentiarily independent of the concepts of false-paternal or non-false-paternal births within a family lineage for, as we have seen, these cannot be completely or reliably detected by retrospective group genetic tests.

(However, I suspect that if these indices could be compared with a real generation-by-generation delineation of false-paternity, we would discover that the ratio of inbreeding and the ratio of false-paternity actually would vary inversely with each other. Or, to put it bluntly, a high level of Y-chromosome preservation in any genealogical lineage may simply suggest that the members of the extended family screwed around with each other rather than with outsiders. That, however, is necessarily speculative.)

This brings us to the incendiary matter of incest. It is a volatile matter for family historians because it is emotionally fraught and is something most of them do not wish to think about. And it is finally and fatally explosive to the employment of present-day genetic signatures in Y-chromosome transmission within a family lineage as an indicator of marital fidelity several generations in the past. For: the conclusion we inferred from Table E.1 is made exponentially, if painfully, more clear when we deal with the potentiality for the form of inbreeding societally-denominated as incest. The table shows most (but not the most outré) forms of incest that might be committed in a family lineage and which would leave no variation in the Y-chromosome signature and thus would not be detectable by the collection of Y-chromosome samples several generations later. Table E.2 provides examples of the potentialities abounding in the middle of any long male-defined genealogy. That is: at any place but the very beginning when the line was narrow and in the present day when individualized genetic testing using non-Y markers could detect incest. We will instance the situation of "Mr and Mrs. Sykes 5," with the understanding that the possibilities shown here actually held for a dozen-and-a-half more generations in the Sykes lineage and for hundreds of families in that lineage.

Because incest is a genealogical and genetic matter that is unpleasant for many readers to deal with, I have walled a fuller discussion off the subject; it is found in Appendix B.

Nevertheless, the conclusion deriving from our short conspectus of the matters of both non-incestuous and incestuous paths of nonpaternal birth is inescapable: that an assemblage of samples of Y-chromosome material from present day males of a specific lineage can never result in the confirmation that the genetic pedigree is the same as the social lineage that forms the documented genealogical narrative of the family involved (and this no matter how high the documentary standard of the paper genealogy). This is because, as we have seen, the Y-chromosomal signature of the family can have been preserved by three methods: (1) by passage through licit and socially sanctioned and well-recorded marriage relationships; (2) by non-incestuous adulterous relationships between the wife and any of the descendants of the male genitor of the family, from first cousins outward; and (3) by incestuous relationships between the wife and any of the several members of her nuclear and extended family who were descendants of the male genitor of the family. Methods "2" and "3" are rarely recorded in family genealogies and are not detectable by the existing method of using Y-chromosome signatures as assembled from present-day males. Perhaps this evidentiary indeterminancy will be reduced by fast-advancing genetic technologies, but it is unlikely ever to be totally erased.

Table E.2
Possible incestuous extra-marital relationships that would preserve
the Y-chromosome through non-paternal births.

"Sykes 5"

"Mrs Sykes 5" can have non-detectable non-paternal offspring
with "Sykes 5's"

(1) grandfather

(2) father

(3) father's brothers

(brothers paternal uncles)

(4) brothers

(5) sons (by a previous or a subsequent marriage)

(6) grandsons (via a previous or a subsequent marriage)

And also can have non-detectable non-paternal offspring with
"Mr and Mrs Sykes 5's" own

(1) sons

(2) grandsons

(3) nephews on paternal side

(4) grand-nephews on paternal side

All of which brings us once again to the message that has been argued from several perspectives in earlier chapters and appendices:
that genealogical lineages and biological pedigrees can never be
equated with each other. They can be related to each other in some
cases, but only tentatively, gently, and certainly not by *force majeure*.[14]

Here, Miguel de Cervantes, writing in the early seventeenth century, serves us well:

Sancho, I want you to know there are two kinds
of lineage in the world: those of persons who trace
and derive their ancestry from kings and princes
of the sort that time has gradually undone. In the end,
they end-up in a point, thusly: a pyramid turned upside
down. Others have their origin in low-born ancestors,
but they have risen by degrees until they have become great
lords. The difference between them is that some were and
are no longer – and others that once were, now are not.[15]

Don Quixote may have been at times quixotic, but as a genealogist, he was no fool.

Notes

CHAPTER ONE

1 Bryan Sykes, *The Seven Daughters of Eve* (New York: W.W. Norton, 2001), 191.
2 Carl Haub, "How Many People Have Ever Lived on Earth?" *Population Today* (February 1995), archived electronically as http://members. bellatlantic.net/bjmcg/story2peoplelived ... 24/03/05; Glen Paige, "How many people have ever lived? Keyfitz's calculation updated (done June 18, 1999)." http://www.math.hawaiiedu/ramsey/ People.html ... 24/03/05.
3 Based on Alex Shoumatoff, *The Mountain of Names. A History of the Human Family* (New York: Simon and Shuster, 1985), 252. Shoumatoff, who gathered his information in the early 1980s, found that the Mormons had one-and-a-half billion names collected in their archives in Salt Lake City. These were in a variety of forms – microfilm and paper, mostly. My own observation of LDS activities in the 1990s and 2000s is that they have acquired at least half a billion more names since then.

Here a word about Shoumatoff's book. It is a fine piece of writing and, in places where I can check it, accurate. The problem, however, is that the author provides no direct citations for any specific quotation or statement of fact, so one has to take a good deal on faith. That said, the book began as a long article for the *New Yorker* in the era when that magazine was known for its fiercely accurate fact-checking, so one's leap-of-faith is not all that big.
4 The exact number of vetted names is a constantly-increasing figure. In 2004, there were 800 million names available to researchers and the

number was growing at about 50 million a year. Donna Potter Phillips, "The IGI, Friend or Foe?" *Family Chronicle* (March-April 2004), 29–31.

5 See Haub and Paige, cited above, note 2.

6 The lines of descent in the diagram are schematic. The actual number of lines equals the numbers of human beings alive today, plus all those included in any line that has gone extinct.

7 The lines of genealogical ascent are schematic. The actual number will vary for each person whose lineage is being traced. Many lines will end before the horizon line. I am grateful to Dr Roger Martin for designing the schematics for this study.

8 The diagram is schematic. In reality, the diamond will not be symmetrical. Also, its edges will not be smooth. And both the lineage collapse and the end of human knowledge of each line will occur irregularly.

9 See both items, note 2, supra. The historical demographers are careful to make clear that their guesstimates are at best "semi-scientific," so any inferences we draw from them are even less provable. Their exercise is useful, however, both heuristically and for voiding certain "common knowledge" myths – such as the idea that most of the people who ever lived are alive today.

CHAPTER TWO

1 James B. Allen and Glen B. Leonard, *The Story of the Latter-day Saints* (Salt Lake City: Deseret Book Co., 1976), 47. This volume is an official history and within that genre is admirable. It recognizes controversial matters without becoming enmeshed in church apologetics. For an introductory history by Mormon believers, see Claudia L. Bushman and Richard L. Bushman, *Building the Kingdom. A History of Mormons in America* (New York: Oxford University Press, 1999).

2 Keen observers of the public presentation of the LDS in the last decade will note (for example, on signs outside church buildings) that there is a concerted effort at "Christianizing" the church's name. That is, the local signboards now say in relatively large letters, "Church of Jesus Christ" and relegate the Latter-day Saints' denominator to small print. This is part of a larger process which some Mormon observers describe as the "Protestantization" of their church's public image.

3 James E. Talmage, *A Study of the Articles of Faith. Being a Consideration of the Principal Doctrines of Jesus Christ of Latter-day Saints* (Salt Lake City: Church of Jesus Christ of Latter-day Saints, 49th edition, 1968), 7. This authoritative commentary was first published in 1899 and has not been

out of print since that time. It has almost – but not quite – acquired the status of a Mormon Standard Work. Talmage, among Mormons, has a status equivalent to Augustine or Maimonides in, respectively, Roman Catholic and Jewish theology.

4 Fawn Brodie, *No Man Knows My History. The Life of Joseph Smith, the Mormon Prophet* (New York: Alfred Knopf, 1963), 24n. Orig. ed., 1945. (A slightly amended edition was published in 1971, but the changes were so minor as to leave the original pagination unchanged.) Brodie's study is still the best biography of Smith, not least because it engages a central issue that bothers many Mormons: namely, how can a set of texts that have a demonstrably fictional origin nevertheless contain material that has immensely convincing spiritual power? Written in an era when the LDS authorities were less confident of their position within the Christian world generally and American society particularly than they are today, Brodie's book resulted in her excommunication from the LDS church.

A large corpus of apologetic historical writing exists within the Mormon world and most of it resembles in character the way that the history of Christianity in the Roman world was written before Edward Gibbon's *The Decline and Fall of the Roman Empire* (1776–88). The *ne plus ultra* of Mormon apologetics history is a fine work of art, if not of professional scholarship: Richard L. Bushman ("with the assistance of Jed Woodworth"), *Joseph Smith. Rough Stone Rolling* (New York: Alfred A. Knopf, 2005). It incorporates his earlier work, *Joseph Smith and the Beginnings of Mormonism* (Chicago and Urbana: University of Illinois Press, 1984), and greatly expands upon it. [Hereafter, when Bushman is cited, it is the 2005 volume that is being referenced.] Bushman is a fine historian when dealing with "secular" (i.e., non-Mormon) topics, but as a devout Mormon he cannot find a stone that does not fit into the Mormon mosaic or an interpretation that does not square with LDS theology or origin-mythology. Despite his intellectual antinomianism concerning Mormon history, his compiling of factual data is extremely useful; and he tells a story very well indeed.

5 Salt Lake City: Deseret Book Co.,1909–12, edited by B.H. Roberts. Revised edition, Salt Lake City: Deseret Book Co., 1971.

6 This is the *desideratum* of the distinguished historian of Mormonism, Klaus Hansen. See his *Mormonism and the American Experience* (Chicago: University of Chicago Press, 1981), 246. The project is now said by LDS authorities to be "in progress."

7 The articles are to be found at the conclusion of The Pearl of Great Price. They are grouped with items whose documented provenance is

1842, but the Articles of Faith could have been circulated earlier and in variant forms. They are also to be found attached to the famous "Wentworth Letter" of 1 March 1842 which the Prophet wrote to John Wentworth, a Chicago newspaper editor. The letter and the Articles of Faith are found in Smith's History of the Church, vol 4, 535–41.

8 Because we are dealing in the text with only the four foundational Mormon scriptures, reference is not made to Joseph Smith's most hubristic work, namely his new "translation and correction" of the entire Old and New Testaments. This was begun in early 1830, but was not published until 1867 under the title *The Holy Scriptures, Translated and Corrected by the Spirit of Revelation, by Joseph Smith, Jr, the Seer* (published by the LDS Church). It was subsequently reprinted several times and the transcription of the full original manuscript is now available. See Scott H. Faulring, Kent P. Jackson, and Robert J. Mathews (eds.), *Joseph Smith's New Translation of the Bible: Original Manuscripts* (Provo: Religious Studies Center, Brigham Young University, 2004). Whole chapters were added to the Bible and other material cut out. Nevertheless, the devout present-day editors are able to claim that the Prophet's work was a translation in the scholarly sense, although the numerous additions did not involve any renderings from Greek or Hebrew manuscripts. For a discerning commentary, see the review essay on the latest version, published by H. Michael Marqurdt in *Journal of Mormon History*, 32 (Fall 2005), 278–81.

9 Allen and Leonard, 46–7.

10 Harold Bloom, *The American Religion. The Emergence of the Post-Christian Nation* (New York: Simon and Schuster, 1992), 84. LDS scholars have had a love-hate relationship with Bloom's appreciation of Mormonism, but mostly the latter. On the one hand, those who are more adept at worldly scholarship (such as Richard Bushman in his 2005 biography of the Prophet), have preened at Mormonism's being taken seriously by one of the English-speaking world's most influential cultural observers. Most, however, have been defensive and somewhat offended at Bloom's daring to claim an understanding of any part of Mormonism. For an example, in no way extreme, see Alan Goff, "Reduction and Enlargement: Harold Bloom's Mormons," *FARMS* (1993), 96–108.

11 The reader who wishes to examine in detail the matter I have so briefly summarized above should read my *Surpassing Wonder: The Invention of the Bible and the Talmuds* (Montreal & Kingston: McGill-Queen's University Press, 1998, New York: Harcourt Brace, 1998, and Chicago: University of Chicago Press, 2001). Harold Bloom, in a recent

gem, *Jesus and Yahweh: The Names Divine* (New York: Riverhead-
Penguin, 2005), 44, disagrees with my appreciation of the structural
and aesthetic virtues of the New Testament (as argued in *Surpassing
Wonder,* 244–69).

12 The author of the Book of Mormon found the "Old Testament" prophets a special comfort when he needed material. Compare, for example, 2
Nephi: 27:2 with Isaiah 29:6 and 3 Nephi 24 with Malachi 3. There are
several other instances. More textually interesting is the Prophet's having the Risen Christ visit the Nephites and deliver to them the Beati-
tudes. Compare 3 Nephi 12:3ff and the Gospel of Matthew 5:3ff. The
other material placed in Christ's voice in 3 Nephi is mostly a conflation
of bits and pieces from the Gospels, with some additions from the Epistles of St. Paul and from the Book of Revelation. Brodie (58) states that
about 25,000 words from the "Old Testament" and 2,000 from the
"New" are found in the Book of Mormon. She means in large chunks,
not simply in fugitive phrasing.

13 See K.H. Connell, "Ether-drinking in Ulster," in *"Irish Peasant Society.
Four Historical Essays* (Oxford: Clarendon Press, 1968), esp. 87–9.

14 As, for example, Mark Twain's "Chloroform in Print."

15 Doctrine and Covenants, sect. 32.

16 Hansen, 182.

17 Leonard J. Arrington and Davis Bitton, *The Mormon Experience: A History
of the Latter-day Saints* (Chicago: University of Illinois Press, second ed.,
1992), chapter 8, "Mormons and Native Americans," 145–60.

18 Brodie, 20.

19 Ibid, 21.

20 When Fawn Brodie in 1945 published a synopsis of the Joseph Smith
fraud trial, the LDS authorities were apoplectic. Her material came
from court records of Bainbridge, Chenango County, New York, as
published in the *New Schaff-Herzog Encyclopedia of Religious Knowledge*
(New York, 1883), vol. 2, 1576. The church authorities, 11 May 1946,
denounced the whole business as a fabrication that had never been
part of any court record. In subsequent editions of her biography,
Brodie produced confirmatory evidence. (See 1963 edition, 405–18
for the whole argument.) However, more importantly, in 1971 a researcher found in the basement of the Chenango County jail a bundle
of documents ancillary to the Smith case that included the Justice of
the Peace's charges of $2.68 for dealing with the case. See David
Persuitte, *Joseph Smith and the Origins of the Book of Mormon* (Jefferson,
N.C., sec. ed., 2000), 48–52. Bushman, (51–2, 575*n*91) passes quickly

over the trial and avoids mentioning the conviction. Other recent Mormon historians have dealt with Smith's peer-stoning by attempting to integrate the existence of a magical world-view in the world of Joseph Smith, Jr. with the foundation of Mormon theology and institutions. See Roger D. Launius, "From Old to New Mormon History. Fawn Brodie and the Legacy of Scholarly Analysis of Mormonism," in Newell G. Bringhurst (ed.), *Reconsidering "No Man Knows My History." Fawn M. Brodie and Joseph Smith in Retrospect* (Logan: Utah State University Press, 1996), 195–233.

21 The Spaulding theory began not long after the Book of Mormon was published. Its early twentieth-century formulations and its rebuttal are found in A. Theodore Shroeder, "Origins of the Book of Mormon," *American Historical Magazine*, 1 and 2 (1906–07), with effective rebuttal (1908–09) by B.H. Roberts. The late twentieth-century's best efforts at promoting the Spaulding theory are by Howard A. Davis, Donald R. Scales, and Wayne L. Cowdrey, *Who Really Wrote the Book of Mormon?* (Santa Ana, Cal: Vision House, 1977). It is not a lunatic argument, but its just-barely plausible case hangs on six holograph pages of the original Book of Mormon that handwriting experts adjudge may – or may not – be in the hand of the Rev. Mr. Spaulding and not in the handwriting of the various scribes whom Joseph Smith eventually engaged.

Incidentally, the everyday reader of historical books and journals will find that when one encounters what passes for historical argument among Mormon officials and their opponents, one is entering a netherworld of gargoyles and dragons: that is, of virtual paranoia on the part of LDS church authorities and of intricate conspiracy theories on the part of their critics. There are some very fine, albeit very few, professional historians who deal with Mormon history from within the LDS and at an evidentiary level demanded by the historical profession. On the other hand, if one wishes to observe just how crazy the non-professionals can be, note the church's desperate reaction to the 1983 forgery by Mark Hoffman of a letter that claimed to show that Joseph Smith learned of the golden plates from an encounter with a white salamander. See Robert Lindsey, *A Gathering of Saints* (New York: Simon and Shuster, 1988); Linda Sillitoe and Allen Roberts, *Salamander: The Story of the Mormon Forgery Murders* (New York: Signature Books, sec. ed., 1989); Steven Naifeh and Gregory Smith, *The Mormon Murders* (London: Weidenfeld and Nicolson, 1988).

22 Brodie reported in 1945 that B.H. Roberts, who was one of the LDS church's most trusted internal historians of the late nineteenth and

early twentieth centuries, compiled a list of parallels between *Views of the Hebrews* and the Book of Mormon. This the church did not permit to be published, but it was circulated privately (Brodie, 47*n*). The best case for the Prophet's dependance on Ethan Smith's work is David Persuitte's book (see above, note 20). Even if it does not show the compelling line-by-line textual lifts, or even close paraphrases that true plagiarism involves, Persuitte's case for structural similarity in certain sections is strong; but whether they are causal (that is, stolen) or coincidental is not, in my judgment, probatively determined in most instances. However, it is more than accidental that Ethan Smith had his book effectively start with the discovery of copper breastplates in an Indian mound and that these had buttons attached to each of them which were "in resemblance of the Urim and Thummim." (Brodie, 47.)

23 Arrington and Bitton, 13.

24 Photographs are found in Brodie, 50 and in Persuitte, 73.

25 Arrington and Bitton, 13; Bushman, 66.

26 Brodie, 54, quoting the biography of Lucy Smith. There is no opposition in LDS sources to the basic story (see, for example. Arrington and Bitton, 13), although Mrs Harris is usually presented as a harpy, not a long-suffering wife who was thoroughly sick of seeing her husband lose the housekeeping money. See also, Bushman, 66–8.

27 Brodie, 62–3. Bushman, 72–4, 590*n*24, re Smith's acquiring a new "translation stone" after he lost the Urim and Thummim.

28 "Memorandum made by John H. Gilbert, Esq.," quoted in Persuitte, 95; Bushman, 90, 581*n*88.

29 Joseph Smith, History of the Church, vol 1, 286. The influence of Smith's followers in England is a continuing minor theme in the history of Mormonism. They centred on Lancashire, especially Liverpool, which was the hub of the British Empire's migrant trade. Not only did 11,000 converts migrate from England to U.S. Mormon sites in 1848, but those who stayed in England provided something of an intellectual elite that was useful in helping to edit the various Mormon scriptures into textual forms that were more acceptable to Victorian literary standards. Interestingly, it was the early Mormons of Upper Canada who were the first to promote a mission to the British, and Upper Canadians provided four of the seven original missionaries whose work began in 1834. For a valuable discussion of Canadian Mormon development, see Brigham Young Card, "Mormons," in Paul R. Magosci (ed.), *Encyclopedia of Canada's Peoples* (Toronto: University of Toronto Press, 1999), 979–97; and

Brigham Young Card (ed.), *The Mormon Presence in Canada* (Edmonton: University of Alberta Press, 1990).

30 Persuitte, 86.

31 Smith had applied for a personal copyright and asserted authorship in New York State court, 11 June 1829 (Bushman, 80). The title page of the book as it eventually appeared in 1830 is found in the photograph section of Bushman's study, 231d.

32 The paradigms that underlie the Hebrew scriptures' grammar of biblical invention are discussed in detail in my *Surpassing Wonder.* See esp. 51ff.

33 This 1830 denial is printed in full in Brodie, 56. It was published in expanded and biblicalized form later as section 10 of The Doctrine and Covenants.

34 Joseph Smith, History of the Church, vol. 4, 461.

35 B of M, 2 Nephi 3:15.

36 Like all Smith's writing, the material in The Pearl of Great Price was cleaned up by later LDS editors. The most important portions of this work – straightening out the spelling, grammar, and punctuation – were done silently. Smith's original manuscripts were (like the Book of Mormon) a run-on affair. In this case, the church records that in 1902 the material in The Pearl of Great Price was divided into chapters and verses (with footnotes to related texts added) and that the book was double-columned and indexed in 1921. Thus, like the Book of Mormon, it came to visually resemble the Bible.

37 Brodie, 96. Bushman, 134–42. See Smith, History of the Church, vol. 1, 133ff for extracts that confirm this.

38 Even the most enthusiastic of LDS commentators are at a loss to justify Joseph Smith's belief that a lost book called the "Prophecy of Enoch" was referred to in the Book of Jude in the Christian scriptures. (See Smith, History of the Church, vol. 1, 132.) What the author of Jude says (1:14) is merely that Enoch prophesied. Rather than admit that Joseph Smith had misread a biblical text, B.H. Roberts, who annotated Smith's History of the Church, was reduced to the vacuous query, "May not the prophecy of Enoch have been among the scriptures with which Abraham was acquainted?"

39 I am taking the Book of Enoch as running from Smith's Book of Moses 6:12 to 8:1, inclusive. Thereafter, what I think was the original form of the Book of Moses resumes. There is no sense in having a textual war about a few verses one way or another, but what I am saying is that when the Book of Enoch was interpolated by LDS authorities into the

Book of Moses sometime between 1844 and 1851, the interpolation most probably occurred after verse 6:11 and ended after 8:1. My estimate means that the Book of Enoch in Joseph Smith's original form ran to 114 verses. Bushman suggests 110 verses (138), which is reasonable. However, he does not explain where the vanished Book of Enoch is found in the Book of Moses. Here Bushman is typical of Mormon historians and theologians in being a touch embarrassed by much of the contents of The Pearl of Great Price and he hurries by it with uncharacteristically vague citations and loose discussion of its sources and contents.

40 The best modern English-language edition of the *Book of Enoch*, with translation and an excellent introduction by E. Isaac, is found in James H. Charlesworth (ed.), *The Old Testament Pseudepigrapha* (New York: Doubleday, 1985), vol. 1, 5–98. For my own discussion of its singular qualities, see *Surpassing Wonder: The Invention of the Bible and the Talmuds*, 156–8, 183–90. Incidentally, the *Book of Enoch* is well-attested by the Dead Sea Scrolls, so that the book is now accepted as authentic by Jewish as well as Christian scholars.

41 Hansen, 31; Bushman, 285–6.

42 Brodie, 171*n*, quoting Smith's secretary, Warren Parrish, in a letter of 5 February 1838, printed in *Painsville Republican*, 5 February 1838 and reprinted in *Zion's Watchman*, 24 March 1838.

43 Brodie, 171.

44 Persuitte, 290–6.

45 Hansen, 31–2. With no conscious sense of irony, Bushman (193) comments: "Full of wonders as it was, the Book of Abraham complicated the problem of regularizing Mormon doctrine."

46 On the interaction of Christian theology and apartheid, see the relevant chapters in my *God's Peoples. Covenant and Land in South Africa, Israel, and Ulster* (Ithaca and London: Cornell University Press, 1992; Montreal & Kingston: McGill-Queen's University Press, 1992.).

47 Hansen is quite brilliant on these developments. See, esp., 184–204.

48 Brodie, 55*n* and 467; Bushman, 128, 563.

49 The Articles of Faith, 1842, are included at the back of The Pearl of Great Price. They are a codification of a doctrine that had been less formally stated since the early 1830s.

50 In the present arrangement of The Doctrine and Covenants, these are sections 3, 5, 6, 8, 9, 10, 11, 12, 13, 14, 15, 16, 17, 18, 19.

51 Bushman, 570*n*34.

52 Persuitte, 22–3. In Allen and Leonard, 28, there is a photograph of a
written account of Joseph Smith's 1820 vision asserted to be in the
Prophet's own handwriting and to be from the year 1832. The authenticity of this 1832 holograph being granted, it is worth noting
that the report of the vision involves only one heavenly messenger, not
two, as Smith elaborated in 1838 and in the early 1840s. Marvin S.
Hill, "Secular or Sectarian History: A Critique of 'No Man Knows My
History,'" in Bringhurst (ed)., 65. This is reprinted from *Church History*, 43 (March 1974).

Actually, the development of belief in this First Vision of Joseph
Smith of 1820 has an ideational history parallel (both in morphologi-
cal evolution and in its nineteenth- and early twentieth-century context) in the innovative Roman Catholic doctrine of the Immaculate
Conception of the Virgin Mary. Kathleen Flake summarizes the scholarship as follows: "James Allen, author of the most extensive study
[states] that the weight of evidence would suggest that it [the First
Vision] was not a matter of common knowledge even among church
members, in the earliest years of Mormon history." Allen further concludes that this oversight continued until 1883 when the First Vision
was employed to teach the Latter-day Saints' doctrine of deity: "While
appreciation for Smith's First Vision continued to grow in the last decade of the nineteenth century, not until the early twentieth century did
it move to the fore of Latter-day Saint self-representation." Kathleen
Flake, *The Politics of American Religious Identity. The Seating of Senator Reed
Smoot, Mormon Apostle* (Chapel Hill: University of North Carolina Press,
2004), 118, quoting James Allen, "Emergence of a Fundamental: The
Expanding Role of Joseph Smith's First Vision in Mormon Religious
Thought," *Journal of Mormon History*, 7 (1980), 53. [The entire article is
43–61.] Flake (203*n*39) notes that at least eight variant accounts of the
First Vision were produced during Joseph Smith's lifetime.

53 The "Wentworth letter" of 1842 is found in full in Smith, History of the
Church, vol. 4, 536–41. It is found in a somewhat expanded form at the
end of The Pearl of Great Price. Incidentally, Harold Bloom views the
Wentworth letter as something of a small masterpiece. "The Wentworth
letter, which prints up as six pages, is marked by the dignity of a simple
eloquence and by the self-possession of a religious innovator who is so secure in the truth of his doctrine that he can state its pith with an almost
miraculous economy" (Bloom, *The American Religion*, 82).

54 In addition to the Wentworth letter which I have been citing, there is
a bit of additional material on this 1823 vision in The Doctrine and

Covenants, section 2. See also the expanded version at the back of The
Pearl of Great Price.

CHAPTER THREE

1 Joseph Smith, History of the Church, vol. 4, 231.
2 James B. Allen, Jessie L. Embry, and Kahlile B. Mehr, *Hearts Turned to
   the Fathers*, book edition of *BYU Studies* (Salt Lake City, 1995), 19, 343.
3 Ibid., 19.
4 Klaus Hansen, *Mormonism and the American Experience* (Chicago: University of Chicago Press, 1981), 104–5.
5 Joseph Smith, History of the Church, vol. 4, 426.
6 Allen, Embry, and Mehr, 19–21.
7 B.H. Roberts, preface, xxxviii, to Joseph Smith, History of the Church,
   vol. 4.
8 For a controversial argument that early Mormonism was much more
   dependent for its ideational base upon the Masonic tradition than is
   generally accepted, see Clyde R. Forsberg, Jr., *Equal Rites. The Book of
   Mormon, Masonry, Gender, and American Culture* (New York: Columbia
   University Press, 2004).
9 James B. Allen and Glen B. Leonard, *The Story of the Latter-day Saints*
   (Salt Lake City: Deseret Books Co., 1976), 160–1.
10 Fawn Brodie, *No Man Knows my History: The Life of Joseph Smith, the Mormon Prophet* (New York, Alfred Knopf, 1963; orig.ed. 1945), 280.
11 S.H. Goodwin, *Mormonism and Masonry* (Salt Lake City: 1938), cited in
   Brodie, 281–2. She lists other relevant sources as well.
12 Allen, Embry, and Mehr, 20; Richard L. Bushman ("with the assistance
   of Jed Woodworth") *Joseph Smith: Rough Stone Rolling* (New York: Alfred
   A. Knopf, 2005), 497.
13 Allen, Embry, and Mehr, 21.
14 Bushman, 323–6. This girl, Fanny Alger, left the Smith household in
   September 1836 and "had no trouble remarrying."
15 Kathleen Flake, *The Politics of American Religious Identity. The Seating
   of Senator Reed Smoot, Mormon Apostle* (Chapel Hill: University of
   North Carolina Press, 2004) cites the sources for the 1833 date
   (187nn.24–7).
16 Bushman, 437–40. The quotation is from 440.
17 Allen, Embry, and Mehr, 22.
18 See Klaus Hansen's breakthrough study on the Council of Fifty, *Quest for
   Empire. The Political Kingdom of God and the Council of Fifty in Mormon History*

(Lincoln: University of Nebraska Press, sec. ed., 1974; orig. pub. 1967). In addition to his acute analysis, especially valuable are Hansen's bibliographic essay and also his preface to the second edition which deals with official LDS reaction to his discoveries.

19 Allen and Leonard, 331.

20 *Journal of Discourses by President Brigham Young, his Counselors, and the Twelve Apostles and Others* (Liverpool: Joseph F. Smith, 1886), vol. 16, 161–71. The entire sermon is worth reading. After Young's death, his idea that a male "Saint" would be punished (or at least reduced in celestial rank to being a mere angel) for having had only one marriage was quietly dropped.

21 On the anti-Mormon federal campaign, see Mark P. Leone, *Roots of Modern Mormonism* (Cambridge: Harvard University Press, 1979), 148–66.

22 Allen and Leonard, 413–16. See also later printings of The Doctrine and Covenants. As late as the 1973 edition, it was still being put away at the back as an unnumbered item and thus, by implication, not of the same majesty as the revelations given to the Prophet and to Brigham Young.

23 Kathleen Flake (2004) makes a compelling argument that between 1890 and 1908 the LDS did not simply surrender to the US government but worked out a compromise with the federal authorities that allowed the church as an institution to redefine its doctrine (especially concerning the First Vision and, as I suggest below, genealogical work) without the church's losing its internal discipline or dignity in the face of the "Gentile" world.

24 Allen and Leonard, 424.

25 Allen, Embry, and Mehr, 43, citing four separate sources. This is the appropriate point to pay tribute to their fine book, *Hearts Turned to the Fathers*, for it provides both a wealth of information otherwise unobtainable by the general public on the history of Mormon genealogical practices and also, through their citations and bibliography, an entrance into available source material on this topic.

26 Ibid., 60–70.

27 Susa Young Gates, *Surname Book and Racial History* (Salt Lake City: General Board of Relief, with the approval of the Genealogical Society of Utah, 1918).

28 Allen, Embry, and Mehr, 70.

29 Ibid. 71–6.

30 Doctrine and Covenants, 138:30. Although the vision was received and publicly articulated in 1918, it was not accepted into The Doctrine and

Covenants and into The Pearl of Great Price (that is, officially made scripture) until 1976. Also, note that the church's leading theologian of the time, James E. Talmage, argued that "It is not to be supposed that by these ordinances the departed are in any way compelled to accept the obligation, nor that they are in the least hindered in the exercise of their will." See James E. Talmage, *A Study of the Articles of Faith* ... (Salt Lake City: Church of Jesus Christ of Latter-day Saints, 49th ed., orig.ed., 1899), 153. The problem that is shrewdly ignored here is: what occurs in the case of a dead individual's saying "no" to the "Saints'" spirit-missionaries, unbeknownst, of course, to the earthly "Saints" who are performing all the ordinances for him and thus obtaining for him spiritual benisons that he wishes to reject? Given the problem free will has provided for centuries of theologians, walking quickly past the issue probably was wise.

31 Allen, Embry, and Mehr, 131.

32 See Talmage, passim.

33 Hansen (1981), 78.

34 Allen and Leonard, 428.

35 Allen, Embry, and Mehr, 119.

36 "Twelve Genealogical Lessons included in the New Outline for the Lesser Priesthood," *Utah Genealogical and Historical Magazine* (1931), 46. I have elided steps in the program that were purely devotional in nature.

37 Allen and Leonard, 601; Allen, Embry, and Mehr, 168. One should note that in 1944, the Genealogical Society of Utah (the church's international genealogical arm, despite its limited title) has been transformed at the direction of the First Presidency from a public corporation into an integral arm of the church. Its new name became the Genealogical Society of the Church of Jesus Christ of Latter-day Saints. This change did not reflect any diminished enthusiasm for the genealogical aspect of the society, but a fear of what the historical material in its archives might reveal to outsiders. The First Presidency was worried that it would be harder to restrict certain institutional records of the church if the society and its holdings were public. (Allen, Embry, and Mehr, 141.) Although one does not want to be too simplistic in describing this new costiveness about the church's institutional history, I suspect it has a good deal to do with the knowledge that Fawn Brodie's breakthrough book on the Prophet was in galleys and would soon appear. And, given what she had found out about early Mormon history, the First

Presidency shuddered at what could be discovered by later researchers, especially non-Mormons.

38 On the planning and construction, see Allen, Embry, and Mehr,
236–41.

39 Ibid., 187–90.

40 Ibid., 304–8.

41 Ibid., 345.

CHAPTER FOUR

1 Christopher J.P. Booker, *The Seven Basic Plots. Why We Tell Stories*
(London: Continuum, 2004), 703.

2 Ibid, 8–9.

3 Georges Polti, tr. by Lucille Ray, *The Thirty-Six Dramatic Situations*
(Franklin, Ohio: J.K. Reeve, 1921). The full list, in terse form, is: suppli-
cation to a greater power; deliverance; crime and vengeance; vengeance
of kin upon kin; pursuit; disaster; prey to misfortune; revolt; daring enterprise; abduction; riddles; obtaining; kinship enmity; kinship rivalry;
murderous adultery; madness; fatal imprudence; innocent sins of love;
slaying an unrecognized relative; sacrifice of self for an idea; sacrifice of
self for kindred; sacrifice of self for a passion; sacrifice of loved ones by
necessity; rivalry of superior and inferior; adultery; crimes of love; discovery of dishonourableness of loved one; love blocked by obstacles;
love for an enemy; ambition; conflict with God; erroneous jealousy; erroneous judgement; remorse; recovery of a lost one; loss of loved ones.

4 William Foster-Harris, *The Basic Patterns of Plot* (Norman, OK.: University of Oklahoma Press, 1959).

5 Booker, 700.

6 Ibid, 701.

7 Two examples of opportunism in this area: Ronald B. Tobias, *20 Master
Plots* (Cincinnati: Writer's Digest Books, 1993); and C. Hugh Homan
and William Harmon, *A Handbook to Literature* (New York: MacMillan,
sixth ed., 1992) which posits a single plot for all literature: Exposition-
Rising action-Climax-Falling action.

8 Vladimir Propp, *The Morphology of the Folktale* (Bloomington, Ind.: Research Center, Indiana University, 1958), tr. by Laurence Scott; edited
with an introduction by Svatava Pirkova-Jakobson.

9 This volume had the same title, but now was re-edited and given a
new preface by Louise A. Wagner and an additional introduction by
Alan Dundes.

10 The full list is as follows: (1) a member of a family leaves home (the hero is introduced, but is not here central); (2) an interdiction is addressed to the hero; (3) the interdiction is violated (villain appears); (4) villain attempts a reconnaissance of his victims or of the prizes he will purloin; (5) the villain acquires information about his victim; (6) the villain attempts to inveigle the victim; (7) the victim is taken in by deception; (8) the villain causes harm to the victim's family, or finds that a family member desires something; (9) misfortune or deficit is made known to the hero; (10) the hero agrees to counteraction; (11) the hero leaves home; (12) the hero is tested by a future helper, or magical agent; (13) the hero passes the test; (14) the hero acquires the help or magical agent's aid; (15) the hero is delivered or led to an object for which he is searching; (16) the hero and villain engage in combat; (17) the hero is wounded or scarred; (18) the villain is defeated or killed or banished; (19) the initial issue is therefore resolved; (20) the hero returns towards home; (21) the hero is pursued; (22) the hero is rescued from pursuit; (23) the hero arrives home, unrecognized; (24) a false hero presents false claims; (25) a difficult test is proposed; (26) the hero engages the test successfully; (27) the hero is recognized; (28) the false hero is exposed; (29) the hero is given a new appearance, healed, or given new raiment; (30) the villain is punished; (31) the hero marries and is rewarded, promoted, or accedes to a princedom.

11 S. Mellor, "Vladimir Propp," http://scandanavian.wisc.edu/hca/glossary/propp.html, 30/03/05.

12 The key phrase is "for our present purposes." Probably the reader will have noticed that I have not referred to Claude Levi-Strauss's attempts to formulate a scheme that would cover every form of narrative, and especially the structure of myth. This is found in his collected papers and in most focused form in his essay "The Structure of Myth," in his *Structural Anthropology*, vol. 1, 202ff (New York: Basic Books, 1963 and London: Allen Lane, 1968, orig. Fr. Ed., 1958), trans. Claire Jacobson and Brooke Grundfest Schoepf. As will be seen below, when I discuss Levi-Strauss's grammar of kinship systems, his work is indispensable. However, on myth – which is to say, on narrative – his all-encompassing system does not here help us. The reason is that Levi-Strauss breaks with the sequential presentation of narrative employed by Propp and his successors and uses a paradigmatic scheme in which sequence is only a surface product of deeper, latent content. Levi-Strauss explains that, in his view, most major religious myths and origin myths are strikingly similar because they all come out of a set of binary oppositions – male vs. female,

life vs. death, and so on. Perhaps he is correct and he is providing the deeper latent paradigms, as opposed to the surface content of narrative. For us, however, in our search for a grammar of genealogy, we have no use for deep patterns that scramble the sequence that we can observe either directly or in archives or in oral myths. Put simply, in the human sequence of events, life always precedes death (unless one believes in reincarnation or in an unseemly degree of composting). We need sequence. So the sequential structure of Propp, even if it is merely a descriptive ethnography, suits our needs. (For a discerning essay on the basic differences between the narratology of Propp and of Levi-Strauss, see Alan Dundes's introduction to the second revised translation of Propp's *Morphology* ..., cited above, note 9.)

13 The hugely influential work of Noam Chomsky was his *Syntactic Structures* (Berlin and New York: Mouton Publishers, 1957). This is the work that has had the most influence in the humanities and social sciences, particularly in its distinction between the "deep structure" of a sentence and its "surface structure," and also in its development of formal rules governing how deep structures are transformed into surface structures. In the 1960s and 1970s, Chomsky lost much of his wider audience by changing his notion of deep-and-surface structures and by turning to mathematical formulations that can be followed by few social scientists or humanists.

14 Gerald Prince, *Narratology. The Form and Functioning of Narrative* (Berlin, Amsterdam, and New York: Mouton Publishers, 1982), 4. Emphasis mine. For the sake of completeness (and to recognize his pioneering place in the field), one should note that Prince published a number of the ideas in his 1982 volume in his *A Grammar of Stories. An Introduction* (Berlin, the Hague, and New York: Mouton Publishers, 1973).

15 For an excellent example of a defence of structurally based narratology combined with an accommodation of the needs of cultural analyses, see Mieke Bal, *Narrratology. Introduction to the Theory of Narrative* (Toronto: University of Toronto Press, sec. ed., 1997).

16 I am here adapting a phrase used by Curtis Gillespie, "Postmodernism," *Toronto Magazine* (5 June 2003).

17 On the Teskeys and similar families, see Carolyn Heald, *The Irish Palatines in Canada* (Gananoque, Ont.: Langdale Press, 1994).

CHAPTER FIVE

1 For the historical material on the Jaga, including items not mentioned in the text above, see Adrian C. Edwards, *The Ovimbundu under*

Two Sovereignties. A Study of Social Control and Social Change among a People of Angola (Oxford: Oxford University Press, 1962). The two sources referred to in the text are E.G. Ravenstein (ed.), *The Strange Adventures of Andrew Battell* (London: The Hakluyt Society, 1901) and Jean-Baptiste Labat and Giovanni A. Cavazzi, *Relation historique de l'Ethopie occidental* (Paris: C.J.B. Despine, 1732), with original material of Cadornega included.

2 The reader may be surprised that the work which on the surface might appear most apt to offer a possibly overarching way of dealing with the grammar of genealogical narrative is not here employed: Jacques Derrida's *Of Grammatology* (Baltimore: Johns Hopkins University Press, 1977), trans. Gayatri Chakrovorty Spivak. Despite the volume's apparent usefulness, the theory underlining the work cripples it for our present purpose. Derrida presents an argument that no linguistic sign existed before the creation of writing. One simplifies, but his basic points are clear enough: that the western world is ethnocentric in giving precedence to written over verbal linguistic systems and that in the western [read: economically advanced] world [therefore?] writing had to be considered as prior to speech. However much this theory may (or well may not) be of any use to literary theory, it has no relevance to the historical evolution of grammars in general (speech undeniably existed eons before the creation of writing) and most particularly not to the grammar of genealogical narrative: the earliest genealogical narratives were oral, and the written narratives that are most prized in European, Semitic, Amerindian, Polynesian, Chinese, and Japanese culture are those that are supposed to be transcriptions of oral texts. Further, despite Derrida's assertion that signification depends on writing, there exist in all the cultures mentioned above individuals who are not literate, but who are nevertheless the repositories of long genealogical narratives. Moreover, even in the case of literate remembrancers, they often refuse to put their knowledge into written form.

3 Lewis Carroll, *Through the Looking Glass and What Alice Found There* (Harmondsworth: Puffin Books ed., 1994), 87.

4 George Peter Murdock, *Ethnographic Atlas* (Pittsburgh: University of Pittsburgh Press, 1967).

5 Murdock's material was tallied by Jack Goody in *Comparative Studies in Kinship* (London: Routledge and Kegan Paul, 1969), 93. Two points should be noted: although Goody counted accurately, he employed somewhat different terms than are found in Murdock's work; and, secondly, I have myself used labels different both from Murdock and from

Goody. These stay true to the data, but are more appropriate for gene-alogical work than are those that stem from the ethnographic way of describing the material. In any case, the categorization is intended to be more indicative than definitive. It provides a general idea of the pre-vailing way human societies have narrated their lineages over the last 500 years.

6 There are many systems of diagramming biological descent and the countervailing cognition of genealogical ascent. I have chosen the sim-plest ones applicable and the schematics used here are virtually self-explanatory. For a useful basic system, see *Notes and Queries on Anthro-pology* (London: Routledge and Kegan Paul, 1951), "revised and rewrit-ten by by a Committee of the Royal Anthropological Institute of Great Britain and Ireland," 53ff, entitled "Technique of the Genealogi-cal Method."

7 Bronislaw Stefaniszny, *Social and Ritual Life of the Ambo of Northern Rhode-sia* (Oxford: Oxford University Press, 1964), 1.

8 Ibid., 133.

9 V.W. Turner, *Schism and Continuity in an African Society. A Study of Ndem-bdu Village Life* (Manchester: Manchester University Press, 1957), 82.

10 J. Clyde Mitchell, *The Yao Village. A Study in the Social Structure of a Nyasa-land Tribe* (Manchester: Manchester University Press, 1956), 184.

11 Alex Shoumatoff, *The Mountain of Names. A History of the Human Family* (New York: Simon and Schuster, 1985), 60. Updated for recent developments.

12 Audrey I. Richards, *Land, Labour and Diet in Northern Rhodesia. An Eco-nomic Study of the Bemba Tribe* (London: Oxford University Press, 1939), 112.

13 Robert A. Lystad, *The Ashanti. A Proud People* (New Brunswick, N.J.: Rut-gers University Press, 1958), 46. The anecdote dates from roughly mid-twentieth century.

14 Mitchell, 185.

15 David Schneider, in David M. Schneider and Kathleen Gough, *Matrilin-eal Kinship* (Berkeley: University of California Press, 1961), 5.

16 Ibid., 5.

17 A.R. Radcliffe-Brown, "Introduction" to A.R. Radcliffe-Brown and Daryll Forde, *African Systems of Kinship and Marriage* (London: Oxford University Press, 1950), 5. Emphasis mine. Because I have been em-ploying the case of polyandry to make the point about genealogical grammars being superordinate over "marriage" forms, the reader may wish to consult Eugene Hillman, *Polygamy Reconsidered. African Plural*

Marriage and the Christian Churches (Maryknoll: Orbis Books, 1975). Father Hillman's book is something of a classic, for it considers African polygamy within the long view of Christian theological and social teachings. Although anything but an ethical relativist, Hillman's view is based on St. Augustine's conclusion concerning polygamy: "When polygamy was a common custom, it was no crime; it ranks as a crime now because it is no longer customary." (Hillman, 21–2, quoting Augustine's "Constra Faustum Manichaeum," lib. xxii, c.47, in P.L. 42, col. 428 in the standard editions of his works.)

18 Robin Fox, *Kinship and Marriage. An Anthropological Perspective* (Cambridge: Cambridge University Press, sec. ed., 1983), 121. Fox's formulation deals with an Ideal Type. In the real world, the father acquired some rights and in the case of divorce, there could be conflict between a husband and a woman's brother(s) over custody or property rights. See Turner, 85. For a clear and admirably economical study of the socioeconomic and cognitive advantages of matrilineality, contextualized in the case of a Zambian group, see Karla O. Poewe, *Matrilineal Ideology: Male-Female Dynamics in Luapula, Zambia* (London: pub. by Academic Press for the International African Institute, 1981).

19 Edmund Wilson, *Apologies to the Iroquois* (London: W.H. Allen, 1960), 68.

20 See, for example, the Luvale of Northern Rhodesia, as of the mid-twentieth century. C.M.N. White, *A Preliminary Survey of Luvale Rural Economy* (Manchester: Manchester University Press, 1959).

21 See Mary McCarthy, *Social Change and the Growth of British Power in the Gold Coast. The Fante States, 1807–1874* (Langham: University Press of America, 1983).

22 For an indication of how the Fante involvement in the slave trade could have effects into the present day, see "Why am I Who I am?" *Observer* (London) 15 May 2005. This concerns Ekow Eshun (recently appointed director of the Institute for Contemporary Arts, London) who made the unsettling discovery that his G5 grandfather was a Fante-Dutch mulatto who was a slave trader and major link between Fante slave catchers and European slave purchasers.

23 Fox, 121.

24 Hugh Ashton, *The Basuto. A Social Study of Traditional and Modern Lesotho* (London: Oxford University Press, sec. ed., 1967), 26.

25 Matthew 1:18–25.

26 Emma Hatfield, *Among the Natives of the Loyalty Group* (London: St. Martin's Press, 1920), 14.

27 Fox, 116–17; Shoumatoff, 64–7.

28 Shoumatoff, 67.

29 Ian Whittaker, "Tribal Structure and National Politics in Albania, 1910–1950," in Iban M. Lewis (ed.), *History and Anthropology* (London: Tavistock Publications, 1968), 265. Whittaker's entire article, 253–93, is highly recommended.

30 Claire Holden, "Spread of cattle led to the loss of matrilineal descent in Africa: a coevolutionary analysis," *Proceedings* [biological sciences] of the Royal Society, vol 270, no. 1532, 7 December 2003.

31 Lystad, 52.

32 David F. Aberle, "Matrilineal Descent in Cross-cultural Perspective," in Schneider and Gough, 702.

33 I have not taken space in the text to discuss systems of genealogy in which (as in some groups in Papua New Guinea) the males trace their descent through the mother and the females through the father. See *Notes and Queries on Anthropology*, 91. And, one can have a genealogical narrative that runs from fathers to sons and mothers to daughters. (See Fox, diagram 31, 149). I think these are both best comprehended as grammars of unilineal genealogy, as for any given *ego* there is only one possible line of genealogical ascent into the past.

34 For a classic discussion that places the "English system" in comparative perspective, see A.R. Radcliffe-Brown, "Introduction," in A.R. Radcliffe-Brown and Daryll Forde (eds.), 1–85.

35 "Genghis Khan's hordes conquer the phone book," *Observer* (London), 17 October 2004.

36 Robert Sandin, *The Sea Dayaks of Borneo before White Rajah Rule* (London: MacMillan, 1967). The genealogies are on 96–118.

37 For a brilliant analysis of pre-twentieth century New Zealand society, see James Belich, *Making Peoples. A History of the New Zealanders. From Polynesian Settlement to the End of the Nineteenth Century* (Aukland: Penguin Books, 1996).

38 See Belich, 23–4, and the references, 451–52nn20–21. This is a point of some sensitivity. Maori genealogists with whom I have talked agree that whakapapa have been, are, and always will be treated as somewhat plastic: cultural material that can be shaped to serve the purposes of healing or of peace-making, as well as made the basis of economic self-interest. However, this is not a matter upon which public discussion is encouraged.

39 For a very useful compilation of the main Maori genealogical lines, see William A. Cole and Elwin W. Jenson, *Israel in the Pacific. A Genealogical Text for Polynesia* (Salt Lake City: Genealogical Society, 1961), esp. 395–418.

One would do well when using this source to prescind the material before the arrival of the origin-canoes in New Zealand. With more enthusiasm than judgement, the authors employ several incompatible strands of Polynesian mythology to trace all the Polynesians back to the mythological Tiki, who is then traced back to North-American figures found in the Book of Mormon, and thence to Adam and Eve.

40 Daryll Forde, "Double Descent among the Yako," in Radcliffe-Brown and Forde, 285–332.

41 Dennis O'Neil, "Descent Principles," http://anthro.palomar.edu/ kinship/kinship_2.htm, 13/12/04.

42 C.E. Fox, *The Threshold of the Pacific. An account of the Social Organization, Magic, and Religion of the People of San Cristoval in the Solomon Islands* (London: Kegan Paul, Trench, Trubner and Co., 1924), 55.

43 G. William Skinner, "Family and Reproduction in East Asia: China, Korea and Japan compared," a lecture delivered 8 October 2002, University of California, Davis. www.info.gov.hk/sfa/en/schemes/sey/ m14.htm–54k.

44 Lewis H. Morgan, *Ancient Society, or Researches in the lines of Human Progress from Savagery, through barbarism to Civilization* (London: MacMillan and Co., 1877).

45 Frederick Engels, *The Origin of the Family, Private Property and the State, in the Light of the Researches of Lewis H. Morgan* (London: International Publishers, reprint edition, 1972, based on the translation by Alec West, 1942). The original German edition was published in 1844 and was in a fourth revised edition in 1891. The material on group marriage is in chapter two of both editions.

46 For an admirably efficient summary of Irish fosterage, see "Fostering," in S.J. Connolly (ed.), *The Oxford Companion to Irish History* (Oxford: Oxford University Press, 1998), 204.

47 T.M. Charles-Edwards, *Early Christian Ireland* (Cambridge: Cambridge University Press, 2000), 83. I am grateful to Dr. Kyla Madden for calling this and related items to my attention.

48 E.E. Evans-Pritchard, *Man and Woman among the Azande* (London: Faber and Faber, 1974), 36–7.

49 E.P. Thompson, *The Poverty of Theory and other essays* (New York: Monthly Review Press, 1978).

50 Claude Levi-Strauss, *The Elementary Structures of Kinship*, trans. James H. Bell, John R von Sturmey and edited by Rodney Needham (London: Eyre and Spottiswoode, 1969, from the second Fr. ed of 1967; orig. Fr. ed., 1949).

51 Claude Levi-Strauss, *Structural Anthropology*, vol. 1, trans. Claire Jacobsen and Brooke G. Schoepf (London: Allen Lane, 1968, orig. Fr. ed., 1958).

52 Claude Levi-Strauss, *Structural Anthropology*, vol. 2, trans. Monique Layton (London: Allen Lane, 1977, orig, Fr. ed., 1973).

53 Giorgio Ausenda, "Kinship and Marriage among the Visigoths," in Peter Heather (ed.), *The Visigoths from the Migration Period to the Seventh Century. An Ethnographic Perspective* (London: Boydell Press, 1999), 132–3.

54 Levi-Strauss, *Elementary Structures*, 182.

55 Levi-Strauss, *Structural Anthropology*, vol. 2, 83. This repeats a similar formulation in *Structural Anthropology*, vol. 1, 46.

56 R.F. Barton, *The Kalingas. Their Institutions and Custom Law* (Chicago: University of Chicago Press, 1949), 38.

57 Levi-Strauss, *Elementary Structures*, 112.

58 For a formulation that finds its way into Levi-Strauss see, for example, Frazer on the Urabunna tribe. J. G. Frazer, *Totemism and Exogamy. A Treatise on Certain Early Forms of Superstition and Society* (London: MacMillan, 1920), vol. 1, 176ff.

59 Levi-Strauss, *Elementary Structures*, 112.

60 Simply put, the reasons that in Levi-Strauss's system two adult male brothers or two adult female sisters could not exchange children was (a) that Levi-Strauss's definition of the marriage alliance demanded that a young female be passed from a male to another male, so the exchange by sisters was excluded; and (b) the brothers' exchanging children would not work because in the next generation, the side of the family that had been given a female would owe a female back and that would result in a degree of endogamy that violated what Levi-Strauss believed were universal incest taboos. (Mind you, it is a bit difficult to see how this incest taboo is overcome in a set of multi-generational exchanges of females as occurs in a line of cross-cousin marriages, but that is not here germane.)

61 See the cases cited in Ausenda, 137–8.

CHAPTER SIX

1 Frank O'Connor [pseud. of Michael O'Donovan], *The Backward Look* (London: MacMillan, 1967). Published in the USA as *A Short History of Irish Literature. A Backward Look* (New York: G.P. Putnam's Son, 1967).

2 The concept of generative paradigms runs through many of the volumes of Neusner's oeuvre. I am here using a lecture he gave in Helsinki, Finland, 31 May 2005, entitled "The Secular and the Religious Narrative in Contention." A useful conspectus of Neusner's work on generative category formation is his *The Theology of the Oral Torah. Revealing the Justice of God* (Montreal and Kingston: McGill-Queen's University Press, 1999).

3 E.A. Thompson, *The Visigoths in the Time of Ulfila* (Oxford: Clarendon Press, 1966).

4 Richard Dawkins, *The Selfish Gene* (Oxford: Oxford University Press, 1976. Second revised edition, 1989). Incidentally, Dawkins, being a very ethical scientist, was sensitive to a suggestion that he had not himself been the first person to use the concept of meme, but had perhaps lifted it from the work of Eugene Marais (1927) or from a German biologist, Richard Semon (1904). In a letter to the *Times Literary Supplement* (9 November 2001), he argued convincingly that he had never read a word of either of those authors, so he certainly was not guilty of plagiarism. Good scientific ethics, but most scholars in the humanities would have told him not to worry: the wheel has been independently invented hundreds of times and so have most concepts related to human social organization.

5 See, for example, Susan Blackmore, *The Meme Machine* (Oxford: Oxford University Press, 1999); Daniel C. Dennett, *Consciousness Explained* (Boston: Little Brown, 1991); and Richard Dawkins, *Unweaving the Rainbow. Science, Delusion and the Appetite for Wonder* (Boston: Houghton Mifflin, 1998). In a review of a recent festschrift for Dawkins (Alan Grates and Mark Ridley, eds., *Richard Dawkins. How a Scientist Changed the Way We Think* (Oxford: Oxford University Press, 2006), Jerry A. Coyne suggests that the idea of memes "has definitely been a scientific flop, despite its perennial popularity." (*Times Literary Supplement,* 16 June 2006.) This judgment is in equal parts largely right and largely irrelevant. Good ideas in science are frequently inapplicable to the more reflective disciplines of the humanities, and vice versa. Occasionally questionable ideas in the humanities have made interesting science, as when cosmologists apply the concept of free will to fundamental physics.

6 Will Bourne,"The Gospel according to Prum," *Harper's* (January 1995), 60–70; Edward Rice, *John Frum He Come* (Garden City: Doubleday, 1974); "Vanuata," http://numbmagazine.net, 24/05/2005.

7 For the purposes of discussing the genealogical imperialism of the Hebrew scriptures, the Tanakh and the Old Testament can be considered

identical. However, one should make it clear that in their macrostructure they are slightly different. In the Hebrew scriptures, Genesis-Kings is a literary unity, while in the Christian version, the Book of Ruth interrupts the original narrative unity. Also 1 and 2 Chronicles come at the end of the Hebrew Bible, whereas they follow Kings in the Christian text. There are other minor differences. These matters noted, the real difference between the Tanakh and the Old Testament is not in substance, but in the way they are read: the Tanakh is read by Jews as an item that has an integrity of its own and comes to an end with Second Chronicles' reprise of the return from Exile. Story done: full stop. The Christian version, the Old Testament, concludes with the words of the prophet Malachi and is read as pointing to a future "fulfillment" in the figure of Jesus Christ. Thus, the Tanakh and the Old Testament can never really be the same. (On this unbridgeable disjuncture, see Harold Bloom, *Jesus and Yahweh. The Names Divine* (London: Penguin, 2005). Still, we have to have some common vocabulary, so one employs "Old Testament" as likely to be the more familiar to readers of this book.

8 Donald Harman Akenson, *Surpassing Wonder. The Invention of the Bible and the Talmuds* (New York: Harcourt Brace and Montreal and Kingston: McGill-Queen's University Press, 1998), esp. 19–63. I am heartened that a leading scholar of the Hebrew scriptures, Richard Elliott Friedman, employing philological rather than narratological analysis, came independently to the same conclusion that I had reached concerning the textual unity of Genesis-Kings. He and I would differ on the dating of the final redaction, however. See Richard Elliott Friedman, *The Hidden Book in the Bible* (San Francisco: HarperSanFrancisco, 1998). If the necessarily compressed character of the text's succeeding discussion of the Tanakh (the Old Testament) makes the reader uneasy, he ir she is referred to the full discussion in *Surpassing Wonder* (Chicago: University of Chicago Press, softcover ed., 2001).

9 There is a medieval Jewish tradition that Adam and God were the same person. That arcane matter is relevant to the present study because both Joseph Smith and Brigham Young seemed to believe this to be the case.

10 How long the practices of polygamy and of concubinage lasted in Eretz Israel is impossible to determine. There was no recorded reform movement on these matters before the writing of the last book of the Hebrew scriptures (the Book of Daniel) in the mid-second century BCE. However, it is clear that the practice of Levirate marriage still was a live issue in the late Second Temple era. See the Sadducees questioning

Yeshua of Nazareth on the matter in Matthew 22:23–28. And the Levirite practice still is followed today in some hyper-Orthodox sects.

11 Harold Bloom, *A Map of Misreading* (New York: Oxford University Press, 1975), 46.

12 Robert R. Wilson, "Genealogy, Genealogies," *Anchor Bible Dictionary* (1992), 2:929–32.

13 Robert Alter, *The Five Books of Moses. A Translation with Commentary* (New York: W.W. Norton, 2004), 200n.

14 Calculated from Mordecai Cogan, "Chronology," *Anchor Bible Dictionary*, 1:1004. Cogan's entire article on Old Testament chronology, 1:1003–11, deserves attention. As an aside, I would emphasize that there are contradictory versions of the various genealogies in the Hebrew scriptures. In this case, in chapter 4 of Genesis, there are seven generations between Adam and Noah (seven being a magic number in the Hebrew scriptures), but in chapter 5 there are ten generations (another magical number).

15 Calculated from Cogan, 1:1004. His sources are: Genesis 17:17; 23:1; 25:7; 25:26; 35:8; 47:28; and 50:22.

16 One says "Twelve Tribes" with just a touch of hesitation, as the compilers of the Old Testament recognized that there were more then twelve tribes in the nation; and further, when naming the twelve main ones, they were not always consistent. Compare, for instance, Genesis chapters 46 and 49 and Exodus chapter 6 and Joshua chapters 13–19.

17 See the commentary on Genesis 36 in Alter, 200–205.

18 The relevant regnal lists and others that both precede and follow the split kingship are found in *Surpassing Wonder*, Appendix B, Table 2.

19 On these distinctions, as they affect literary texts in general, see Wolfgang Iser, "Indeterminancy and the Reader's Response," in J. Hillis Miller, *Aspects of Narrative* (New York: Columbia University Press, 1971), 1–45.

20 E. Stuart Bates, *Inside Out. An Introduction to Autobiography* (Oxford: Basil Blackwell, 1936), 6.

21 Alter, 54n.

22 See *Surpassing Wonder*, 211–69.

23 It is an ironic parallel to the Twelve Tribes whose membership numbers cannot ever quite be agreed upon (entire camel loads of papyri were spent parsing the ambiguous lists in the Tanakh), that one cannot draw up from the Synoptics and the Gospel of John a single agreed list of Twelve Disciples. And what does one make of St. Paul's affirmation in the earliest written account of the Resurrection that the Risen

Yeshua was seen first by Peter and then by "The Twelve"? (1 Corinthians 15:5). On all this, bales and bales of vellum were expended by early church commentators. In fact, once it had been agreed by ancient authorities that there were twelve tribes of Israel, the only possible number of disciples Yeshua could have had was twelve, no matter how many actual persons are named as having a claim to be in that band.

24 Harold Bloom, *The Anxiety of Influence. A Theory of Poetry* (New York: Oxford University Press, 1973; revised edition, 1997). The long-term shelf-life of this work has probably been somewhat reduced by its being compact in size and lucid in expression. Neither of these characteristics is admired or imitated by Bloom's critics.

25 Ibid., 5.

26 Ibid., 94.

27 It makes for confusion that the arbiters of the Christian canon did not follow St. Paul and reject the idea of the Virgin Conception. He abhorred it, presumably as a pagan infiltration that was unacceptable to anyone whose faith was based on ancient Hebrew foundations. See Romans 1:3, where Paul explicitly states that Yeshua "was made of the seed of David according to the flesh." This is as explicit a denial of the Virgin Conception as one can imagine within the Christian canon, and it must have been made necessary by early Christians' already starting to borrow from pagan myths the idea of divine impregnation. For a discussion of Paul's beliefs according to the evidentiary methods of present-day professional historians, see Donald Harman Akenson, *Saint Saul. A Skeleton Key to the Historical Jesus* (New York: Oxford University Press, 2000). The study engages in detail the traditional and the "liberal" biblical scholarship on early Christian evidence.

28 A necessary parenthesis: please note that I am dealing with Ireland and not with "Celtic" countries in general, although Ireland undeniably was, and in many ways, still is, Celtic. The reason for this limitation on my part is that I really do not know what "Celtic" means and have not yet encountered anyone who has convincingly defined it. Yes, Celtic covers certain present-day linguistic groups who feel some cultural affinity with each other (language and music, mostly): some Welsh, some Bretons, a few Manx, fewer Cornish persons, some highland Scots and an undefined proportion of Irish persons. This identity began to arise in the eighteenth century and is largely a result of the Romantic revival and the cultural foxfire it left behind. If you take the earlier period, when the Irish were conquering large parts of Scotland, it is hardly worthwhile calling anyone Celtic, since Irish is a

more accurate and specific term. And if one wants to be left dangling, try to find any indication of how the people who conquered Ireland – traditionally between 500 BCE and 100 CE, broadly – did so, since there is almost no evidence of military struggle. Evidently, some people speaking a tongue that is known to linguists as "Celtic," culturally conquered a pre-existing group. If that is the case, then "Celtic" is simply a linguistic term and has no major genetic implications – after all, the pre-Celts took up using the tongue and themselves became Celts, apparently. Therefore, we had best use "Celtic" to mean a linguistic group and "Irish" to mean someone who lived in Ireland, neither more nor less.

29 I wrote the phrases down at the time and was pleased to see that they agreed with the later published version. For the entire sequence, see John V. Kelleher, "Edwin O'Connor and the Irish-American Process," *Atlantic Monthly*, vol. 222 (July 1968), 48–52. This, and a number of Kelleher's other pieces are found in an homage edited by Charles Fanning, *Selected Writings of John V. Kelleher on Ireland and Irish America* (Carbondale: Southern Illinois University Press, 2002).

30 John V. Kelleher, "The Pre-Norman Irish Genealogies," *Irish Historical Studies*, vol.16 (September 1968), 140.

31 Ibid., 145.

32 Ibid.

33 R.A. MacAlister (ed.) *Lebor Gabála Érenn. The Book of the Taking of Ireland* (Dublin: Irish Texts Society, 1938ff). MacAlister's edition is preceded by a brilliant introduction which includes the following indication of the borrowings of Ireland's ancient "history" from the Old Testament (xxvii-xxviii)

Old Testament	*Lebor Gabala*

The biblical history from the Creation to the Sons of Noah is borrowed by the Irish historians: after which –

Shem is selected and his genealogy is followed out …	Japhet is selected and his genealogy is followed out …
until we reach Terah and his son Abram, upon whose family the historian specializes …	until we reach Nel and his son Gaedel, upon whose family the historian specializes …

down to the two wives and the
numerous sons of Jacob.

down to the two wives and the
numerous sons of Mil.

A servitude in Egypt begins
with a friendly invitation from
an Egyptian king ...

An oppression in Egypt begins with
a friendly invitation from an
Egyptian king ...

and the children of Israel are
delivered by the adopted son of
an Egyptian princess.

and the children of Nel are
delivered by the son-in-law of the
Egyptian king. This deliverer
meets

and almost joins forces with his
prototype Moses.

They wander for a long time,
beset by enemies ...

They wander for a long time,
beset by enemies ...

and sojourn at a mountain
(Sinai)

and sojourn at a mountain
(Riphi)

where they receive the doom
that not they but their children shall reach the Promised
Land; so they wander ...

where they receive the doom that
not they but their children shall
reach the Promised Land; so they
wander ...

till their leader sees the
Promised Land from the
top of a mountain afar off.

till their leader sees the Promised
Land from the top of a mountain
afar off.

He dies: but his successor con-
ducts the people to a subjugation of the former inhabitants
of Canaan, amid circum-
stances of marvel and
mystery ...

He dies: but his successor con-
ducts the people to a subjugation
of the former inhabitants of
Ireland, amid circumstances of
marvel and mystery ...

and to a successful colonization of the country.
The history then concludes
with a brief record of the successive kings (beginning with
a partition of the country),
allotting in most

and to a successful colonization
of the country.
The history then concludes with
a brief record of the successive
kings (beginning with a partition
of the country), allotting in
most cases not more than

cases not more than a single
paragraph to individual kings.

a single paragraph to
individual kings.

34 Denis Murphy (ed.), *The Annals of Clonmacnoise, being annals of Ireland from the earliest period to AD 1408, translated into English, AD 1627 by Conell Mageoghan* (Dublin: orig. ed. 1896, reprinted Felinfach: Llanerch, 1993); Sean Mac Airt, *The Annals of Inisfallen* (Dublin: Institute for Advanced Studies, orig. ed. 1951, reprinted 1988); Whitley Stokes (ed.), *The Annals of Tigernach*, first printed in *Review Celtique*, 1895–97; (reprinted Felinfach: Llanerch, 1993); William M. Hennessy and Bartholomew MacCarthy, *Annala Uladh: Annals of Ulster ... a Chronicle of Irish affairs, 431–1131, 1155–1541* (Dublin: orig. pub. 4 vols, 1887–1901). New edition Sean Mac Airt (ed.), (Dublin: Institute for Advanced Studies, 1983).

35 The classic collection is *Ancient Irish Tales* (ed.) Tom Pete Cross and Clark Harris Slover (New York: Henry Holt and Co., 1936).

36 For saints' lives and for comprehensive listings of primary sources such as minor annals, hagiography, genealogy and regnal lists, see the bibliography by Daibhi O'Croinin, F.J. Byrne, and Peter Harbinson in Daibhi O'Croinin (ed.), *A New History of Ireland*, vol.1, *Prehistoric and Early Ireland* (Oxford: Oxford University Press, 2005), 996–1045.

37 Morton W. Bloomfield and Charles W. Dunn, *The Role of the Poet in Early Societies* (Cambridge, Eng.: D.S. Brewster, 1989), 1–6.

38 Ibid., 9.

39 Nollaig O'Muraile (ed. and trans.), *The Great Book of Genealogies compiled (1645–66) by Dubhaltach Mac* (Dublin: De Burca, 2003, 5 vols.), "Foreword," 1:9–10.

40 John V. Kelleher, "Humor in the Ulster Saga," in Fanning (ed.), 187.

41 I am grateful to Joseph Kukhta for pointing this out to me. On Irish kingship, see Francis John Byrne, *Irish Kings and High Kings* (London: B.T. Batsford, 1973). On Keating, see Bernadette Cunningham, *The World of Geoffrey Keating. Myth and religion in seventeenth-century Ireland* (Dublin: Four Courts Press, 2000).

42 Bloomfield and Dunn, 32–33.

43 Kathleen Hughes, "The Irish church, 800–c.1050," in Daibhi O'Croinin (ed.), 652.

44 O'Muraile, 11. The author's point being accepted, it is relevant to note that over the past three decades a modest swing has occurred among scholars in the direction of finding some of the Irish genealogies more accurate than previously was thought.

45 James Carney, "Language and Literature to 1169," in Daibhi O'Croinin (ed.), 464.

46 See the genealogy in the excellent article by T.M Charles-Edwards, "Early Irish Saints' Cults and their Constituencies," *Eriu*, vol.14 (2004), Fig. 1, 87.

47 The seminal discussion of the Brigit material is Kim McCone, "Brigit in the Seventeenth Century; A Saint with Three Lives?" *Peritia*, vol. 1 (1982), 107–45.

48 Byrne, quoted in O'Muraile, 11.

49 Daibhi O'Croinin, "Ireland, 400–800," in Daibhi O'Croinin (ed.), 184. The six methods were: to insert base-born folk as aristocrats simply by taking their betters' names; to multiply the claimed number of serfs someone had (thus jumping them up the social scale); to make the names of certain aristocrats falsely extinct; to demean an aristocratic line by understating the tribes under its suzerainty; to permit ignorant folk to write as if they were learned; and, for money, to have the learned perpetuate the false-learning of the ignorant.

50 John V. Kelleher, "Early Irish History and Pseudo-History," orig. pub. *Studia Hibernica* (1963), reproduced in Fanning, 167.

CHAPTER SEVEN

1 Samuel Laing (tr. and ed.), *The Olaf Sagas* (London: J.M. Dent, 1915, 2 vols.; Erling Monson (tr. and ed.), *Heimskringla, or, The Lives of the Norse Kings by Snorri Sturluson* (Cambridge: W. Heffer and Sons, 1932) [hereafter *Heimskringla*]; trans. Hermann Palsson and Paul Edwards, *Egil's Saga*, (Harmondsworth: Penguin, 1970).

2 Robert Kellog, "Introduction" to *The Sagas of Icelanders* (London: Allen Lane, 2000), esp. the diagram, pp. lxii.-lxiii.

3 For example, Anthony Faulkes (tr. and ed.), *Snorri Sturloson: Edda* (London: Dent, 1987), p.xliii, and Verseinn Olasson, "Family Sagas," in Rory McTurk (ed.), *A Companion to Old Norse-Icelandic Literature and Culture* (Oxford Blackwell Publishing, 2005), 105.

4 *Heimskringla*, 12.

5 Jean I. Young (tr.and ed.), *The Prose Edda of Snorri Sturluson* (Cambridge: Bowes and Bowes, 1954), 23. [Hereafter: *Prose Edda*.]

6 *Prose Edda*, 26–27.

7 Bryan Sykes, *Adam's Curse* (New York: W.W. Norton, 2004), 174–81 on the genetic lines of Clan Donald.

8 Ibid., 181.

9 *Heimskringla*, 3.

10 Four comments that are useful for keeping the Icelandic material in larger perspective. First, in contrast to the Irish material, women are found frequently in the Norse material. Men still outnumber women by a good margin and are the focus of most sagas, but gaps in lineages are sometimes continued in the female line. Second, by the time of the settlement of Iceland, the structure of Icelandic lineages had become the Standard Double sort. The terminology used for positions in the family structure had by that time coalesced into a form that is very close to that of the Scandinavian family of the nineteenth and twentieth centuries. (Compare the diagram by Robert Kellog, p. xi, with the Swedish family definitions in Appendix A to the present work.) Third, like the Irish, the Norse frequently practised fosterage (at least at the aristocratic level), so ghost-genealogies based on these foster relationships must have floated behind the formal genealogies. (Kellog, p. xl.) And fourth, although exceptional in its own way, the Norse genealogical narratives were part of a general trend in Europe. As Gabrielle M. Spiegel suggests, "Genealogy intrudes into historical narrative at precisely the time when noble families in France were beginning to organize themselves into vertical structures based on agnatic consanguinity, to the form, in other words, of *lignanes*." And, "moreover, genealogy employed as a perceptual 'grid' inevitably affected the chronicler's organization of chronological time ... resulting in a narrative controlled by dynastic rather than annalistic or calendar time." Gabrielle M. Spiegel, "Genealogy: Form and Function in Medieval Historical Narrative," *History and Theory*, vol.22 (February 1983), 47, 50.

11 Quoted by Jonathan Freedland in "Sara's Legacy," *The Guardian Weekend* (12 February 2005), 18.

12 Jacob Neusner to author, 28 July 2005.

13 As a small qualification to the discussion of ways in which genetics (or its social equivalent, genealogy) are tied to religious groups' self-definitions, the cases that are of importance are of the positive type, as discussed in the text. Positive here means that certain genetic/genealogical qualifications or attributes or interests are desirable for group membership or are benign by-products of group membership. There is also the occasional negative case, wherein genetics are considered just plain bad by the denomination, sect or ethno-religious group involved. The best example of this is the Shakers (more properly, the United Society of Believers in Christ's Second Appearing). Founded in England in 1747, they spun out their etiolated history in the United States.

They abhorred genetics, in the sense that they did not approve of sexual congress and thus rejected sexual reproduction. Thus, their membership could grow only by attracting outsiders. This worked for a while, but their strict rejection of sexual activity resulted in their going extinct in the second half of the twentieth century, although there are still occasional reports of individuals self-converting themselves to Shakerism.

14 Paul Johnson, in a review of a book on Josephus, makes the telling point that the Roman army required to conquer Jerusalem was the largest siege force assembled during the Roman imperial period and was much bigger than the force that had been required to conquer Britain a quarter-century previously. (*Times Literary Supplement*, 29 July 2005), 7. The point is that one should not see the control of Jerusalem as some minor squabble fought on the periphery of empire.

15 To be strictly accurate, it was the Third Temple: the second being that of Zerubbabel, built after the Babylonian Exile and replaced by Herod's Temple (which was not yet finished when it was destroyed in 70 CE). The virtually universal practice is to call Herod's Temple the Second Temple. The term Third Temple is used by certain Jewish and Christian sects in an apocalyptic or Messianic sense to refer to a new temple to be built in the future where the ruins of Herod's Temple now lie.

16 The apologetic literature that deals with this historical process is immense and is fascinating in its own way. The two most easily accessible volumes that deal with it in a vocabulary that is compatible with professional historical thought are my *Surpassing Wonder: The Invention of the Bible and the Talmuds* (New York: Harcourt Brace, and Montreal and Kingston: McGill-Queen's University Press, 1998) and Jacob Neusner's brilliant *Transformations in Ancient Judaism* (Peabody, Mass: Hendrikson Publishers, 2005).

17 Meir Soloveichik, "The Jewish Mother: A Theology," *Azure* (Spring 2005), 101.

18 R. Kendall Soulen, "Israel and the Church," in Tikva Frymer-Kensky (ed.), *Christianity in Jewish Terms* (Boulder: Westview, 2002), 172, quoted in Soloveichik, 101.

19 Soloveitchik, 101.

20 I am fully aware that since, roughly, the end of World War II, the question "Who is a Jew?" has been the most divisive of issues in the world Jewish community. It was first fought as part of the formation of the state of Israel. A complex compromise between the several factions was

negotiated. Insofar as certain genealogical requirements had to be met for a marriage to be celebrated in the new state and for the offspring to be recognized as Jewish, the decision was left to Orthodox Rabbinic authorities. Secondly, in 1968, the Federation of Reconstructionist Congregations and Havurot rejected traditional Rabbinic genealogical requirements, the most important of which (as we shall discuss in the text) was that the mother be Jewish. Thirdly, and most consequentially, in 1983 the largest sector of the American Jewish community, represented by the Central Conference of American Rabbis, also voted to depart from the traditional genealogical requirements. This latter move caused a major disruption, one that continues to this day.

As part of the debate that arose from the 1983 Reform decision, the quarterly *Judaism* produced a special issue (vol. 34, winter 1985) that gave all sides a forum for expression of their own views and for the criticism of those of their opponents. I am indebted to that publication for providing an entry into the topic. Of the contributors to that special issue, Shaye J.D. Cohen was the only one who operated in his approach and in his patterns of proof in the way that a professional historian does. He has since produced a number of relevant essays and these are brought together in *The Beginnings of Jewishness. Boundaries, Varieties, Uncertainties* (Berkeley: University of California Press, 1999). Although my admiration for the work is obvious, I should make it clear, first, that the analysis of various texts is mine and he is in no way to blame for any errors that I make; and, secondly, that I concede completely that the historical method is only one method and that theologians and canon-lawyers have their own fields of expertise which operate differently from historical analysis.

21 Cohen, *Beginnings*, 264, and in *Judaism*, 7.

22 The only plausible exception is the case of Esau, who married a Hittite woman and founded the Edomites. However, this instance is not germane in the matter of genealogical requirements for being an Israelite, since Esau had voluntarily given up his relationship to the covenant system prior to his forming his own family (see Genesis, chapters 27 and 36).

23 The text here is that of the King James Bible (also called the Authorized Version). It corresponds on family matters to the text of the Tanakh published by the Jewish Publication Society (1985). In this and the other quotations from the "Old Testament," I am employing the KJB for three reasons. First, because it is the version most familiar to most English-language readers; second, because, as Gerald Hammond and

Robert Alter have argued, the KJB, despite being out of fashion at the present time, is still the best translation available of the full text of the Tanakh, given that any translation must thread the needle between ancient Hebrew locution and English prose (Alter, p. xvii); thirdly, because the best translation of the Tanakh, Robert Alter's *The Five Books of Moses* (New York: W.W. Norton, 2004) thus far encompasses only the Pentateuch. Hence, for standardization of language and imagery throughout the entire Old Testament, it is best to use the KJB.

24 I am using the neologism "Female Licence Principle" to avoid enmeshing our wide-scope examination of world genealogical patterns in the intra-Jewish vocabulary with which groups argue about this matter. Anyone who enters the present-day Jewish literature should be warned that the in-house vocabulary uses "matrilineal" to mean that one has to have a Jewish mother to be birthright Jewish. Their opponents argue for the "patrilineal" principle, by which they mean that a Jewish father is sufficient. Both of these usages are appropriate to present-day Jewish socio-theological concerns, but are not those of the genealogical or ethnographic conventions that predominate in the social sciences and in genealogical history.

25 On the relative numbers who were taken into captivity and those who were not, and also on the number who returned, see Akenson, *Surpassing Wonder,* 71–77.

26 See Shaye J.D. Cohen in *Judaism,* 8 and the reluctant acceptance by his opponent Robert Gordis in "Patrilineal Descent – a Solution or a Problem?" in *Judaism,* 36.

Limitations of space preclude my parsing the few references in the vast para-biblical literature of the Late Second Temple period that are in any way concerned with the matter of mixed marriages. Actually, the apparent lack of interest in this matter is in itself the texts' most intriguing characteristic. The references and a compact discussion are found in Cohen, *The Beginnings of Jewishness,* 268–72. The texts that display even a passing interest in the intermarriage matter are few: the Book of Jubilees (found both in the Pseudepigrapha and later among the Dead Sea Scrolls, and probably the most copied and most popular item of non-biblical religious literature of the Late Second Temple) and the Temple Scroll (a large document found among the Dead Sea Scrolls) and Joseph and Aseneth (found both in the Pseudepigrapha and the DSS). These items are conveniently available in translation either in James H. Charlesworth (ed.), *The Old Testament Pseudepigrapha,* 2 vols. (New York: Doubleday, 1985) and in various translations of the

DSS, such as Florentino Garcia Martinez (trans. to English by Wilfred G.E. Watson), *The Dead Sea Scrolls Translated* (Leiden: E.J. Brill, 1994). For an historical discussion of the Late Second Temple religious literature, see Akenson, *Surpassing Wonder*, 133–207.

27 Observe Robert Gordis in *Judaism*, 37, citing the argument of Morton Smith in his *Palestinian Parties and Politics that Shaped the Old Testament* (New York: Columbia University Press, 1971).

28 Lest I enter into a methodological argument with critics, I should make it clear that the evidential principle here means that *unless* there is background evidence that a phenomenon is a general one, then lack of evidence is not evidence for a phenomenon's existence. Only in the case of a phenomenon for which there *is* background evidence of its being general (such as, to take an extreme and obvious case, the sun's rising daily in the east), can be the absence of evidence for a deviation from the pattern is taken as implying that the phenomenon still continues.

29 Josephus, *Jewish Antiquities*, 14:2, 403, Loeb Library edition.

30 See, for example, Lawrence Schiffman, "Jewish Identity and Jewish Descent," in *Judaism*, 79.

31 See Peter Richardson, *Herod. King of the Jews and Friend of the Romans* (Columbia: University of South Carolina Press, 1996).

32 Cohen, "Was Herod Jewish?" in *The Beginnings of Jewishness*, 13–24, esp. 18.

33 On the extraordinary nature and origin of the Mishnah, see my chapter "The Hermetic, Perfect Mishnah," in *Surpassing Wonder*, 295–327.

34 In the quotations and citations from the Mishnah, I am using the translation by Jacob Neusner (New Haven: Yale University Press, 1988). This and the other major translations Neusner has edited have encountered scholarly criticism at points, as should any work on texts of this importance. However, what Neusner has done here and in several other massive documents (the Tosefta, the Yerushalmi, and others) is not simply to translate, but to provide a referencing system that is comparable in usefulness to that which the Christian commentators introduced into the Hebrew scriptures in the Middle Ages. Neusner's system is the only one that permits citation of quotations at the level of specificity required by scholarly work in the academic world. Otherwise, the sprawling unspecificity of the original texts severely discourages critical scrutiny of the materials by anyone except ideologically committed insiders.

35 Jacob Neusner, *Introduction to Rabbinic Literature* (New York: Doubleday, 1994), 129–52.

36 Jacob Neusner (ed. and trans.), *The Tosefta, translated from the Hebrew. Third Division. Nashim (The Order of Women)* (New York: KTAV Publishing House, 1979).

37 Again, the field's indebtedness to Jacob Neusner is great. He edited (and did most of the translation of) the first edition of the Jerusalem Talmud to be rendered in any modern European language. Jacob Neusner (ed.), *The Talmud of the Land of Israel* (Chicago: University of Chicago Press, 1983–93).

38 On the compositional relationship of the major items in the Rabbinic corpus, of which the Bavli is the capstone, see Akenson, *Surpassing Wonder*, 396, 606–25.

39 See Jacob Neusner, *Judaism in the Matrix of Christianity* (Philadelphia: Fortress Press, 1986). Also relevant is his *Judaism and Christianity in the Age of Constantine: Issues of the Initial Confrontation* (Chicago: University of Chicago Press, 1987).

40 Babylonian Talmud, Yebamoth 45a trans. I. Epstein (London: Soncino Press, 1936), 291–92.

41 On the multiple Judahist sects, see Akenson, *Surpassing Wonder*, 109–11, 190–207.

42 Jaroslav Pelikan, *The Christian Tradition. A History of the Development of Doctrine*, vol 1, *The Emergence of the Catholic Tradition* (Chicago: University of Chicago Press, 1971), 13.

43 Yacov's being stoned to death is referred to in Josephus' *Jewish Antiquities*, 20:200–203. There is no comparable ancient mention of the deaths of Peter and Paul in Rome in the 60s, but these two events are among the few pieces of "tradition" that have not been seriously contested.

44 In the discussion that follows, I am indebted to two excellent sources. One of these is the collection of virtually all the relevant documentation in translation by James J. Shotwell and Louise R. Loomis, *The See of Peter* (New York: Columbia University Press, 1927, reprinted New York: Octagon Books, 1965). The other is one of the best pieces of popular history I have ever encountered. It is by the distinguished historian, Eamon Duffy: *Saints and Sinners. A History of the Popes* (New Haven: Yale University Press, 1997).

45 Duffy, 1.

46 The genuine letters of Paul are the only documents of the Christian faith that predate the Destruction of 70 CE. The seven epistles that are granted near-consensus on their being truly Pauline in origin are, in probable order of their composition: 1 Thessalonians, 1 and 2

Corinthians, Philippians, Philemon, Galatians, Romans. On the way in which scholars have developed their views on these texts, see D. H. Akenson, *Saint Saul. A Skeleton Key to the Historical Jesus* (New York: Oxford University Press, 2000), 119–45.

47 Duffy, 16.

48 Irenaeus of Lyon, *Contra Haereses* 3:1–4, tr. And reproduced in Shotwell and Loomis, 265–74.

49 Duffy, 16.

50 See, for example, Donald Attwater, *A Dictionary of the Popes. From Peter to Pius XII* (London: Catholic Book Club, 1939) and Charles A. Colombe, *Vicars of Christ. A History of the Popes* (New York: Citadel Press, 2003).

CHAPTER EIGHT

1 For an appreciation of some Mormon primary sources that are available to secular historians, see Larry R. Gerlach and Michael L. Nicholls, "The Mormon Genealogical Society and Research Opportunities in Early American History," *William and Mary Quarterly*, 3rd. ser., vol 32 (October 1975), 625–29.

2 Donald Harman Akenson, *The Irish in Ontario. A Study in Rural History* (Montreal and Kingston: McGill-Queen's University Press, orig. ed 1984, 2nd ed. 1999).

3 Robert Alter, *The Five Books of Moses. A Translation with Commentary* (New York: W.W. Norton, 2004), 34–35n.

4 Derek Freeman, *Margaret Mead and Samoa. The Making and Unmaking of an Anthropological Myth* (Cambridge, Mass: Harvard University Press, 1983).

5 Jon Wiener, *Historians in Trouble. Plaigarism, Fraud, and Politics in the Ivory Tower* (New York: New Press, 2005).

6 Anthony W. Ivins, "Israel in History and Genealogy," *Utah Genealogical and Historical Magazine* (January 1932), 1–9.

7 Armand L. Mauss, *All Abraham's Children. Changing Mormon Conceptions of Race and Lineage* (Urbana: University of Illinois Press, 2003), quotation from 17.

8 Ibid., 272 ff.

9 For a presentation of the elements of Mormon genealogy in the Promised Land of America, see Jessie M. Lindsay, *Book of Mormon Genealogy* (Honolulu: Lanakila Ward, Pearl Harbor Stake, 1963). For a summary of the church's integration of biblical genealogy, Book of Mormon lineages, European history and near-Eastern history, see the diagrams and

tables in Victor L. Ludlow, "The Scattering and Gathering of Israel. God's Covenant with Abraham Remembered Through the Ages," in Roy A. Prete (ed.), *Window of Faith. Latter-day Saint Perspective on World History* (Salt Lake City: Religious Studies Center, Brigham Young University, 2005), 97–120.

10 Mauss, 21–29.

11 Klaus Hansen, *Mormonism and the American Experience* (Chicago: University of Chicago Press, 1981), 192–93.

12 Ibid., 193.

13 Mauss, 32–33.

14 It will be interesting to see how the LDS church deals with recent DNA work that confirms what professional archeologists and anthropologists have long held – (1) that the Amerindians are certainly not descended from sea-faring Israelites and (2) that the Polynesians originated in southeast Asia. My own guess is that the church will fight a rearguard action and then, as in the case of admitting blacks to full fellowship, will have a belief-reversing revelation which will become regnant without there being any admission of earlier error. For a sympathetic discussion of the problem, written by a former Mormon bishop, see Simon G. Southerton, *Losing a Lost Tribe. Native Americans, DNA, and the Mormon Church* (Salt Lake City: Signature Books, 2004).

15 "Field Notes for Genealogical Committeemen," *Utah Genealogical and Historical Magazine* (1932), 157.

16 Ibid, 156.

17 As the text implies, the one problem that Woodruff and his colleagues in the First Presidency could not cope with was what to do with the old records that showed sealings to "adopted" lines. They decided in the 1890s to leave them standing and to let the wisdom of God eventually deal with them. As late as the 1930s, genealogical workers were still worrying about what to do with these inaccurate (from the genealogical point of view) sealings. See James B. Allen, Jessie L. Embrey, and Kahlile B. Mehr, *Hearts Turned to the Fathers*, book edition of *BYU Studies* (Salt Lake City: 1995), 43–44, 56, 101–3. As far as can be found out, the problem is still under the carpet. Since a liturgical sealing is also a genealogical statement, this has some secular interest. However, it is not really a big issue to non-Mormons, for the odds of their having devout Mormon ancestors who were active in the "adoption" era of LDS genealogy is relatively small. Rather, it represents a problem to old Mormon families whose roots well may lie in that problematic direction.

18 Ibid., 96–98.

19 Ibid., 104–05, 110.

20 LDS Genealogical Society minutes, 2 July 1935, quoted ibid., 111.

21 Ibid., 143. In 1961, a comparable corrections committee found that 42 percent of the submissions had to be rejected and a further 26 percent were duplicates of material already submitted by other "Saints." From their perspective, this was an error rate of 70 percent, although the duplicates may not have been flawed in terms of genealogical accuracy. Ibid., 176.

22 Quoted ibid., 177.

23 Ibid., 147–48.

24 Ibid., 143–87, passim. It is worth noting that LDS microfilms until, roughly, the 1960s, were of fairly poor quality. Also, the early material (into the 1960s) is often maddening to use because the camera operators worked with large cameras affixed to a tripod with a focus point that was not very adjustable. Thus, one will find that in many early films of large record books, the operator set up camera so as to take the left-hand page first and went through an entire record book that way: then, at the back, he moved his camera to the right-hand side of the page and came back towards the front. That means that one has to read, say, page 1 at the front of a film and page 2 at the back. Only in the middle does one stop cursing.

25 Procedure for participation in one such ward-level name-extraction programs is found in "Dear Myrtle," http://www.dearmyrtle.com/01/0313.htm.

26 Joe Berkofsky, "Baptism controversy flares anew between Jews, Mormons." *Cleveland Jewish News*, 31 December 2003.

27 Allen, Embry and Mehr, 146, 179.

28 William G. Hartley, "The Church Grows in Strength," *Ensign* (September 1999) 46; Timothy L. Gall (ed.), *Worldmark Encyclopedia of Culture and Daily Life*, vol 2, *Americas* (Cleveland: Eatwood Publications, 1998).

29 "Hinkley Addresses 175th Mormon Conference," http://www4utah.com, 4/3/2005.

30 *The Times* (London) 25 February 2005.

31 Kathleen Flake, *The Politics of American Religious Identity. The Seating of Senator Reed Smoot, Mormon Apostle* (Chapel Hill: University of North Carolina Press, 2004), 209n30.

32 Ibid.

33 "Hinkley Address," cited above and "LDS Church Updated Statistics," http://www4utah.com, 4 April 2005.

34 Allen, Embry and Mehr, 304–19; Donna Potter Philips, "The IGI: Friend or Foe?" *Family Chronicle* (March-April 2004), 29–31. See also chapter one, notes 3 and 4.

35 Allen, Embry and Mehr, 319.

36 The present address of their website is http://www.NewEngland Ancestors.org.

37 One can obtain all the relevant forms at http://www.familysearch.org under the "Research Helps" section. Rather more revealing is the pamphlet *A Member's Guide to Temple and Family History Work. Ordinances and Covenants* (Salt Lake City: Church of Jesus Christ of Latter-day Saints, 1993), and subsequent editions.

38 Phillips, 31.

39 Allen, Embry and Mehr, 290.

40 Philips, 31.

41 *A Member's Guide*, 14.

42 See T.W. Moody, F.X. Martin, and F.J. Byrne, *A New History of Ireland*, vol. 9, *Maps, Genealogies, Lists* (Oxford: Clarendon Press, 1984), part II, 134.

43 The caveat here is that the king-lists provided by the Mormons make it appear as if the pre- Norman Irish kingships (there were several) passed from father to son, as in primogeniture. Actually, the kingships were elective and the kingship bounced around between various lines, often several times in a single generation. See the concluding section in chapter six in the present study.

44 Allen, Embry, and Mehr, 318.

APPENDIX A

1 R. F. Barton, *The Kalingas. Their Institutions and Custom Law* (Chicago: University of Chicago Press, 1949). See 66–69, and esp. Figure 3. Even this system has its ambiguities.

2 Pierre de Charlevoix, *Journal of a Voyage to North America* (London, 1761), vol 2, 54–57, 109–10, reprinted and edited in James Axtell, *The Indian Peoples of Eastern America. A Documentary History of the Sexes* (New York: Oxford University Press, 1981), 14–17.

3 Emma Hadfield, *Among the Natives of the Loyalty Group* (London: MacMillan, 1920), 180.

4 W.E. Armstrong, *Rossel Island. An Ethnological Study* (Cambridge: Cambridge University Press, 1928), 52.

5 André Krause, *The Tlinglit Indians. Results of a Trip to the Northwest Coast of America and the Bering Straits*, trans. Aurel Krause (Seattle:

University of Washington Press, for the American Ethnological
Society, 1956), 152.
6 A.B. Brewster, *The Hill Tribes of Fiji* (London: Seeley Service and Co.,
1922), 188.
7 Hadfield, 182.
8 C.E. Fox, *The Threshold of the Pacific. An Acount of the Social Organization,
Magic, and Religion of the People of San Cristoval in the Solomon Islands*
(London: Kegan Paul, Trench, Trubner and Co., 1924), 56.
9 Ibid., 54.
10 Ibid.

APPENDIX B

1 This is lucidly explained in Spencer Wells, *The Journey of Man. A Genetic
Odyssey* (Princeton: Princeton University Press, 2002), 15–45.
2 The study is found in the Research reports section of *Nature*, no. 437
(15 September 2005), 408–11, research conducted by Stephen
Rossiter.
3 See Richard Agarwala, Alejandroa A. Schaffer, and James F. Tomlin,
"Towards a Complete North American Anabaptist Genealogy: Analysis
of Inbreeding," *Human Biology*, vol.73 (August 2001), 533–45; Lisa
Belkin, "A Doctor for the Future," *New York Times Magazine*, 6 November 2005, 68–115, passim; John A. Hostetler, John M. Opitz, and James
F. Reynolds, "History and relevance of the Hutterite population for genetic studies," *American Journal of Medical Genetics*, vol.33 (June 2005),
453–62.
4 Yoko Imaizumi, "Reasons for consanguineous Marriages in Japan,"
Journal of Biosocial Science, vol. 19 (1987), 97–106; William J. Schull and
James V. Neel, *The Effects of Inbreeding on Japanese Children* (New York:
Harper and Row, 1965), cited in Martin Ottenheimer, *Forbidden Relatives. The American Myth of Cousin Marriage* (Urbana: University of
Illinois Press, 1996), 125.
5 As cited by Ottenheimer, 124. The first study, by S.M. Bemiss, was
published in 1857 as "On Marriages of Consanguinity," in *North American Medico-Churugical Review* (January 1857) and followed by his "Report on the Influence of Marriages of Consanguinity among
Offspring," *Transactions of the American Medical Association* (vol. 11
(1858), 319–425. It may be that the problem here is that traditional
geneticists think of these incidences of genetic defects as
being detectable either by linear probability calculations or as the

mechanistic results of a specific combination of parental genes. A more productive way of dealing with genetic defects that seem to skip generations would be to work with mathematical models of wave theory and with the various resonances that waves inevitably produce in all media through which they move.

6 I am here paraphrasing Robin Fox in his chapter, "The Incest Problem," in his *Kinship and Marriage. An Anthropological Perspective* (Cambridge: Cambridge University Press, sec. ed., 1982, first pub.1967), 55–56.

7 Jaroslav Cerny, "Consanguineous Marriages in Pharonic Egypt," *Journal of Egyptian Archeology*, vol. 40 (1954), 23–29; Keith Hopkins, "Brother-sister Marriage in Roman Egypt," *Comparative Studies in Society and History*, vol. 22 (1980), 303–54; Brent D. Shaw, "Explaining Incest: Brother-sister Marriage in Graeco-Roman Egypt," *Man*, New Series, vol. 19 (1984), 267–99. All cited in Ottenheimer, 62.

8 Shaw, 283, cited in Oppenheimer, 61–62.

9 *United States report under the International Covenant on Civil and Political Rights* (July 1994), section 1, report *re* Mays Estates, 114 ne. 2ndR (Ct. App. N.Y. 1953), citing the Rhode Island statute as precedent; Michael G. Farrow and Richard C. Juberg, "Genetics and Laws Prohibiting Marriage in the United States," *Journal of the American Medical Association*, vol. 209 (1969), 534–38.

10 Steve Sailer, "Cousin Marriage Conundrum," *The American Conservative*, 13 January 2003. 21. The article is reprinted in Steven Pinker (ed.), *Best Science and Nature Writing, 2004.*

11 See Jack Goody, *The Development of the Family and Marriage in Europe* (Cambridge: Cambridge University Press, 1983), 50–51 *n*2 and 82 *n*21.

12 UK Statutes, 5 and 6 William IV., c. 54.

13 UK Statutes, 7 Edward VII, c. 47.

14 UK Statutes, 11 and 12 George V, c. 24.

15 The advantages of consanguineal first-cousin marriage are brilliantly summarized in Sailer, 20–22.

16 Goody, 82 *n*21.

17 Sailer, 20–22.

18 "Hospital staff," *Journal of the Faculty of Medicine, Baghdad*, vol. 28 (1986), no. 4, 29–36.

19 Alan H. Bittles, quoted in Sailer, 21.

20 The genetic literature on the Cohens is growing exponentially and promises to be one of the most interesting locales in which cultural origin narratives and genetic investigation overlap. This is a topic that I

will approach only in skeleton form. In part, this is because it is an extremely rapidly developing area; in part because any discussion of Jewish heredity and genetics is a very fraught area by virtue of the nineteenth- and twentieth-centuries' pseudo-science on the matter; and in part, because, as we will see in Appendix E's discussion of the Sykes' Y-chromosome marker, when genealogical records fail, even the most disciplined of scientists are in danger of filling in the blanks in a way that is emotionally satisfying but evidentiarily weak. In this case, the danger is a form of *shtetl* romanticism from within the Jewish Community. The following is an outline of the main points in the matter.

1. One mainline version of Jewish origin mythology points to *Aharon, haCohen* – Aaron-the-priest, brother of Moses, as being the founder of a line of high priests whose lineage passed from father-to-son (Numbers 3:2–3). The sons-of-Aaron (Cohens) were an elite class of the tribe of Levi (all of whom were said to descend from the patriarch Jacob.) From a second level of the tribe of Levi was said to descend a subordinate hereditary priestly line, the Levites. The traditional dating for the creation of the Cohen line is between 1300 and 1500 BCE.

2. In terming this an origin myth, one is not making any judgment about the accuracy of the posited genealogy: myths can be factually-based or not. Their power is independent of their accuracy. However one should note (a) that there is no external confirmation, either archeological or in the records of non-Israelite cultures of the existence of Aaron, Moses or any of the other patriarchal figures. They may have been euhumerized gods; (b) in the Hebrew scriptures there is nothing approaching a continuous genealogy of the sons-of-Aaron; (c) indeed, within the Hebrew scriptures, a third priestly line, the Zadokites, is prepotent in the nation's luminary hour, the era of the United Kingdom and down to the Babylonian exile. Zadok was one of the two high priests under King David (the other high priest was cashiered by King Solomon) and the line of Zadok monopolized the high priesthood until the Babylonian exile of 586/7 BCE. Thereafter, they were dominant over the Aaronites, but did not have a monopoly on the high priesthood. The Zadokites were deposed by the Maccabeans, the last Zadokite high priest in Jerusalem being murdered. Onias IV, son of the last Zadokite, sought refuge in Egypt and there at Leontopolis set up a diaspora Temple that operated until 73 CE, three years after the demise of the Jerusalem Temple. (Geza Vermes, *The Dead Sea Scrolls* (Sheffield: JSOT, third ed., 1987), 21–22; *(Encyclopaedia Judaica*, 12: 1404–05). Only after the Destruction of the Jerusalem Temple in 70 CE and

the subsequent creation of Rabbinic Judaism does the Cohen line become dominant, now as Rabbis rather than functional priests. (The Temple was gone.) Even then, substantive subsequent links of descent were sketchy or non-existent, hardly surprising given the position of the Jews in the medieval and early-modern eras.

3. Yet, today there are tens of thousands of Cohen men (var: Coen, Kohn, Cowen, Cowan, Kagan, and more) who are granted special privileges in Orthodox congregations (such as rendering the first reading from the Torah at service). There is also an equivalent group who serve as Levites. (They carry Levy and similar names, but with greater variation than among the Cohens.) So, one has a large number of men who base their religious privilege upon direct father-to-son linkages, but can do so only by assertion, not documentation. Their genealogies have a missing patch that runs from between a millennium-and-a-half to three millennia, depending on one's mode of reckoning. (That is, whether one considers them to be descendants of the ancient priests or of the elite of post-Destruction Rabbis.) Their assertion of genealogical continuity is intriguing to genetic scientists and, simultaneously, there is a deep yearning within the Jewish community for third-party confirmation of this important aspect of Jewish traditional belief.

4. In 1996, a new era in genetic thought concerning Jews (the bad-old form being the "scientific" racisms of the nineteenth and twentieth centuries) began. Karl Skoreki and Michael Hammer employed variously by top-line universities in the USA, Canada, England and Israel (good scientists move around a lot), put together a series of Y-chromosome studies through which they said they had determined a Cohen Model Hapoltype ("CMH"). This was not a single gene, but polymorphisms from all over the Y-chromosome (an early version of their work specified six generic markers, but they later expanded to twelve). About 5 percent of Jewish males worldwide (of a total male population of about 7 million) are Cohens or Levites. The CMH was found in over 97 percent of the Cohens tested and in less than one-third of non-Cohen Jews. (Admittedly the work was small-sample, just over 100 in its initial probe; other studies found a 50 percent rate in Cohens, still very high.) The general rate in the Jewish population was about 12 percent. Skorecki and Hammer and their several associates have suggested: (a) that Ashkenazi and Sephardic Levites are genetically separate, implying that each caste emerged after the split between Ashkenazi and Sephardim in the fifth through ninth centuries of the Common Era; (b) that, in contrast, the Cohens go back at least to the

era of the Temple (that is, pre-70 CE), well before the Ashkenazi-Sephardic divide; (c) that, given certain assumptions about the rate of mutation in the CMH, the first Cohen lived about 2,100–3,250 years ago, which is during the periods usually called the First and Second Temple eras. (Religious enthusiasts have tried to pin the number down to almost 3,300 years exactly, but that should not be laid at the doorstep of the geneticists.) See Karl Skorecki and Michael F. Hammer *et. al.*, "Y-chromosomes of Jewish Priests," *Nature*, vol. 385 (2 January 1998), 32; Mark G. Thomas, Karl Skorecki, Tudor Parfitt, Neil Bradman, and David Goldstein "Origins of Old Testament Priests, "*Nature*, vol. 394 (9 July 1998), 138–9; Doron M. Beher, Mark G. Thomas, Karl Skorecki, Michael F. Hammer *et. al.*, "Multiple Origins of Ashkenazi Levites: Y-Chromosome Evidence for both Near Eastern and European Ancestries," *American Journal of Human Genetics*, vol. 73 (2003), 768–79.

5. Since then researchers have found the CMH occurs in high incidences in the Lemba of southern Africa. These are a Bantu-speaking group of about 50,000 that are sometimes called the "black Jews" of Africa. Their senior clan keeps a number of Jewish customs and self-identifies as Jewish (even though not recognized as such by Rabbinic authorities. See Mark G. Thomas, Tudor Parfitt, Deborah A. Weeiss, Karl Skorecki *et. al.*, "Y-Chromosomes Travelling South: The Cohen Modal Haplotype and the Origins of the Lemba – the Black Jews of Southern Africa," *American Journal of Human Genetics*, vol. 66 (2000), 674–86. The CMH marker has also been found in high concentrations in the 4,000 Bene Israel, a self-declared Jewish community in India. See Kevin Davies, *Cracking the Genome: Inside the Race to Unlock Human DNA* (New York: Free Press, 2001), 182–83, quoting Michael Hammer.

6. A complicating factor is that research has indicated that a version of the CMH is found quite frequently in Palestinian Moslem Arabs and that this close-CMH is also common in Iraqui Kurds. See C. Brinkman *et. al.*, "Human Y-Chromosomal STR Haplotypes in a Kurdish Population Sample," *International Journal of Legal Medicine*, vol. 113 (1999), 38–42; Almut Nebel, Ariella Oppenheim *et. al.*, "High-resolution Y-chromosome haplotypes of Israeli and Palestinian Arabs reveal geographic substructure and substantial overlap with haplotypes of Jews," *Human Genetics*, vol. 107 (December 2000), 630–41. The implication is that the CMH may be *characteristic* of genetically descended Cohens, but that it is not *distinctive* of them. In this entire matter, we may be witnessing the parallax that bedevils so much scholarly work: namely, that

what one holds closest to one's eye is what one sees most. Since the great interest has been in studying Jewish populations (in relation to their numbers, they are much the most highly-studied group in post-1990 human population genetics), it is not surprising that items that are characteristic of wider population groups are, at present, being seen as distinctively Jewish.

7. Nevertheless, the Cohens are special, no question. Michael Hammer and his colleagues have been careful to explain that they are identifying a specific genetic marker and are hypothesizing its probable genetic family tree, but that they are not constructing a genealogical narrative. Where the problems occur is with the enthusiasts who hang baubles on the tree and also play about with the scientific results. Therefore, we should repeat some obvious warnings: (a) the genetic results have nothing to do with proving that there ever was, or was not, an historical figure named Aaron the high priest; it may be a god-name for someone whose divine characteristics have been diminished in turning him into a high priest, the brother of the mythic law-giver, Moses; (b) even if there was a real Aaron, the ur-figure in the Cohen genetic line has no necessary relationship to him. "Aaron" is simply a name that is attached to a Y-chromosome linkage that could have begun before or after the "real Aaron." The genetic line is called Aaronite only as a name of convenience; (c) that Cohen males today have a high frequency of the CMH marker indicates only one thing: that they have been remarkably inbred for a long period of time; and (d) to claim that this is "a testament to the devotion of the wives of the Cohens over the years. Even a low rate of infidelity would have dramatically lowered the percentages" is risible. All that the prevalence of the CMH marker indicates is that the high degree of inbreeding was maintained by a mixture of close marriages (especially first-cousin and uncle-niece pairings) and that infidelities were kept mostly within the Cohen cohort. (The quotation is from Oxford's Dr. David Goldstein, *Science News*, 3 October 1998.)

8. In sum, the Cohen research promises to be one of the most fascinating pieces of genetic research in the next decade as far as genealogists are concerned. The one sure way to make the entire effort valueless would be to declare in advance what the research will prove. Faith without works is dead, it has been said.

21 I am here excluding as rational the practices of southern-mountain inbreds of the United States, for the genetic deficiencies have far outweighed any benefits. See James S. Brown, *Beech Creek: A Study of a*

Kentucky Mountain Neighborhood (Berea, Kentucky: Berea College Press, 1988). This is based on research for a 1950 PhD thesis. "Beech Creek" is actually Clay County, Kentucky.

22 Goody, 55.

23 Ibid., 55–75.

24 Goody's entire book, which is well-tempered and not an anti-church diatribe, deserves close reading.

25 Ottenheimer, 69–70.

26 "Kindred and Affinity," in *Oxford Dictionary of the Christian Church*, 767.

27 For a reproduction of the 1761 version, see James B. Twitchell, *Forbidden Partners. The Incest Taboo in Modern Culture* (New York: Columbia University Press, 1987), 129.

28 The Church of England's prohibited degrees as of 1940, as compared to earlier eras, is found in Goody, Table 2, 178–79.

29 For a précis of all US incest statutes, see Leigh B. Bienen, "The Incest Statutes," in Judith L. Herman, with Lisa Hirschman, *Father-Daughter Incest* (Cambridge: Harvard University Press, 1981), 221–59. See also Ottenheimer, Table 3, 38–39.

30 Ottenheimer, Table 2, 32–33.

31 Ottenheimer, passim.

32 Ottenheimer, 41.

33 Fox, 71.

APPENDIX C

1 Mark A. Bellis, Karen Hughes, Sara Hughes, and R. Ashton , "Measuring paternal discrepancy and its public health consequences," *Journal of Epidemiology and Community Health*, vol. 59 (2005), 749–54). This article uses the term "paternal discrepancy" as the preferred designator of non-paternal births and of false-paternity. That neologism obscures the more familiar and less ambiguous commonly employed terms and thus will not here be employed.

2 Even the quality papers took this route. See the *Independent* (London), 11 August 2005 and the *Guardian* (London), 25 August 2005.

3 The John Moores University group cited for this number Sally MacIntyre and Anne Sooman, "Non-paternity and prenatal genetic screening," *Lancet*, no. 338 (1991), 869–71. Actually, these authors said that 10 percent is used widely in standard texts and that 10–15 percent is usually taught to medical students. Thus, the revision of the conventional wisdom that was being attempted by

the John Moores group was even greater than their own
presentation claimed.

4 According to Bradley Popovich, vice-president of the American College of Medical Genetics. *Santa Barbara News Press*, 27 February 2000.

5 The study was reported in a CIBA Foundation Symposium as E.E. Philip,
"Law and Ethics of A.I.D. and Embryo Transfer: Discussion: Moral, Social and Ethical Issues," in G.E.W. Wostenholme and D.W. FitzSimons
(eds), *CIBA Foundation Symposium*, vol. 17 (1973), 63–66.

6 The reason for up-levelling the estimates is that blood testing according to blood type (which was what was used in the Philip study) could
not at that time detect all instances of non-paternal births. This is indicated in the following table that provides the possibilities of identification as they existed at the time of Philip's work.

Blood type of the two parents	Possible blood types of children produced by these two parents	Blood types of children who could not be produced by these two parents
A&A	A, O	B, AB
A&B	A, B, AB, O	NONE
A&AB	A, B, AB	O
A&O	A, O	B, AB
B&B	B, O	A, AB
B&AB	A, B, AB	O
B&O	B, O	A, AB
AB&AB	A, B, AB	O
AB&O	A, B	AB, O
O&O	O	A, B, AB

The reason one cannot provide a single coefficient of correction for
blood type is that the degree of correction necessary varies for each of
the parental pairings given above, and the mix varies.

7 For example, Robin Baker, *Sperm Wars: The Science of Sex* (New York:
Basic Books, 1996) makes this point. The existence of this socioeconomic gradient is not controversial. It is one of the few things about
false-paternity on which there is consensus. For an interesting statement of this gradient in terms of a designated variable called
"Reproductive Success" – the relationship between a man's power,
status, resource-access and his producing children – see Laura
Betzig, "Where are the bastards' daddies?," *Behavioral and Brain
Sciences*, vol.16 (1993), 284–85.

8 L.E. Schact and H. Gershowitz, "Frequency of extra-marital children
as determined by blood groups," in L. Gedda (ed.), *Proceedings of the*

Second International Congress on Human Genetics (Rome: Mendel, 1963), 894–97. On the other hand, a German study conducted by the Max Planck Institute of Munich found that the percentages of non-paternal births produced in stable monogamous marriages was about 10 percent for a first child, but rose thereafter, reaching 25 percent with the fourth birth. *Report Newsmagazine*, 24 April 2000.

9 Bryan Sykes, *Adam's Curse. A Future without Men* (New York: W.W. Norton, 2004), 14.

10 Schact and Gershowitz, 894–97.

11 Robert L. Smith, "Human Sperm Competition," in Robert L. Smith (ed.), *Sperm Competition and the Evolution of Animal Mating Systems* (New York: Academic Press, Inc., 1984), 617, reports "an extensive study conducted by the University of Michigan Department of Human Genetics on a rural midwestern population" (other sources identify the locale as rural Michigan and the cohort study as being women born in the 1940s), but then provides no citations and no details save the 10 percent false-paternity rate. This is a good example of the frustratingly low level of documentation that bedevils so much of the discussion of non-paternal births. The only relevant detail provided by Smith is that the study involved first births, so it may have been loaded toward girls who became pregnant before marriage, a group that probably has a tilt towards false-paternity.

12 R. Robin Baker and Mark A. Bellis, *Human Sperm Competition, Copulation, Masturbation and Infidelity* (London: Chapman and Hall, 1995), 200, Box 8.4

13 I would not mention a study that doubles in spades the errors of the John Moore's University research, except that somehow the *New York Times Sunday Magazine* (10 December 2006), 64) decided to list it as one of the 100 good things done in 2006. This was a report in *Current Anthropology* (June 206, 513–19) by Kermyt G. Anderson, "How Well Does Paternity Confidence Match Actual Paternity?" This worked with essentially the same old studies that the Moore group's work employed and, like the Moores study, mashed large and small data sets together, and then found the median number where half fell one way, half the other, and that was taken as the meaningful non-paternity figure. The richly misleadingly innovative aspect of Anderson's work was that he separated studies in which men could be expected to be confident of non-paternity being absent and those in which men thought non-paternity was likely. In the former case, the median number in the various studies (a useless figure) was 1.7%, or 3.7% (depending on what studies he discarded),

while in the latter case it was 29.8% (an equally meaningless number). Then Anderson integrated these figures intuitively and stated that the usual 10% real non-paternity figure is too high because it could only be reached, based on his procedures, if 75% of the men in the population had high-paternity confidence and 25% had low-paternity confidence. Somehow he knows that the level of non-paternity confidence worldwide (he is dealing with a wide range of international samples) is higher than that. Anderson then introduces a massive non-sequitor: he has done a study that implies a 3.75% non-paternity rate in Albuquerque, New Mexico. End of story. All one can do in the face of this cascade of errors of method and illogic is to repeat the point in the text: until wide-sample DNA studies are done, we really have no idea what the non-paternity rate is in any given culture, much less worldwide.

14 This example follows the method of Thomas H. Roderick, "Estimations of the Percentage of Genetically False Pedigrees," *The American Genealogist*, vol. 37 (October 1961, 241–43.

15 In order to avoid double-counting (and thus overstating the impact of false-paternity upon genealogical narratives), two practices are necessary. First, although it sounds slightly counter-intuitive, the effect of false-paternity stemming from the mother's side of the family becomes statistically relevant only with her birth which, from the standpoint of Ego is Generation 2, *not* Generation 1. Secondly, the deflator for invalidity (.95 in this example) should be applied sequentially to each generational entry in the genealogy as the narrative ascends. That keeps the probability pool at 100 percent. Cumulating the invalidity rates for each line separately results in a probability pool of several times that, depending on how far back one takes it. And 100 percent is as high as probability can go in standard mathematics.. This example follows the method of Thomas H. Roderick, "Estimations of the Percentage of Genetically False Pedigrees," *The American Genealogist*, vol. 37 (October 1961), 241-43.

16 The same cautions against double-counting hold for this exercise as for Table C.2.

17 The reader may have noticed that I have ignored entirely in the text the issue of false-maternity. The matter is, however, discussed in Appendix D.

APPENDIX D

1 The false-maternity matters I noticed but did not find worth written commentary, arose while doing: *Between Two Revolutions: Islandmagee,*

Co. *Antrim, 1798-1920* (Toronto: P.D. Meany Co., and Dublin: Academy Press, 1979); *The Irish in Ontario: A Study in Rural History* (Montreal and Kingston: McGill-Queen's University Press, 1984, second ed., 1999); *If the Irish Ran the World. Montserrat, 1630-1730* (Liverpool: Liverpool University Press; Mona, Jamaica: The Press of the University of the West Indies; Montreal and Kingston: McGill-Queen's University Press, 1997). Having previously set aside the matter of false-maternity, I presented the social and historical context of possible simultaneous false-paternity and false-maternity in fictionalized form in *At Face Value: The Life and Times of Eliza McCormack/John White* (Montreal and Kingston: McGill-Queen's University Press, 1990). None of this material proves the anecdotal observations that I make in the text above, but it does give the reader a chance to see how I have operated when doing micro-histories and (in *At Face Value*) when speculating upon the stories hidden beneath official records.

2 This set of observations is well established in Irish studies and is not controversial. For a convenient summary of the legal, social and religious mechanisms that made this situation possible, see my *The United States and Ireland* (Cambridge: Harvard University Press, 1973), 129-67.

3 *Dail Eireann. Debates*, volume 200, 14 March 1963.

4 Allan C. Brownfield, "Non-Jewish Immigrants Forcing Israel to Choose between Being a 'Jewish' State and a Democracy," *Washington Report on Middle East Affairs* (April, 2000), 66-67; Chris McGreal, "Sharon takes on Rabbis over Jewish Identity," *Guardian*, 31 December 2002; Jessica Steinberg, "Israelis re-examine Russian aliyah," *Canadian Jewish News*, 19 September 2002, taken from Jewish Telegraphic Agency; David Golinkin, "On Conversion, Intermarriage and 'Who is a Jew,'" *Insight Israel* online edition, 12/10/05, citing as sources: *Moment* (April 1997), 48ff; *Jerusalem Post*, 14 January 2000 and 11 January 2001; *Aviad Hacohen Meimad*, no. 19 (April 2000), pp. 4-7); *Ha'aretz*, 24 December 2000; *Jewish Week*, 19 January 2001; *Jerusalem Report*, 29 January 2001, 26-29.

APPENDIX E

1 One should pay respect to the use of genetic thinking to define and treat medical problems that occurred long before the genome age. In the present, no less than in the past, the genetic assessment can only occur if there is some family knowledge. The requirements for the

medical application of genealogy are found in Luanne McNabb, Elizabeth B.J. Curtis and Kathleen R. Barclay-Bowley, *Family Health Trees. Genetics and Genealogy* (Toronto: Ontario Genealogy Society, 1995).

2 The "Genographic Project," launched jointly by the IBM Corporation and the National Geographic Society of the United States is attempting to collect more than 100,000 DNA samples from around the world as part of the charting of human history through genetics. For a thoughtful popular description of the thinking behind this project, see Spencer Wells, *The Journey of Man. A Genetic Odyssey* (Princeton: Princeton University Press, 2002).

3 *Sunday Telegraph* (London), 17 April 2005.

4 Bryan Sykes, *The Seven Daughters of Eve* (New York: W.W. Norton, 2001).

5 For products available, see www.oxfordancestors.com.

6 Bryan Sykes, *Adam's Curse. A Future Without Men* (New York: W.W. Norton, 2001) 318.

7 For an excellent summary of the logic behind the Y-chromosome research program, see Mark A. Jobling and Chris Tyler-Smith, "Fathers and Sons: the Y-chromosome and human evolution," *Trends in Genetics*, vol. 11 (November 1995), 449-56. See also Wells, 174-78.

8 Bryan Sykes and Catherine Irven, "Surnames and the Y-Chromsome," *American Journal of Human Genetics*, vol. 66 (2000), 1417-19.

9 See note 6.

10 Sykes and Irven, "Surnames...," 1418; Sykes, *Adam's Curse*, 14. The potential overstatement is because "genuine adoptions" (Sykes's term) could have been included in the cohort from which he computed the non-paternity rate.

11 Sykes, *Adam's Curse*, 14.

12 A very strange aspect of Sykes's presentation of his calculation and conclusions concerning rates of false-paternity is that: (a) in his original article with Catherine Irven, he granted that various forms of inbreeding "involving other males with the core Sykes haplotype would not be detected" (1418) and (b) in his book he admitted that the deviant Sykes-chromosome "might be the Y-chromosome of several different 'original' Mr Sykeses, each passed down to the present day through a direct paternal line unbroken by non-paternity events. From this [his] evidence alone, it is impossible to tell the difference."

Each of these admissions on its own dictates a straight conclusion: one cannot use his data to calculate a false-paternity rate.

Yet he does so. Each of the two caveats appears innocuous when wedged into longer disparate discussions. But there is something

distasteful about his inserting them as a prophylactic shield before proceeding to engage in the presentation of a proposition which they
(and other additional considerations) render patently invalid.

And the whole presentation is worrisome because the popular version of his work is bound to find its way into the field of family history
and to be used as an analgesic by family historians who wish to ignore,
or, at least, to minimize any thoughts of what non-paternal events do to
genealogical narratives. For that reason, close attention is being paid
to Sykes's work. I am grateful to professors R. Marvin McInnis and
Chris Ferrall for their help in understanding Sykes's sometimes
opaque statistical procedures and experimental design. Any errors of
interpretation are mine.

13 Sykes, *Adam's Curse*, 13-14.

14 For an example of the sensible and modest integration of genealogical
and genetic information, see Ugo A. Perego, Natalie M. Myers and
Scott R. Woodward, "Reconstructing the Y-Chromosome of Joseph
Smith: Genealogical Applications," *Journal of Mormon History*, vol. 32
(Fall 2005), 42-60. For the way that Mormon family researchers at
the ward level are being told to deal with DNA data, see S.C. Meates,
"Exploring Your Family Tree with DNA," *Family Chronicle* (Jan. Feb.
2006), 11–16. Thus far, the LDS response is a combination of optimistic awareness of the possibilities of genetic analysis and a realization
that genetic analysis can solve only sharply-defined segments of the
whole range of genealogical puzzles. One worries less about the Mormons being overly credulous than about avocational enthusiasts who
are apt to use genetic testing (with its statements of large-group evolution) to give ropey genealogies of specific family lines an authority that
they should never have. The other worry one has about historical genetics of human populations is that they quickly play into arguments
about claims for sovereignty over land based on claim of primacy of occupation. Think aboriginal land claims in North and South America
and in Australasia; or conjure with the claims to territorial occupation
in Eurasia and the Middle East. For a thoughtful discussion of how genetic history and the claims of nationalist rights and of geographic possession can interrelate, see Diana Muir Appelbaum and Paul S.
Appelbaum, "The Gene Wars," *Azure* (Winter 2007), 51-79.

15 I am grateful to my colleague, the distinguished geographer of the His-
panic world, Professor George Lovell, for this translation.

Index